Webster's
Standard American
Style Manual

Webster's
Standard American
Style Manual

A Merriam-Webster®

Merriam-Webster Inc., Publishers
Springfield, Massachusetts

A GENUINE MERRIAM-WEBSTER

The name *Webster* alone is no guarantee of excellence. It is used by a number of publishers and may serve mainly to mislead an unwary buyer.

A Merriam-Webster® is the registered trademark you should look for when you consider the purchases of dictionaries and other fine reference books. It carries the reputation of a company that has been publishing since 1831 and is your assurance of quality and authority.

Library of Congress Cataloging in Publication Data
Main entry under title:

Webster's standard American style manual.

    Bibliography: p. 413
    Includes index.
    1. Authorship—Handbooks, manuals.
I. Merriam-Webster Inc.
PN147.W36   1985   808'.02   85-15512
ISBN 0-87779-033-7

Printed and bound in the United States of America

6789AG/F93929190

Index/Coleen K. Withgott

Contents

Chapter 13

Composition, Printing, and Binding   376

Overview of the Processes. Composition. Platemaking and Printing.
Binding.

Preface

Webster's Standard American Style Manual is designed to be a practical guide to the conventions of the English language in its written form. Writers and editors generally use the word *style* to refer to these conventions, which include such day-to-day matters as punctuating sentences, capitalizing names and terms, using italics or underlining, spelling compound words and the plural and possessive forms of words, and deciding when to use abbreviations and numerals. The term *style* is also used to describe the conventions that writers and editors follow in carrying out more specialized tasks, such as copyediting mathematical and scientific copy, writing bibliographies and footnotes, and designing tables and indexes.

This book offers information and advice across this entire range of topics as well as on a selection of other editing- and publishing-related topics. For each topic, the manual offers concise and comprehensive descriptions of the rules and conventions that writers and editors have developed for themselves to help them prepare copy that is clear, consistent, and attractive. Where the rules and conventions have exceptions, variations, and fine points that readers need to know of, these are also presented.

The manual is divided into 13 chapters, each of which discusses in detail one aspect of style or a style-related topic. Each chapter is introduced by its own table of contents, listing all of the major sections in the chapter and the number of the page on which each section begins. Directional cross-references are placed throughout the text to guide the reader from one subject to a related subject. Cross-references usually refer the reader either to a major section of a chapter or to a specific page or range of pages within a chapter. In Chapters 1 through 5, which describe the most basic aspects of style, each paragraph describes a single point of style and is designated with a boldface numeral; hence, cross-references to points of style within these chapters often include a specific paragraph number.

In many cases, the styling conventions discussed in this book offer choices rather than a single rule, as over the years writers and editors have developed differing sets of rules to guide them in matters of style. One writer may favor a particular way of deciding when to use numerals and when to spell out numbers or how to form possessives of proper names ending in *s*, while another writer may favor other ways. Neither of these writers is necessarily wrong; each may simply be following a different style.

There are, of course, limits on the range of acceptable styles available to writers. In punctuating a list such as "license, title, and taxes," writers are often free to choose between a style that calls for placing a comma before *and* and a style that calls for omitting that comma. However, short of rewording the list, there is no practical alternative to using the other comma. One either uses it or risks confusing the reader. Moreover, most writers and editors try to be consistent in the choices they make regarding style rules. In other words, having decided on one page to use the comma before *and,* writers and editors try to use that comma for all other similar lists in the text they are working on.

Style manuals are designed to meet this need of writers and editors to choose acceptable and consistent styling practices. Writers know that as long as they consult a reputable style manual the stylings they choose will be among the acceptable ones and that as long as they always consult the same manual the choices they make are more likely to be consistent.

Most style manuals are written by editors working for a particular publication or at a particular publishing house, and they are usually written to describe the style rules in effect for that publication or publishing house. Many of today's best-known style manuals began as this sort of in-house set of style rules. Most of them have been revised and expanded to meet the needs of writers and editors in general, and some even describe styling alternatives that are not the preferred style of that publication or house; however, most style manuals that originated as in-house manuals retain the distinctive flavor of their house.

Like the style manuals just described, *Webster's Standard American Style Manual* was written and edited by working editors, the editors at Merriam-Webster Inc., and it reflects their experience in writing and editing for publication. However, the styling conventions described in this book are by no means meant to be exhaustive of or limited to the style rules followed in Merriam-Webster® publications. Instead this manual is based on Merriam-Webster's continuous study of the ways that Americans use their language. It draws on our extensive citation files, which include over 13 million examples of English words used in context gathered from books by respected authors, major metropolitan newspapers, and widely circulated general-interest magazines. In addition, a special reading-and-marking program for this book produced citations focusing on styling conventions followed in newsletters, annual reports, and special mailings by corporations and associations. Working from these sources, Merriam-Webster editors were able to establish which styling conventions are most commonly followed in standard American prose. This book records those results and constitutes, so far as we know, the first commercial attempt to develop a major style manual by means of the methods of descriptive lexicography that are the hallmark of this company's dictionaries.

Based as it is on this descriptive method, the manual recognizes both the consensus and the variety that are apparent in standard American style. The consensus in this book is recorded with simple descriptive statements, such as "A period terminates a sentence or a sentence fragment that is neither interrogative nor exclamatory."

In some cases, these statements have to be qualified, as in "The abbreviations A.D. and B.C. are usually styled in typeset matter as punctuated, unspaced, small capitals. . . ." The term *usually* is used throughout this manual to indicate that we have evidence that some writers and editors follow a different styling practice than the one we are describing. However, *usually* appears only in statements describing a styling practice that is clearly the prevalent practice. Hence, the writer who prefers AD or A.D. or AD knows that he or she is departing from the prevalent style but that such departures are not unprecedented in standard practice.

In describing styling practices that are clearly not prevalent, we have used the word *sometimes* to qualify the descriptive statement, as in "Commas are sometimes used to separate main clauses that are not joined by conjunctions." In most cases, a descriptive statement qualified with *sometimes* is also accompanied by an additional explanation that tells the reader what are the circumstances under which this styling is most likely to occur and what are the common alternatives to this styling. In the case of the example just cited, the reader is told that this styling is likely to be used if the main clauses are short and feature obvious parallelism. The reader is also told that using a comma to join clauses that are not short or obviously parallel is usually considered an error, that most writers avoid it, and that clauses not joined by conjunctions are usually separated with a semicolon.

The qualifiers *often* and *frequently* are used throughout the manual without meaning to suggest anything about the prevalence of the styling practice being described except that it is not universally followed. In saying, for instance, that "a comma is often used to set off the word *Incorporated* or the abbreviation *Inc.* from the rest of a corporate name; however, many companies elect to omit this comma from their names," we are not saying whether most companies do or do not favor using a comma in this position. We are saying that both practices are so well-established within standard style that their relative frequency is fundamentally irrelevant.

Finally, some styling practices raise questions that demand explanations that go beyond the use of a simple qualifier. In these cases we have appended a note to the description. Notes are introduced by the all-capitalized designation "NOTE," and they serve to explain, in as much detail as needed, variations, exceptions, and fine points that relate to or qualify the descriptive statement that precedes them.

The devices explained above are most in evidence in the first five chapters, which cover the most basic aspects of style. However, the approach taken in the first five chapters carries through the rest of the chapters even as they adopt a more discursive and less rigorous tone. Throughout these later chapters, we continue to describe both consensus and variety and to offer whatever additional information we can to help readers choose among alternatives when alternatives are available. This approach is certainly in evidence in Chapters 6 through 10, which describe the conventions followed in more specialized styling situations, such as presenting extended quotations or writing footnotes and bibliographies. The reader will encounter a slightly different flavor in Chapters 11, 12, and 13, as these chapters take up topics such as proofreading and typography which are not really questions of style but which are nevertheless of interest to many writers and editors.

Like all Merriam-Webster® publications, this manual is a product of the efforts of the entire editorial department. In addition to the people whose names are listed below, each member of this department has made a contribution to this book in some way—by offering suggestions during the planning stages of the book, by reviewing portions of the manuscript or responding to specific questions raised by the writers and editors of the book, or by contributing citational evidence that might otherwise have been missed. Writers and editors who assisted in preparing copy for this book include Madeline L. Novak and Stephen J. Perrault, Assistant Editors; Julie A. Collier and Kathleen M. Doherty, Associate Editors; James G. Lowe, Senior Editor; and Coleen K. Withgott, a free-lance colleague of this department. Proofreading was done by Kara L. Puskey, Editorial Assistant, and Peter D. Haraty, Daniel J. Hopkins, Madeline L. Novak, and Stephen J. Perrault, Assistant Editors, all of whom went beyond the strict call of duty to make good suggestions for improving the text. Manuscript typing was done by Helene Gingold, Department Secretary, and by Georgette B. Boucher and Barbara A. Winkler; other kinds of invaluable assistance were provided by Gloria J. Afflitto, Head of the Typing Room, and Ruth W. Gaines, Senior General Clerk. E. Ward Gilman, Senior Editor and Supervisor of Defining, provided expert copyreading and masterly rewriting of large portions of Chapters 1 through 4. Frederick C. Mish, Editorial Director, reviewed the entire manuscript, offered many excellent suggestions, and provided much support and wise counsel that were crucial to the successful completion of this project. Finally, while the colophon at the back of this book acknowledges the contributions of our typesetter and printer, special mention should be made of Carmen Vaccarelli of P&M Typesetting, whose careful attention and good judgment contributed greatly to the appearance of this book.

John M. Morse
Editor

Chapter 1

Punctuation

CONTENTS

Punctuation marks are used in the English writing system to help clarify the structure and meaning of sentences. To some degree, they achieve this end by corresponding to certain elements of the spoken language, such as pitch, volume, pause, and stress. To an even greater degree, however, punctuation marks serve to clarify structure and meaning by virtue of the fact that they conventionally accompany certain grammatical elements in a sentence, no matter how those elements might be spoken. In many cases, the relationship between punctuation and grammatical structure is such that the choice of which mark of punctuation to use in a sentence is clear and unambiguous. In other cases, however, the structure of a sentence may be such that it allows for several patterns of punctuation. In cases like these, varying notions of correctness have grown up, and two writers might, with equal correctness and with equal clarity, punctuate the same sentence quite differently.

This chapter is designed to help writers and editors make decisions about which mark of punctuation to use. In situations where more than one pattern of punctuation may be used, each is explained; if there are reasons to prefer one over another, the reasons are presented. However, even after having read this chapter, writers and editors will find that they still encounter questions requiring them to exercise their judgment and taste.

The descriptions in this chapter focus on the ways in which punctuation marks are used to convey grammatical structure. The chapter does not explain in any detailed way the use of some punctuation marks to style individual words and compounds. Specifically, this chapter does not discuss the use of quotation marks to style titles and other kinds of proper nouns, the use of apostrophes to form plurals and possessives, the use of hyphens to form compounds, or the use of periods to punctuate abbreviations. For a discussion of these topics, see Chapter 2, "Capitals, Italics, and Quotation Marks"; Chapter 3, "Plurals, Possessives, and Compounds"; and Chapter 4, "Abbreviations."

General Principles

In addition to the rules that have been developed for individual marks of punctuation, there are also conventions and principles that apply to marks of punctuation in general, and these are explained in the paragraphs that follow.

Open and Close Punctuation

Two terms frequently used to describe patterns of punctuation, especially in regard to commas, are *open* and *close*. An open punctuation pattern is one in which commas and other marks of punctuation are used sparingly, usually only to separate major syntactical units, such as main clauses, or to prevent misreading. A close punctuation pattern, on the other hand, makes liberal use of punctuation marks, often putting one wherever the grammatical structure of the sentence will allow it. Close punctuation is often considered old-fashioned, and open punctuation more modern; however, contemporary writing displays a wide range of practices in regard to commas, and some grammatical constructions are still punctuated in ways traditionally associated with close punctuation (see paragraphs 8 and 22 under Comma in this chapter).

Multiple Punctuation

The term *multiple punctuation* describes the use of two or more marks of punctuation following the same word in a sentence. A conventional rule says that multiple punctuation is to be avoided except in cases involving brackets, parentheses, quotation marks, and sometimes dashes. Unfortunately, it is not possible to formulate any simple general instructions that would allow writers and editors to apply this rule. This book addresses the question of multiple punctuation by including a section entitled "With

Other Marks of Punctuation" at the end of the treatment of each mark of punctuation for which there is a specific convention regarding multiple punctuation.

Boldface and Italic Punctuation

In general, marks of punctuation are set in the same typeface (lightface or boldface, italic or roman) as the word that precedes them, but most writers and editors allow themselves a number of exceptions to this rule. Brackets and parentheses are nearly always set in the font of the surrounding text, usually lightface roman, regardless of the text they enclose. Quotation marks are usually handled in the same manner; however, if the text they enclose is entirely in a contrasting typeface, they are set in a typeface to match. Some writers and editors base decisions regarding the typeface of exclamation points and question marks on the context in which they are used. If the exclamation point or question mark is clearly associated with the word or words that precede it, it is set in a matching typeface. If, on the other hand, it punctuates the sentence as a whole, it is set in the typeface of the sentence.

> **Summary:** Recently completed surveys confirm the theory that . . .
> You did *that!*
> We were talking with the author of the book *Who Did That?*
> Have you seen the latest issue of *Saturday Review?*

Spacing

The conventions regarding the amount of space that precedes or follows a mark of punctuation vary from mark to mark. In general, the usual spacing around each mark of punctuation should be clear from the example sentences included for each mark of punctuation. In cases where additional explanation is needed, it is included at the end of the discussion, often under the heading "Spacing."

Ampersand

An ampersand is typically written &, although it has other forms, as *&*, *&*, and &. The character represents the word *and*; its function is to replace the word when a shorter form is desirable. However, the ampersand is an acceptable substitute for *and* only in a few constructions.

1. The ampersand is used in the names of companies but not in the names of agencies that are part of the federal government.

> American Telephone & Telegraph Co.
> Gulf & Western Corporation
> Occupational Safety and Health Administration
> Securities and Exchange Commission

NOTE: In styling corporate names, writers and editors often try to reproduce the form of the name preferred by the company (taken from an annual report or company letterhead). However, this information may not be available and, even if it is available, following the different preferences of different companies can lead to apparent inconsistencies in the text. Publications that include very many corporate names usually choose one styling, usually the one with the ampersand, and use it in all corporate names that include *and*.

2. Ampersands are frequently used in abbreviations. Style varies regarding the spacing around the ampersand. Publications that make heavy use of abbreviations, such as business or technical publications, most often omit the spaces. In general-interest publications, both the spaced and the unspaced stylings are common.

   The R&D budget looks adequate for the next fiscal year.
   Apply for a loan at your bank or S & L.

3. The ampersand is often used in cases where a condensed text is necessary, as in tabular material. While bibliographies, indexes, and most other listings use *and*, some systems of parenthetical documentation do use the ampersand. For more on parenthetical documentation, see Chapter 8, "Notes and Documentation of Sources."

   (Carter, Good & Robertson 1984)

4. When an ampersand is used between the last two elements in a series, the comma is omitted.

   the law firm of Shilliday, Fraser & French

Apostrophe

1. The apostrophe is used to indicate the possessive case of nouns and indefinite pronouns. For details regarding this use, see the section on Possessives, beginning on page 79, in Chapter 3, "Plurals, Possessives, and Compounds."

2. Apostrophes are sometimes used to form plurals of letters, numerals, abbreviations, symbols, and words referred to as words. For details regarding this use, see the section on Plurals, beginning on page 74 in Chapter 3, "Plurals, Possessives, and Compounds."

3. Apostrophes mark omissions in contractions made of two or more words that are pronounced as one word.

   didn't   you're   o'clock   shouldn't've

4. The apostrophe is used to indicate that letters have been intentionally omitted from the spelling of a word in order to reproduce a per-

ceived pronunciation or to give a highly informal flavor to a piece of writing.

"Head back to N'Orleans," the man said.

Get 'em while they're hot.

dancin' till three

NOTE: Sometimes words are so consistently spelled with an apostrophe that the spelling with the apostrophe becomes an accepted variant.

fo'c'sle for *forecastle*
bos'n for *boatswain*
rock 'n' roll for *rock and roll*

5. Apostrophes mark the omission of numerals.

class of '86 politics in the '80s

NOTE: Writers who use the apostrophe for styling the plurals of words expressed in numerals usually avoid the use of the apostrophe illustrated in the second example above. Either they omit the apostrophe that stands for the missing figures, or they spell the word out.

80's *or* eighties *but not* '80's

6. Apostrophes are used to produce the inflected forms of verbs that are made of numerals or individually pronounced letters. Hyphens are sometimes used for this purpose also.

86'ed our proposal
OK'ing the manuscript
TKO'd his opponent

7. An apostrophe is often used to add an *-er* ending to an abbreviation, especially if some confusion might result from its absence. Hyphens are sometimes used for this purpose also. If no confusion is likely, the apostrophe is usually omitted.

4-H'er AA'er CBer DXer

8. The use of apostrophes to form abbreviations (as *ass'n* for *association* or *sec'y* for *secretary*) is avoided in most formal writing.

Brackets

Brackets work like parentheses to set off inserted material, but their functions are more specialized. Several of their principal uses occur with quoted material, as illustrated below. For other aspects of styling quotations, see Chapter 7, "The Treatment of Quotations."

With Editorial Insertions

1. Brackets enclose editorial comments, corrections, clarifications, or other material inserted into a text, especially into quoted matter.

> "Remember, this was the first time since it became law that the Twenty-first Amendment [outlining procedures for the replacement of a dead or incapacitated President or Vice President] had been invoked."

> "But there's one thing to be said for it [his apprenticeship with Samuels]: it started me thinking about architecture in a new way."

> He wrote, "I am just as cheerful as when you was [sic] here."

NOTE: While the text into which such editorial insertions are made is almost always quoted material, they are sometimes also used in nonquoted material, particularly in cases where an editor wishes to add material to an author's text without disturbing the author's original wording.

> Furthermore the Committee anticipates additional expenses in the coming fiscal year [October 1985–September 1986] and seeks revenues to meet these expenses.

2. Brackets set off insertions that supply missing letters.

> "If you can't persuade D[israeli], I'm sure no one can."

3. Brackets enclose insertions that take the place of words or phrases that were used in the original version of a quoted passage.

> The report, entitled "A Decade of Progress," begins with a short message from President Stevens in which she notes that "the loving portraits and revealing accounts of [this report] are not intended to constitute a complete history of the decade. . . . Rather [they] impart the flavor of the events, developments, and achievements of this vibrant period."

4. Brackets enclose insertions that slightly alter the form of a word used in an original text.

> The magazine reported that thousands of the country's children were "go[ing] to bed hungry every night."

5. Brackets are used to indicate that the capitalization or typeface of the original passage has been altered in some way.

> As we point out on page 164, "The length of a quotation usually determines whether it is run into the text or set as a block quotation . . . . [L]ength can be assessed in terms of number of words, the number of typewritten or typeset lines, or the number of sentences in the passage."

> They agreed with and were encouraged by her next point: "In the past, many secretaries have been placed in positions of responsibility *without being delegated enough authority to carry out the responsibility.* [Italics added.] The current pressures affecting managers have caused them to rethink the secretarial function and to delegate more responsibility and authority to their secretaries."

NOTE: The use of brackets to indicate altered capitalization is optional in many situations. For more on this use of brackets, see the section on Alterations, Omissions, and Interpolations, beginning on page 167, in Chapter 7, "The Treatment of Quotations."

As a Mechanical Device

6. Brackets function as parentheses within parentheses.

> The company was incinerating high concentrations of pollutants (such as polychlorinated biphenyls [PCBs]) in a power boiler.

7. Brackets set off phonetic symbols or transcriptions.

> [t] in British *duty*

8. Brackets are used in combination with parentheses to set off units in mathematical expressions. They are also used in chemical formulas. For more on the use of brackets in mathematical expressions and chemical formulas, see Chapter 6, "Mathematics and Science."

> $x + 5[(x + y)(2x - y)]$ $Ag[Pt(NO_2)_4]$

With Other Marks of Punctuation

9. No punctuation mark (other than a period after an abbreviation) precedes bracketed material within a sentence. If punctuation is required, the mark is placed after the closing bracket.

> The report stated, "If we fail to find additional sources of supply [of oil and gas], our long-term growth will be limited."

10. When brackets enclose a complete sentence, the required punctuation should be placed within the brackets.

> [A pawprint photographed last month in the Quabbin area has finally verified the cougar's continued existence in the Northeast.]

NOTE: Unlike parentheses, brackets are rarely used to enclose complete sentences within other sentences.

Spacing

11. No space is left between brackets and the material they enclose or between brackets and any mark of punctuation immediately following.

12. In typewritten material, two spaces precede an opening bracket and follow a closing bracket when the brackets enclose a complete sentence. In typeset material, one space is used.

```
We welcome the return of the cougar.  [A paw print
photographed last month has verified its existence
locally.]  Its habitation in this area is a good sign
for the whole environment.
```

> We welcome the return of the cougar. [A paw print photographed last month has verified its existence locally.] Its habitation in this area is a good sign for the whole environment.

Colon

The colon is a mark of introduction. It indicates that what follows it—whether a clause, a phrase, or even a single word—is linked with some element that precedes it. Many uses of the colon are similar to those of the dash. Like the dash, the colon gives special emphasis to whatever follows it; lengthy material introduced by a colon is often further emphasized by indention. (For information on the question of capitalizing the first word following a colon, see the section on Beginnings, starting on page 49, in Chapter 2, "Capitals, Italics, and Quotation Marks.")

With Phrases and Clauses

1. A colon introduces a clause or phrase that explains, illustrates, amplifies, or restates what has gone before.

   The sentence was poorly constructed: it lacked both unity and coherence.

   Throughout its history, the organization has combined a tradition of excellence with a dedication to human service: educating the young, caring for the elderly, assisting in community-development programs.

   Disk cartridges provide high-density storage capacity: up to 16 megabytes of information on some cartridges.

   Time was running out: a decision had to be made.

2. A colon directs attention to an appositive.

   The question is this: where will we get the money?

   He had only one pleasure: eating.

3. A colon is used to introduce a series. The introductory statement often includes a phrase such as *the following* or *as follows*.

   The conference was attended by representatives of five nations: England, France, Belgium, Spain, and Portugal.

   Anyone planning to participate should be prepared to do the following: hike five miles with a backpack, sleep on the ground without a tent, and paddle a canoe through rough water.

   NOTE: Opinion varies regarding whether a colon should interrupt the grammatical continuity of a clause (as by coming between a verb and its objects). Although most style manuals and composition handbooks advise against this practice and recommend that a full independent clause precede the colon, the interrupting colon is common. It is especially likely to be used before a lengthy and complex list, in which case the colon serves to set the list distinctly apart from the normal flow of running text. With shorter or less complex lists, the colon is usually not used.

   Our programs to increase profitability include: continued modernization of our manufacturing facilities; consolidation of distribution terminals; discontinuation of unprofitable retail outlets; and reorganization of our personnel structure, along with across-the-board staff reductions.

Our programs to increase profitability include plant modernization, improved distribution and retailing procedures, and staff reductions.

Our programs to increase profitability include the following: continued modernization of our manufacturing facilities; consolidation of distribution terminals; discontinuation of unprofitable retail outlets; and reorganization of our personnel structure, along with across-the-board staff reductions.

4. A colon is used like a dash to introduce a summary statement following a series.

Physics, biology, sociology, anthropology: he discusses them all.

With Quotations

5. A colon introduces lengthy quoted material that is set off from the rest of a text by indentation but not by quotation marks. For more on the treatment of lengthy quoted material, see Chapter 7, "Treatment of Quotations."

> He took the title for his biography of Thoreau from a passage in *Walden*:
> I long ago lost a hound, a bay horse, and a turtle-dove, and am still on their trail.... I have met one or two who had heard the hound, and the tramp of the horse, and even seen the dove disappear behind a cloud, and they seemed as anxious to recover them as if they had lost them themselves.
> However, the title *A Hound, a Bay Horse, and a Turtle-Dove* probably puzzled some readers.

6. A colon may be used before a quotation in running text, especially when (1) the quotation is lengthy, (2) the quotation is a formal statement or is being given special emphasis, or (3) the quotation is an appositive.

> Said Murdoch: "The key to the success of this project is good planning. We need to know precisely all of the steps that we will need to go through, what kind of staff we will require to accomplish each step, what the entire project will cost, and when we can expect completion."

> The inscription reads: "Here lies one whose name was writ in water."

> In response, he had this to say: "No one knows better than I do that changes will have to be made soon."

As a Mechanical Device

7. In transcriptions of dialogue, a colon follows the speaker's name.

> Robert: You still haven't heard from her?
> Michael: No, and I'm beginning to worry.

8. A colon follows a brief heading or introductory term.

> NOTE: The library will be closed on the 17th while repairs are being made to the heating system.
> 1977: New developments in microchip technology lead to less-expensive manufacturing.

9. A colon separates elements in page references, bibliographical and biblical citations, and fixed formulas used to express ratios and time.

> *Journal of the American Medical Association* 48:356
> Springfield, Mass.: Merriam-Webster Inc.
> John 4:10
> 8:30 a.m.
> a ratio of 3:5

10. A colon separates titles and subtitles (as of books).

> *The Tragic Dynasty: A History of the Romanovs*

11. A colon is used to join terms that are being contrasted or compared.

> Seventeenth-century rhymes include *prayer : afar* and *brass : was : ass.*

12. A colon follows the salutation in formal correspondence.

> Dear General Smith: Dear Product Manager:
> Dear Mr. Jiménez: Ladies and Gentlemen:

13. A colon punctuates memorandum and government correspondence headings and subject lines in general business letters.

> TO: VIA:
> SUBJECT: REFERENCE:

14. A colon separates writer/dictator/typist initials in the identification lines of business letters.

> WAL:jml
> WAL:WEB:jml

15. A colon separates carbon-copy or blind carbon-copy abbreviations from the initials or names of copy recipients in business letters.

> cc:RWP
>   JES
>
> bcc:MWK
>   FCM

With Other Marks of Punctuation

16. A colon is placed outside quotation marks and parentheses.

> There's only one thing wrong with "Harold's Indiscretion": it's not funny.
>
> I quote from the first edition of *Springtime in Savannah* (published in 1952):

Spacing

17. In typewritten material, two spaces follow a colon used in running text, bibliographical references, publication titles, and letter or memorandum headings. In typeset material, only one space follows.

```
The answer is simple:  don't go.
SUBJECT:  Project X
```

New York: Macmillan, 1980.
Typewriting: A Guide

18. When a colon is being used between two correlated terms (see paragraph 11), it is centered with equal spacing on each side.

The stature of the two sexes shows the same female : male proportions.

19. No space precedes or follows a colon when it is used between numerals.

9:30 a.m.   a ratio of 2:4

20. No space precedes or follows a colon in a business-letter identification line or in a carbon-copy notation that indicates a recipient designated by initials.

FCM:hg   cc:FCM

21. Two spaces follow a colon in a carbon-copy notation that indicates a recipient designated by a full name.

cc: Mr. Johnson

Comma

The comma is the most frequently used punctuation mark in the English writing system. Its most common uses are to separate items in a series and to set off syntactical elements within sentences. Within these two broad categories, there are a great many specific uses to which commas can be put. This section explains the most common aspects of the comma, listed under the following headings.

Between Main Clauses
With Compound Predicates
With Subordinate Clauses and
   Phrases
With Appositives
With Introductory and
   Interrupting Elements
With Contrasting Expressions
With Items in a Series

With Compound Modifiers
In Quotations, Questions, and
   Indirect Discourse
With Omitted Words
With Addresses, Dates, and Numbers
With Names, Degrees, and Titles
In Correspondence
Other Uses
With Other Marks of Punctuation

Between Main Clauses

1. A comma separates main clauses joined by a coordinating conjunction (as *and, but, or, nor,* and *for*). For use of commas with clauses joined by correlative conjunctions, see paragraph 24 below.

> She knew very little about him, and he volunteered nothing.
>
> We will not respond to any more questions on that topic this afternoon, nor will we respond to similar questions at any time in the future.
>
> His face showed disappointment, for he knew that he had failed.

NOTE: Some reference books still insist that *so* and *yet* are adverbs rather than conjunctions and that therefore they should be preceded by a semicolon when they join main clauses. However, our evidence indicates that the use of *so* and *yet* as conjunctions preceded by a comma is standard.

> The acoustics in this hall are good, so every note is clear.
>
> We have requested this information many times before, yet we have never gotten a satisfactory reply.

2. When one or both of the clauses are short or when they are closely related in meaning, the comma is often omitted.

> The sun was shining and the birds were singing.
>
> We didn't realize it at the time but the spot we had picked for our home was the same spot one of our ancestors had picked for his home.
>
> Six thousand years ago, the top of the volcano blew off in a series of powerful eruptions and the sides collapsed into the middle.
>
> Many people want to take their vacations in August so it may be difficult for some of them to find good accommodations.

NOTE: In punctuating sentences such as the ones illustrated above, writers have to use their own judgment regarding whether clauses are short enough or closely related enough to warrant omitting the comma. There are no clear-cut rules to follow; however, factors such as the rhythm, parallelism, or logic of the sentence often influence how clearly or smoothly it will read with or without the comma.

3. Commas are sometimes used to separate main clauses that are not joined by conjunctions. This styling is especially likely to be used if the clauses are short and feature obvious parallelism.

> One day you are a successful corporate lawyer, the next day you are out of work.
>
> The city has suffered terribly in the interim. Bombs have destroyed most of the buildings, disease has ravaged the population.

NOTE: Using a comma to join clauses that are neither short nor obviously parallel is usually called *comma fault* or *comma splice* and most writers and editors avoid such a construction. In general, clauses not joined by conjunctions are separated by semicolons.

4. If a sentence is composed of three or more clauses, the clauses may be separated by either commas or semicolons. Clauses that are short and relatively free of commas can be separated by commas even if they are not joined by a conjunction. If the clauses are long or heavily punctuated, they are separated with semicolons, except for the last

two clauses which may be separated by either a comma or a semicolon. Usually a comma will be used between the last two clauses only if those clauses are joined by a conjunction. For more examples of clauses separated with commas and semicolons, see paragraph 5 under Semicolon in this chapter.

> The pace of change seems to have quickened, the economy is uncertain, the technology seems sometimes liberating and sometimes hostile.

> Small fish fed among the marsh weed, ducks paddled along the surface, and a muskrat ate greens along the bank.

> The policy is a complex one to explain; defending it against its critics is not easy, nor is it clear the defense is always necessary.

With Compound Predicates

5. Commas are not usually used to separate the parts of a compound predicate.

> The firefighter tried to enter the burning building but was turned back by the thick smoke.

NOTE: Despite the fact that most style manuals and composition handbooks warn against separating the parts of compound predicates with commas, many authors and editors use commas in just this way. They are particularly likely to do so if the predicate is especially long and complicated, if they want to stress one part of the predicate, or if the absence of a comma could cause even a momentary misreading of the sentence.

> The board helps to develop the financing, new product planning, and marketing strategies for new corporate divisions, and issues periodic reports on expenditures, revenues, and personnel appointments.

> This is an unworkable plan, and has been from the start.

> I try to explain to him what I want him to do, and get nowhere.

With Subordinate Clauses and Phrases

6. Adverbial clauses and phrases that precede a main clause are usually set off with commas.

> As cars age, they depreciate.

> Having made that decision, we turned our attention to other matters.

> To understand the situation, you must be familiar with the background.

> From the top of this rugged and isolated plateau, I could see the road stretching out for miles across the desert.

> In 1919, his family left Russia and moved to this country.

> In addition, staff members respond to queries, take new orders, and initiate billing.

7. If a sentence begins with an adverbial clause or phrase and can be easily read without a comma following it, writers will often omit the comma. In most cases where the comma is omitted, the phrase will be short—four words or less. But some writers will omit the comma even after a longer phrase if the sentence can be easily read or seems more forceful that way.

> In January the company will introduce a new line of entirely redesigned products.

> On the map the town appeared as a small dot in the midst of vast emptiness.

> If the project cannot be done profitably perhaps it should not be done at all.

8. Adverbial clauses and phrases that introduce a main clause other than the first main clause are usually set off with commas. However, if the adverbial clause or phrase follows a conjunction, style varies regarding how many commas are required to set it off. In most cases, two commas are used: one before the conjunction and one following the clause or phrase. Writers who prefer close punctuation usually use three commas: one before the conjunction and two more to enclose the clause or phrase. If the writer prefers open punctuation, the phrase may not be set off at all. In this case, only one comma that separates the main clauses is used. For more on open and close punctuation, see page 2.

> His parents were against the match, and had the couple not eloped, their plans for marriage would have come to nothing.

> They have redecorated the entire store, but, to the delight of their customers, the store retains much of its original flavor. [close]

> We haven't left Springfield yet, but when we get to Boston we'll call you. [open]

9. A comma is not used after an introductory phrase if the phrase immediately precedes the main verb.

> In the road lay a dead rabbit.

10. Subordinate clauses and phrases that follow a main clause or that fall within a main clause are usually not set off by commas if they are restrictive. A clause or phrase is considered restrictive if its removal from the sentence would alter the meaning of the main clause. If the meaning of the main clause would not be altered by removing the subordinate clause or phrase, the clause or phrase is considered nonrestrictive and usually is set off by commas.

> We will be delighted if she decides to stay. [restrictive]

> Anyone who wants his or her copy of the book autographed by the author should get in line. [restrictive]

> Her new book, *Fortune's Passage*, was well received. [nonrestrictive]

> That was a good meal, although I didn't particularly like the broccoli in cream sauce. [nonrestrictive]

11. Commas are used to set off an adverbial clause or phrase that falls between the subject and the verb.

> The weather, fluctuating from very hot to downright chilly, necessitated a variety of clothing.

12. Commas enclose modifying phrases that do not immediately precede the word or phrase they modify.

> Hungry and tired, the soldiers marched back to camp.
>
> We could see the importance, both long-term and short-term, of her proposal.
>
> The two children, equally happy with their lunches, set off for school.

13. Absolute phrases are set off with commas, whether they fall at the beginning, middle, or end of the sentence.

> Our business being concluded, we adjourned for refreshments.
>
> We headed southward, the wind freshening behind us, to meet the rest of the fleet in the morning.
>
> I still remember my first car, its bumpers sagging, its tires worn, its body rusting.

With Appositives

14. Commas are used to set off a word, phrase, or clause that is in apposition to a noun and that is nonrestrictive.

> My husband, Larry, is in charge of ticket sales for the fair.
>
> The highboy, or tallboy, is a tall chest of drawers typically made between 1690 and 1780.
>
> George Washington, first president of the United States, has been the subject of countless biographies.
>
> We were most impressed by the third candidate, the one who brought a writing sample and asked so many questions.

NOTE: A nonrestrictive appositive sometimes precedes the word with which it is in apposition. It is set off by commas in this position also.

> A cherished landmark in the city, the Hotel Sandburg has managed once again to escape the wrecking ball.

15. Restrictive appositives are not set off by commas.

> My daughter Andrea had the lead in the school play.
>
> Alfred Hitchcock's thriller "Psycho" will be screened tonight.

With Introductory and Interrupting Elements

16. Commas set off transitional words and phrases (as *finally, meanwhile,* and *after all*).

> Indeed, close coordination between departments can minimize confusion during this period of expansion.

We are eager to begin construction; however, the necessary materials have not yet arrived.

The most recent report, on the other hand, makes clear why the management avoids such agreements.

NOTE: Adverbs that can serve as transitional words can often serve in other ways as well. When these adverbs are not used to make a transition, no comma is necessary.

The materials had finally arrived.

17. Commas set off parenthetical elements, such as authorial asides and supplementary information, that are closely related to the rest of the sentence.

All of us, to tell the truth, were completely amazed by his suggestion.

The headmaster, now in his sixth year at the school, was responsible for the changes in the curriculum.

NOTE: When the parenthetical element is digressive or otherwise not closely related to the rest of the sentence, it is often set off by dashes or parentheses. For contrasting examples, see paragraph 3 under Dash and paragraphs 1 and 9 under Parentheses in this chapter.

18. Commas are used to set off words or phrases that introduce examples or explanations.

He expects to visit three countries this summer, namely, France, Spain, and Germany.

I would like to develop a good, workable plan, i.e., one that would outline our goals and set a timetable for their accomplishment.

NOTE: Words and phrases such as *i.e., e.g., namely, for example,* and *that is* are often preceded by a dash, open parenthesis, or semicolon, depending on the magnitude of the break in continuity represented by the examples or explanations that they introduce; however, regardless of the punctuation that precedes the word or phrase, a comma always follows it. For contrasting examples of dashes, parentheses, and semicolons with these words and phrases, see paragraph 6 under Dash, paragraph 2 under Parentheses, and paragraph 6 under Semicolon in this chapter.

19. Commas are used to set off words in direct address.

We would like to discuss your account, Mrs. Reid.

The answer, my friends, lies within us.

20. Commas set off mild interjections or exclamations such as *ah* or *oh.*

Ah, summer—season of sunshine and goodwill.
Oh, what a beautiful baby.

NOTE: The vocative *O* is not set off by commas.

O Time! O Death!
Have mercy, O Lord.

With Contrasting Expressions

21. A comma is used to set off contrasting expressions within a sentence.

This project will take six months, not six weeks.
He has merely changed his style, not his ethics.

22. Style varies regarding use of the comma to set off two or more contrasting phrases used to describe a single word that follows immediately. In open punctuation, a comma follows the first modifier but is not used between the final modifier and the word modified. In close punctuation, the contrasting phrase is treated as a nonrestrictive modifier and is, therefore, both preceded and followed by a comma. For more on open and close punctuation, see page 2.

The harsh, although eminently realistic critique is not going to make you popular. [open]
The harsh, although eminently realistic, critique is not going to make you popular. [close]
This street takes you away from, not toward the capitol building. [open]
This street takes you away from, not toward, the capitol building. [close]

23. Adjectives and adverbs that modify the same word or phrase and that are joined by *but* or some other coordinating conjunction are not separated by a comma.

a bicycle with a light but sturdy frame
a multicolored but subdued rag rug
errors caused by working carelessly or too quickly

24. A comma does not usually separate elements that are contrasted through the use of a pair of correlative conjunctions (as *either . . . or, neither . . . nor,* and *not only . . . but also*).

The cost is either $69.95 or $79.95.

Neither my brother nor I noticed the mistake.

He was given the post not only because of his diplomatic connections but also because of his great tact and charm.

NOTE: Correlative conjunctions are sometimes used to join main clauses. If the clauses are short, a comma is not added; however, if the clauses are long, a comma usually separates them.

Either you do it my way or we don't do it at all.

Not only did she have to see three salesmen and a visiting reporter during the course of the day, but she also had to prepare for the next day's meeting with the president.

25. Long parallel contrasting and comparing clauses are separated by commas; short parallel phrases are not.

> The more I heard about this new project, the greater was my desire to volunteer.
>
> "The sooner the better," I said.

With Items in a Series

26. Words, phrases, and clauses joined in a series are separated by commas. If main clauses are joined in a series, they may be separated by either semicolons or commas. For more on the use of commas and semicolons to separate main clauses, see paragraphs 1, 3, and 4 above and paragraph 5 under Semicolon in this chapter.

> Men, women, and children crowded aboard the train.
>
> Her job required her to pack quickly, to travel often, and to have no personal life.
>
> He responded patiently while reporters shouted questions, flashbulbs popped, and the crowd pushed closer.

NOTE: Style varies regarding the use of the comma between the last two items in a series if those items are also joined by a conjunction. In some cases, as in the example below, omitting the final comma (often called the serial comma) can result in ambiguity. Some writers feel that in most sentences the use of the conjunction makes the comma superfluous, and they favor using the comma only when a misreading could result from omitting it. Others feel that it is easier to include the final comma routinely rather than try to consider each sentence separately to decide whether a misreading is possible without the comma. Most reference books, including this one, and most other book-length works of nonfiction use the serial comma. In all other categories of publishing, according to our evidence, usage is evenly or nearly evenly divided on the use or omission of this comma.

> We are looking for a house with a big yard, a view of the harbor, and beach and docking privileges. [with serial comma]
>
> We are looking for a house with a big yard, a view of the harbor and beach and docking privileges. [without serial comma]

27. A comma is not used to separate items in a series that are joined with conjunctions.

> I don't understand what this policy covers or doesn't cover or only partially covers.
>
> I have talked to the president and the vice president and three other executives.

28. When the elements in a series are long or complex or consist of clauses that themselves contain commas, the elements are usually separated by semicolons, not commas. For more on this use of the semicolon, see paragraphs 7 and 8 under Semicolon in this chapter.

With Compound Modifiers

29. A comma is used to separate two or more adjectives, adverbs, or phrases that modify the same word or phrase. For the use of commas with contrasting modifiers, see paragraphs 22 and 23 above.

> She spoke in a calm, reflective manner.
> We watched the skier move smoothly, gracefully through the turns.
> His story was too fantastic, too undersupported by facts for us to take seriously.

30. A comma is not used between two adjectives when the first modifies the combination of the second adjective plus the word or phrase it modifies.

> a little brown jug
> a modern concrete-and-glass building

31. A comma is not used to separate an adverb from the adjective or adverb that it modifies.

> a truly distinctive manner
> running very quickly down the street

In Quotations, Questions, and Indirect Discourse

32. A comma separates a direct quotation from a phrase identifying its source or speaker. If the quotation is a question or an exclamation and the identifying phrase follows the quotation, the comma is replaced by a question mark or an exclamation point.

> Mary said, "I am leaving."
> "I am leaving," Mary said.
> Mary asked, "Where are you going?"
> "Where are you going?" Mary asked.
> "I am leaving," Mary said, "even if you want me to stay."
> "Don't do that!" Mary shouted.

NOTE: In some cases, a colon can replace a comma preceding a quotation. For more on this use of the colon, see paragraph 6 under Colon in this chapter.

33. A comma does not set off a quotation that is tightly incorporated into the sentence in which it appears.

> Throughout the session his only responses were "No comment" and "I don't think so."
> Just because he said he was "about to leave this minute" doesn't mean he actually left.

34. Style varies regarding the use of commas to set off shorter sentences that fall within longer sentences and that do not constitute actual dialogue. These shorter sentences may be mottoes or maxims, unspoken or imaginary dialogue, or sentences referred to as sentences; and they may or may not be enclosed in quotation marks. (For more on the use of quotation marks with sentences like these, see paragraph 6 under Quotation Marks, Double, in this chapter.) Typically the shorter sentence functions as a subject, object, or complement within the larger sentence and does not require a comma. Sometimes the structure of the larger sentence will be styled like actual quoted dialogue, and in such cases a comma is used to separate the shorter sentence from the text that introduces or identifies it. In some cases, where an author decides not to use quotation marks, a comma may be inserted simply to mark the beginning of the shorter sentence clearly.

> "The computer is down" was the response she dreaded.
> Another confusing idiom is "How do you do?"
> He spoke with a candor that seemed to insist, This actually happened to me and in just this way.
> The first rule is, When in doubt, spell it out.

When the shorter sentence functions as an appositive in the larger sentence, it is set off with a comma when nonrestrictive and not when restrictive. (For more on restrictive modifiers and appositives, see paragraphs 10, 14, and 15 above.)

> He was fond of the slogan "Every man a king, but no man wears a crown."
> We had the club's motto, "We make waves," printed on our T-shirts.

35. A comma introduces a direct question regardless of whether it is enclosed in quotation marks or if its first word is capitalized.

> I wondered, what is going on here?
> The question is, How do we get out of here?
> What bothered her was, who had eaten all of the cookies?

36. The comma is omitted before quotations that are very short exclamations or representations of sounds.

> He jumped up suddenly and cried "Yow!"
> When she was done, she let out a loud "Whew!"

37. A comma is not used to set off indirect discourse or indirect questions introduced by a conjunction (such as *that* or *what*).

> Mary said that she was leaving.
> I wondered what was going on there.
> The clerk told me that the book I had ordered had just come in.

With Omitted Words

38. A comma indicates the omission of a word or phrase, especially in parallel constructions where the omitted word or phrase appears earlier in the sentence.

> Common stocks are preferred by some investors; bonds, by others.

39. A comma often replaces the conjunction *that*.

> The road was so steep and winding, we thought for sure that we would go over the edge.
>
> The problem is, we don't know how to fix it.

With Addresses, Dates, and Numbers

40. A comma is used to set off the individual elements of an address except for zip codes. In current practice, no punctuation appears between a state name and the zip code that follows it. If prepositions are used between the elements of the address, commas are not needed.

> Mrs. Bryant may be reached at 52 Kiowa Circle, Mesa, Arizona.
>
> Mr. Briscoe was born in Liverpool, England.
>
> The collection will be displayed at the Wilmington, Delaware, Museum of Art.
>
> Write to the Bureau of the Census, Washington, DC 20233.
>
> The White House is located at 1600 Pennsylvania Avenue in Washington, D.C.

NOTE: Some writers omit the comma that follows the name of a state when no other element of an address follows it. This is most likely to happen when a city name and state name are being used in combination to modify a noun that follows; however, our evidence indicates that retaining this comma is still the more common practice.

> We visited their Enid, Oklahoma plant.
> *but more commonly*
> We visited their Enid, Oklahoma, plant.

41. Commas are used to set off the year from the day of the month. When only the month and the year are given, the comma is usually omitted.

> On October 26, 1947, the newly hired employees began work on the project.
>
> In December 1903, the Wright brothers finally succeeded in keeping an airplane aloft for a few seconds.

42. A comma groups numerals into units of three to separate thousands, millions, and so on; however, this comma is generally not used in page numbers, street numbers, or numbers within dates. For more on the styling of numbers, see Chapter 5, "The Treatment of Numbers."

> a population of 350,000   the year 1986
> 4509 South Pleasant Street   page 1419

With Names, Degrees, and Titles

43. A comma punctuates an inverted name.

> Sagan, Deborah J.

44. A comma is used between a surname and *Junior, Senior,* or their abbreviations.

> Morton A. Williams, Jr.
> Douglas Fairbanks, Senior

45. A comma is often used to set off the word *Incorporated* or the abbreviation *Inc.* from the rest of a corporate name; however, many companies elect to omit this comma from their names.

> Leedy Manufacturing Company, Incorporated
> Tektronics, Inc.
> Merz-Fortunata Inc.

46. A comma separates a surname from a following academic, honorary, military, or religious degree or title.

> Amelia P. Artandi, D.V.M.
> John L. Farber, Esq.
> Sister Mary Catherine, S.C.
> Robert Menard, M.A., Ph.D.
> Admiral Herman Washington, USN

In Correspondence

47. The comma follows the salutation in informal correspondence and follows the complimentary close in both informal and formal correspondence. In formal correspondence, a colon follows the salutation. For more on this use of the colon, see paragraph 12 under Colon in this chapter.

> Dear Rachel,
> Affectionately,
> Very truly yours,

Other Uses

48. The comma is used to avoid ambiguity when the juxtaposition of two words or expressions could cause confusion.

> Whatever will be, will be.
> To John, Marshall was someone special.
> I repaired the lamp that my brother had broken, and replaced the bulb.

49. A comma often follows a direct object or a predicate nominative or predicate adjective when they precede the subject and verb in the sentence. If the meaning of the sentence is clear without this comma, it is often omitted.

> That we would soon have to raise prices, no one disputed.
> Critical about the current state of affairs, we might have been.
> A disaster it certainly was.

With Other Marks of Punctuation

50. Commas are used in conjunction with brackets, ellipsis points, parentheses, and quotation marks. Commas are not used in conjunction with colons, dashes, exclamation points, question marks, or semi-colons. If one of these latter marks falls at the same point in a sentence at which a comma would fall, the comma is dropped and the other mark is retained. For more on the use of commas with other marks of punctuation, see the heading With Other Marks of Punctuation in the sections of this chapter covering those marks of punctuation.

Dash

In many of its uses, the dash functions like a comma, a colon, or a pair of parentheses. Like commas and parentheses, dashes set off parenthetic material such as examples, supplemental facts, or appositional, explanatory, or descriptive phrases. Like colons, dashes introduce clauses that explain or expand upon some element of the material that precedes them. The dash is sometimes considered to be a less formal equivalent of the colon and parenthesis, and it does frequently take their place in advertising and other informal contexts. However, dashes are prevalent in all kinds of writing, including the most formal, and the choice of which mark to use is usually a matter of personal preference.

The dash exists in a number of different lengths. The dash in most general use is the em dash, which is approximately the width of an uppercase M in typeset material. In typewritten material, it is represented by two hyphens. The en dash and the two- and three-em dashes have more limited uses which are explained in paragraphs 15–18 below.

Abrupt Change or Suspension

1. The dash marks an abrupt change in the flow of a writer's thought or in the structure of a sentence.

> The mountain that we climbed is higher than—well, never mind how high it is.
>
> The students seemed happy with the change, but the alumni—there was the problem.

2. Dashes mark a suspension in the writer's flow of thought or in the sentence structure. Such suspensions are frequently caused by an authorial aside.

> He was—how shall we put it?—a controversial character to say the least.
>
> If I had kept my notes—and I really wish that I had—I would be able to give you the exact date of the sale.

Parenthetic and Amplifying Elements

3. Dashes are used in place of other punctuation (such as commas or parentheses) to emphasize parenthetic or amplifying material or to make such material stand out more clearly from the rest of the sentence.

> She is willing to discuss all problems—those she has solved and those for which there is no immediate solution.
>
> In 1976, they asked for—and received—substantial grants from the federal government.
>
> The privately owned consulting firm—formerly known as Aborjaily and Associates—is now offering many new services.

NOTE: When dashes are used to set off parenthetic elements, they often indicate that the material is more digressive than elements set off with commas but less digressive than elements set off by parentheses. For contrasting examples see paragraph 17 under Comma and paragraphs 1 and 9 under Parentheses in this chapter.

4. Dashes are used to set off or to introduce defining and enumerating phrases.

> The fund sought to acquire controlling positions—a minimum of 25% of outstanding voting securities—in other companies.
>
> The essay dealt with our problems with waste—cans, bottles, discarded tires, and other trash.

5. A dash is often used in place of a colon or semicolon to link clauses, especially when the clause that follows the dash explains, summarizes, or expands upon the clause that precedes it.

> The test results were surprisingly good—none of the tested models displayed serious problems.
>
> The deterioration of our bridges and roads has been apparent for many years—parts of the interstate highway system are 30 years old, after all, and most of our bridges are older than that.

6. A dash or a pair of dashes often sets off parenthetic or amplifying material introduced by such phrases as *for example, namely, that is, e.g.,* and *i.e.*

> After some discussion the motion was tabled—that is, it was removed indefinitely from the board's consideration.
>
> Sports develop two valuable traits—namely, self-control and the ability to make quick decisions.
>
> Not all "prime" windows—i.e., the ones installed when a house is built—are equal in quality.

NOTE: Commas, parentheses, and semicolons are often used for the same purpose. For contrasting examples, see paragraph 18 under Comma, paragraph 2 under Parentheses, and paragraph 6 under Semicolon in this chapter.

7. A dash introduces a summary statement that follows a series of words or phrases.

> Unemployment, strikes, inflation, stock prices, mortgage rates—all are part of the economy.

Once into bankruptcy, the company would have to pay cash for its supplies, defer maintenance, and lay off workers—moves that could threaten its long-term profitability.

As a Mechanical Device

8. A dash precedes the name of an author or source at the end of a quoted passage.

> Winter tames man, woman and beast.
>
> > —William Shakespeare
>
> "A comprehensive and beautifully written biography."—*National Review*

NOTE: This method of attribution is most often used when the quoted material is not part of the main text. Examples of such situations are quotations set as epigraphs and quotations set as extracts. The attribution may appear immediately after the quotation, or it may appear on the next line. For more on the treatment of quotations, see Chapter 7, "The Treatment of Quotations."

9. A dash is used to indicate interrupted speech or a speaker's confusion or hesitation.

> "The next point I'd like to bring up—" the speaker started to say. "I'm sorry. I'll have to stop you there," the moderator broke in.
>
> "Yes," he went on, "yes—that is—I guess I agree."

NOTE: There is some disagreement among style manuals regarding the use of a comma between a quotation ending with a dash and its attribution. Our evidence indicates that the comma is usually omitted in such circumstances. This follows the general practice regarding the use of commas with dashes described in paragraph 11 below.

10. Dashes are used variously as elements in page design. They may, for example, precede items in a vertical enumeration, set off elements in the dateline of a newspaper report, or separate words from their definitions in a glossary. The use of dashes in such circumstances is usually determined by the editor or designer of the publication.

> Required skills are:
> —Shorthand
> —Typing
> —Transcription

With Other Marks of Punctuation

11. If a dash appears at a point in a sentence where a comma could also appear, the dash is retained and the comma is dropped. For one situation in which this practice is not always followed, see paragraph 9 above.

> If we don't succeed—and the critics say we won't—then the whole project is in jeopardy.

> Our lawyer has read the transcript—all 1200 pages of it—and he has decided that an appeal would not be useful.
>
> Some of the other departments, however—particularly Accounting, Sales, and Credit Collection—have expanded their computer operations.

12. If the second of a pair of dashes appears at a point in a sentence where a period or semicolon would also appear, the period or semicolon is retained and the dash is dropped.

> His conduct has always been exemplary—near-perfect attendance, excellent productivity, a good attitude; nevertheless, his termination cannot be avoided.

13. Dashes are used with exclamation points and question marks. When a pair of dashes sets off parenthetic material calling for either of these marks of punctuation, the exclamation point or the question mark is placed inside the second dash. If the parenthetic material falls at the end of a sentence ending with an exclamation point or question mark, the closing dash is not required.

> His hobby was getting on people's nerves—especially mine!—and he was extremely good at it.
>
> When the committee meets next week—are you going to be there?—I will present all of the final figures.
>
> Is there any way to predict the future course of this case—one which we really cannot afford to lose?

14. Dashes and parentheses are used in combination to indicate parenthetic material appearing within parenthetic material. Our evidence indicates that dashes within parentheses and parentheses within dashes occur with about equal frequency.

> We were looking for a narrator (or narrators—sometimes a script calls for more than one) who could handle a variety of assignments.
>
> On our trip south we crossed a number of major rivers—the Hudson, the Delaware, and the Patapsco (which flows through Baltimore)—without paying a single toll.

NOTE: If the inner parenthetic element begins with a dash and its closing dash would fall in the same position as the closing parenthesis, the closing dash is omitted and the parenthesis is retained, as in the first example above. If the inner phrase begins with a parenthesis and its closing parenthesis would coincide with the closing dash, the closing parenthesis and the closing dash are both retained, as in the second example above.

En Dash

15. En dashes appear only in typeset material. The en dash is shorter than the em dash but slightly longer than the hyphen, and it is used in place of the hyphen in some situations. The most common use of the en dash is as an equivalent to "(up) to and including" when used between numbers, dates, or other notations that indicate range.

1984–85	8:30 a.m.–4:30 p.m.	GS 12–14
$20–$40	Monday–Friday	ages 10–15
levels D–G	35–40 years	pages 128–34

NOTE: The use of the en dash to replace the hyphen in such cases, although urged by most style manuals, is by no means universal. Writers and editors who wish to have en dashes set in their copy need to indicate on their manuscripts which hyphens should be set as en dashes (see Chapter 11, "Production Techniques," page 309), and this need to mark en dashes can obviously be an inconvenience and an invitation to errors. However, many writers and editors prefer to use en dashes because of the visual clarity they provide between numbers and because of the distinction they make between en dashes used to mean "to" and hyphens used to connect elements in compound words.

16. Publishers make various uses of the en dash, and no one set of rules can be said to be standard. Some common uses of the en dash include using it as a replacement for the hyphen following a prefix that is added to an open compound, as a replacement for the word *to* between capitalized names, and to indicate linkages, such as boundaries, treaties, or oppositions.

> pre–Civil War architecture
> the New York–Connecticut area
> Chicago–Memphis train
> Washington–Moscow diplomacy
> the Dempsey–Tunney fight

Long Dashes

17. A two-em dash is used to indicate missing letters in a word and, less frequently, to indicate a missing word.

> Mr. P—— of Baltimore
> That's b——t and you know it.

18. A three-em dash indicates that a word has been left out or that an unknown word or figure is to be supplied. For the use of this dash in bibliography listings, see Chapter 8, "Notes and Documentation of Sources," pages 206–207.

> The study was carried out in ———, a fast-growing Sunbelt city.
> We'll leave New York City on the ——— of August.

Spacing

19. Style varies as to spacing around the dash. Some publications insert a space before and after the dash, others do not. Our evidence indicates that the majority of publishers style the dash without spaces.

Ellipsis Points

Ellipsis points is the name most often given to periods when they are used, usually in groups of three, to signal an omission from quoted material or to indicate a pause or trailing off of speech. Other names for periods used in this way include *ellipses, points of ellipsis,* and *suspension points.* Ellipsis points are often used in conjunction with other marks of punctuation, including periods used to mark the ends of sentences. When ellipsis points are used in this way with a terminal period, the omission is sometimes thought of as being marked by four periods. This discussion of ellipsis points is illustrated with examples of ellipsis points used with quoted material enclosed in quotation marks. For examples of ellipsis points used to indicate omissions from quoted material set as extracts, see Chapter 7, "The Treatment of Quotations," especially the section on Alterations, Omissions, and Interpolations, beginning on page 167.

> NOTE: The examples given below present passages in which ellipsis points indicate omission of material. In most cases, the full text from which these omissions have been made is some portion of the headnote above.

1. Ellipsis points indicate the omission of one or more words within a quoted sentence.

   > One book said, "Other names . . . include *ellipses, points of ellipsis,* and *suspension points.*"

2. Ellipsis points are usually not used to indicate the omission of words that precede the quoted portion. However, style varies on this point, and in some formal contexts, especially those in which the quotation is introduced by a colon, ellipsis points are used.

   > The book maintained that "the omission is sometimes thought of as being marked by four periods."
   >
   > The book maintained: ". . . the omission is sometimes thought of as being marked by four periods."

3. Punctuation used in the original that falls on either side of the ellipsis points is often omitted; however, it may be retained, especially if such retention helps clarify the sentence.

   > According to the book, "*Ellipsis points* is the name most often given to periods when they are used . . . to signal an omission from quoted material or to indicate a pause or trailing off of speech."
   >
   > According to the book, "When ellipsis points are used in this way . . . , the omission is sometimes thought of as being marked by four periods."
   >
   > According to the book, "*Ellipsis points* is the name most often given to periods when they are used, usually in groups of three, . . . to indicate a pause or trailing off of speech."

4. If an omission comprises an entire sentence within a passage, the last part of a sentence within a passage, or the first part of a sentence other than the first quoted sentence, the end punctuation preceding or following the omission is retained and is followed by three periods.

> That book says, "Other names for periods used in this way include *ellipses, points of ellipsis,* and *suspension points*. . . . When ellipsis points are used in this way with a terminal period, the omission is sometimes thought of as being marked by four periods."

> That book says, "*Ellipsis points* is the name given to periods when they are used, usually in groups of three, to signal an omission from quoted material. . . . Other names for periods used in this way include *ellipses, points of ellipsis,* and *suspension points*."

> That book says, "Ellipsis points are often used in conjunction with other marks of punctuation, including periods used to mark ends of sentences. . . . The omission is sometimes thought of as being marked by four periods."

NOTE: The capitalization of the word *The* in the third example is acceptable. For more on the capitalization of words in quotations, see the section on Alterations, Omissions, and Interpolations, beginning on page 167, in Chapter 7, "The Treatment of Quotations."

5. If the last words of a quoted sentence are omitted and if the original sentence ends with a period, that period is retained and three ellipsis points follow. However, if the original sentence ends with punctuation other than a period, the end punctuation often follows the ellipsis points, especially if it helps clarify the quotation.

> Their book said, "Ellipsis points are often used in conjunction with other marks of punctuation. . . ."

> He always ends his harangues with some variation on the question, "What could you have been thinking when you . . . ?"

NOTE: Many writers and editors, especially those writing in more informal contexts, choose to ignore the styling considerations presented in paragraphs 4 and 5. They use instead an alternative system in which all omissions are indicated by three periods and all terminal periods that may precede or follow an omission are dropped.

6. Ellipsis points are used to indicate that a quoted sentence has been intentionally left unfinished. In situations such as this the terminal period is not included.

> In that section, the introductory paragraph begins, "*Ellipsis points* is the name most often given . . ."

7. A line of ellipsis points indicates that one or more lines of poetry have been omitted from a text. For more on this use of ellipsis points, see the section on Quoting Verse, beginning on page 172, in Chapter 7, "The Treatment of Quotations."

8. Ellipsis points are used to indicate faltering speech, especially if the faltering involves a long pause between words or a sentence that trails off or is left intentionally unfinished. In these kinds of sentences most writers treat the ellipsis points as terminal punctuation, thus removing the need for any other punctuation; however, style does vary on this point, and some writers routinely use other punctuation in conjunction with ellipsis points.

> The speaker seemed uncertain how to answer the question. "Well, that's true . . . but even so . . . I think we can do better."
> "Despite these uncertainties, we believe we can do it, but . . ."
> "I mean . . ." he said, "like . . . How?"

9. Ellipsis points are sometimes used as a stylistic device to catch and hold a reader's attention.

> They think that nothing can go wrong . . . but it does.

10. Each ellipsis point is set off from other ellipsis points, from adjacent punctuation (except for quotation marks, which are closed up to the ellipsis points), and from surrounding text by a space. If a terminal period is used with ellipsis points, it precedes them with no space before it and one space after it.

Exclamation Point

The exclamation point is used to mark a forceful comment. Writers and editors usually try to avoid using the exclamation point too frequently, because its heavy use can weaken its effect.

1. An exclamation point can punctuate a sentence, phrase, or interjection.

> This is the fourth time in a row he's missed his cue!
> No one that I talked to—not even the accounting department!—seemed to know how the figures were calculated.
> Oh! you startled me.
> Ah, those eyes!

2. The exclamation point replaces the question mark when an ironic or emphatic tone is more important than the actual question.

> Aren't you finished yet!
> Do you realize what you've done!
> Why me!

3. Occasionally the exclamation point is used with a question mark to indicate a very forceful question.

> How much did you say?!
> You did what!?

NOTE: The interrobang, printed ‽ , was created to punctuate the types of sentences described in paragraphs 2 and 3 above. However, the character is not available to most typesetters, and it is rarely used.

4. In mathematical expressions, the exclamation point indicates a factorial. For an example of this use, see page 138 in Chapter 6, "Mathematics and Science."

5. The exclamation point is enclosed within brackets, dashes, parentheses, and quotation marks when it punctuates the material so enclosed rather than the sentence as a whole. It should be placed outside them when it punctuates the entire sentence.

> All of this proves—at long last!—that we were right from the start.
> Somehow the dog got the gate open (for the third time!) and ran into the street.
> He shouted, "Wait!" and sprinted toward the train.
> The correct word is "mousse," not "moose"!

6. Exclamatory phrases that occur within a sentence are set off by dashes or parentheses.

> And now our competition—get this!—wants to start sharing secrets.
> The board accepted most of the recommendations, but ours (alas!) was not even considered.

7. If an exclamation point falls at a place in a sentence where a comma or a terminal period could also go, the comma or period is dropped and the exclamation point is retained.

> "Absolutely not!" he snapped.
> She has written about sixty pages so far—and with no help!

NOTE: If the exclamation point is part of a title, as of a play, book, or movie, it may be followed by a comma. If the title falls at the end of a sentence, the terminal period is usually dropped.

> Marshall and Susan went to see the musical *Oklahoma!*, and they enjoyed it very much.
> They enjoyed seeing the musical *Oklahoma!*

8. In typewritten material, two spaces follow an exclamation point that ends a sentence. If the exclamation point is followed by a closing bracket, closing parenthesis, or closing quotation marks, the two spaces follow the second mark. In typeset material, only one space follows the exclamation point.

> `The time is now!  Decide what you are going to do.`
> `She said, "The time is now!"  That meant we had to`
> `decide what to do.`
> The time is now! Decide what you are going to do.
> She said, "The time is now!" That meant we had to decide what to do.

Hyphen

1. Hyphens are used to link elements in compound words. For more on the styling of compound words, see the section on Compounds, beginning on page 82, in Chapter 3, "Plurals, Possessives, and Compounds."
2. A hyphen marks an end-of-line division of a word when part of the word is to be carried down to the next line.

   > We visited several showrooms, looked at the prices (it wasn't a pleasant experience; prices in this area have not gone down), and asked all the questions we could think of.

3. A hyphen divides letters or syllables to give the effect of stuttering, sobbing, or halting speech.

   > S-s-sammy   ah-ah-ah   y-y-es

4. Hyphens indicate a word spelled out letter by letter.

   > p-r-o-b-a-t-i-o-n

5. A hyphen indicates that a word element is a prefix, suffix, or medial element.

   > anti-   -ship   -o-

6. A hyphen is used in typewritten material as an equivalent to the phrase "(up) to and including" when placed between numbers and dates. In typeset material this hyphen is very often replaced by an en dash. For more on the use of the en dash, see paragraphs 15 and 16 under Dash in this chapter.
7. Hyphens are sometimes used to produce inflected forms of verbs that are made of individually pronounced letters or to add an -er ending to an abbreviation; however, apostrophes are more commonly used for this purpose. For more on these uses of the apostrophe, see paragraphs 6 and 7 under Apostrophe in this chapter.

   > D.H.-ing for the White Sox   a loyal AA-er

Parentheses

Parentheses enclose supplementary elements that are inserted into a main statement but that are not intended to be part of the statement; in fact, parenthetic elements often interrupt the main structure of the sentence. For some of the cases described below, especially those listed under the heading "Parenthetic Elements," commas and dashes are frequently used instead of parentheses. (For contrasting examples, see paragraph 17 under Comma and paragraph 3 under Dash in this chapter.) In general, commas tend to be used when the inserted material is closely related, logically or grammatically, to the main clause; parentheses are more often used when the inserted material is incidental or digressive. Some newspapers and news magazines avoid the use of parentheses in straight news reporting and rely instead on the dash. In most cases, however, the choice of dashes or parentheses to enclose parenthetic material is a matter of personal preference.

Parenthetic Elements

1. Parentheses enclose phrases and clauses that provide examples, explanations, or supplementary facts. Supplementary numerical data may also be enclosed in parentheses.

   > Nominations for the association's principal officers (president, vice president, treasurer, and secretary) were heard and approved at the last meeting.
   > Although we liked the restaurant (their Italian food was the best), we seldom went there.
   > Three old destroyers (all now out of commission) will be scrapped.
   > Their first baseman was hitting well that season (.297, 84 RBIs), and their left fielder was doing well also (21 HRs, 78 RBIs).

2. Parentheses enclose phrases and clauses introduced by expressions such as *namely, that is, e.g.,* and *i.e.* Commas, dashes, and semicolons are also used to perform this function. (For contrasting examples, see paragraph 18 under Comma, paragraph 6 under Dash, and paragraph 6 under Semicolon in this chapter.)

   > In writing to the manufacturer, be as specific as possible (i.e., list the missing or defective parts, describe the nature of the malfunction, and provide the name and address of the store where the unit was purchased).

3. Parentheses set off definitions, translations, or alternate names for words in the main part of a sentence.

   > The company sold off all of its retail outlets and announced plans to sell off its houseware (small appliance) business as well.
   > He has followed the fortunes of the modern renaissance (*al-Nahdad*) in the Arab-speaking world.
   > The hotel was located just a few blocks from San Antonio's famous Paseo del Rio (river walk).
   > They were scheduled to play Beethoven's Trio in B-flat major, Opus 97 ("The Archduke").

4. Parentheses enclose abbreviations synonymous with spelled-out forms and occurring after those forms, or they may enclose the spelled-out form occurring after the abbreviation.

She referred to a ruling by the Federal Communications Commission (FCC).

They were involved with a study regarding the manufacture and disposal of PVC (polyvinyl chloride).

5. Parentheses are used in running text to set off bibliographical or historical data about books, articles, or other published or artistic works. (For full information regarding the use of parentheses with bibliographical references, see the section on Parenthetical References, beginning on page 192, in Chapter 8, "Notes and Documentation of Sources.")

His work was influenced by several of Freud's essays, including "Some Character Types Met with in Psychoanalytic Work" (1916).

Ohio Impromptu (1981) was written for a special performance at Ohio State University.

Another book in this category is Alice Schick's *Serengeti Cats* (Lippincott, $10.53).

6. Parentheses often set off cross-references.

Telephone ordering service is also provided (refer to the list of stores at the end of this catalog).

Textbooks are available at the bookstore for all on-campus courses. (See page 12 for hours.)

The diagram (Fig. 3) illustrates the action of the pump.

7. Parentheses enclose Arabic numerals that confirm a spelled-out number in a text.

Delivery will be made in thirty (30) days.

8. Parentheses enclose the name of a city or state that is inserted into a proper name for identification.

the Norristown (Pa.) State Hospital
the *Tulsa* (Okla.) *Tribune*

9. Some writers use parentheses to set off personal asides.

It was largely as a result of this conference that the committee was formed (its subsequent growth in influence is another story).

10. Parentheses are used to set off quotations, either attributed or unattributed, that illustrate or support a statement made in the main text.

After he had had a few brushes with the police, his stepfather had him sent to jail as an incorrigible ("It will do him good").

As a Mechanical Device

11. Parentheses enclose unpunctuated numbers or letters in a series within running text.

We must set forth (1) our long-term goals, (2) our immediate objectives, and (3) the means at our disposal.

NOTE: Some writers and editors use only a single parenthesis following the number; however, most style books advise that parentheses be used both before and after, and most publications do follow that style.

12. Parentheses indicate alternative terms.

Please indicate the lecture(s) you would like to attend.

13. Parentheses are used in combination with numbers for several mechanical purposes, such as setting off area codes in telephone numbers, indicating losses in accounting, and grouping elements in mathematical expressions.

(413) 256-7899 $3(a+b) + 4(a+b)$

Operating Profits (in millions)
Cosmetics 26.2
Food products 47.7
Food services 54.3
Transportation .... (17.7)
Sporting goods .... (11.2)

Total   99.3

With Other Marks of Punctuation

14. If a parenthetic expression is an independent sentence, its first word is capitalized and a period is placed *inside* the last parenthesis. On the other hand, a parenthetic expression that occurs within a sentence—even if it could stand alone as a separate sentence—does not end with a period. It may, however, end with an exclamation point, a question mark, a period after an abbreviation, or a set of quotation marks. A parenthetic expression within a sentence does not require capitalization unless it is a quoted sentence. (For more on the use of capitals with parenthetic expressions, see the section on Beginnings, starting on page 49, in Chapter 2, "Capitals, Italics, and Quotation Marks.")

The discussion was held in the boardroom. (The results are still confidential.)

Although several trade organizations worked actively against the legislation (there were at least three paid lobbyists working on Capitol Hill at any one time), the bill passed easily.

After waiting in line for an hour (why do we do these things?), we finally left.

The conference was held in Vancouver (that's in B.C.).

He was totally confused ("What can we do?") and refused to see anyone.

15. If a parenthetic expression within a sentence is composed of two independent clauses, capitalization and periods are avoided. To separate the clauses within the parentheses, semicolons are usually used. If the parenthetic expression occurs outside of a sentence, normal patterns of capitalization and punctuation prevail.

We visited several showrooms, looked at the prices (it wasn't a pleasant experience; prices in this area have not gone down), and asked all the questions we could think of.

We visited several showrooms and looked at the prices. (It wasn't a pleasant experience. Prices in this area have not gone down.) If salespeople were available, we asked all of the questions we could think of.

16. No punctuation mark (other than a period after an abbreviation) is placed before parenthetic material within a sentence; if a break is required, the punctuation is placed after the final parenthesis.

I'll get back to you tomorrow (Friday), when I have more details.

17. Parentheses sometimes appear within parentheses, although the usual practice is to replace the inner pair of parentheses with a pair of brackets. (For an example of brackets within parentheses, see paragraph 6 under Brackets in this chapter.)

Checks must be drawn in U.S. dollars. (PLEASE NOTE: In accordance with U.S. Department of Treasury regulations, we cannot accept checks drawn on Canadian banks for amounts less than four U.S. dollars ($4.00). The same regulation applies to Canadian money orders.)

18. Dashes and parentheses are often used together to set off parenthetic material within a larger parenthetic element. For details and examples, see paragraph 14 under Dash in this chapter.

Spacing

19. In typewritten material, a parenthetic expression that is an independent sentence is followed by two spaces. In typeset material, the sentence is followed by one space. In typewritten or typeset material, a parenthetic expression that falls within a sentence is followed by one space.

```
We visited several showrooms and looked at the prices.
(It wasn't a pleasant experience.  Prices in this area
have not gone down.)  We asked all the questions we
could think of.
```

We visited several showrooms and looked at the prices. (It wasn't a pleasant experience. Prices in this area have not gone down.) We asked all the questions we could think of.

NOTE: Paragraphs 14 and 15 above are followed by examples that illustrate the appearance in typeset material of parenthetic expressions that are independent sentences.

Period

This section describes uses of the period in running text. For rules regarding use of the period in bibliographies, see Chapter 8, "Notes and

Documentation of Sources." For uses of the period in tables and captions, see Chapter 9, "Tables and Illustrations." For the use of three periods to indicate a pause or omission, see the section on Ellipsis Points in this chapter.

1. A period terminates a sentence or a sentence fragment that is neither interrogative nor exclamatory.

   Do your best.
   I did my best.
   Total chaos. Nothing works.

2. A period punctuates some abbreviations. For more on the punctuation of abbreviations, see the section on Punctuation, beginning on page 97, in Chapter 4, "Abbreviations."

a.k.a.	Assn.	Dr.	Jr.	Ph.D.
fig.	in.	No.	e.g.	ibid.
N.W.	U.S.	Inc.	Co.	Corp.

3. A period is used with an individual's initials. If all of the person's initials are used instead of the name, however, the unspaced initials may be written without periods.

   F. Scott Fitzgerald   Susan B. Anthony
   F.D.R. *or* FDR   T. S. Eliot

4. A period follows Roman and Arabic numerals and also letters when they are used without parentheses in outlines and vertical enumerations.

   I. Objectives
     A. Economy
        1. Low initial cost
        2. Low maintenance cost
     B. Ease of operation

   Required skills are:
        1. Shorthand
        2. Typing
        3. Transcription

5. A period is placed within quotation marks even when it does not punctuate the quoted material.

   The charismatic leader was known to his followers as "the guiding light."
   "I said I wanted to fire him," Henry went on, "but she said, 'I don't think you have the contractual privilege to do that.'"

6. When brackets or parentheses enclose a sentence that is independent of surrounding sentences, the period is placed inside the closing parenthesis or bracket. However, when brackets or parentheses enclose a sentence that is part of a surrounding sentence, the period for the enclosed sentence is omitted.

On Friday the government ordered a 24-hour curfew and told all journalists and photographers to leave the area. (Authorities later confiscated the film of those who did not comply.)

I took a good look at her (she was standing quite close to me at the time).

7. In typewritten material, two spaces follow a period that ends a sentence. If the period is followed by a closing bracket, closing parenthesis, or quotation marks, the two spaces follow the second mark. In typeset material, only one space follows this period.

```
Here is the car.    Do you want to get in?
He said, "Here is the car."    I asked if I should get
in.
```
Here is the car. Do you want to get in?

8. One space follows a period that comes after an initial in a name. If a name is composed entirely of initials, no space is required; however, the usual styling for such names is to omit the periods.

Mr. H. C. Matthews   F.D.R. *or* FDR

9. No space follows an internal period within a punctuated abbreviation.

f.o.b.   i.e.   Ph.D.   A.D.   p.m.

Question Mark

1. The question mark terminates a direct question.

What went wrong?
"When do they arrive?" she asked.

NOTE: The intent of the writer, not the word order of the sentence, determines whether or not the sentence is a question. Polite requests that are worded as questions, for instance, usually take periods, because they are not really questions. Similarly, sentences whose word order is that of a statement but whose force is interrogatory are punctuated with question marks.

Will you please sit down.
He did that?

2. The question mark terminates an interrogative element that is part of a sentence. An indirect question is not followed by a question mark.

The old arithmetic books were full of How-much-wallpaper-will-it-take-to-cover-a-room? questions.
How did she do it? was the question on everybody's mind.
She wondered, will it work?
She wondered whether it would work.

3. The question mark punctuates each element of an interrogative series that is neither numbered nor lettered. When an interrogative series is numbered or lettered, only one question mark is used, and it is placed at the end of the series.

> Can you give us a reasonable forecast? back up your predictions? compare them with last year's earnings?
>
> Can you (1) give us a reasonable forecast, (2) back up your predictions, (3) compare them with last year's earnings?

4. The question mark indicates a writer's or editor's uncertainty about a fact.

> Geoffrey Chaucer, English poet (1340?–1400)

5. The question mark is placed inside a closing bracket, dash, parenthesis, or pair of quotation marks when it punctuates only the material enclosed by that mark and not the sentence as a whole. It is placed outside that mark when it punctuates the entire sentence.

> What did Andrew mean when he called the project "a fiasco from the start"?
>
> I had a vacation in 1975 (was it really that long ago?), but I haven't had time for one since.
>
> "She thought about it for a moment," Alice continued, "and finally she said, 'Can you guarantee this will work?' "
>
> He asked, "Do you realize the extent of the problem [the housing shortage]?"

6. In typewritten material, two spaces follow a question mark that ends a sentence. If the question mark is followed by a closing bracket, closing parenthesis, or quotation marks, the two spaces follow the second mark. In typeset material, only one space follows the question mark.

> ```
> She wondered, will it work?   He said he thought it
> would.
> She asked, "Will it work?"   He said he thought it
> would.
> ```
> She wondered, will it work? He said he thought it would.

7. One space follows a question mark that falls within a sentence.

> Are you coming today? tomorrow? the day after?

Quotation Marks, Double

This section describes the use of quotation marks to enclose quoted matter in running text. It also describes the mechanical uses of quotation marks, such as to set off translations of words or to enclose single letters within sentences. For the use of quotation marks to enclose titles of

poems, paintings, or other works, see the section on Proper Nouns, Pronouns, and Adjectives, beginning on page 52, in Chapter 2, "Capitals, Italics, and Quotation Marks." For a discussion of extended quotations set
off from the rest of the text by indention, see Chapter 7, "The Treatment
of Quotations."

Basic Uses

1. Quotation marks enclose direct quotations but not indirect quotations.

> She said, "I am leaving."
> "I am leaving," she said, "and I'm not coming back."
> "I am leaving," she said. "This has gone on long enough."
> She said that she was leaving.

2. Quotation marks enclose fragments of quoted matter when they are
reproduced exactly as originally stated.

> The agreement makes it clear that he "will be paid only upon receipt of
> an acceptable manuscript."
> As late as 1754, documents refer to him as "yeoman" and "husbandman."

3. Quotation marks enclose words or phrases borrowed from others,
words used in a special way, or words of marked informality when
they are introduced into formal writing.

> That kind of corporation is referred to as "closed" or "privately held."
> Be sure to send a copy of your résumé, or as some folks would say, your
> "biodata summary."
> They were afraid the patient had "stroked out"—had had a cerebrovascu-
> lar accident.

4. Quotation marks are sometimes used to enclose words referred to as
words. Italic type is also frequently used for this purpose. For more
on this use of italics, see the section on Other Uses of Italics, beginning on page 70, in Chapter 2, "Capitals, Italics, and Quotation
Marks."

> He went through the manuscript and changed every "he" to "she."

5. Quotation marks enclose short exclamations or representations of
sounds. Representations of sounds are also frequently set in italic
type. For more on this use of italics, see the section on Other Uses of
Italics, beginning on page 70, in Chapter 2, "Capitals, Italics, and
Quotation Marks."

> "Ssshh!" she hissed.
> They never say anything crude like "shaddap."

6. Quotation marks enclose short sentences that fall within longer sentences, especially when the shorter sentence is meant to suggest spoken dialogue. Kinds of sentences that may be treated in this way in-

clude mottoes and maxims, unspoken or imaginary dialogue, or sentences referred to as sentences.

Throughout the camp, the spirit was "We can do."

She never could get used to his "That's the way it goes" attitude.

In effect, the voters were saying "You blew it, and you don't get another chance."

Their attitude could only be described as "Kill the messenger."

Another example of a palindrome is "Madam, I'm Adam."

NOTE: Style varies regarding the punctuation of sentences such as these. In general, the force of the quotation marks is to set the shorter sentence off more distinctly from the surrounding sentence and to give the shorter sentence more of the feel of spoken dialogue; omitting the quotation marks diminishes the effect. (For a description of the use of commas in sentences like these, see paragraphs 33 and 34 under Comma in this chapter.)

The first rule is, When in doubt, spell it out.

They weren't happy with the impression she left: "Don't expect favors, because I don't have to give them."

7. Quotation marks are not used to enclose paraphrases.

Build a better mouse trap, Emerson says, and the world will beat a path to your door.

8. Direct questions are usually not enclosed in quotation marks unless they represent quoted dialogue.

The question is, What went wrong?

As we listened to him, we couldn't help wondering, Where's the plan?

She asked, "What went wrong?"

NOTE: As in the sentences presented in paragraph 6 above, style varies regarding the use of quotation marks with direct questions; and in many cases, writers will include the quotation marks.

As we listened to him, we couldn't help wondering, "Where's the plan?"

9. Quotation marks are used to enclose translations of foreign or borrowed terms.

The term *sesquipedalian* comes from the Latin word *sesquipedalis*, meaning "a foot and a half long."

While in Texas, he encountered the armadillo ("little armored one") and developed quite an interest in it.

10. Quotation marks are sometimes used to enclose single letters within a sentence.

The letter "m" is wider than the letter "i."

We started to work on the dictionary, beginning with the letter "A."

Put an "x" in the right spot.

The metal rod was shaped into a "V."

NOTE: Style varies on this point. Sans serif type is most often used when the shape of the letter is being stressed. Letters referred to as letters are commonly set in italic type. (For more on this use of italics, see the section on Other Uses of Italics, beginning on page 70, in Chapter 2, "Capitals, Italics, and Quotation Marks.") Finally, letters often appear in the same typeface as the surrounding text if no confusion would result from the styling.

> a "V"-shaped blade
> He was happy to get a B in the course.
> How many e's are in her name?

With Other Marks of Punctuation

11. When quotation marks follow a word in a sentence that is also followed by a period or comma, the period or comma is placed within the quotation marks.

> He said, "I am leaving."
>
> Her camera was described as "waterproof," but "moisture-resistant" would have been a better description.

NOTE: Some writers draw a distinction between periods and commas that belong logically to the quoted material and those that belong to the whole sentence. If the period or comma belongs to the quoted material, they place it inside the quotation marks; if the period belongs logically to the sentence that surrounds the quoted matter, they place it outside the quotation marks. This distinction was previously observed in a wide range of publications, including U.S. Congressional publications and Merriam-Webster® dictionaries. In current practice, the distinction is made in relatively few publications, although the distinction is routinely made for dashes, exclamation points, and question marks used with quotation marks, as described in paragraph 13 below.

> The package was labeled "Handle with Care".
>
> The act was referred to as the "Army-Navy Medical Services Corps Act of 1947".
>
> Her camera was described as "waterproof", but "moisture-resistant" would have been a better description.
>
> He said, "I am leaving."

12. When quotation marks follow a word in a sentence that is also followed by a colon or semicolon, the colon or semicolon is placed outside the quotation marks.

> There was only one thing to do when he said, "I may not run": promise him a larger campaign contribution.
>
> She spoke of her "little cottage in the country"; she might better have called it a mansion.

13. The dash, question mark, and exclamation point are placed inside quotation marks when they punctuate the quoted matter only. They are placed outside the quotation marks when they punctuate the whole sentence.

> He asked, "When did she leave?"
> What is the meaning of "the open door"?
> Save us from his "mercy"!
> "I can't see how—" he started to say.
> He thought he knew where he was going—he remembered her saying, "Take two lefts, then stay to the right"—but the streets didn't look familiar.

14. One space follows a quotation mark that is followed by the rest of a sentence.

> "I am leaving," she said.

15. In typewritten material, two spaces follow a quotation mark that ends a sentence. In typeset material one space follows.

> ```
> He said, "Here is the car."   I asked if I should get
> in.
> ```
> He said, "Here is the car." I asked if I should get in.

Quotation Marks, Single

1. Single quotation marks enclose a quotation within a quotation in conventional English.

> The witness said, "I distinctly heard him say, 'Don't be late,' and then I heard the door close."
> The witness said, "I distinctly heard him say, 'Don't be late.' "

NOTE: When both single and double quotation marks occur at the end of a sentence, the period typically falls *within* both sets of marks.

2. Single quotation marks are sometimes used in place of double quotation marks especially in British usage.

> The witness said, 'I distinctly heard him say, "Don't be late," and then I heard the door close.'

3. On rare occasions, authors face the question of how to style a quotation within a quotation within a quotation. Standard styling practice would be to enclose the innermost quotation in double marks; however, this construction can be confusing, and in many cases rewriting the sentence can remove the need for it.

> The witness said, "I distinctly heard him say, 'Don't you say "Shut up" to me.' "
> The witness said that she distinctly heard him say, "Don't you say 'Shut up' to me."

4. In some specialized fields, such as theology, philosophy, and linguistics, special terminology or words referred to as words are enclosed within single quotation marks. When single quotation marks are used in this way, any other punctuation following the word enclosed is placed outside the quotation marks.

> She was interested in the development of the word 'humongous', especially during the 1960s.

Semicolon

The semicolon is used in ways that are similar to those in which periods and commas are used. Because of these similarities, the semicolon is often thought of as either a weak period or a strong comma. As a weak period, the semicolon marks the end of a complete clause and signals that the clause that follows it is closely related to the clause that precedes it. As a strong comma, the semicolon clarifies meaning usually by distinguishing major sentence divisions from the minor pauses that are represented by commas.

Between Clauses

1. A semicolon separates independent clauses that are joined together in one sentence without a coordinating conjunction.

> He hemmed and hawed for over an hour; he couldn't make up his mind.
>
> The river rose and overflowed its banks; roads became flooded and impassable; freshly plowed fields disappeared from sight.
>
> Cream the shortening and sugar; add the eggs and beat well.

2. Ordinarily a comma separates main clauses joined with a coordinating conjunction. However, if the sentence might be confusing with a comma in this position, a semicolon is used in its place. Potentially confusing sentences include those with other commas in them or with particularly long clauses.

> We fear that this situation may, in fact, occur; but we don't know when.
>
> In a society that seeks to promote social goals, government will play a powerful role; and taxation, once simply a means of raising money, becomes, in addition, a way of furthering those goals.
>
> As recently as 1978 the company felt the operation could be a successful one that would generate significant profits in several different markets; but in 1981 the management changed its mind and began a program of shutting down plants and reducing its product line.

3. A semicolon joins two statements when the grammatical construction of the second clause is elliptical and depends on that of the first.

The veal dishes were very good; the desserts, too.

In many cases the conference sessions, which were designed to allow for full discussions of topics, were much too long and tedious; the breaks between them, much too short.

4. A semicolon joins two clauses when the second begins with a conjunctive adverb, as *accordingly, also, besides, consequently, furthermore, hence, however, indeed, likewise, moreover, namely, nevertheless, otherwise, still, then, therefore,* and *thus.* Phrases such as *by the same token, in that case, as a result, on the other hand,* and *all the same* can also act as conjunctive adverbs.

Most people are covered by insurance of one kind or another; indeed, many people don't even see their medical bills.

It won't be easy to sort out the facts of this confusing situation; however, a decision must be made.

The case could take years to work its way through the court system; as a result, many plaintiffs will accept out-of-court settlements.

NOTE: Style varies regarding the treatment of clauses introduced by *so* and *yet.* Although many writers continue to treat *so* and *yet* as adverbs, it has become standard to treat these words as coordinating conjunctions that join clauses. In this treatment, a comma precedes *so* and *yet* and no punctuation follows them. (For examples, see paragraph 1 under Comma in this chapter.)

5. When three or more clauses are separated by semicolons, a coordinating conjunction may or may not precede the final clause. If a coordinating conjunction does precede the final clause, the final semicolon is often replaced with a comma. (For the use of commas to separate three or more clauses without conjunctions, see paragraph 4 under Comma in this chapter.)

Their report was one-sided and partial; it did not reflect the facts; it distorted them.

They don't understand; they grow bored; and they stop learning.

The report recounted events leading up to the incident; it included observations of eyewitnesses, but it drew no conclusions.

NOTE: The choices of whether to use a conjunction and whether to use a semicolon or comma with the conjunction are matters of personal preference. In general, the force of the semicolon is to make the transition to the final clause more abrupt, which often serves to place more emphasis on that clause. The comma and conjunction ease the transition and make the sentence seem less choppy.

With Phrases and Clauses Introduced by *for example, i.e.,* etc.

6. A semicolon is sometimes used before expressions (as *for example, for instance, that is, namely, e.g.,* or *i.e.*) that introduce expansions or series. Commas, dashes, and parentheses are also used in sentences like

these. For contrasting examples, see paragraph 18 under Comma, paragraph 6 under Dash, and paragraph 2 under Parentheses in this chapter.

> On one point only did everyone agree; namely, that too much money had been spent already.
>
> We were fairly successful on that project; that is, we made our deadlines and met our budget.
>
> Most of the contestants had traveled great distances to participate; for example, three had come from Australia, one from Japan, and two from China.

In a Series

7. A semicolon is used in place of a comma to separate phrases in a series when the phrases themselves contain commas. A comma may replace the semicolon before the last item in a series if the last item is introduced with a conjunction.

> She flung open the door; raced up the stairs, taking them two at a time; locked herself in the bathroom; and, holding her sides, started to laugh uncontrollably.
>
> The visitor to Barndale was offered three sources of overnight accommodation: The Rose and Anchor, which housed Barndale's oldest pub; The Crawford, an American-style luxury hotel; and Ellen's Bed and Breakfast on Peabody Lane.
>
> We studied mathematics and geography in the morning; English, French, and Spanish right after lunch, and science in the late afternoon.

8. When the individual items in an enumeration or series are long or are sentences themselves, they are usually separated by semicolons.

> Among the committee's recommendations: more hospital beds in urban areas where there are waiting lists for elective surgery; smaller staff size in half-empty rural hospitals; review procedures for all major purchases.
>
> There is a difference between them: she is cross and irritable; he is merely moody.

As a Mechanical Device

9. A semicolon separates items in a list in cases where a comma alone would not clearly separate the items or references.

> (Friedlander 1957; Ballas 1962)
> (Genesis 3:1–19; 4:1–16)

With Other Marks of Punctuation

10. A semicolon is placed outside quotation marks and parentheses.

> They referred to each other as "Mother" and "Father"; they were the archetypal happily married elderly couple.
>
> She accepted the situation with every appearance of equanimity (but with some inward qualms); however, all of that changed the next day.

Virgule

The virgule is known by many names, including *diagonal, solidus, oblique, slant, slash,* and *slash mark.* Most commonly, the virgule is used to represent a word that is not written out or to separate or set off certain adjacent elements of text. For use of the virgule in copyediting and proofreading, see Chapter 11, "Production Techniques."

In Place of Missing Words

1. A virgule represents the word *per* or *to* when used with units of measure or when used to indicate the terms of a ratio.

40,000 tons/year	9 ft./sec.	a 50/50 split
14 gm/100 cc	price/earnings ratio	risk/reward tradeoff

2. A virgule separates alternatives. In this context, the virgule usually represents the words *or* or *and/or.*

alumni/ae	introductory/refresher courses
his/her	oral/written tests

3. A virgule replaces the word *and* in some compound terms.

molybdenum/vanadium steel
in the May/June issue
1973/74
in the Falls Church/McLean, Va., area
an innovative classroom/laboratory

4. A virgule is used, although less commonly, to replace a number of prepositions, such as *at, versus, with,* and *for.*

U.C./Berkeley	parent/child issues
table/mirror	Vice President/Editorial

With Abbreviations

5. A virgule punctuates some abbreviations.

c/o	A/V	d/b/a
A/R	A/1C	S/Sgt
w/	V/STOL	

NOTE: In some cases the virgule may stand for a word that is not represented in the abbreviation (e.g., *in* in *W/O,* the abbreviation for *water in oil*).

To Separate Elements

6. The virgule is used in a number of mechanical ways to separate groups of numbers, such as elements in a date, numerators and denominators in fractions, and area codes in telephone numbers. For more on the use of virgules with numbers, see Chapter 5, "The Treatment of Numbers."

7. The virgule serves as a divider between lines of poetry that are run in with the text around them. This method of quoting poetry is usually limited to passages of no more than three or four lines. Longer passages are usually set off from the text as extract quotations, as shown in Chapter 7, "The Treatment of Quotations."

> When Samuel Taylor Coleridge wrote in "Christabel" that "'Tis a month before the month of May, /And the Spring comes slowly up this way," he could have been describing New England.

8. The virgule sets off certain elements—such as the parts of an address that are normally placed on separate lines—when they appear run in with the surrounding text.

> Mlle Christine Lagache/20, Passage des Écoliers/75051 Paris/France

9. The virgule sets off phonemes and phonemic transcriptions.

> /b/ as in *but*
> pronounced /ˌekə'nämik/ or /ˌēkə'nämik/

Spacing

10. In general, no space is used between the virgule and the words, letters, or figures separated by it. Some authors and editors prefer to place spaces around a virgule used to separate lines of poetry, but most omit the space. In the case of virgules used to set off phonemes and phonemic transcriptions, however, a space precedes the first virgule and follows the second virgule.

Chapter 2

Capitals, Italics, and Quotation Marks

CONTENTS

Words and phrases are capitalized, italicized, or enclosed in quotation marks in order to indicate that they have a special significance in a particular context. Some rules regarding capitals, italics, and quotation marks are backed by long tradition and are quite easy to apply ("The first word of a sentence or sentence fragment is capitalized"); others require arbitrary decisions or personal judgment ("Foreign words and phrases that have not been fully adopted into the English language are italicized"). Careful writers and editors usually make notes or keep a style sheet to record the decisions that they make so they can be consistent in their use of capitals, italics, and quotation marks. For more on keeping and using style sheets, see Chapter 11, "Production Techniques," page 297.

This chapter is divided into four sections. The first section explains the use of capitalized words to begin sentences and phrases. The second section explains the use of capitals, italics, and quotation marks to indicate that a word or phrase is a proper noun, pronoun, or adjective. The third and fourth sections explain other uses of capital letters and italics. For other uses of quotation marks, see the section on Quotation Marks beginning on page 39, in Chapter 1, "Punctuation." For a discussion of the treatment of extended quotations, see Chapter 7, "Treatment of Quotations."

Beginnings

1. The first word of a sentence or sentence fragment is capitalized.

> The meeting was postponed.
> No! I cannot do it.

Will you go?
Total chaos. Nothing works.

2. The first word of a sentence contained within parentheses is capitalized; however, a parenthetical sentence occurring inside another sentence is not capitalized unless it is a complete quoted sentence.

The discussion was held in the boardroom. (The results are still confidential.)

Although we liked the restaurant (their Italian food was the best), we could not afford to eat there often.

After waiting in line for an hour (why do we do these things?), we finally left.

He was totally demoralized ("There is just nothing we can do") and was contemplating resignation.

3. The first word of a direct quotation is capitalized; however, if the quotation is interrupted in midsentence, the second part does not begin with a capital.

The President said, "We have rejected this report entirely."

"We have rejected this report entirely," the President said, "and we will not comment on it further."

4. When a quotation, whether a sentence fragment or a complete sentence, is syntactically dependent on the sentence in which it occurs, the quotation does not begin with a capital.

The President made it clear that "there is no room for compromise."

5. The first word of a sentence within a sentence is usually capitalized. Examples of sentences within sentences include mottoes and rules, unspoken or imaginary dialogue, sentences referred to as sentences, and direct questions. (For an explanation of the use of commas and quotation marks with sentences such as these, see paragraphs 34 and 35 in the section on Comma, beginning on page 11, and paragraph 6 in the section on Quotation Marks, Double, beginning on page 39, in Chapter 1, "Punctuation."

You know the saying, "A stitch in time saves nine."

The first rule is, When in doubt, spell it out.

The clear message coming back from the audience was "We don't care."

My question is, When can we go?

She kept wondering, how did they get here so soon?

NOTE: In the cases of unspoken or imaginary dialogue and of direct questions, it is a matter of individual preference whether or not to capitalize the first word; however, the most common practice is to capitalize it.

6. The first word of a line of poetry is conventionally capitalized.

The best lack all conviction, while the worst
Are full of passionate intensity.
                                                 —W. B. Yeats

7. The first word following a colon may be either lowercased or capitalized if it introduces a complete sentence. While the former is the
   usual styling, the latter is also quite common, especially when the sentence introduced by the colon is fairly lengthy and distinctly separate
   from the preceding clause.

   The advantage of this particular system is clear: it's inexpensive.
   The situation is critical: This company cannot hope to recoup the fourth-
   quarter losses that were sustained in five operating divisions.

   NOTE: For the sake of consistency, many authors and editors prefer
   to use one style or the other in all cases, regardless of sentence length.
   The capitalized style is more common in newspapers, but overall the
   lowercased styling is more frequently used.

8. If a colon introduces a series of sentences, the first word of each sentence is capitalized.

   Consider the following steps that we have taken: A subcommittee has been
   formed to evaluate our past performance and to report its findings to the
   full organization. New sources of revenue are being explored, and relevant organizations are being contacted. And several candidates have been
   interviewed for the new post of executive director.

9. The first words of run-in enumerations that form complete sentences
   are capitalized, as are the first words of phrasal lists and enumerations arranged vertically beneath running texts. Phrasal enumerations
   run in with the introductory text, however, are lowercased.

   Do the following tasks at the end of the day: 1. Clean your typewriter.
   2. Clear your desktop of papers. 3. Cover office machines. 4. Straighten
   the contents of your desk drawers, cabinets, and bookcases.
   This is the agenda:
      Call to order
      Roll call
      Minutes of the previous meeting
      Treasurer's report
   On the agenda will be (1) call to order, (2) roll call, (3) minutes of the previous meeting, (4) treasurer's report . . .

10. The introductory words *Whereas* and *Resolved* are capitalized in min-
    utes and legislation, as is the word *That* or an alternative word or
    expression which immediately follows either.

    Resolved, That . . .
    Whereas, Substantial benefits . . .

11. The first word in an outline heading is capitalized.

    I. Editorial tasks
   II. Production responsibilities
      A. Cost estimates
      B. Bids

12. The first word of the salutation of a letter and the first word of a complimentary close are capitalized.

Dear Mary,	Dear Sir or Madam:	Ladies and Gentlemen:
Gentlemen:	Sincerely yours,	Very truly yours,

13. The first word and each subsequent major word following a SUBJECT or TO heading (as in a memorandum) are capitalized.

    SUBJECT: Pension Plans
    TO: All Department Heads and Editors

Proper Nouns, Pronouns, and Adjectives

This section describes the ways in which a broad range of proper nouns, pronouns, and adjectives are styled—with capitals, italics, quotation marks, or some combination of these devices. In almost all cases, proper nouns, pronouns, and adjectives are capitalized. The essential distinction in the use of capitals and lowercase letters lies in the particularizing or individualizing significance of capitals as against the generalizing significance of lowercase. A capital is used with a proper noun because it distinguishes some individual person, place, or thing from others of the same class. A capital is used with a proper adjective because it takes its descriptive meaning from a proper noun.

In many cases, proper nouns are italicized or enclosed in quotation marks in addition to being capitalized. No clear distinctions can be drawn between the kinds of words that are capitalized and italicized, capitalized and enclosed in quotation marks, or simply capitalized, as styling on these points is governed almost wholly by tradition.

The paragraphs in this section are grouped under the following alphabetically arranged headings:

Abbreviations	Topographical	Numerical Designations
Abstractions and	References	Organizations
Personifications	Governmental, Judicial,	People
Academic Degrees	and Political Bodies	Pronouns
Animals and Plants	Historical Periods	Religious Terms
Awards, Honors, and	and Events	Scientific Terms
Prizes	Hyphenated Compounds	Time Periods and Zones
Derivatives of Proper	Legal Material	Titles
Names	Medical Terms	Trademarks
Geographical and	Military Terms	Transportation

Abbreviations

1. Abbreviated forms of proper nouns and adjectives are capitalized, just as the spelled-out forms would be. For more on the capitalization of abbreviations, see the section on Capitalization, beginning on page 98, in Chapter 4, "Abbreviations."

Dec. for *December*   Wed. for *Wednesday*
Col. for *Colonel*   Brit. for *British*

Abstractions and Personifications

2. Abstract terms, such as names of concepts or qualities, are usually not capitalized unless the concept or quality is being presented as if it were a person. If the term is simply being used in conjunction with other words that allude to human characteristics or qualities, it is usually not capitalized. For more on the capitalization of abstract terms, see the section on Other Uses of Capitals in this chapter.

a time when Peace walked among us
as Autumn paints each leaf in fiery colors
an economy gripped by inflation
hoping that fate would lend a hand

3. Fictitious names used as personifications are capitalized.

Uncle Sam   Ma Bell   John Bull   Jack Frost
Big Oil squirmed under the new regulations.

Academic Degrees

4. The names of academic degrees are capitalized when they follow a person's name. The names of specific academic degrees not following a person's name are capitalized or not capitalized according to individual preference. General terms referring to degrees, such as *doctorate, master's degree,* or *bachelor's* are not capitalized. Abbreviations for academic degrees are always capitalized.

Martin Bonkowski, Doctor of Divinity
earned her Doctor of Laws degree *or* earned her doctor of laws degree
working for a bachelor's degree
Susan Wycliff, M.S.W.
received her Ph.D.

Animals and Plants

5. The common names of animals and plants are not capitalized unless they contain a proper noun as a separate element, in which case the proper noun is capitalized, but any element of the name following the proper noun is lowercased. Elements of the name preceding the proper noun are usually but not always capitalized. In some cases, the common name of the plant or animal contains a word that was once a proper noun but is no longer thought of as such. In these cases, the word is usually not capitalized. When in doubt about the capitalization of a plant or animal name, consult a dictionary. (For an explanation of the capitalization of genus names in binomial nomenclature or of New Latin names for groups above genera in zoology and botany, see paragraphs 67 and 68 below.)

cocker spaniel	lily of the valley	ponderosa pine
great white shark	Hampshire hog	Kentucky bluegrass
Steller's jay	Bengal tiger	Japanese beetle
Rhode Island red	Great Dane	Brown Swiss
black-eyed Susan	wandering Jew	holstein

NOTE: In references to specific breeds, as distinguished from the animals that belong to the breed, all elements of the name are capitalized.

Gordon Setter	Rhode Island Red	Holstein

Awards, Honors, and Prizes

6. Names of awards, honors, and prizes are capitalized. Descriptive words and phrases that are not actually part of the award's name are lowercased. (For an explanation of capitalizing the names of military decorations, see paragraph 44 below.)

Academy Award	Emmy
Nobel Prize	Nobel Prize in medicine
Nobel Prize winner	Nobel Peace Prize
Rhodes Scholarship	Rhodes scholar
New York Drama Critics' Circle Award	

Brand Names—See Trademarks below.

Computer Terms—See Scientific Terms below.

Derivatives of Proper Names

7. Derivatives of proper names are capitalized when they are used in their primary sense. However, if the derived term has taken on a specialized meaning, it is usually not capitalized.

Roman architecture	Victorian customs	Keynesian economics
an Americanism	an Egyptologist	french fries
manila envelope	pasteurized milk	a quixotic undertaking

Geographical and Topographical References

8. Terms that identify divisions of the earth's surface and distinct areas, regions, places, or districts are capitalized, as are derivative nouns and adjectives.

Chicago, Illinois	Tropic of Capricorn
the Middle Eastern situation	the Western Hemisphere
the Southwest	the Sun Belt

9. Popular names of localities are capitalized.

the Big Apple	the Loop	Hell's Kitchen
the Village	the Twin Cities	the Valley

10. Compass points are capitalized when they refer to a geographical region or when they are part of a street name. They are lowercased when they refer to a simple direction.

back East	West Columbus Avenue
up North	South Pleasant Street
out West	down South
east of the Mississippi	traveling north on I-91

11. Nouns and adjectives that are derived from compass points and that designate or refer to a specific geographical region are usually capitalized.

a Southern accent	a Western crop
Northerners	part of the Eastern establishment

12. Words designating global, national, regional, or local political divisions are capitalized when they are essential elements of specific names. However, they are usually lowercased when they precede a proper name or when they are not part of a specific name.

the British Empire	New York City
Washington State	Ward 1
Hampden County	Ohio's Ninth Congressional District
the fall of the empire	the city of New York
the state of Washington	fires in three wards
the county of Hampden	carried her district

NOTE: In legal documents, these words are often capitalized regardless of position.

the State of Washington   the County of Hampden   the City of New York

13. Generic geographical terms (as *lake, mountain, river, valley*) are capitalized if they are part of a specific proper name.

Crater Lake	Lake Como	Rocky Mountains
the Columbia River	Ohio Valley	Long Island
Great Barrier Reef	Atlantic Ocean	Niagara Falls
Hudson Bay	Strait of Gibraltar	Bering Strait

14. Generic geographical terms preceding names are usually capitalized.

Lakes Mead and Powell   Mounts Whitney and Shasta

NOTE: When *the* precedes the generic term, the generic term is lowercased.

the river Thames

15. Generic geographical terms that are not used as part of a proper name are not capitalized. These include plural generic geographical terms that follow two or more proper names and generic terms that are used descriptively or alone.

the Himalaya and Andes mountains   the Missouri and Platte rivers
the Atlantic coast of Labrador   the Arizona desert
the Mississippi delta   the Caribbean islands
the river valley   the valley

16. The names of streets, monuments, parks, landmarks, well-known buildings, and other public places are capitalized. However, generic terms that are part of these names (as *avenue, bridge,* or *tower*) are low-ercased when they occur after multiple names or are used alone (but see paragraph 17 below).

Golden Gate Bridge   the Capitol   Rock Creek Park
Eddystone Lighthouse   the Dorset Hotel   Fanueil Hall
the San Diego Zoo   Coit Tower   the Mall
the Pyramids   the Statue of Liberty Peachtree Street

the Dorset and Drake hotels   Fifth and Park avenues
on the bridge   walking through the park

17. Well-known informal or shortened forms of place-names are capitalized.

the Avenue for *Fifth Avenue*
the Street for *Wall Street*
the Exchange for the *New York Stock Exchange*

Governmental, Judicial, and Political Bodies

18. Full names of legislative, deliberative, executive, and administrative bodies are capitalized, as are easily recognizable short forms of these names. However, nonspecific noun and adjective references to them are usually lowercased.

United States Congress   the Federal Reserve Board
the Congress   the House
the Federal Bureau of Investigation the Fed
congressional hearings   a federal agency

NOTE: Style varies regarding the capitalization of words such as *department, committee,* or *agency* when they are being used in place of the full name of a specific body. They are most often capitalized when the department or agency is referring to itself in print. In most other cases, these words are lowercased.

The Connecticut Department of Transportation is pleased to offer this new booklet on traffic safety. The Department hopes that it will be of use to all drivers.

We received a new booklet from the Connecticut Department of Transportation. This is the second pamphlet the department has issued this month.

19. The U.S. Supreme Court and the short forms *Supreme Court* and *Court* referring to it are capitalized.

> the Supreme Court of the United States
> the United States Supreme Court
> the Supreme Court
> the Court

20. Official and full names of higher courts and names of international courts are capitalized. Short forms of official higher court names are often capitalized in legal documents but lowercased in general writing.

> The International Court of Arbitration
> the United States Court of Appeals for the Second Circuit
> the Virginia Supreme Court
> the Court of Queen's Bench
> a ruling by the court of appeals
> the state supreme court

21. Names of city and county courts are usually lowercased.

> the Lawton municipal court   police court
> the Owensville night court   the county court
> small claims court   juvenile court

22. The single designation *court,* when specifically applicable to a judge or a presiding officer, is capitalized.

> It is the opinion of this Court that . . .
> The Court found that . . .

23. The terms *federal* and *national* are capitalized only when they are essential elements of a name or title.

> Federal Trade Commission   National Security Council
> federal court   national security

24. The word *administration* is capitalized in some publications when it refers to the administration of a specific United States president; however, the word is more commonly lowercased in this situation. If the word does not refer to a specific presidential administration, it is not capitalized except when it is a part of an official name of a government agency.

> the Truman administration   *or*   the Truman Administration
> the administration   *or*   the Administration
> the Farmers Home Loan Administration
>
> The running of the White House varies considerably from one administration to another.

25. Names of political organizations and their adherents are capitalized, but the word *party* may or may not be capitalized, depending on the writer's or publication's preference.

the Democratic National Committee   the Republican platform
Tories   Nazis
the Democratic party   *or*   the Democratic Party
the Communist party   *or*   the Communist Party

26. Names of political groups other than parties are usually lowercased, as are their derivative forms.

rightist   right wing   left winger
   but usually   the Left   the Right

27. Terms describing political and economic philosophies and their derivative forms are usually capitalized only if they are derived from proper names.

authoritarianism   nationalism   isolationist
democracy   supply-side economics   civil libertarian
fascism   *or*   Fascism   social Darwinism   Marxist

Historical Periods and Events

28. The names of conferences, councils, expositions, and specific sporting, historical, and cultural events are capitalized.

the Yalta Conference   the Congress of Vienna
the Minnesota State Fair   the Games of the XXIII Olympiad
the World Series   the Series
the Boston Tea Party   the San Francisco Earthquake
the Bonus March of 1932   the Philadelphia Folk Festival
the Golden Gate International Exposition

29. The names of some historical and cultural periods and movements are capitalized. When in doubt about such a name, consult a dictionary or encyclopedia.

Augustan Age   Renaissance   Stone Age
Prohibition   the Enlightenment   the Great Depression
fin de siècle   space age   cold war *or* Cold War

30. Numerical designations of historical time periods are capitalized only when they are part of a proper name; otherwise they are lowercased.

the Third Reich   Roaring Twenties
seventeenth century   eighties

31. Full names of treaties, laws, and acts are capitalized.

Treaty of Versailles   The Controlled Substances Act of 1970

32. The full names of wars are capitalized; however, words such as *war, revolution, battle,* and *campaign* are capitalized only when they are part of a proper name. Descriptive terms such as *assault, seige,* and *engagement* are usually lowercased even when used in conjunction with the name of the place where the action occurred.

the French and Indian War
the War of the Roses
the American Revolution
the Revolution of 1688
the Battle of the Bulge
the Peninsular Campaign
the second battle of Manassas
the Meuse-Argonne offensive
the assault on Iwo Jima
was in action throughout most of the war

the Spanish American War
the War of the Spanish Succession
the Whiskey Rebellion
the Battle of the Coral Sea
the naval battle of Guadalcanal
the American and French
revolutions
the seige of Yorktown
the winter campaign

Hyphenated Compounds

33. Elements of hyphenated compounds are capitalized if they are proper nouns or adjectives.

Arab-Israeli negotiations
East-West trade agreements
an eighteenth-century poet

Tay-Sachs disease
U.S.-U.S.S.R. détente
American-plan rates

NOTE: If the second element in a two-word compound is not a proper noun or adjective, it is lowercased.

French-speaking peoples
an A-frame house
Thirty-second Street

34. Word elements (as prefixes and combining forms) may or may not be capitalized when joined to a proper noun or adjective. Common prefixes (as *pre-* or *anti-*) are usually not capitalized when so attached. Geographical and ethnic combining forms (as *Anglo-* or *Afro-*) are capitalized; *pan-* is usually capitalized when attached to a proper noun or adjective.

the pro-Soviet faction
un-American activities
Sino-Soviet relations
Pan-Slavic nationalism

post–Civil War politics
Afro-Americans
Greco-Roman architecture
the Pan-African Congress

Languages—See **People** below.

Legal Material—See also **Governmental, Judicial, and Political Bodies** above.

35. The names of both plaintiff and defendant in legal case titles are italicized. The *v.* for *versus* may be roman or italic. Cases that do not involve two opposing parties have titles such as *In re Watson* or *In the matter of John Watson*; these case titles are also italicized. When the person involved rather than the case itself is being discussed, the reference is not italicized.

Jones v. *Massachusetts*
In re Jones

Smith et al. v. Jones
She covered the Jones trial for the newspaper.

NOTE: In running text a case name involving two opposing parties may be shortened.

The judge based his ruling on a precedent set in the *Jones* decision.

Medical Terms

36. Proper names that are elements in terms designating diseases, symptoms, syndromes, and tests are capitalized. Common nouns are lowercased.

Down's syndrome   Parkinson's disease
Duchenne-Erb paralysis   Rorschach test
German measles   syndrome of Weber
acquired immunodeficiency syndrome   mumps
measles   herpes simplex

37. Taxonomic names of disease-causing organisms follow the rules established for binomial nomenclature discussed in paragraph 67 below. The names of diseases or pathological conditions derived from taxonomic names of organisms are lowercased and not italicized.

a neurotoxin produced by *Clostridium botulinum*
nearly died of botulism

38. Generic names of drugs are lowercased; trade names should be capitalized.

a prescription for chlorpromazine
had been taking Thorazine

Military Terms

39. The full titles of branches of the armed forces are capitalized, as are easily recognized short forms of full branch designations.

U.S. Air Force   the Air Force   U.S. Navy
the Navy   U.S. Army   the Army
U.S. Coast Guard   the Coast Guard   U.S. Marine Corps
the Marine Corps   the Marines   the Corps

40. The terms *air force, army, coast guard, marine(s),* and *navy* are lowercased unless they form a part of an official name or refer back to a specific branch of the armed forces previously named. They are also lowercased when they are used collectively or in the plural.

the combined air forces of the NATO nations
the navies of the world
the American army

In some countries the duty of the coast guard may include icebreaking in inland waterways.

41. The adjectives *naval* and *marine* are lowercased unless they are part of a proper name.

    naval battle   marine barracks   Naval Reserves

42. The full titles of units and organizations of the armed forces are capitalized. Elements of full titles are lowercased when they stand alone.

U.S. Army Corps of Engineers	the corps
the Reserves	a reserve commission
First Battalion	the battalion
4th Marine Regiment	the regiment
Eighth Fleet	the fleet
Cruiser Division	the division
Fifth Army	the army

43. Military ranks are capitalized when they precede the names of their holders, and when they take the place of a person's name (as in direct address). Otherwise they are lowercased.

    Admiral Nimitz
    General Creighton W. Abrams
    I can't get this rifle any cleaner, Sergeant.
    The major arrived precisely on time.

44. The specific names of decorations, citations, and medals are capitalized.

    Medal of Honor   Purple Heart   Silver Star
    Navy Cross   Distinguished Service Medal

Nicknames—See paragraphs 49, 51, and 52 below.

Numerical Designations

45. A noun introducing a reference number is usually capitalized.

    Order 704   Flight 409   Form 2E   Policy 118-4-Y

46. Nouns used with numbers or letters to designate major reference headings (as in a literary work) are capitalized. However, nouns designating minor reference headings are typically lowercased.

Book II	Table 3	paragraph 6.1
Volume V	page 101	item 16
Division 4	line 8	question 21
Figure 1	note 10	

Organizations

47. Names of firms, corporations, schools, and organizations and terms derived from those names to designate their members are capitalized. However, common nouns used descriptively or occurring after the names of two or more organizations are lowercased.

Merriam-Webster Inc.	Rotary International
University of Michigan	Kiwanians
Smith College	American and United airlines
Washington Huskies	Minnesota North Stars
played as a Pirate last year	

NOTE: The word *the* at the beginning of such names is capitalized only when the full legal name is used.

48. Words such as *agency, department, division, group,* or *office* that designate corporate and organizational units are capitalized only when they are used with a specific name.

> while working for the Criminal Division in the Department of Justice
> a notice to all department heads

NOTE: Style varies regarding the capitalization of these words when they are used in place of the full name of a specific body. For more on this aspect of styling, see the note following paragraph 18 above.

49. Nicknames, epithets, or other alternate terms for organizations are capitalized.

> referred to IBM as Big Blue
> the Big Three auto makers
> trading stocks on the Big Board

People

50. The names and initials of persons are capitalized. If a name is hyphenated, both elements are capitalized. Particles forming the initial elements of surnames (as *de, della, der, du, la, ten, ter, van,* and *von*) may or may not be capitalized, depending on the styling of the individual name. However, if a name with a lowercase initial particle begins a sentence, the particle is capitalized.

Thomas de Quincey	E. I. du Pont de Nemours
Sir Arthur Thomas Quiller-Couch	Gerald ter Hoerst
James Van Allen	Heinrich Wilhelm Von Kleist
the paintings of de Kooning	De Kooning's paintings are . . .

51. The name of a person or thing can be added to or replaced entirely by a nickname or epithet, a characterizing word or phrase. Nicknames and epithets are capitalized.

Calamity Jane	the Golden Bear	Doctor J.
Buffalo Bill	Wilt the Stilt	Attila the Hun
Louis the Fat	Murph the Surf	Dizzy Gillespie
Bubba Smith	Dusty Rhodes	Rusty Staub
Goose Gossage	Bird Parker	Meadowlark Lemon
Big Mama Thornton	Night Train Lane	Lefty Grove

52. Nicknames and epithets are frequently used in conjunction with both the first and last name of a person. If it is placed between the first and last name, it will often be enclosed in quotation marks or parentheses; however, if the nickname is expected to be very well known to readers, the quotation marks or parentheses are often omitted. If the nickname precedes the first name, it is sometimes enclosed in quotation marks, but more often it is not.

Thomas P. "Tip" O'Neill	Joanne "Big Mama" Carner
Earl ("Fatha") Hines	Dennis (Oil Can) Boyd
Mary Harris ("Mother") Jones	Anna Mary Robertson "Grandma" Moses
Kissin' Jim Folsom	Blind Lemon Jefferson
Slammin' Sammy Snead	Mother Maybelle Carter

53. Words of family relationship preceding or used in place of a person's name are capitalized. However, these words are lowercased if they are part of a noun phrase that is being used in place of a name.

Cousin Mercy   Grandfather Barnes

I know when Mother's birthday is.

I know when my mother's birthday is.

54. Words designating languages, nationalities, peoples, races, religious groups, and tribes are capitalized. Descriptive terms used to refer to groups of people are variously capitalized or lowercased. Designations based on color are usually lowercased.

Latin	Canadians	Ibo	Afro-American
Caucasians	Muslims	Christians	Navajo

Bushman (for a nomadic hunter of southern Africa)

bushman (for an inhabitant of the Australian bush)

the red man in America   black, brown, and white people

55. Corporate, professional, and governmental titles are capitalized when they immediately precede a person's name, unless the name is being used as an appositive.

President Roosevelt	Queen Elizabeth	Senator Henry Jackson
Doctor Malatesta	Professor Greenbaum	Pastor Linda Jones

They wanted to meet the new pastor, Linda Jones.

Almost everyone has heard of Chrysler's president, Lee Iacocca.

56. When corporate or governmental titles are used as part of a descriptive phrase to identify a person rather than as a person's official title, the title is lowercased.

Senator Ted Stevens of Alaska   *but*   Ted Stevens, senator from Alaska
Lee Iacocca, president of Chrysler Corporation

NOTE: Style varies when governmental titles are used in descriptive phrases that precede a name.

Alaska senator Ted Stevens   *or*   Alaska Senator Ted Stevens

57. Specific governmental titles may be capitalized when they are used in place of particular individuals' names. In minutes and official records of proceedings, corporate titles are capitalized when they are used in place of individuals' names.

> The Secretary of State gave a news conference.
> The Judge will respond to questions in her chambers.
> The Treasurer then stated his misgivings about the project.

58. Some publications always capitalize the word *president* when it refers to the United States presidency. However, the more common practice is to capitalize the word *president* only when it refers to a specific individual.

> It is one of the duties of the President to submit a budget to Congress.
> It is one of the duties of the president to submit a budget to Congress.

59. Titles are capitalized when they are used in direct address.

> Tell me the truth, Doctor.
> Where are we headed, Captain?

Personifications—See **Abstractions and Personifications** above.

Prefixes—See **Hyphenated Compounds** above.

Pronouns

60. The pronoun *I* is capitalized. For pronouns referring to the Deity, see rule 62 below.

> He and I will attend the meeting.

Religious Terms

61. Words designating the Deity are capitalized.

> Allah   God Almighty   Christ
> Jehovah   Yahweh   the Holy Spirit

62. Personal pronouns referring to the Deity are usually capitalized. Relative pronouns (as *who, whom,* and *whose*) usually are not.

> God in His mercy
> when God asks us to do His bidding
> believing that it was God who created the universe

NOTE: Some style manuals maintain that the pronoun does not need to be capitalized if it is closely preceded by its antecedent; however, in current practice, most writers capitalize the pronoun regardless of its position.

63. Traditional designations of apostles, prophets, and saints are capitalized.

> our Lady   the Prophet   the Lawgiver

64. Names of religions, denominations, creeds and confessions, and religious orders are capitalized, as are adjectives derived from these names. The word *church* is capitalized only when it is used as part of the name of a specific body or edifice or, in some publications, when it refers to organized Christianity in general.

Judaism
the Church of Christ
Apostles' Creed
the Poor Clares
Hunt Memorial Church
Islamic
the Thirty-nine Articles of the Church of England

Catholicism
the Southern Baptist Convention
the Society of Jesus
Franciscans
a Buddhist monastery
the Baptist church on the corner

65. Names of the Bible or its books, parts, versions, or editions of it and other sacred books are capitalized but not italicized. Adjectives derived from the names of sacred books are variously capitalized and lowercased. When in doubt, consult a dictionary.

Authorized Version
Talmud
Gospel of Saint Mark
talmudic

Old Testament
Genesis
Koran
Koranic

Apocrypha
Pentateuch
biblical
Vedic

66. The names of prayers and well-known passages of the Bible are capitalized.

Ave Maria
Ten Commandments
the Lord's Prayer

the Sermon on the Mount
the Beatitudes
the Our Father

Scientific Terms

67. Genus names in biological binomial nomenclature are capitalized; species names are lowercased, even when derived from a proper name. Both genus and species names are italicized.

Both the wolf and the domestic dog are included in the genus *Canis.*
The California condor (*Gymnogyps californianus*) is facing extinction.
Trailing arbutus (*Epigaea repens*) and rue anemone (*Anemonella thalictroides*) are among the earliest wildflowers to bloom in the spring.

NOTE: When used, the names of races, varieties, or subspecies are lowercased. Like genus and species names, they are italicized.

Hyla versicolor chrysoscelis
Otis asio naevius

68. The New Latin names of classes, families, and all groups above the genus level in zoology and botany are capitalized but not italicized. Their derivative adjectives and nouns in English are neither capitalized nor italicized.

Gastropoda
Thallophyta

gastropod
thallophyte

69. The names, both scientific and informal, of planets and their satellites, asteroids, stars, constellations, groups of stars, and other unique celestial objects are capitalized. However, the words *sun, earth,* and *moon* are usually lowercased unless they occur with other astronomical names. Generic terms that are the final element in the name of a celestial object are usually lowercased.

Ganymede	Sirius	Great Bear
the Milky Way	Venus	Ursa Major
Pleiades	Big Dipper	Barnard's star
probes heading for the Moon and Mars		

70. Names of meteorological phenomena are lowercased.

aurora australis	northern lights
aurora borealis	parhelic circle

71. Terms that identify geological eras, periods, epochs, and strata are capitalized. The generic terms that follow them are lowercased. The words *upper, middle,* and *lower* are capitalized when they are used to designate an epoch or series within a period; in most other cases, they are lowercased. The word *age* is capitalized in names such as *Age of Reptiles* or *Age of Fishes*.

Mesozoic era	Quaternary period	Oligocene epoch
Upper Cretaceous	Middle Ordovician	Lower Silurian

72. Proper names forming essential elements of scientific laws, theorems, and principles are capitalized. However, the common nouns *law, theorem, theory,* and the like are lowercased.

Boyle's law	Planck's constant
the Pythagorean theorem	Einstein's theory of relativity

NOTE: In terms referring to popular or fanciful theories or observations, descriptive words are usually capitalized as well.

Murphy's Law	the Peter Principle

73. The names of chemical elements and compounds are lowercased.

hydrogen fluoride
ferric ammonium citrate

74. The names of computer services and data bases are usually trademarks and should always be capitalized. The names of computer languages are irregularly styled either with an initial capital letter or with all letters capitalized. The names of some computer languages are commonly written either way. When in doubt, consult a dictionary.

CompuServe	TeleTransfer	Dow Jones News Retrieval Service
Atek	Pascal	
BASIC	COBOL *or* Cobol	APL
PENTA	PL/1	FORTRAN *or* Fortran

Time Periods and Zones

75. The names of days of the week, months of the year, and holidays and holy days are capitalized.

Easter	Independence Day	June
Passover	Memorial Day	Thanksgiving
Tuesday	Yom Kippur	Ramadan

76. The names of time zones are capitalized when abbreviated but usually lowercased when written out except for words that are themselves proper names.

CST	central standard time
mountain time	Pacific standard time

77. Names of the seasons are lowercased if they simply declare the time of year; however, they are capitalized if they are personified.

My new book is scheduled to appear this spring.

the sweet breath of Spring

Titles—For titles of people, see **People** above.

78. Words in titles of books, long poems, magazines, newspapers, plays, movies, novellas that are separately published, and works of art such as paintings and sculpture are capitalized except for internal articles, conjunctions, prepositions, and the *to* of infinitives. The entire title is italicized. For the styling of the Bible and other sacred works, see paragraph 65 above.

The Lives of a Cell	*Of Mice and Men*
Saturday Review	*Christian Science Monitor*
Shakespeare's *Othello*	*The Old Man and the Sea*
Gainsborough's *Blue Boy*	the movie *Wait until Dark*

NOTE: Some publications also capitalize prepositions of five or more letters (as *about* or *toward*).

79. An initial article that is part of a title is often omitted if it would be awkward in context. However, when it is included it is capitalized and italicized. A common exception to this style regards books that are referred to by an abbreviation. In this case, the initial article is neither capitalized nor italicized.

The Oxford English Dictionary
the 13-volume *Oxford English Dictionary*
the *OED*

80. Style varies widely regarding the capitalization and italicization of initial articles and city names in the titles of newspapers. One style rule that can be followed is to capitalize and italicize any word that is part of the official title of the paper as shown on its masthead. However, this information is not always available, and even if it is available it can lead to apparent inconsistencies in styling. Because of this, many publications choose one way of styling newspaper titles regardless of their official titles. The most common styling is to italicize the city name but not to capitalize or italicize the initial article.

the *New York Times*   the *Wall Street Journal*
the *Des Moines Register*   the *Washington Post*

81. Many publications, especially newspapers, do not use italics to style titles. They either simply capitalize the words of the title or capitalize the words and enclose them in quotation marks.

the Heard on the Street column in the Wall Street Journal
our review of "The Lives of a Cell" in last week's column

82. The first word following a colon in a title is capitalized.

John Crowe Ransom: An Annotated Bibliography

83. The titles of short poems, short stories, essays, lectures, dissertations, chapters of books, articles in periodicals, radio and television programs, and novellas that are published in a collection are capitalized and enclosed in quotation marks. The capitalization of articles, conjunctions, and prepositions is the same as it is for italicized titles, as explained in paragraph 78 above.

Robert Frost's "Dust of Snow"
Katherine Anne Porter's "That Tree"
John Barth's "The Literature of Exhaustion"
The talk, "Labor's Power: A View for the Eighties," will be given next week.
the third chapter of *Treasure Island,* entitled "The Black Spot"
Her article, "Computer Art on a Micro," was in last month's *Popular Computing.*
listening to "A Prairie Home Companion"
watching "The Tonight Show"
D. H. Lawrence's "The Woman Who Rode Away"

84. Common titles of sections of books (as a preface, introduction, or index) are capitalized but not enclosed in quotation marks when they refer to a section of the same book in which the reference is made. If they refer to another book, they are usually lowercased.

See the Appendix for further information.
In the introduction to her book, the author explains her goals.

85. Style varies regarding the capitalization of the word *chapter* when it is used with a cardinal number to identify a specific chapter in a book. In some publications the word is lowercased, but more commonly it is capitalized.

See Chapter 3 for more details.
is discussed further in Chapter Four
> *but*   in the third chapter

86. The titles of long musical compositions such as operas and sympho-
nies are capitalized and italicized; the titles of short compositions are
capitalized and enclosed in quotation marks. The titles of musical
compositions identified by the nature of the musical form in which
they were written are capitalized only.

Verdi's *Don Carlos*   "America the Beautiful"
Ravel's "Bolero"   Serenade No. 12 in C Minor

Trademarks

87. Registered trademarks, service marks, and brand names are capitalized.

Band-Aid   Jacuzzi   Kleenex
College Board   Granny   Realtor
Kellogg's All-Bran Diet Pepsi   Lay's potato chips

Transportation

88. The names of individual ships, submarines, airplanes, satellites, and
space vehicles are capitalized and italicized. The designations *U.S.S.,
S.S., M.V.,* and *H.M.S.* are not italicized.

Apollo 11   *Enola Gay*
Mariner 5   *Explorer 10*
Spirit of Saint Louis   M.V. *West Star*

Other Uses of Capitals

1. Full capitalization of a word is sometimes used for emphasis or to indicate that a speaker is talking very loudly. Both of these uses of capitals are usually avoided or at least used very sparingly in formal
prose. Italicization of words for emphasis is more common. For examples of this use of italics, see paragraph 8 of the section on Other
Uses of Italics in this chapter.

Results are not the only criteria for judging performance. HOW we
achieve results is important also.

All applications must be submitted IN WRITING before January 31.

The waiter rushed by yelling "HOT PLATE! HOT PLATE!"

2. A word is sometimes capitalized to indicate that it is being used as a
philosophical concept or to indicate that it stands for an important
concept in a discussion. Style manuals generally discourage this practice, but it is still in common use today even in formal writing.

Many people seek Truth, but few find it.
the three M's of advertising, Message, Media, and Management

3. Full capitals or a mixture of capitals and lowercase letters or sometimes even small capitals are used to reproduce the text of signs, labels, or inscriptions.

a poster reading SPECIAL THRILLS COMING SOON
a Do Not Disturb sign
a barn with CHEW MAIL POUCH on the side
a truck with WASH ME written in the dust

4. A letter used to indicate a shape is usually capitalized. If sans serif
type is available, it is often used for such a letter, because it usually
best approximates the shape that is being referred to.

an A-frame house   a J-bar   V-shaped

Other Uses of Italics

Italic type is used to indicate that there is something out of the ordinary
about a word or phrase or about the way in which it is being used. For
some of the uses listed below, quotation marks can be substituted. For
more on this use of quotation marks, see the section on Quotation Marks,
Double, in Chapter 1, "Punctuation," beginning on page 39. For each of
the uses listed below, underlining is used in place of italicizing when the
text is typewritten instead of typeset.

1. Foreign words and phrases that have not been fully adopted into the
English language are italicized. The decision whether or not to italicize a word will vary according to the context of the writing and the
audience for which the writing is intended. In general, however, any
word that appears in the main A–Z vocabulary section of *Webster's
Ninth New Collegiate Dictionary* does not need to be italicized.

These accomplishments will serve as a monument, *aere perennius*, to the
group's skill and dedication.
They looked upon this area as a *cordon sanitaire* around the city.
"The cooking here is *wunderbar*," he said.
After the concert, the crowd headed en masse for the parking lot.
The committee meets on an ad hoc basis.

NOTE: A complete sentence (such as a motto) can also be italicized.
However, passages that comprise more than one sentence, or even a
single sentence if it is particularly long, are usually treated as quotations; i.e., they are set in roman type and enclosed in quotation
marks.

2. Unfamiliar words or words that have a specialized meaning are set in italics, especially when they are accompanied by a short definition. Once these words have been introduced and defined, they do not need to be italicized in subsequent references.

> *Vitiligo* is a condition in which skin pigment cells stop making pigment.
>
> Another method is the *direct-to-consumer* transaction in which the publisher markets directly to the individual by mail or door-to-door.

3. Style varies somewhat regarding the italicization of Latin abbreviations. During the first half of this century, these abbreviations were most commonly set in italic type. Some authors and publishers still italicize them, either by tradition or on the grounds that they should be treated like foreign words. However, most authors and publishers now set these abbreviations in roman type. (For an explanation of the use of *ibid., op. cit.,* and other Latin bibliographical abbreviations, see Chapter 8, "Notes and Documentation of Sources.")

> et al.   cf.   e.g.   i.e.   viz.

4. Italic type is used to indicate words referred to as words, letters referred to as letters, or numerals referred to as numerals. However, if the word referred to as a word was actually spoken, it is often enclosed in quotation marks. If the letter is being used to refer to its sound and not its printed form, virgules or brackets can be used instead of italics. And if there is no chance of confusion, numerals referred to as numerals are often not italicized. (For an explanation of the ways in which to form the plurals of words, letters, and numerals referred to as such, see the section on Plurals, beginning on page 74, in Chapter 3, "Plurals, Possessives, and Compounds.")

> The panel could not decide whether *data* was a singular or plural noun.
>
> *Only* can be an adverb modifying a verb, as in the case of "I *only* tried to help."
>
> We heard his warning, but we weren't sure what "other repercussions" meant in that context.
>
> You should dot your *i*'s and cross your *t*'s.
>
> She couldn't pronounce her *s*'s.
>
> He was still having trouble with the /p/ sound.
>
> The first *2* and the last *1* are barely legible.

5. A letter used to indicate a shape is usually capitalized but not set in italics. For more on this use of capital letters, see the section on Other Uses of Capitals in this chapter.

6. Individual letters are sometimes set in italic type to provide additional typographical contrast. This use of italics is common when letters are used in run-in enumerations or when they are used to identify elements in an illustration.

providing information about (*a*) typing, (*b*) transcribing, (*c*) formatting, and (*d*) graphics

located at point *A* on the diagram

7. Italics are used to indicate a word created to suggest a sound.

From the nest came a high-pitched *whee* from one of the young birds.

We sat listening to the *chat-chat-chat* of the sonar.

8. Italics are used to emphasize or draw attention to a word or words in a sentence.

Students must notify the dean's office *in writing* of all courses added or dropped from their original list.

She had become *the* hero, the one everyone else looked up to.

NOTE: Italics serve to draw attention to words in large part because they are used so infrequently. Writers who overuse italics for giving emphasis may find that the italics lose their effectiveness.

Chapter 3

Plurals, Possessives, and Compounds

CONTENTS

This chapter describes the ways in which plurals, possessives, and compound words are most commonly formed. In doing so, it treats some of the simplest and some of the most problematic kinds of questions that are faced by writers and editors. For some of the questions raised in this chapter, various solutions have been developed over the years, but no single solution has come to be universally accepted. This chapter describes the range of solutions that are available; however, many of the questions raised in this chapter inevitably require arbitrary decisions and personal judgments. In cases like these, careful writers and editors usually make notes or keep a style sheet so that they can be consistent in the way that they form plurals, possessives, and compounds for certain specific words or categories of words. For more on keeping and using a style sheet, see pages 297–301 in Chapter 11, "Production Techniques."

Writers and editors are frequently told that consulting a good dictionary will solve many of the problems that are discussed in this chapter. To some extent this is true, and this chapter does recommend consulting a dictionary at a number of points. In this regard, the best dictionary to consult is an unabridged dictionary, such as *Webster's Third New International Dictionary*. In the absence of such a comprehensive reference book, writers and editors should consult a good desk dictionary, such as *Webster's Ninth New Collegiate Dictionary*. Any dictionary that is much smaller than the *Ninth Collegiate* will often be more frustrating in what it fails to show than helpful in what it shows.

In giving examples of plurals, possessives, and compounds, this chapter uses both *or* and *also* to separate variant forms of the same word. The word *or* is used when both forms of the word are used with approximately equal frequency in standard prose; the form that precedes the *or* is probably slightly more common than the form that follows it. The word *also* is used when one form of the word is much more common than the other; the more common precedes the less common.

Plurals

The plurals of most English words are formed by adding -*s* to the singular. If the noun ends in -*s*, -*x*, -*z*, -*ch*, or -*sh*, so that an extra syllable must be added in order to pronounce the plural, -*es* is added to the singular. If the noun ends in a -*y* preceded by a consonant, the -*y* is changed to -*i*- and -*es* is added. Most proper nouns ending in -*y* (as *Mary* or *Germany*), however, simply add -*s* to the singular.

Many English nouns do not follow the general pattern for forming plurals. Most good dictionaries give thorough coverage to irregular and variant plurals, so they are often the best place to start to answer questions about the plural form of a specific word. The paragraphs that follow describe the ways in which plurals are formed for a number of categories of words whose plural forms are most apt to raise questions.

The symbol → is used throughout this section of the chapter. In each case, the element that follows the arrow is the plural form of the element that precedes the arrow.

Abbreviations

1. The plurals of abbreviations are commonly formed by adding -*s* or an apostrophe plus -*s* to the abbreviation; however, there are some significant exceptions to this pattern. For more on the formation of plurals of abbreviations, see the section on Plurals, Possessives, and Compounds, beginning on page 98, in Chapter 4, "Abbreviations."

COLA → COLA's	CPU → CPUs	bldg. → bldgs.
f.o.b. → f.o.b.'s	Ph.D. → Ph.D.'s	p. → pp.

Animals

2. The names of many fishes, birds, and mammals have both a plural formed with a suffix and one that is identical with the singular. Some have only the -*s* plural; others have only an uninflected plural.

flounder → flounder *or* flounders		mink → mink *or* minks	
quail → quail *or* quails		buffalo → buffalo *or* buffalos	
cow → cows	hen → hens	rat → rats	monkey → monkeys
bison → bison	sheep → sheep	shad → shad	moose → moose

3. Many of the animals that have both plural forms are ones that are hunted, fished, or trapped, and those who hunt, fish for, and trap them are most likely to use the uninflected form. The -*s* form is especially likely to be used to emphasize diversity of kinds.

caught four trout
   but
trouts of the Rocky Mountains
a place where fish gather
   but
the fishes of the Pacific Ocean

Compounds and Phrases

4. Most compounds composed of two nouns, whether styled as one word or two words or as hyphenated words, are pluralized by pluralizing the final element.

matchbox → matchboxes   spokeswoman → spokeswomen
judge advocate → judge advocates   tree house → tree houses
city-state → city-states   crow's-foot → crow's-feet
face-lift → face-lifts   battle-ax → battle-axes

5. The plural form of a compound consisting of an *-er* agent noun and an adverb is made by pluralizing the noun element.

hanger-on → hangers-on   looker-on → lookers-on
onlooker → onlookers   passerby → passersby

6. Nouns made up of words that are not nouns form their plurals on the terminal element.

also-ran → also-rans   ne'er-do-well → ne'er-do-wells
put-down → put-downs   set-to → set-tos
changeover → changeovers   blowup → blowups

7. Plurals of compounds that are phrases consisting of two nouns separated by a preposition are regularly formed by pluralizing the first noun.

aide-de-camp → aides-de-camp   base on balls → bases on balls
auto-da-fe → autos-da-fe   mother-in-law → mothers-in-law
man-of-war → men-of-war   coup d'état → coups d'état
attorney-at-law → attorneys-at-law
lady-in-waiting → ladies-in-waiting
power of attorney → powers of attorney

8. Compounds that are phrases consisting of two nouns separated by a preposition and a modifier form their plurals in various ways.

flash in the pan → flashes in the pan
jack-in-the-box → jack-in-the-boxes *or* jacks-in-the-box
jack-of-all-trades → jacks-of-all-trades
son of a gun → sons of guns
stick-in-the-mud → stick-in-the-muds

9. Compounds consisting of a noun followed by an adjective are regularly pluralized by adding a suffix to the noun.

cousin-german → cousins-german
heir apparent → heirs apparent
knight-errant → knights-errant

NOTE: If the adjective in such a compound tends to be construed as a noun, the compound may have more than one plural form.

attorney general → attorneys general *or* attorney generals

sergeant major → sergeants major   *or*   sergeant majors
poet laureate → poets laureate   *or*   poet laureates

Foreign Words and Phrases

10. Many nouns of foreign origin retain the foreign plural; most of them also have a regular English plural.

alumnus → alumni
beau → beaux   *or*   beaus
crisis → crises
emporium → emporiums   *or*   emporia
index → indexes   *or*   indices
larynx → larynges   *or*   larynxes
phenomenon → phenomena   *or*   phenomenons
schema → schemata   *also*   schemas
seraph → seraphim   *or*   seraphs
series → series
tempo → tempi   *or*   tempos

NOTE: A foreign plural may not be used for all senses of a word or may be more commonly used for some senses than for others.

antenna (on an insect) → antennae
antenna (on a radio) → antennas

11. Phrases of foreign origin may have a foreign plural, an English plural, or both.

beau monde → beau mondes   *or*   beaux mondes
carte blanche → cartes blanches
charlotte russe → charlottes russe
felo-de-se → felones-de-se   *or*   felos-de-se
hors d'oeuvre → hors d'oeuvres

-ful Words

12. A plural *-fuls* can be used for any noun ending in *-ful*, but some of these nouns also have an alternative, usually less common plural with -s- preceding the suffix.

eyeful → eyefuls	mouthful → mouthfuls
barnful → barnfuls	worldful → worldfuls
barrelful → barrelfuls *or* barrelsful	
bucketful → bucketfuls *or* bucketsful	
cupful → cupfuls *also* cupsful	
tablespoonful → tablespoonfuls *also* tablespoonsful	

Irregular Plurals

13. A small group of English nouns form their plurals by changing one or more of their vowels.

foot → feet	man → men	woman → women
goose → geese	mouse → mice	tooth → teeth
louse → lice		

14. A few nouns have *-en* or *-ren* plurals.

> ox → oxen
> child → children
> brother → brethren

15. Some nouns ending in *-f*, *-fe*, and *-ff* have plurals that end in *-ves*. Some of these also have regularly formed plurals.

elf → elves	beef → beefs *or* beeves
knife → knives	staff → staffs *or* staves
life → lives	wharf → wharves *also* wharfs
loaf → loaves	dwarf → dwarfs *or* dwarves

Italic Elements

16. Italicized words, phrases, abbreviations, and letters in roman context are variously pluralized with either an italic or roman *s*. Most stylebooks urge use of a roman *s*, and our evidence indicates that that is the form used most commonly. If the plural is formed with an apostrophe and an *-s*, the *-s* is almost always roman.

> fifteen *Newsweek*s on the shelf
> answered with a series of *uh-huh*s
> a row of *x*'s

Letters

17. The plurals of letters are usually formed by the addition of an apostrophe and an *-s*, although uppercase letters are sometimes pluralized by the addition of an *-s* alone.

> p's and q's
> V's of geese flying overhead
> dot your *i*'s
> straight As

Numbers

18. Numerals are pluralized by adding an *-s*, or, less commonly, an apostrophe and an *-s*.

> two par 5s   1960's
> 1970s   the mid-$20,000s
> in the 80s   DC-10's

19. Spelled-out numbers are usually pluralized without an apostrophe.

> in twos and threes
> scored two sixes

-o Words

20. Most words ending in an *-o* are pluralized by adding an *-s*; however, some words ending in an *-o* preceded by a consonant have *-s* plurals, some have *-es* plurals, and some have both. When you are in doubt about such a word, consult a dictionary.

alto → altos
echo → echoes
motto → mottoes *also* mottos
tornado → tornadoes *or* tornados

Proper Nouns

21. The plurals of proper nouns are usually formed with *-s* or *-es*.

Bruce → Bruces
Charles → Charleses
John Harris → John Harrises
Hastings → Hastingses
Velasquez → Velasquezes

22. Proper nouns ending in *-y* usually retain the *-y* and add *-s*.

Germany → Germanys
Mary → Marys
Mercury → Mercurys
  but
Ptolemy → Ptolemies
Sicily → The Two Sicilies
The Rockies

NOTE: Words that were originally proper nouns and that end in *-y* are usually pluralized by changing *-y* to *-i-* and adding *-es*, but a few retain the *-y*.

bobby → bobbies
Jerry → Jerries
Bloody Mary → Bloody Marys
Typhoid Mary → Typhoid Marys

johnny → johnnies
Tommy → Tommies

Quoted Elements

23. Style varies regarding the plural form of words in quotation marks. Some writers form the plural by adding an *-s* or an apostrophe plus *-s* within the quotation marks; others add an *-s* outside the quotation marks. Both arrangements look awkward, and writers generally try to avoid this construction.

too many "probably's" in the statement
didn't hear any "nays"
One "you" among millions of "you"s
a response characterized by its "yes, but"s

Symbols

24. Although symbols are not usually pluralized, when a symbol is being referred to as a character in itself without regard to meaning, the plural is formed by adding an *-s* or an apostrophe plus *-s*.

used &'s instead of *and*'s
his π's are hard to read
printed three *s

Words used as Words

25. Words used as words without regard to meaning usually form their plurals by adding an apostrophe and an -*s*.

> five *and*'s in one sentence
> all those *wherefore*'s and *howsoever*'s

NOTE: When a word used as a word has become part of a fixed phrase, the plural is usually formed by adding a roman -*s* without the apostrophe.

> oohs and aahs
> dos and don'ts

Possessives

The possessive case of most nouns is formed by adding an apostrophe or an apostrophe plus -*s* to the end of the word. For most other uses of the apostrophe, such as to form contractions, see the section on Apostrophe, beginning on page 4, in Chapter 1, "Punctuation." For the use of the apostrophe to form plurals, see the section on Plurals in this chapter.

Common Nouns

1. The possessive case of singular and plural common nouns that do not end in an *s* or *z* sound is formed by adding an apostrophe plus -*s* to the end of the word.

> the boy's mother   at her wit's end   the potato's skin
> men's clothing   children's books   the symposia's themes

2. The possessive case of singular nouns ending in an *s* or *z* sound is usually formed by adding an apostrophe plus -*s* to the end of the word. Style varies somewhat on this point, as some writers prefer to add an apostrophe plus -*s* to the word only when the added -*s* is pronounced; if it isn't pronounced, they add just an apostrophe. According to our evidence, both approaches are common in contemporary prose, although always adding an apostrophe plus -*s* is the much more widely accepted approach.

> the press's books   the index's arrangement
> the boss's desk   the horse's saddle
> the audience's reaction   *also*   the audience' reaction
> the waitress's duties   *also*   the waitress' duties
> the conference's outcome   *also*   the conference' outcome

NOTE: Even writers who follow the pattern of adding an apostrophe plus -*s* to all singular nouns will often make an exception for a multisyllabic word that ends in an *s* or *z* sound if it is followed by a word beginning with an *s* or *z* sound.

   for convenience' sake   for conscience' sake
   the illness' symptoms   *or*   the illness's symptoms
   to the princess' surprise   *or* to the princess's surprise

3. The possessive case of plural nouns ending in an *s* or *z* sound is formed by adding only an apostrophe to the end of the word. One exception to this rule is that the possessive case of one-syllable irregular plurals is usually formed by adding an apostrophe plus -*s*.

   horses' stalls   consumers' confidence
   geese's calls   mice's habits

Proper Names

4. The possessive forms of proper names are generally made in the same way as they are for common nouns. The possessive form of singular proper names not ending in an *s* or *z* sound is made by adding an apostrophe plus -*s* to the name. The possessive form of plural proper names is made by adding just an apostrophe.

   Mrs. Wilson's store   Utah's capital   Canada's rivers
   the Wattses' daughter   the Cohens' house   Niagara Falls' location

5. As is the case for the possessive form of singular common nouns (see paragraph 2 above), the possessive form of singular proper names ending in an *s* or *z* sound may be formed either by adding an apostrophe plus -*s* or by adding just an apostrophe to the name. For the sake of consistency, most writers choose one pattern for forming the possessive of all singular names ending in an *s* or *z* sound, regardless of the pronunciation of individual names (for exceptions see paragraphs 6 and 7 below). According to our evidence, adding an apostrophe plus -*s* to all such names is more common than adding just the apostrophe.

   Jones's car   *also* Jones' car
   Bliss's statue   *also* Bliss' statue
   Dickens's novels   *also* Dickens' novels

6. The possessive form of classical and biblical names of two or more syllables ending in -*s* or -*es* is usually made by adding an apostrophe without an -*s*. If the name has only one syllable, the possessive form is made by adding an apostrophe and an -*s*.

   Aristophanes' plays   Achilles' heel   Odysseus' journey
   Judas' betrayal   Zeus's anger   Mars's help

7. The possessive forms of the names *Jesus* and *Moses* are always formed with just an apostrophe.

   Jesus' time   Moses' law

8. The possessive forms of names ending in a silent *-s, -z,* or *-x* usually include the apostrophe and the *-s.*

>   Arkansas's capital   Camus's *The Stranger*
>   Delacroix's paintings   Josquin des Prez's work

9. For the sake of convenience and appearance, some writers will italicize the possessive ending when adding it to a name that is in italics; however, most frequently the possessive ending is in roman.

>   the U.S.S. *Constitution*'s cannons   the *Mona Lisa*'s somber hues
>   *Gone With the Wind*'s ending   *High Noon*'s plot

Pronouns

10. The possessive case of indefinite pronouns such as *anyone, everybody,* and *someone* is formed by adding an apostrophe and an *-s.*

>   everyone's   anybody's   everyone's
>   everybody's   someone's   somebody's

NOTE: Some indefinite pronouns usually require an *of* phrase rather than inflection to indicate possession.

>   the rights of each   the satisfaction of all
>   the inclination of many

11. Possessive pronouns include no apostrophes.

>   mine   yours   his   hers
>   its   ours   theirs

Phrases

12. The possessive form of a phrase is made by adding an apostrophe or an apostrophe plus *-s* to the last word in the phrase.

>   board of directors' meeting
>   his brother-in-law's sidecar
>   from the student of politics' point of view
>   a moment or so's thought

NOTE: Constructions such as these can become awkward, and it is often better to rephrase the sentence to eliminate the need for the possessive ending. For instance, the last two examples above could be rephrased as follows:

>   from the point of view of the student of politics
>   thinking for a moment or so

Words in Quotation Marks

13. Style varies regarding the possessive form of words in quotation marks. Some writers place the apostrophe and *-s* inside the quotation marks; others place them outside the quotation marks. Either arrangement will look awkward, and writers usually try to avoid this construction.

>the "Today Show"'s cohosts
>the "Grande Dame's" escort
>*but more commonly*
>the cohosts of the "Today Show"
>escort to the "Grande Dame"

Abbreviations

14. Possessives of abbreviations are formed in the same way as those of nouns that are spelled out. The singular possessive is formed by adding an apostrophe plus -*s* to the abbreviation; the plural possessive, by adding an apostrophe only.

>the AMA's executive committee
>Itek Corp.'s Applied Technology Division
>the Burns Bros.' stores
>the MPs' decisions

Numerals

15. The possessive form of nouns composed of or including numerals is made in the same way as for nouns composed wholly of words. The possessive of singular nouns is formed by adding an apostrophe plus -*s*; the possessive form of plural nouns, by adding an apostrophe only.

>1985's most popular model
>Louis XIV's Court
>the 1980s' most colorful figure

Individual and Joint Possession

16. Individual possession is indicated when an apostrophe plus -*s* is added to each noun in a sequence. Joint possession is most commonly indicated by adding an apostrophe or an apostrophe plus -*s* to the last noun in the sequence. In some cases, joint possession is also indicated by adding a possessive ending to each name.

>Kepler's and Clark's respective clients
>John's, Bill's, and Larry's boats
>Kepler and Clark's law firm
>Christine and James's vacation home   *or*   Christine's and James's vacation home

Compounds

A compound is a word or word group that consists of two or more parts working together as a unit to express a specific concept. Compounds can be formed by combining two or more words (as in *eye shadow*, *graphic equalizer*, *farmhouse*, *cost-effective*, *blue-pencil*, *around-the-clock*, or *son of a gun*), by combining word elements (as prefixes or suffixes) with words (as in *ex-president*, *shoeless*, *presorted*, *uninterruptedly*, or *meaningless*), or by combining two or more word elements (as in *supermicro* or *photomicrograph*). Compounds are written in one of three ways: solid (as *cottonmouth*), hyphenated (as *player-manager*), or open (as *field day*).

Some of the explanations in this section make reference to permanent and temporary compounds. Permanent compounds are those that are so commonly used that they have become established as permanent parts of the language; many of them can be found in dictionaries. Temporary compounds are those made up to fit the writer's need at the particular moment. Temporary compounds, of course, cannot be found in dictionaries and therefore present the writer with styling problems.

Presenting styling problems similar to those of temporary compounds are self-evident compounds. These are compounds (as *baseball game* or *economic policy*) that are readily understood from the meanings of the words that make them up. Self-evident compounds, like temporary compounds, are not to be found in dictionaries.

In other words, writers faced with having to use compounds such as *farm stand* (*farm-stand? farmstand?*), *wide body* (*wide-body? widebody?*), or *picture framing* (*picture-framing? pictureframing?*) cannot rely wholly on dictionaries to guide them in their styling of compounds. They need, in addition, to develop an approach for dealing with compounds that are not in the dictionary. A few of those approaches are explained below.

One approach is simply to leave open any compound that is not in the dictionary. Many writers do this, but there are drawbacks to this approach. A temporary compound may not be as easily recognized as a compound by the reader when it is left open. For instance if you need to use *wide body* as a term for a kind of jet airplane, a phrase like "the operation of wide bodies" may catch the reader unawares. And if you use the open style for a compound modifier, you may create momentary confusion (or even unintended amusement) with a phrase like "the operation of wide body jets."

Another possibility would be to hyphenate all compounds that aren't in the dictionary. Hyphenation would give your compound immediate recognition as a compound. But hyphenating all such compounds runs counter to some well-established American practice. Thus you would be calling too much attention to the compound and momentarily distracting the reader.

A third approach is to use analogy to pattern your temporary compound after some other similar compound. This approach is likely to be more complicated than simply picking an open or hyphenated form, and will not free you from the need to make your own decisions in most instances. But it does have the advantage of making your compound less distracting or confusing by making it look as much like other more familiar compounds as possible.

The rest of this section is aimed at helping you to use the analogical approach to styling compounds. You will find compounds listed according to the elements that make them up and the way that they function in a sentence.

This section deals first with compounds formed from whole English words, then compounds formed with word elements, and finally with a small collection of miscellaneous styling conventions relating to compounds. The symbol + in the following paragraphs can be interpreted as "followed immediately by."

Compound Nouns

Compound nouns are combinations of words that function in a sentence as nouns. They may consist of two or more nouns, a noun and a modifier, or two or more elements that are not nouns.

1. **noun + noun** Compounds composed of two nouns that are short, commonly used, and pronounced with falling stress—that is, with the most stress on the first noun and less or no stress on the second—are usually styled solid.

teapot	cottonmouth	birdbath	handmaiden
catfish	sweatband	handsaw	farmyard
football	handlebar	railroad	bandwagon

2. When a noun + noun compound is short and common but pronounced with equal stress on both nouns, the styling is more likely to be open.

bean sprouts	beach buggy	head louse
fuel oil	duffel bag	dart board
fuel cell	fire drill	rose fever

3. Many short noun + noun compounds begin as temporary compounds styled open. As they become more familiar and better established, there is a tendency for them to become solid.

data base	*is becoming*	database
chain saw	*is becoming*	chainsaw
lawn mower	*is becoming*	lawnmower

4. Noun + noun compounds that consist of longer nouns, are self-evident, or are temporary are usually styled open.

wildlife sanctuary	reunion committee
football game	television camera

5. When the nouns in a noun + noun compound describe a double title or double function, the compound is hyphenated.

city-state	dinner-dance	player-manager
decree-law	secretary-treasurer	author-critic

6. Compounds formed from a noun or adjective followed by *man, woman, person,* or *people* and denoting an occupation are regularly solid.

salesman	saleswoman	salesperson	salespeople
congresswoman	handyman	spokesperson	policewoman

7. Compounds that are units of measurement are hyphenated.

foot-pound	man-hour	light-year
kilowatt-hour	column-inch	board-foot

8. **adjective + noun** Most temporary or self-evident adjective + noun compounds are styled open. Permanent compounds formed from relatively long adjectives or nouns are also open.

automatic weapons	modal auxiliary	modular arithmetic
religious freedom	automatic pilot	graphic equalizer
pancreatic juice	minor seminary	white lightning

9. Adjective + noun compounds consisting of two short words may be styled solid when pronounced with falling stress. Just as often, however, short adjective + noun compounds are styled open; a few are hyphenated.

bigfoot	blueprint	drywall	highland
longboat	longhand	redline	shortcake
shortcut	shorthand	sickbed	wetland
yellowhammer	big deal	dry cleaner	dry rot
dry run	dry well	high gear	long haul
red tape	short run	short story	sick leave
wet nurse	yellow jacket	red-eye	red-hot

10. **participle + noun** Most participle + noun compounds are styled open, whether permanent, temporary, or self-evident.

frying pan	furnished apartment	shredded wheat
whipped cream	nagging backache	whipping boy

11. **noun's + noun** Compounds consisting of a possessive noun followed by another noun are usually styled hyphenated or open.

crow's-feet	lion's share	fool's gold
cat's cradle	cat's-eye	cat's-paw
stirred up a hornet's nest		

NOTE: Compounds of this type that have become solid have lost the apostrophe.

foolscap	menswear	sheepshead

12. **noun + verb + -er; noun + verb + -ing** Temporary compounds in which the first noun is the object of the verb to which the suffix has been added are most often styled open; however, many writers use a hyphen to make the relationships of the words immediately apparent. Permanent compounds like these are sometimes styled solid as well.

temporary	gene-splicing	opinion maker	cost-cutting
	risk-taking	career planning	English-speakers
permanent	lifesaver	copyediting	flyswatter
	data processing	bird-watcher	fund-raising
	lawn mower	penny-pinching	bookkeeper

13. object + verb   Noun compounds consisting of a verb preceded by a noun that is its object are variously styled.

clambake	car wash	face-lift	turkey shoot

14. verb + object   A few compounds are formed from a verb followed by a noun that is its object. These are mostly older words, and they are solid.

tosspot	breakwater	pinchpenny
cutthroat	carryall	pickpocket

15. noun + adjective   Compounds composed of a noun followed by an adjective are styled open or hyphenated.

battle royal	consul general	secretary-general
governor-designate	heir apparent	letters patent
sum total	mayor-elect	president-elect

16. particle + noun   Compounds consisting of a particle (usually a preposition or adverb having prepositional, adverbial, or adjectival force in the compound) and a noun are usually styled solid, especially when they are short and pronounced with falling stress.

downpour	inpatient	outpatient	input
output	throughput	aftershock	overskirt
offshoot	undershirt	crossbones	upkeep

17. A few particle + noun compounds, especially when composed of longer elements or having equal stress on both elements, may be hyphenated or open.

off-season	down payment	off year	cross-fertilization

18. verb + particle; verb + adverb   These compounds may be hyphenated or solid. Compounds with two-letter particles (*by, to, in, up, on*) are most frequently hyphenated, since the hyphen aids quick comprehension. Compounds with three-letter particles (*off, out*) are hyphenated or solid with about equal frequency. Those with longer particles or adverbs are more often but not always solid.

call-up	lay-up	lead-in	run-on	set-to
sign-on	sit-in	trade-in	turn-on	warm-up
wrap-up	write-in	flyby	letup	pileup
brush-off	shoot-out	show-off	sick-out	write-off
dropout	layout	strikeout	tryout	turnoff
follow-through	get-together	breakdown		breakthrough
gadabout	giveaway	rollback		takeover

19. verb + -er + particle; verb + -ing + particle   Except for *passerby*, these compounds are hyphenated.

hanger-on	diner-out	falling-out	runner-up
summing-up	talking-to	goings-on	looker-on

20. compounds of three or four elements Compounds of three or four elements are styled either hyphenated or open. Those consisting of noun + prepositional phrase are generally open, although some are hyphenated. Those formed from other combinations are usually hyphenated.

base on balls	justice of the peace	lady of the house
lily of the valley	lord of misrule	son of a gun
good-for-nothing	jack-of-all-trades	lady-in-waiting
love-in-a-mist	by-your-leave	Johnny-jump-up
know-it-all	pick-me-up	stick-to-itiveness

21. letter + noun Compounds formed from a single letter (or sometimes a combination of them) followed by a noun are either open or hyphenated.

A-frame	B-girl	H-bomb	T-shirt
C ration	D day	I beam	T square
ABO system	J-bar lift	Rh factor	H and L hinge

Compounds That Function as Adjectives

Compound adjectives are combinations of words that work together to modify a noun—that is, they work as unit modifiers. As unit modifiers they should be distinguished from other strings of adjectives that may also precede a noun. For instance, in "a low, level tract of land" or "that long, lonesome road" the two adjectives each modify the noun separately. We are talking about a tract of land that is both low and level and about a road that is both long and lonesome. These are coordinate modifiers.

In "a low monthly fee" or "a wrinkled red necktie" the first adjective modifies the noun plus the second adjective. In other words, we mean a monthly fee that is low and a red necktie that is wrinkled. These are non-coordinate modifiers. But in "low-level radiation" we do not mean radiation that is low and level or level radiation that is low; we mean radiation that is at a low level. Both words work as a unit to modify the noun.

Unit modifiers are usually hyphenated. The hyphens not only make it easier for the reader to grasp the relationship of the words but also avoid confusion. The hyphen in "a call for more-specialized controls" removes any ambiguity as to which word *more* modifies. A phrase like "graphic arts exhibition" may seem clear to its author, but may have an unintended meaning for some readers.

22. Before the Noun (attributive position) Most two-word permanent or temporary compound adjectives are hyphenated when placed before the noun.

tree-lined streets	fast-acting medication
an iron-clad guarantee	a tough-minded negotiator
class-conscious persons	Spanish-American relations
well-intended advice	the red-carpet treatment
a profit-loss statement	an input-output device
arrested on a trumped-up charge	a risk-free investment

23. Temporary compounds formed of an adverb (as *well, more, less, still*) followed by a participle (or sometimes an adjective) are usually hyphenated when placed before a noun.

more-specialized controls	a just-completed survey
a still-growing company	a well-funded project
these fast-moving times	a now-vulnerable politician

24. Temporary compounds formed from an adverb ending in *-ly* followed by a participle may sometimes be hyphenated but are more commonly open, because adverb + adjective + noun is a normal word order.

a widely-read feature   internationally-known authors
 but more often
generally recognized categories a beautifully illustrated book
publicly supported universities   our rapidly changing plans

25. The combination of *very* + adjective is not a unit modifier.

a very satisfied smile

26. Many temporary compound adjectives are formed by using a compound noun—either permanent or temporary—to modify another noun. If the compound noun is an open compound, it is usually hyphenated so that the relationship of the words is more immediately apparent to the reader.

the farm-bloc vote	a picture-framing shop
a short-run printing press	a secret-compartment ring
a tax-law case	ocean-floor hydrophones

27. Some open compound nouns are considered so readily recognizable that they are frequently placed before a noun without a hyphen.

a high school diploma *or* a high-school diploma
a data processing course *or* a data-processing course
a dry goods store *or* a dry-goods store

28. A proper name placed before a noun to modify it is not hyphenated.

a Thames River marina	a Huck Finn life
a Korean War veteran	a General Motors car

29. Compound adjectives of three or more words are hyphenated when they precede the noun. Many temporary compounds are formed by taking a phrase, hyphenating it, and placing it before a noun.

spur-of-the-moment decisions
higher-than-anticipated costs
her soon-to-be-released movie

30. Compound adjectives composed of foreign words are not hyphenated when placed before a noun unless they are always hyphenated.

the per capita cost   an a priori argument
a cordon bleu restaurant   a ci-devant professor

31. Chemical names used as modifiers before a noun are not hyphenated.

a sodium hypochlorite bleach
a citric acid solution

32. Following the Noun (as a complement or predicate adjective)   When the words that make up a compound adjective follow the noun they modify, they tend to fall in normal word order and are no longer unit modifiers. They are therefore no longer hyphenated.

Controls have become more specialized.
The company is still growing.
a device for both input and output
a statement of profit and loss
arrested on charges that had been trumped up
decisions made on the spur of the moment
They were ill prepared for the journey.

33. Many permanent and temporary compounds keep their hyphens after the noun in a sentence if they continue to function as unit modifiers. Compounds consisting of adjective or noun + participle, adjective or noun + noun + -ed (which looks like a participle), or noun + adjective are most likely to remain hyphenated.

Your ideas are high-minded but impractical.
streets that are tree-lined
You were just as nice-looking then.
metals that are corrosion-resistant
tends to be accident-prone

34. Permanent compound adjectives that are entered in dictionaries are usually styled in the way that they appear in the dictionary whether they precede or follow the noun they modify.

The group was public-spirited.
The problems are mind-boggling.
is well-read in economics

35. Compound adjectives of three or more words are normally not hyphenated when they follow the noun they modify.

These remarks are off the record.

36. Permanent compounds of three or more words may be entered as hyphenated adjectives in dictionaries. In such cases the hyphens are retained as long as the phrase is being used as a unit modifier.

the plan is still pay-as-you-go
   but a plan in which you pay as you go

37. It is possible that a permanent hyphenated adjective from the dictionary may appear alongside a temporary compound in a position where it would normally be open (as "one who is both ill-humored and ill prepared"). Editors usually try to resolve these inconsistencies, either by hyphenating both compounds or leaving both compounds open.

38. When an adverb modifies another adverb that is the first element of a compound modifier, the compound may lose its hyphen. If the first adverb modifies the whole compound, however, the hyphen should be retained.

> a very well developed idea
> a delightfully well-written book
> a most ill-humored remark

39. Adjective compounds that are names of colors may be styled open or hyphenated. Color names in which each element can function as a noun (as *blue green* or *chrome yellow*) are almost always hyphenated when they precede a noun; they are sometimes open when they follow the noun. Color names in which the first element can only be an adjective are less consistently treated; they are often not hyphenated before a noun and are usually not hyphenated after.

> blue-gray paint
> paint that is blue-gray   *also*   paint that is blue gray
> bluish gray paint   *or*   bluish-gray paint
> paint that is bluish gray

40. Compound modifiers that include a number followed by a noun are hyphenated when they precede the noun they modify. When the modifier follows the noun, it is usually not hyphenated. For more on the styling of numbers, see Chapter 5, "The Treatment of Numbers."

> five-card stud   ten-foot pole   twelve-year-old girl
> an 18-inch rule *but* a 10 percent raise
> an essay that is one page
> a child who is ten years old

41. An adjective that is composed of a number followed by a noun in the possessive is not hyphenated.

> a two weeks' wait   a four blocks' walk

Compounds That Function as Adverbs

42. Adverb compounds consisting of preposition + noun are almost always written solid; however, there are a few well-known exceptions.

> downtown   downwind   onstage   overseas
> upstairs   upfield   offhand   underhand
>   *but*
> in-house   off-line   on-line

43. Compound adverbs of more than two words are usually styled open, and they usually follow the words they modify.

every which way	high and dry	off and on
little by little	hook, line, and sinker	over and over

44. A few three-word adverbs are homographs of hyphenated adjectives and are therefore styled with hyphens. But many adverbs are styled open even if an adjective formed from the same phrase is hyphenated.

back-to-back (adverb or adjective)
face-to-face (adverb or adjective)
> *but*

hand-to-hand combat	fought hand to hand
off-the-cuff remarks	spoke off the cuff

Compound Verbs

45. Two-word verbs consisting of a verb followed by an adverb or a preposition are styled open.

get together	run around	run across
set to	run wild	put down
break through	strike out	print out

46. A compound composed of a particle followed by a verb is styled solid.

upgrade	outflank	overcome	bypass

47. A verb derived from an open or hyphenated compound noun—permanent, temporary, or self-evident—is hyphenated.

blue-pencil	double-check	poor-mouth
sweet-talk	tap-dance	water-ski

48. A verb derived from a solid noun is styled solid.

bankroll	roughhouse	mainstream

Compounds Formed with Word Elements

Many new and temporary compounds are formed by adding word elements to existing words or by combining word elements. There are three basic word elements: prefixes (as *anti-*, *re-*, *non-*, *super-*), suffixes (as *-er*, *-ly*, *-ness*, *-ism*), and what the dictionaries call combining forms (as *mini-*, *macro-*, *pseud-*, *ortho-*, *-ped*, *-graphy*, *-gamic*, *-plasty*). Prefixes and suffixes are usually attached to existing words; combining forms are usually combined to form new words.

49. prefix + word Except as specified below, compounds formed from a prefix and a word are usually styled solid.

precondition	refurnish	suborder	postwar
interagency	misshapen	overfond	unhelpful

50. If the prefix ends with a vowel and the word it is attached to begins with the same vowel, the compound is usually hyphenated.

    anti-inflation   co-owner   de-emphasize   multi-institutional

NOTE: Many exceptions to this styling (as *cooperate* and *reentry*) can be found by checking a dictionary.

51. If the base word to which a prefix is added is capitalized, the compound is hyphenated.

    anti-American   post-Victorian   pro-Soviet   inter-Caribbean

NOTE: The prefix is usually not capitalized in such compounds. But if the prefix and the base word together form a new proper name, the compound may be solid with the prefix capitalized (as *Postimpressionist, Precambrian*). Such exceptions can be found in a dictionary.

52. Compounds made with *self-* and *ex-* meaning "former" are hyphenated.

    self-pity   ex-wife

53. If a prefix is added to a hyphenated compound, it may be either followed by a hyphen or closed up solid to the next element. Permanent compounds of this kind should be checked in a dictionary.

    unair-conditioned   non-self-governing
    ultra-up-to-date   unself-conscious

54. If a prefix is added to an open compound, the prefix is followed by a hyphen in typewritten material. In typeset material, this hyphen is often represented by an en dash. (For more on this use of the en dash, see paragraph 16 in the section on Dash, beginning on page 23, in Chapter 1, "Punctuation.")

    ex–Boy Scout   post–coup d'état

55. A compound that would be identical with another word if styled solid is usually hyphenated to prevent misreading.

    a multi-ply fabric   re-collect the money   un-ionized particles

56. Some writers and editors like to hyphenate a compound that might otherwise be solid if they think the reader might be momentarily puzzled (as by consecutive vowels, doubled consonants, or simply an odd combination of letters.)

    coed *or* co-ed   overreact *or* over-react
    coworker *or* co-worker   interrow *or* inter-row

57. Temporary compounds formed from *vice-* are usually hyphenated; however, some permanent compounds (as *vice president* and *vice admiral*) are open.

58. When prefixes are attached to numerals, the compounds are hyphenated.

    pre-1982 expenses   post-1975 vintages   non-20th-century ideas

59. Compounds formed from combining forms like *Anglo-*, *Judeo-*, or *Sino-* are hyphenated when the second element is an independent word and solid when it is a combining form.

    Judeo-Christian   Austro-Hungarian   Sino-Soviet
    Italophile   Francophone   Anglophobe

60. Prefixes that are repeated in the same compound are separated by a hyphen.

    sub-subheading

61. Some prefixes and initial combining forms have related independent adjectives or adverbs that may be used where the prefix might be expected. A temporary compound with *quasi(-)* or *pseudo(-)* therefore may be written open as modifier + noun or hyphenated as combining form + noun. A writer or editor must thus decide which style to follow.

    quasi intellectual *or* quasi-intellectual
    pseudo liberal *or* pseudo-liberal

NOTE: in some cases (as *super, super-*), the independent modifier may not mean quite the same as the prefix.

62. Compounds consisting of different prefixes with the same base word and joined by *and* or *or* are sometimes shortened by pruning the first compound back to the prefix. The missing base word is indicated by a hyphen on the prefix.

    pre- and postoperative care
    anti- or pro-Revolutionary sympathies

63. word + suffix Except as noted below, compounds formed by adding a suffix to a word are styled solid.

    Darwinist   fortyish   landscaper   powerlessness

64. Permanent or temporary compounds formed with a suffix are hyphenated if the addition of the suffix would create a sequence of three like letters.

    bell-like   will-less   a coffee-er coffee

65. Temporary compounds made with a suffix are often hyphenated if the base word is more than three syllables long, if the base word ends with the same letter the suffix begins with, or if the suffix creates a confusing sequence of letters.

tunnel-like	Mexican-ness	jaw-wards
umbrella-like	industry-wide	battle-worthy

66. Compounds made from a number + *odd* are hyphenated whether the number is spelled out or in numerals; a number + *-fold* is solid if the number is spelled out but hyphenated if it is in numerals.

20-odd	twenty-odd
12-fold	twelvefold

67. Most compounds formed from an open or hyphenated compound + a suffix do not separate the suffix by a hyphen. But such suffixes as *-like, -wide, -worthy,* and *-proof,* all of which are homographs of independent adjectives, are attached by a hyphen.

good-humoredness   dollar-a-yearism   do-it-yourselfer
a United Nations-like agency

NOTE: Open compounds often become hyphenated when a suffix is added unless they are proper nouns.

middle age *but* middle-ager   New Englandism
tough guy *but* tough-guyese   Wall Streeter

68. combining form + combining form   Many new terms in technical fields are created by adding combining form to combining form or combining form to a word or a word part. Such compounds are generally intended to be permanent, even though many never get into the dictionary. They are regularly styled solid.

Miscellaneous Styling Conventions

69. Compounds that would otherwise be styled solid according to the principles described above are written open or hyphenated to avoid ambiguity, to make sure of rapid comprehension, or to make the pronunciation more obvious.

meat-ax *or* meat ax	bi-level	tri-city
re-utter	umbrella-like	un-iced

70. When typographical features such as capitals or italics make word relationships in a sentence clear, it is not necessary to hyphenate an open compound (as when it precedes a noun it modifies).

a *Chicago Tribune* story   an "eyes only" memo
I've been Super Bowled to death.
a *noblesse oblige* attitude

71. Publications (as technical journals) aimed at a specialized readership likely to recognize the elements of a compound and their relationship tend to use open and solid stylings more frequently than more general publications would.

electrooculogram   radiofrequency   rapid eye movement

72. Words that are formed by reduplication and so consist of two similar-sounding elements (as *hush-hush, razzle-dazzle,* or *hugger-mugger*) present styling questions like those of compounds. Words like these are hyphenated if each of the elements is made up of more than one syllable. If each element has only one syllable, the words are variously styled solid or hyphenated. The solid styling is slightly more common overall; however, for very short words (as *no-no, go-go,* and *so-so*), for words in which both elements may have primary stress (as *tip-top* and *sci-fi*), and for words coined in the twentieth century (as *ack-ack* and *hush-hush*), the hyphenated styling is more common.

goody-goody	palsy-walsy	teeter-totter	topsy-turvy
agar-agar	ack-ack	boo-boo	tip-top
crisscross	peewee	knickknack	singsong

Chapter 4

Abbreviations

CONTENTS

Abbreviations are used for a variety of reasons. They serve to save space, to avoid repetition of long words and phrases that may distract the reader, and to reduce keystrokes for typists and thereby increase their output. In addition, abbreviations are used simply to conform to conventional usage.

The frequency of abbreviations in typewritten or printed material is directly related to the nature of the material itself. For example, technical literature (as in the military and in the fields of aerospace, engineering, data processing, and medicine) features many abbreviations, but formal literary writing has relatively few. By the same token, the number of abbreviations in a piece of business writing depends on the nature of the business, as do the particular abbreviations employed. A person working in a university English department will often see *ibid.*, *ll.*, and *TESOL*, while the employee of an electronics firm will instead see *CAD*, *CPU*, and *mm* from day to day.

Unfortunately, the contemporary styling of abbreviations is to a large extent inconsistent and arbitrary. No set of rules can hope to cover all the possible variations, exceptions, and peculiarities actually encountered in print. The styling of abbreviations—whether capitalized or lowercased, closed up or spaced, punctuated or unpunctuated—depends most often on the writer's preference or the organization's policy. For example, some companies style the abbreviation for *cash on delivery* as *COD*, while others prefer *C.O.D.*, and still others, *c.o.d.*

All is not confusion, however, and general patterns can be discerned. Some abbreviations (as *a.k.a.*, *e.g.*, *etc.*, *i.e.*, *No.*, and *viz.*) are governed by a strong tradition of punctuation, while others (as *NATO*, *NASA*, *NOW*, *OPEC*, and *SALT*) that are pronounced as words tend to be all-capitalized and unpunctuated. Styling problems can be dealt with by consulting a good general dictionary such as *Webster's Ninth New Collegiate Dictionary*, especially for capitalization guidance, and by following the guidelines of one's own organization or the dictates of one's own preference. An abbreviations dictionary such as *Webster's Guide to Abbreviations* may also be consulted. For more specialized abbreviations dictionaries, see the section on Reference Books in the Bibliography at the back of this book.

Punctuation

The paragraphs that follow describe a few broad principles that apply to abbreviations in general; however, there are many specific situations in which these principles will not apply. For instance, U.S. Postal Service abbreviations for names of states are always unpunctuated, as are the abbreviations used within most branches of the armed forces for the names of ranks. The section on Specific Styling Conventions in this chapter contains more information on particular kinds of abbreviations.

1. A period follows most abbreviations that are formed by omitting all but the first few letters of a word.

   bull. for *bulletin*   fig. for *figure*
   bro. for *brother*   Fr. for *French*

2. A period follows most abbreviations that are formed by omitting letters from the middle of a word.

   secy. for *secretary*   agcy. for *agency*
   mfg. for *manufacturing*   Mr. for *Mister*

3. Punctuation is usually omitted from abbreviations that are made up of initial letters of words that constitute a phrase or compound word. However, for some of these abbreviations, especially ones that are not capitalized, the punctuation is retained.

   GNP for *gross national product*   PC for *personal computer*
   EFT for *electronic funds transfer*   f.o.b. for *free on board*

4. Terms in which a suffix is added to a numeral, such as *1st, 2nd, 3d, 8vo,* and *12mo,* are not abbreviations and do not require a period.

5. Isolated letters of the alphabet used to designate a shape or position in a sequence are not punctuated.

   T square   A 1   I beam   V sign

6. Some abbreviations are punctuated with one or more virgules in place of periods.

   c/o for *care of*   w/o for *without*
   d/b/a for *doing business as*   w/w for *wall to wall*

Capitalization

1. Abbreviations are capitalized if the words they represent are proper nouns or adjectives.

     F for *Fahrenheit*   Nov. for *November*
     NFL for *National Football League*   Brit. for *British*

2. Abbreviations are usually capitalized when formed from the initial letters of the words or word elements that make up what is being abbreviated. There are, however, some very common abbreviations formed in this way that are not capitalized.

     TM for *trademark*   EEG for *electroencephalogram*
     ETA for *estimated time of arrival*   FY for *fiscal year*
     CATV for *community antenna television*
     a.k.a. for *also known as*   d/b/a for *doing business as*

3. Most abbreviations that are pronounced as words, rather than as a series of letters, are capitalized. If they have been assimilated into the language as words in their own right, however, they are most often lowercased.

     OPEC   NATO   MIRV   NOW account
     quasar   laser   sonar   scuba

Plurals, Possessives, and Compounds

1. Punctuated abbreviations of single words are pluralized by adding *-s* before the period.

     bldgs.   bros.   figs.   mts.

2. Punctuated abbreviations that stand for phrases or compounds are pluralized by adding *-'s* after the last period.

     Ph.D.'s   f.o.b.'s   J.P.'s   M.B.A.'s

3. Unpunctuated abbreviations that stand for phrases or compound words are usually pluralized by adding *-s* to the end of the abbreviation.

     COLAs   CPUs   PCs   DOSs

NOTE: Some writers pluralize such abbreviations by adding *-'s* to the abbreviation; however, this styling is far less common than the one described above.

4. The plural form of most lowercase single-letter abbreviations is made by repeating the letter. For the plural form of single-letter abbreviations that are abbreviations for units of measure, see paragraph 5 below.

cc. for *copies*   ff. for *and the following ones*
ll. for *lines*   nn. for *notes*
pp. for *pages*   vv. for *verses*

5. The plural form of abbreviations of units of measure is the same as the singular form.

30 sec.   24 ml   20 min.   200 bbl.
30 d.   24 h.   50 m   10 mi.

6. Possessives of abbreviations are formed in the same way as those of spelled-out nouns: the singular possessive is formed by the addition of -*'s*, the plural possessive simply by the addition of an apostrophe.

the CPU's memory   most CPUs' memories
Brody Corp.'s earnings   Bay Bros.' annual sale

7. Compounds that consist of an abbreviation added to another word are formed in the same way as compounds that consist of spelled-out nouns.

a Kalamazoo, Mich.-based company
an AMA-approved medical school

8. Compounds formed by adding a prefix or suffix to an abbreviation are usually styled with a hyphen.

an IBM-like organization
non-DNA molecules
pre-HEW years

Specific Styling Conventions

The following paragraphs describe styling practices commonly followed for specific kinds of situations involving abbreviations. The paragraphs are arranged under the following alphabetical headings.

A and An	Degrees	Military Ranks and
A.D. and B.C.	Division of Abbreviations	Units
Agencies, Associations,	Footnotes	Number
and Organizations	Full Forms	Personal Names
Beginning a Sentence	Geographical and Topo-	Saint
Books of the Bible	graphical Names	Scientific Terms
Company Names	Latin Words and	Time
Compass Points	Phrases	Titles
Contractions	Latitude and Longitude	Units of Measure
Dates	Laws and Bylaws	Versus

A and An

1. The choice of the article *a* or *an* before abbreviations depends on the *sound* with which the abbreviation begins. If an abbreviation begins with a consonant sound, *a* is normally used. If an abbreviation begins with a vowel sound, *an* is used.

a B.A. degree	a YMCA club	a UN agency
an FCC report	an SAT score	an IRS agent

A.D. and B.C.

2. The abbreviations A.D. and B.C. are usually styled in typeset matter as punctuated, unspaced small capitals; in typed material they usually appear as punctuated, unspaced capitals.

in printed material	41 B.C.	A.D. 185
in typed material	41 B.C.	A.D. 185

3. The abbreviation A.D. usually precedes the date; the abbreviation B.C. usually follows the date. However, many writers and editors place A.D. after the date, thus making their placement of A.D. consistent with their placement of B.C. In references to whole centuries, the usual practice is to place A.D. after the century. The only alternative is not to use the abbreviation at all in such references.

A.D. 185   *but also*   185 A.D.
the fourth century A.D.

Agencies, Associations, and Organizations

4. The names of agencies, associations, and organizations are usually abbreviated after they have been spelled out on their first occurrence in a text. The abbreviations are usually all capitalized and unpunctuated.

EPA	SEC	NAACP	NCAA	USO	NOW

NOTE: In contexts where the abbreviation is expected to be instantly recognizable, it will generally be used without having its full form spelled out on its first occurrence.

Beginning a Sentence

5. Most writers and editors avoid beginning a sentence with an abbreviation that is ordinarily not capitalized. Abbreviations that are ordinarily capitalized, on the other hand, are commonly used to begin sentences.

Page 22 contains . . .   *not*   P. 22 contains . . .
Doctor Smith believes . . .   *or*   Dr. Smith believes . . .
OSHA regulations require . . .
PCB concentrations that were measured at . . .

Books of the Bible

6. Books of the Bible are generally spelled out in running text but abbreviated in references to chapter and verse.

The minister based his sermon on Genesis.
In the beginning God created the heavens and the earth. —Gen. 1:1

Capitalization—See the section on Capitalization in this chapter.

Chemical Elements and Compounds—See **Scientific Terms** below.

Company Names

7. The styling of company names varies widely. Many published style manuals say that the name of a company should not be abbreviated unless the abbreviation is part of its official name; however, many publications routinely abbreviate words such as *Corporation, Company,* and *Incorporated* when they appear in company names. Words such as *Airlines, Associates, Fabricators, Manufacturing,* and *Railroad,* however, are spelled out.

> Ginn and Company   *or*   Ginn and Co.
> The Bailey Banks and Biddle Company   *or*   The Bailey Banks and Biddle Co.
> Gulf & Western Industries, Inc.
> Canon, U.S.A., Inc.

NOTE: An ampersand frequently replaces the word *and* in official company names. For more on this use of the ampersand, see paragraph 1 in the section on Ampersand, beginning on page 3, in Chapter 1, "Punctuation."

8. If a company is easily recognizable from its initials, its name is usually spelled out for the first mention and abbreviated in all subsequent references. Some companies have made their initials part of their official name, and in those cases the initials appear in all references.

> *first reference*   General Motors Corp. released figures today . . .
> *subsequent reference* A GM spokesperson said . . .
> MCM Electronics, an Ohio-based electronics company . . .

Compass Points

9. Compass points are abbreviated when occurring after street names, though styling varies regarding whether these abbreviations are punctuated and whether they are preceded by a comma. When compass points form essential internal elements of street names, they are usually spelled out in full.

> 2122 Fourteenth Street, NW *or* 2122 Fourteenth Street NW
>   *or* 2122 Fourteenth Street, N.W.
> 192 East 49th Street
> 1282 North Avenue

Compounds—See section on Plurals, Possessives, and Compounds above.

Computer Terms—See **Scientific Terms** below.

Contractions

10. Some abbreviations resemble contractions by including an apostrophe in place of omitted letters. These abbreviations are not punctuated with a period.

>   sec'y for *secretary*   ass'n for *association*   dep't for *department*

NOTE: This style of abbreviation is usually avoided in formal writing.

Courtesy Titles—See **Titles** below.

Dates

11. The names of days and months are usually not abbreviated in running text, although some publications do abbreviate names of months when they appear in dates that refer to a specific day or days. The names of months are not abbreviated in date lines of business letters, but they may be abbreviated in government or military correspondence.

>   the December issue of *Scientific American*
>   going to camp in August
>   a report due on Tuesday
>   a meeting held on August 1, 1985   *or*   a meeting held on Aug. 1, 1985
>   *general business date line*   November 1, 1985
>   *military date line*   1 Nov 1985

NOTE: When dates are used in tables or in notes, the names of days and months are commonly abbreviated.

Degrees

12. Except for a few academic degrees with highly recognizable abbreviations (as *A.B., M.S.,* and *Ph.D.*), the names of degrees and professional ratings are spelled out in full when first mentioned in running text. Often the name of the degree is followed by its abbreviation enclosed in parentheses, so that the abbreviation may be used alone later in running text. When a degree or professional rating follows a person's name it is usually abbreviated.

>   Special attention is devoted to the master of arts in teaching (M.A.T.) degree.
>   Julia Ramirez, P.E.

13. Like other abbreviations, abbreviations of degrees and professional ratings are often unpunctuated. In general, punctuated abbreviations are more common for academic degrees, and unpunctuated abbreviations are slightly more common for professional ratings, especially if the latter comprise three or more capitalized letters.

R.Ph.	P.E.	CLA	CMET
Ph.D.	B.Sc.	M.B.A.	BGS

14. The initial letter of each element in abbreviations of all degrees and professional ratings is capitalized. Letters other than the initial letter are usually not capitalized.

D.Ch.E.	Litt.D.	M.F.A.	D.Th.

Division of Abbreviations

15. Division of abbreviations at the end of lines or between pages is usually avoided.

received an M.B.A. degree	*not*	received an M.B.-A. degree

Expansions—See **Full Forms** below.

Footnotes

16. Footnotes sometimes incorporate abbreviations.

ibid.	op. cit.	loc. cit.

NOTE: In current practice these abbreviations are usually not italicized.

Full Forms

17. When using an abbreviation that may be unfamiliar or confusing to the reader, many publications give the full form first, followed by the abbreviation in parentheses; in subsequent references just the abbreviation is used.

first reference   At the American Bar Association (ABA) meeting in June . . .

subsequent reference At that particular ABA meeting . . .

Geographical and Topographical Names

18. U.S. Postal Service abbreviations for states, possessions, and Canadian provinces are all-capitalized and unpunctuated, as are Postal Service abbreviations for streets and other geographical features when these abbreviations are used on envelopes addressed for automated mass handling.

addressed for automated handling   1234 SMITH BLVD
SMITHVILLE, MN 56789

regular address styling   1234 Smith Blvd.
Smithville, MN 56789

19. Abbreviations of states are often used in running text to identify the location of a city or county. In this context they are set off with commas, and punctuated, upper- and lowercase state abbreviations are usually used. In other situations within running text, the names of states are usually not abbreviated.

> John Smith of 15 Chestnut St., Sarasota, Fla., has won . . .
> the Louisville, Ky., public library system
> Boston, the largest city in Massachusetts, . . .

20. Terms such as *street* and *parkway* are variously abbreviated or un-abbreviated in running text. When they are abbreviated, they are usually punctuated.

> our office at 1234 Smith Blvd. (*or* Boulevard)
> an accident on Windward Road (*or* Rd.)

21. Names of countries are typically abbreviated in tabular data, but they are usually spelled in full in running text. The most common exceptions to this pattern are the abbreviations *U.S.S.R.* and *U.S.* (see paragraph 23 below).

> *in a table*   Gt. Brit. *or* U.K. *or* UK
> *in text*   Great Britain and the U.S.S.R. announced the agreement.

22. Abbreviations for the names of most countries are punctuated. Abbreviations for countries whose names include more than one word are often not punctuated if the abbreviations are formed from only the initial letters of the individual words.

Mex.	Can.	Scot.
Ger.	Gt. Brit.	U.S. *or* US
U.S.S.R. *or* USSR	U.K. *or* UK	U.A.E. *or* UAE

23. *United States* is often abbreviated when it is being used as an adjective, such as when it modifies the name of a federal agency, policy, or program. When *United States* is used as a noun in running text, it is usually spelled out, or it is spelled on its initial use and then abbreviated in subsequent references.

> U.S. Department of Justice
> U.S. foreign policy
> The United States has offered to . . .

24. *Saint* is usually abbreviated when it is part of the name of a geographical or topographical feature. *Mount, Point,* and *Fort* are variously spelled out or abbreviated according to individual preference. *Saint, Mount* and *Point* are routinely abbreviated when space is at a premium. (For more on the abbreviation of *Saint,* see paragraph 36 below.)

St. Louis, Missouri	St. Kitts	Mount McKinley
Mount St. Helens	Fort Sumter	Point Pelee

Latin Words and Phrases—See also **Footnotes** above.

25. Words and phrases derived from Latin are commonly abbreviated in contexts where readers can reasonably be expected to recognize them. They are punctuated, not capitalized, and usually not italicized.

> etc.   i.e.   e.g.   viz.   et al.   pro tem.

Latitude and Longitude

26. Latitude and longitude are abbreviated in tabular data but written out in running text.

in a table lat. 10°20′N *or* lat. 10-20N
in text   from 10°20′ north latitude to 10°30′ south latitude

Laws and Bylaws

27. Laws and bylaws, when first mentioned, are spelled in full; however, subsequent references to them in a text may be abbreviated.

first reference   Article I, Section 1
subsequent reference Art. I, Sec. 1

Military Ranks and Units

28. Military ranks are usually given in full when used with a surname only but are abbreviated when used with a full name.

Colonel Howe   Col. John P. Howe

29. In nonmilitary publications, abbreviations for military ranks are punctuated and set in capital and lowercase letters. Within the military (with the exception of the Marine Corps) these abbreviations are all-capitalized and unpunctuated. The Marine Corps follows the punctuated, capital and lowercase styling.

in the military BG John T. Dow, USA
       LCDR Mary I. Lee, USN
       Col. S. J. Smith, USMC
outside the military Brig. Gen. John T. Dow, USA
       Lt. Comdr. Mary I. Lee, USN
       Col. S. J. Smith, USMC

30. Abbreviations for military units are capitalized and unpunctuated.

USA   USAF   SAC   NORAD

Number

31. The word *number,* when used with figures such as *1* or *2* to indicate a rank or rating, is usually abbreviated. When it is, the *N* is capitalized, and the abbreviation is punctuated.

The No. 1 priority is to promote profitability.

32. The word *number* is usually abbreviated when it is part of a set unit (as a contract number), when it is used in tabular data, or when it is used in bibliographic references.

Contract No. N-1234-76-57   Publ. Nos. 12 and 13
Policy No. 123-5-X   Index No. 7855

Period with Abbreviations—See section on Punctuation above.

Personal Names

33. Personal names are not usually abbreviated.

> George S. Patterson   *not*   Geo. S. Patterson

34. Unspaced initials of famous persons are sometimes used in place of their full names. The initials may or may not be punctuated.

> FDR   *or*   F.D.R.

35. Initials used with a surname are spaced and punctuated.

> F. D. Roosevelt

Plurals—See section on Plurals, Possessives, and Compounds above.

Possessives—See section on Plurals, Possessives, and Compounds above.

Saint

36. The word *Saint* is often abbreviated when used before the name of a saint or when it is the first element of the name of a city or institution named after a saint. However, when it forms part of a surname, it may or may not be abbreviated, and the styling should be the one used by the person or the institution.

> St. Peter   *or*   Saint Peter   St. Cloud, Minnesota
> St. John's University   Saint Joseph College
> Ruth St. Denis   Louis St. Laurent
> Augustus Saint-Gaudens

Scientific Terms—See also **Units of Measure** below.

37. In binomial nomenclature, a genus name may be abbreviated with its initial letter after the first reference to it is spelled out. The abbreviation is always punctuated.

> *first reference*   *Escherichia coli*
> *subsequent reference*   *E. coli*

38. Abbreviations for the names of chemical compounds or mechanical or electronic equipment or processes are usually not punctuated.

> OCR   PCB   CPU   PBX

39. The symbols for chemical elements are not punctuated.

> H   Cl   Pb   Na

Time—See also **A.D. and B.C.** and **Dates** above and **Units of Measure** below.

40. When time is expressed in figures, the abbreviations that follow are most often styled as punctuated lowercase letters; punctuated small capital letters are also common. For more on the use of *a.m.* and *p.m.*, see paragraph 44 in the section on Specific Styling Conventions, beginning on page 119, in Chapter 5, "The Treatment of Numbers."

> 8:30 a.m.   10:00 p.m.   8:30 A.M.   10:00 P.M.

41. In transportation schedules *a.m.* and *p.m.* are generally styled in capitalized, unpunctuated, unspaced letters.

    8:30 AM   10:00 PM

42. Time zone designations are usually styled in capitalized, unpunctuated, unspaced letters.

    EST   PST   CDT

Titles—See also **Degrees** and **Military Ranks and Units** above.

43. The only courtesy titles that are invariably abbreviated in written references are *Mr., Ms., Mrs.,* and *Messrs.* Other titles, such as *Doctor, Representative,* or *Senator,* may be either written out or abbreviated.

    Ms. Lee A. Downs
    Messrs. Lake, Mason, and Nambeth
    Doctor Howe   *or*   Dr. Howe
    Senator Long   *or*   Sen. Long

44. Despite some traditional injunctions against the practice, the titles *Honorable* and *Reverend* are often abbreviated when used with *the.*

    the Honorable Samuel I. O'Leary   *or*   the Hon. Samuel I. O'Leary
    the Reverend Samuel I. O'Leary   *or*   the Rev. Samuel I. O'Leary

NOTE: There is also a traditional injunction against using the titles *Honorable* and *Reverend* without *the* preceding them. However, in current practice, *Reverend* and *Rev.* are commonly used without *the.*

    the Reverend Samuel I. O'Leary   *or*   Rev. Samuel I. O'Leary

45. The designations *Jr.* and *Sr.* may be used in conjunction with courtesy titles, with abbreviations for academic degrees, and with professional rating abbreviations. They may or may not be preceded by a comma according to the writer's preference. They are terminated with a period, and they are commonly only used with a full name.

    Mr. John K. Walker, Jr.
    Dr. John K. Walker, Jr.
    General John K. Walker Jr.
    The Honorable John K. Walker, Jr.
    John K. Walker Jr., M.D.

46. When an abbreviation for an academic degree, professional certification, or association membership follows a name, it is usually preceded by a comma. No courtesy title should precede the name.

    Dr. John Smith   *or*   John Smith, M.D.   *but not*   Dr. John Smith, M.D.
    Katherine Derwinski, CLU
    Carol Manning, M.D., FACPS

47. The abbreviation *Esq.* for *Esquire* is used in the United States after the surname of professional persons such as attorneys, architects, consuls, clerks of the court, and justices of the peace. It is not used, however, if *the Honorable* precedes the first name. If a courtesy title such as *Dr.,* *Hon., Miss, Mr., Mrs.,* or *Ms.* is used in correspondence, *Esq.* is omitted. *Esquire* or *Esq.* is frequently used in the United States after the surname of a woman lawyer, although the practice has not yet gained acceptance in all law offices or among all state bar associations.

> Carolyn B. West, Esq.

Units of Measure

48. Measures and weights may be abbreviated in figure plus unit combinations; however, if the numeral is written out, the unit should also be written out.

> 15 cu ft   *or*   15 cu. ft.   *but*   fifteen cubic feet
> How many cubic feet does the refrigerator hold?

49. Abbreviations for metric units are usually not punctuated. In many scientific and technical publications, abbreviations for traditional non-metric units are also unpunctuated. However, in most nonscientific publications, abbreviations for traditional units are punctuated.

> 14 ml   12 km   22 mi.   8 ft.   4 sec.   20 min.

Versus

50. *Versus* is abbreviated as the lowercase roman letter *v.* in legal contexts; it is either spelled out or abbreviated as lowercase roman letters *vs.* in general contexts.

> *in a legal context*   *Smith* v. *Vermont*
> *in a general context*   honesty versus dishonesty
> > *or*
> > honesty vs. dishonesty

Chapter 5

The Treatment of Numbers

CONTENTS

The styling of numbers presents special difficulties to writers and editors because there are so many conventions to follow, some of which may conflict when applied to particular passages. The writer's major decision is whether to write out numbers in running text or to express them in figures. Usage varies considerably, in part because no single neat formula covers all the categories in which numbers are used. In general, the more formal the writing the more likely that numbers will be spelled out. In scientific, technical, or statistical contexts, however, numbers are likely to be expressed as figures. This chapter explains most of the conventions used in the styling of numbers. A discussion of general principles is followed by detailed information on specific situations involving numbers.

Numbers as Words or Figures

At one extreme of styling, all numbers, sometimes even including dates, are written out. This usage is uncommon and is usually limited to proclamations, legal documents, and some other types of very formal writing. This styling is space-consuming and time-consuming; it can also be ungainly or, worse, unclear. At the other extreme, some types of technical writing, such as statistical reports, contain no written-out numbers except at the beginning of a sentence.

In general, figures are easier to read than the spelled-out forms of numbers; however, the spelled-out forms are helpful in certain circumstances, such as in distinguishing different categories of numbers or in providing relief from an overwhelming cluster of numerals. Most writers follow one or the other of two common conventions combining numerals and written-out numbers. The conventions are described in this section, along with the situations that provide exceptions to the general rules.

Basic Conventions

1. The first system requires that a writer use figures for exact numbers that are greater than nine and words for numbers nine and below (a variation of this system sets the number ten as the dividing point). In this system, numbers that consist of a whole number between one and nine followed by *hundred, thousand, million,* etc. may be spelled out or expressed in figures.

> She has performed in 22 plays on Broadway, seven of which won Pulitzer prizes.
>
> The new edition will consist of 25 volumes which will be issued at a rate of approximately four volumes per year.
>
> The cat show attracted an unexpected two thousand entries.
>
> They sold more than 2,000 units in the first year.

2. The second system requires that a writer use figures for all exact numbers 100 and above (or 101 and above) and words for numbers from one to ninety-nine (or one to one hundred) and for numbers that consist of a whole number between one and ninety-nine followed by *hundred, thousand, million,* etc.

> The artist spent nearly twelve years completing these four volumes, which comprise 435 hand-colored engravings.
>
> The 145 participants in the seminar toured the area's eighteen period houses.
>
> In the course of four hours, the popular author signed twenty-five hundred copies of her new book.

Sentence Beginnings

3. Numbers that begin a sentence are written out, although some make an exception for the use of figures for dates that begin a sentence. Most writers, however, try to avoid spelled-out numbers that are lengthy and awkward by restructuring the sentence so that the number appears elsewhere than at the beginning and may then be styled as a figure.

> Sixty-two species of Delphinidae inhabit the world's oceans.
> *or*
> The Delphinidae consist of 62 ocean-dwelling species.
>
> Twelve fifteen was the year King John of England signed the Magna Carta.
> *or*
> 1215 was the year King John of England signed the Magna Carta.
> *or*
> In 1215 King John of England signed the Magna Carta.
>
> One hundred fifty-seven illustrations, including 86 color plates, are contained in the book.
> *or*
> The book contains 157 illustrations, including 86 color plates.

Adjacent Numbers and Numbers in Series

4. Generally, two separate sets of figures should not be written adjacent to one another in running text unless they form a series. So that the juxtaposition of unrelated figures will not confuse the reader, either the sentence is restructured or one of the figures is spelled out. Usually the figure with the written form that is shorter and more easily read is converted. When one of two adjacent numbers is an element of a compound modifier, the first of the two numbers is often expressed in words, the second in figures. But if the second number is the shorter, the styling is often reversed.

original	*change to*
16 ½-inch dowels	sixteen ½-inch dowels
25 11-inch platters	twenty-five 11-inch platters
20 100-point games	twenty 100-point games
78 20-point games	78 twenty-point games
By 1997, 300 more of the state's schools will have closed their doors.	By 1997, three hundred more of the state's schools will have closed their doors.

5. Numbers paired at the beginning of a sentence are usually styled alike. If the first word of the sentence is a spelled-out number, the second, related number is also spelled out. However, some writers and editors prefer that each number be styled independently, even if that results in an inconsistent pairing.

Sixty to seventy-five acres were destroyed.
Sixty to 75 acres were destroyed.

6. Numbers that form a pair or a series referring to comparable quantities within a sentence or a paragraph should be treated consistently. The style of the largest number usually determines the style of the other numbers. Thus, a series of numbers including some which would ordinarily be spelled out might all be styled as figures. Similarly, figures are used to express all the numbers in a series if one of those numbers is a mixed or simple fraction.

Graduating from the obedience class were 3 corgis, 20 Doberman pinschers, 19 German shepherds, 9 golden retrievers, 10 Labrador retrievers, and 1 Rottweiler.
The three jobs took 5, 12, and 4½ hours, respectively.

Round Numbers

7. Approximate or round numbers, particularly those that can be expressed in one or two words, are often written out in general writing; in technical and scientific writing they are more likely to be expressed as numerals.

seven hundred people
five thousand years
four hundred thousand volumes

seventeen thousand metric tons
four hundred million dollars
but in technical writing
50,000 people per year
20,000 species of fish

8. For easier reading, numbers of one million and above may be expressed as figures followed by the word *million, billion,* and so forth. The figure may include a decimal fraction, but the fraction is not usually carried past the first digit to the right of the decimal point, and it is never carried past the third digit. If a more exact number is required, the whole amount should be written in figures.

about 4.6 billion years old
1.2 million metric tons of grain
the last 600 million years
$7.25 million
$3,456,000,000
but 200,000 years   *not*   200 thousand years

NOTE: In the United Kingdom, the word *billion* refers to an amount that in the United States is called *trillion.* In the American system each of the denominations above 1,000 millions (the American billion) is one thousand times the one preceding (thus, one trillion equals 1,000 billions; one quadrillion equals 1,000 trillions). In the British system the first denomination above 1,000 millions (the British milliard) is one thousand times the preceding one, but each of the denominations above 1,000 milliards (the British billion) is one million times the preceding one (thus, one trillion equals 1,000,000 billions; one quadrillion equals 1,000,000 trillions).

Ordinal Numbers

1. Ordinal numbers generally follow the styling rules for cardinal numbers that are listed above in the section on Numbers as Words or Figures: if a figure would be required for the cardinal form of a number, it should also be used for the ordinal form; if conventions call for a written-out form, it should be used for both cardinal and ordinal numbers. In technical writing, however, as well as in footnotes and tables, all ordinal numbers are written as figure-plus-suffix combinations. In addition, certain ordinal numbers—those specifying percentiles and latitudinal lines are common ones—are conventionally set as figures in both general and technical writing.

the sixth Robert de Bruce   the 20th century
the ninth grade   the 98th Congress

the 9th and 14th chapters

his twenty-third try

the 12th percentile

the 40th parallel

2. The forms *second* and *third* may be written with figures as *2d* or *2nd, 3d* or *3rd, 22d* or *22nd, 93d* or *93rd, 102d* or *102nd.* A period does not follow the suffix.

Roman Numerals

Roman numerals, which may be written either in capital or lowercase letters, are conventional in the specific situations described below. Roman numerals are formed by adding the numerical values of letters as they are arranged in descending order going from left to right. If a letter with a smaller numerical value is placed to the left of a letter with a greater numerical value, the value of the smaller is subtracted from the value of the larger. A bar placed over a numeral ($\bar{V}$) multiplies its value by one thousand. A list of Roman numerals and their Arabic equivalents, is given in the table on page 114.

1. Roman numerals are traditionally used to differentiate rulers and popes that have identical names.

    Elizabeth II

    Henry VIII

    Innocent X

    Louis XIV

2. Roman numerals are used to differentiate related males who have the same name. The numerals are used only with a person's full name and, unlike the similar forms *Junior* and *Senior,* they are placed after the surname with no intervening comma. Ordinals are sometimes used instead of Roman numerals.

    James R. Watson II

    James R. Watson III

    James R. Watson IV

    James R. Watson 2nd *or* 2d

    James R. Watson 3rd *or* 3d

    James R. Watson 4th

    NOTE: Possessive patterns for these names are the following:

    singular   James R. Watson III's (*or* 3rd's *or* 3d's) house

    plural   the James R. Watson IIIs' (*or* 3rds' *or* 3ds') house

3. Roman numerals are used to differentiate certain vehicles and vessels, such as yachts, that have the same name. If the name is italicized, the numeral is italicized also. Names of American spacecraft formerly bore Roman numerals, but Arabic numerals are now used.

    Shamrock V

    The U.S. spacecraft *Rangers VII, VIII,* and *IX* took pictures of the moon.

    On July 20, 1969, *Apollo 11* landed on the moon.

Arabic and Roman Numerals

Name	Arabic Numeral	Roman Numeral
zero	0	
one	1	I
two	2	II
three	3	III
four	4	IV
five	5	V
six	6	VI
seven	7	VII
eight	8	VIII
nine	9	IX
ten	10	X
eleven	11	XI
twelve	12	XII
thirteen	13	XIII
fourteen	14	XIV
fifteen	15	XV
sixteen	16	XVI
seventeen	17	XVII
eighteen	18	XVIII
nineteen	19	XIX
twenty	20	XX
twenty-one	21	XXI
twenty-two	22	XXII
twenty-three	23	XXIII
twenty-four	24	XXIV
twenty-five	25	XXV
twenty-six	26	XXVI
twenty-nine	29	XXIX
thirty	30	XXX
thirty-one	31	XXXI
thirty-two	32	XXXII
forty	40	XL
fifty	50	L
sixty	60	LX
seventy	70	LXX
eighty	80	LXXX
ninety	90	XC
one hundred	100	C
one hundred one *or* one hundred and one	101	CI
one hundred two *or* one hundred and two	102	CII
two hundred	200	CC
three hundred	300	CCC
four hundred	400	CD
five hundred	500	D
six hundred	600	DC
seven hundred	700	DCC
eight hundred	800	DCCC
nine hundred	900	CM
one thousand	1,000	M
two thousand	2,000	MM
five thousand	5,000	$\bar{V}$
ten thousand	10,000	$\bar{X}$
one hundred thousand	100,000	$\bar{C}$
one million	1,000,000	$\bar{M}$

4. Lowercase Roman numerals are often used to number book pages that precede the regular Arabic sequence, as in a foreword, preface, or introduction.
5. Roman numerals are often used in enumerations to list major headings. An example of an outline with Roman-numeral headings is shown on page 125.
6. Roman numerals are sometimes used to specify a particular act and scene of a play or a particular volume in a collection. In this system, capitalized Roman numerals are used for the number of the act, and lowercase Roman numerals for the number of the scene. Arabic numerals are increasingly used for these purposes, however.

Roman style	*Arabic style*
Richard II, Act II, scene i	Act 2, scene 1
Hamlet, I.i.63	Act 1, scene 1, line 63 *or* 1.1.63
II, iii, 13-20	2, 3, 13-20

7. Roman numerals are found as part of a few established technical terms such as blood-clotting factors, quadrant numbers, and designations of cranial nerves. Also, chords in the study of music harmony are designated by capital and lowercase Roman numerals. For the most part, however, technical terms that include numbers express them in Arabic form. The technical manuals listed in the Bibliography at the end of this book provide more information about specialized styling problems involving Roman numerals.

> blood-clotting factor VII
> quadrant III
> the cranial nerves II, IV, and IX
> Population II stars
> type I error
>   *but*
> adenosine 3', 5'-monophosphate
> cesium 137
> PL/1 programming language

Punctuation, Spacing, and Inflection

This section explains general rules for the use of commas, hyphens, and spacing in compound and large numbers, as well as the plural forms of numbers. For the styling of specific categories of numbers, such as dates, money, and decimal fractions, see the section on Specific Styling Conventions in this chapter.

Commas and Spaces in Large Numbers

1. In general writing, with the exceptions explained in paragraph 3 below, figures of four digits may be styled with or without a comma; the

punctuated form is more common. In scientific writing, these numerals are usually styled with a comma (but see paragraph 4 below). If the numerals form part of a tabulation, commas are necessary so that four-digit numerals can align with numerals of five or more digits. (For information about the alignment of tabular material, see pages 224–226 of Chapter 9, "Illustrations and Tables.")

2,000 case histories   *or less commonly*   1253 people

2. Whole numbers of five digits or more (but not decimal fractions) use a comma or a space to separate three-digit groups, counting from the right. Commas are used in general writing; either spaces or commas are used in technical writing.

a fee of $12,500
15,000 units   *or*   15 000 units
a population of 1,500,000   *or*   1 500 000

3. Certain types of numbers do not conform to these conventions. Decimal fractions and serial and multidigit numbers in set combinations, such as the numbers of policies, contracts, checks, streets, rooms, suites, telephones, pages, military hours, and years, do not contain commas. Numerals used in binary notation are also written without commas or spaces.

check 34567	the year 1929
page 209	Policy No. 33442
Room 606	10011
1650 hours	111010

NOTE: Year numbers of five or more digits (as geological or archeological dates) do contain a comma.

The Wisconsin glaciation lasted from approximately 70,000 to 10,000 years B.P.

4. In technical and scientific writing, lengthy figures are usually avoided by the use of special units of measure and by the use of multipliers and powers of ten. When long figures are written, however, each group of three digits may be separated by a space counting from the decimal point to the left and the right. If the digits are separated by a comma instead of a space, neither commas nor spaces are placed to the right of the decimal point. Whichever system is used should be applied consistently to all numbers with four or more digits.

27 483 241	27,483,241
23.000 003	23.000003
27 483.241 755	27,483.241755

Hyphens

5. Hyphens are used with written-out numbers between 21 and 99.

forty-one   forty-first

four hundred twenty-two
the twenty-fifth day

6. A hyphen is used between the numerator and the denominator of a fraction that is written out when that fraction is used as a modifier. A written-out fraction consisting of two words only (as *two thirds*) is usually styled open, although the hyphenated form is common also. Multiword numerators and denominators are usually hyphenated. If either the numerator or the denominator is hyphenated, no hyphen is used between them. For more on fractions, see pages 125–126.

   a two-thirds majority of the staff
   three fifths of her paycheck
   seven and four fifths
   forty-five hundredths
   four five-hundredths

7. Numbers that form the first part of a compound modifier expressing measurement are followed by a hyphen. An exception to this practice is that numbers are not followed by a hyphen when the second part of the modifier is the word *percent*.

   a 5-foot board   an eight-pound baby
   a 28-mile trip   a 680-acre ranch
   a 10-pound weight   a 75 percent reduction

8. An adjective or adverb made from a numeral plus the suffix *-fold* contains a hyphen, while a similar term made from a written-out number is styled solid. (For more on the use of suffixes with numbers, see page 94 in Chapter 3, "Plurals, Possessives, and Compounds.")

   a fourfold increase
   increased 20-fold

9. Serial numbers, such as social security or engine numbers, often contain hyphens that make lengthy numerals more readable.

   020-42-1691

10. Numbers are usually not divided at the end of a line. If division is unavoidable, the break occurs only after a comma. End-of-line breaks do not occur at decimal points, and a name with a numerical suffix (as *Elizabeth II*) is not divided between the name and the numeral.

Inclusive Numbers

11. Inclusive numbers—those which express a range—are separated either by the word *to* or by an en dash, which serves as an arbitrary equivalent of the phrase "(up) to and including" when used between dates and other inclusive numbers. (The en dash is explained further in the section on Dash, beginning on page 23, in Chapter 1, "Punctuation.") En dashes are used in tables, parenthetical references, and

footnotes to save space. In running text, however, the word *to* is more often used.

pages 40 to 98   the years 1960–1965
pages 40–98   spanning the years 1915 to 1941
pp. 40–98   the decade 1920–1930
14–18 months   the fiscal year 1984–1985

NOTE: Inclusive numbers separated by an en dash are not used in combination with the words *from* or *between,* as in "from 1955–60" or "between 1970–90." Instead, phrases like these are written as "from 1955 to 1960" or "between 1970 and 1990."

12. Units of measurement expressed in words or abbreviations are usually used only after the second element of an inclusive number. Symbols, however, are repeated.

an increase in dosage from 200 to 500 mg
running 50 to 75 miles every week
ten to fifteen dollars
30 to 35 degrees Celsius
    but
$50 to $60 million
45° to 48° F
45°–48°
3′–5′ long

13. Numbers that are part of an inclusive set or range are usually styled alike: figures with figures, spelled-out words with other spelled-out words. Similarly, approximate numbers are usually not paired with exact numbers.

from 8 to 108 absences
five to twenty guests
300,000,000 to 305,000,000   *not*   300 million to 305,000,000

14. Inclusive page numbers and dates that use the en dash may be written in full (1981–1982) or elided (1981–82). Guidelines for the elision of inclusive numbers are explained beginning on page 258 in Chapter 10, "Indexes." Both stylings are widely used. However, inclusive dates that appear in titles and other headings are almost never elided. Dates that appear with era designations are also not elided.

467–68   *or*   467–468   1724–27   *or*   1724–1727
550–602   1463–1510
203–4   *or*   203–204   1800–1801
552–549 B.C.

Plurals

15. The plurals of written-out numbers are formed by the addition of *-s* or *-es*.

Back in the thirties these roads were unpaved.
Christmas shoppers bought the popular toy in twos and threes.

16. The plurals of figures are formed by adding *-s*. Some writers and publications prefer to add an apostrophe before the *-s*. For more on the plurals of figures, see the section on Plurals, beginning on page 74, in Chapter 3, "Plurals, Possessives, and Compounds," and the section on Apostrophe, beginning on page 4, in Chapter 1, "Punctuation."

This ghost town was booming back in the 1840s.
The first two artificial hearts to be implanted in human patients were Jarvik-7s.
but also
linen manufacture in France in the 1700's
1's and 7's that looked alike

Specific Styling Conventions

The following paragraphs describe styling practices commonly followed for specific types of situations involving numbers. The paragraphs are arranged under the following alphabetical headings:

Addresses
Dates
Degrees of Temperature
   and Arc
Enumerations and
   Outlines
Fractions and Decimal
   Fractions

Money
Percentages
Proper Names
Ratios
Serial Numbers and
   Miscellaneous Numbers
Time of Day
Units of Measurement

Addresses

1. Arabic numerals are used for all building, house, apartment, room, and suite numbers except for *one*, which is written out.

6 Lincoln Road
1436 Fremont Street
Apt. 281, Regency Park Drive
Room 617, McClaskey Building
but
One Bayside Drive
One World Trade Center

NOTE: When the address of a building is used as its name, the number in the address is written out.

Fifty Maple Street

2. Numbered streets have their numbers written as ordinals. There are two distinct conventions for the styling of numbered street names. The first, useful where space is limited, calls for Arabic numerals to denote all numbered streets above Twelfth; numbered street names from First through Twelfth are written out. A second, more formal, convention calls for the writing out of all numbered street names up to and including One Hundredth.

19 South 22nd Street	145 East 145th Street
167 West Second Avenue	122 East Forty-second Street
One East Ninth Street	36 East Fiftieth
in the Sixties (streets from 60th to 69th)	
in the 120s (streets from 120th to 129th)	

NOTE: A disadvantage of the first convention is that the direct juxtaposition of the house or building number and the street number may occur when there is no intervening word such as a compass direction. In these cases, a spaced hyphen or en dash may be inserted to distinguish the two numbers, or the second convention may be used and the street number written out.

2018–14th Street
2018 Fourteenth Street

3. Arabic numerals are used to designate interstate, federal, and state highways and, in some states, county roads.

U.S. Route 1   *or*   U.S. 1
Interstate 91   *or*   I-91
Massachusetts 57
Indiana 60
County 213

Dates

4. Year numbers are styled as figures. However, if a number representing a year begins a sentence, it may be written in full or the sentence rewritten to avoid beginning it with a figure. (For additional examples, see paragraph 3 in the section on Numbers as Words or Figures in this chapter.)

in 323 B.C.
before A.D. 40
1888–96
Fifteen eighty-eight marked the end to Spanish ambitions for the control of England.
  or
Spanish ambitions for the control of England ended in 1588 with the destruction of their "Invincible Armada."

5. A year number may be abbreviated, or cut back to its last two digits, in informal writing or when an event is so well-known that it needs no century designation. In these cases an apostrophe precedes the numerals. For more on this use of the apostrophe, see the section on Apostrophe, beginning on page 4, in Chapter 1, "Punctuation."

> He always maintained that he'd graduated from Korea, Clash of '52.
> the blizzard of '88

6. Full dates (month, day, and year) may be styled in one of two distinct patterns. The traditional styling is the month-day-year sequence, with the year set off by commas that precede and follow it. An alternate styling is the inverted date, or day-month-year sequence, which does not require commas. This sequence is used in Great Britain, in U.S. government publications, and in the military.

> *traditional style*
> July 8, 1776, was a warm, sunny day in Philadelphia.
> the explosion on July 16, 1945, at Alamogordo
> *military style*
> the explosion on 16 July 1945 at Alamogordo
> Lee's surrender to Grant on 9 April 1865 at Appomattox

7. Ordinal numbers are not used in expressions of full dates. Even though the numbers may be pronounced as ordinals, they are written as cardinal numbers. Ordinals may be used, however, to express a date without an accompanying year, and they are always used when preceded in a date by the word *the*.

> December 4, 1829
> on December 4th   *or*   on December 4
> on the 4th of December
> on the 4th

8. Commas are usually omitted from dates that include the month and year but not the day. Alternatively, writers sometimes insert the word *of* between month and year.

> in November 1805
> back in January of 1981

9. Once a numerical date has been given, a reference to a related date may be written out.

> After the rioting of August 3 the town was quiet, and by the seventh most troops had been pulled out.

10. All-figure dating (as 6-8-85 or 6/8/85) is inappropriate except in the most informal writing. It also creates a problem of ambiguity, as it may mean either June 8, 1985, or August 6, 1985.

11. References to specific centuries are often written out, although they may be expressed in figures, especially when they form the first element of a compound modifier.

> the nineteenth century
> a sixteenth-century painting
> > *but also*
>
> a 12th-century illuminated manuscript
> 20th-century revolutions

12. In general writing, the name of a specific decade often takes a short form. Although many writers place an apostrophe before the shortened word and a few capitalize it, both the apostrophe and the capitalization are often omitted when the context clearly indicates that a date is being referred to.

> in the turbulent seventies
> growing up in the thirties
> > *but also*
>
> back in the 'forties
> in the early Fifties

13. The name of a specific decade is often expressed in numerals, usually in plural form. (For more on the formation of plural numbers, see paragraphs 15 and 16 in the section on Punctuation, Spacing, and Inflection in this chapter.) The figure may be shortened with an apostrophe to indicate the missing numerals, but any sequence of such numbers should be styled consistently. (For more on this use of the apostrophe, see the section on Apostrophe, beginning on page 4, in Chapter 1, "Punctuation.")

> during the 1920s   *or*   during the 1920's
> the 1950s and 1960s   *or*   the '50s and '60s
> > *but not*
>
> the 1950s and '60s
> the 1930s and forties
> > *and not*
>
> the '50's and '60's

14. Era designations precede or follow words that specify centuries or numerals that specify years. Era designations are unspaced and are nearly always abbreviated; they are usually printed as small capitals and typed as regular capitals, and they may or may not be punctuated with periods. Any date that is given without an era designation or context is understood to mean A.D. The two most commonly used abbreviations are B.C. (before Christ) and A.D. (*anno Domini*, "in the year of our Lord"). The abbreviation B.C. is placed after the date, while A.D. is usually placed before the date but after a century designation. (For more on the use of these abbreviations, see page 100 of Chapter 4, "Abbreviations.")

> 1792–1750 B.C.
> between 600 and 400 B.C.
> from the fifth or fourth millennium to c. 250 B.C.
> 35,000 B.C.

between 7 B.C. and A.D. 22
c. A.D. 1100
the second century A.D.
the seventeenth century

15. Less commonly used era designations include A.H. (*anno Hegirae*, "in the year of [Muhammad's] Hegira," or *anno Hebraico*, "in the Hebrew year"); B.C.E. (before the common era; a synonym for B.C.); C.E.(of the common era; a synonym for A.D.); and B.P. (before the present; often used by geologists and archeologists, with or without the word *year*). The abbreviation A.H. in both its meanings is usually placed before the year number, while B.C.E., C.E., and B.P. are placed after it.

the tenth of Muharram, A.H. 61 (October 10, A.D. 680)
the first century A.H.
from the first century B.C.E. to the fourth century C.E.
63 B.C.E.
the year 200 C.E.
5,000 years B.P.
two million years B.P.

Degrees of Temperature and Arc

16. In technical writing figures are generally used for quantities expressed in degrees. In addition, the degree symbol (°) rather than the word *degree* is used with the figure. With the Kelvin scale, however, neither the word *degree* nor the symbol is used with the figure.

a 45° angle
6°40′10″N
32° F
0° C
Absolute zero is zero kelvins or 0 K.

NOTE: In many technical and scientific publications, the figure, degree symbol, and the *F* or *C* that follows are usually written without any space between them or with a space before the degree symbol but not after it. Another style followed in some scientific publications is to omit the degree symbol in expressions of temperature.

100°F   *or*   100 °F   *or*   100F
39°C   *or*   39 °C   *or*   39C

17. In general writing the quantity expressed in degrees may or may not be written out, depending upon the styling conventions being followed. A figure is followed by the degree symbol or the word *degree*; a written-out number is always followed by the word *degree*.

latitude 43°19″ N
latitude 43 degrees N
a difference of 43 degrees latitude
The temperature has risen thirty degrees since this morning.

Enumerations and Outlines

18. Both run-in and vertical enumerations are often numbered. In run-in enumerations, each item is preceded by a number (or an italicized letter) enclosed in parentheses. The items in the list are separated by commas if the items are brief and have little or no internal punctuation; if the items are complex, they are separated by semicolons. The entire run-in enumeration is introduced by a colon if it is preceded by a full clause.

> We feel that she should (1) increase her administrative skills, (2) pursue additional professional education, and (3) increase her production.
>
> The oldest and most basic word-processing systems consist of the following: (1) a typewriter for keyboarding information, (2) a console to house the storage medium, and (3) the medium itself.
>
> The vendor of your system should (1) instruct you in the care and maintenance of your system; (2) offer regularly scheduled maintenance to ensure that the system is clean, with lubrication and replacement of parts as necessary; and (3) respond promptly to service calls.

19. In vertical enumerations, the numbers are usually not enclosed in parentheses but are followed by a period. Each item in the enumeration begins its own line, which is either flush left or indented. Runover lines are usually aligned with the first word that follows the number, and figures are aligned on the periods that follow them. Each item on the list is usually capitalized if the items on the list are syntactically independent of the words that introduce them; however, style varies on this point, and use of a lowercase style for such items is fairly common. There is no terminal punctuation following the items unless at least one of the items is a complete sentence, in which case a period follows each item. Items that are syntactically dependent on the words that introduce them begin with a lowercase letter and carry the same punctuation marks that they would if they were a run-in series in a sentence.

> Required skills include the following:
> 1. Shorthand
> 2. Typing
> 3. Transcription
>
> To type a three-column table, follow this procedure:
> 1. Clear tab stops.
> 2. Remove margin stops.
> 3. Determine precise center of the page. Set a tab stop at center.
>
> The vendor of your system should
> 1. instruct you in the care and maintenance of your system;
> 2. offer regularly scheduled maintenance to ensure that the system is clean, with lubrication and replacement parts as necessary; and
> 3. respond promptly to service calls.

20. Outlines make use of Roman numerals, Arabic numerals, and letters.

I. Editorial tasks
   A. Manuscript editing
   B. Author contact
      1. Authors already under contract
      2. New authors
II. Production responsibilities
   A. Scheduling
      1. Composition
      2. Printing and binding
   B. Cost estimates and bids
      1. Composition
      2. Printing and binding

Fractions and Decimal Fractions—See also Chapter 6, "Mathematics and Science."

21. In running text, fractions standing alone are usually written out. Common fractions used as nouns are usually styled as open compounds, but when they are used as modifiers they are usually hyphenated. For more on written-out fractions, see page 117.

> two thirds of the paint
> a two-thirds majority
> three thirty-seconds
> seventy-two hundredths
> one one-hundredth

NOTE: Most writers try to find ways to avoid the necessity of writing out complicated fractions (as *forty-two seventy-fifths*).

22. Mixed fractions (fractions with a whole number, such as $3\frac{1}{2}$) and fractions that form part of a unit modifier are expressed in figures in running text. A *-th* is not added to a figure fraction.

> waiting $2\frac{1}{2}$ hours   a $\frac{7}{8}$-mile course
> $1\frac{1}{4}$ million population   a $2\frac{1}{2}$-kilometer race

NOTE: When mixed fractions are typewritten, the typist leaves a space between the whole number and the fraction. The space is closed up when the number is set in print. Fractions that are not on the typewriter keyboard may be made up by typing the numerator, a virgule, and the denominator in succession without spacing.

23. Fractions used with units of measurement are expressed in figures.

> $\frac{1}{10}$ km $\frac{1}{4}$ mile

24. Decimal fractions are always set as figures. In technical writing, a zero is placed to the left of the decimal point when the fraction is less than a whole number. In general writing, the zero is usually omitted.

> An example of a pure decimal fraction is 0.375, while 1.402 is classified as a mixed decimal fraction.

0.142857
0.2 gm
received 0.1 mg/kg diazepam i.v.
but
a .40 gauge shotgun

25. A comma is never inserted in the numbers following a decimal point, although spaces may be inserted as described and illustrated in paragraph 4 in the section on Punctuation, Spacing, and Inflection in this chapter.

26. Fractions and decimal fractions are usually not mixed in a text.

5½ lb. 2⅕ oz.
5.5 lb. 2.2 oz.
but not
5½ lb. 2.2 oz.

Money

27. Sums of money are expressed in words or figures, according to the conventions described in the first section of this chapter. If the sum can be expressed in one or two words, it is usually written out in running text. But if several sums are mentioned in the sentence or paragraph, all are usually expressed as figures. When the amount is written out, the unit of currency is also written out. If the sum is expressed in figures, the symbol of the currency unit is used, with no space between it and the numerals.

We paid $175,000 for the house.
My change came to 87¢.
The shop charged $67.50 for hand-knit sweaters.
The price of a nickel candy bar seems to have risen to more like forty cents.
Fifty dollars was stolen from my wallet.
forty thousand dollars
fifty-two dollars

28. Monetary units of mixed dollars-and-cents amounts are expressed in figures.

$16.75 $307.02 $1.95

29. Even-dollar amounts are often expressed in figures without a decimal point and zeros. But when even-dollar amounts are used in a series with or are near to amounts that include dollars and cents, the decimal point and zeros are usually added for consistency. The dollar sign is repeated before each amount in a series or inclusive range; the word *dollar* may or may not be repeated.

The price of the book rose from $7.95 in 1970 to $8.00 in 1971 and then to $8.50 in 1972.

The bids were eighty, ninety, and one hundred dollars.
or
The bids were eighty dollars, one hundred dollars, and three hundred dollars.

30. Sums of money given in round units of millions or above are usually expressed in a combination of figures and words, either with a dollar sign or with the word *dollars*. For more on the handling of round numbers, see paragraphs 7 and 8 in the section on Numbers as Words or Figures in this chapter.

> 60 million dollars
> a $10 million building program
> $4.5 billion

31. In legal documents a sum of money is usually written out fully, with the corresponding figures in parentheses immediately following.

> twenty-five thousand dollars ($25,000)

Percentages

32. In technical writing and in tables and footnotes, specific percentages are styled as figure plus unspaced percent sign (%). In general writing, the percentage number may be expressed as a figure or spelled out, depending upon the conventions that apply to it. The word *percent* rather than the symbol is used in nonscientific texts.

technical	*general*
15%	15 percent
13.5%	87.2 percent
	Twenty-five percent of the office staff was out with the flu.
	a four percent increase

33. The word *percentage* or *percent*, used as a noun without an adjacent numeral, should never be replaced by a percent sign.

> Only a small percentage of the test animals exhibited a growth change.
> The clinic treated a greater percentage of outpatients this year.

34. In a series or unit combination the percent sign should be included with all numbers, even if one of the numbers is zero.

> a variation of 0% to 10%

Proper Names

35. Numbers in the names of religious organizations and of churches are usually written out in ordinal form. Names of specific ruling houses and governmental bodies may include ordinals, and these are written out if they are one hundred or below. A few ruling houses, however, are traditionally designated by Roman numerals that follow the name.

First Church of Christ, Scientist
Third Congregational Church
Seventh-Day Adventists
Fifth Republic
Third Reich
First Continental Congress
  but
Egyptian tombs from Dynasty XI

36. Names of electoral, judicial, and military units may include ordinal numbers that precede the noun. Numbers of one hundred or below may be either written out or styled as numerals.

First Congressional District
Twelfth Precinct
Ninety-eighth Congress   *or*   98th Congress
Circuit Court of Appeals for the Third Circuit
United States Eighth Army   *or*   8th United States Army

At H hour, the 32d would drive forward to seize the 77th Division's position southeast of Maeda.

The assault was led by the 54th Massachusetts, the first black regiment recruited in a free state.

37. Specific branches of labor unions and fraternal organizations are conventionally identified by an Arabic numeral usually placed after the name.

International Brotherhood of Electrical Workers Local 42
Elks Lodge No. 61
Local 98 Operating Engineers

Ratios

38. Ratios expressed in figures use a colon, a hyphen, a virgule, or the word *to* as a means of comparison. Ratios expressed in words use a hyphen, or the word *to*.

a 3:1 chance
odds of 100 to 1
a 6-1 vote
22.4 mi/gal
a ratio of ten to four
a fifty-fifty chance

Serial Numbers and Miscellaneous Numerals

39. Figures are used to refer to things that are numbered serially, such as chapter and page numbers, addresses, years, policy and contract numbers, and so forth.

Serial No. 5274   vol. 5, p. 202
Permit No. 63709   column 2
paragraphs 5–7   Table 16
pages 420–515

40. Figures are also used to express stock market quotations, mathematical calculations, scores, and tabulations.

> won by a score of 8 to 2   3⅛ percent bonds
> the tally: 322 ayes, 80 nays 3 × 15 = 45

Time of Day

41. In running text the time of day is usually spelled out when expressed in even, half, or quarter hours.

> Quitting time is four-thirty.
> By half past eleven we were all getting hungry.
> We should arrive at a quarter past five.

42. The time of day is also usually spelled out when it is followed by the contraction *o'clock* or when *o'clock* is understood.

> I plan to leave here at eight o'clock.
> He should be here by four at the latest.
> My appointment is at eleven o'clock.
> *or*
> My appointment is at 11 o'clock.

43. Figures are used to delineate a precise time.

> The patient was discharged at 9:15 in the morning.
> Her plane is due in at 3:05 this afternoon.
> The program starts at 8:30 in the evening.

44. Figures are also written when the time of day is used in conjunction with the abbreviations *a.m. (ante meridiem)* and *p.m. (post meridiem)*. The punctuated lowercase styling for these abbreviations is most common, but punctuated small capital letters are also frequently used. These abbreviations should not be used in conjunction with the words *morning* or *evening*; and the word *o'clock* should not be combined with either *a.m.* or *p.m.*

> 8:30 a.m. *or* 8:30 A.M.
> 10:30 p.m. *or* 10:30 P.M.
> 8 a.m. *or* 8 A.M.
> *but*
> 9:15 in the morning
> 11:00 in the evening
> nine o'clock

NOTE: When twelve o'clock is written, it is often helpful to add the designation *midnight* or *noon*, as *a.m.* and *p.m.* sometimes cause confusion.

> twelve o'clock (midnight) *or* 12:00 midnight
> twelve o'clock (noon) *or* 12:00 noon

45. For consistency, even-hour times should be expressed with a colon and two zeros, when used in a series or pairing with any odd-hour times.

He came at 7:00 and left at 9:45.

46. The 24-hour clock system—also called military time—uses no punctuation and is expressed without the use of *a.m., p.m.,* or *o'clock.*

from 0930 to 1100   at 1600 hours

Units of Measurement

47. In technical writing, numbers used with units of measurement—even numbers below ten—are expressed as numerals.

2 liters	12 miles
55 pounds	6 hectares
60 watts	15 cubic centimeters
20 kilometers	35 milligrams

48. General writing, on the other hand, usually treats these numbers according to the basic conventions explained in the first section of this chapter. However, in some cases writers achieve greater clarity by styling all numbers—even those below ten—that express quantities of physical measurement as numerals.

The car was traveling in excess of 80 miles an hour.

The old volume weighed three pounds and was difficult to hold in a reading position.

but also in some general texts
3 hours, 25 minutes
saw 18 eagles in 12 minutes
a 6-pound hammer
weighed 3 pounds, 5 ounces

49. When units of measurement are written as abbreviations or symbols, the adjacent numbers are always figures, in both general and technical texts.

6 cm	67.6 fl oz
1 mm	4'
10 cm^3	98.6°
3 kg	$4.25

50. When two or more quantities are expressed, as in ranges or dimensions or series, an accompanying symbol is usually repeated with each figure.

2' x 4'
4" by 6" cards
temperature on successive days of 30°, 55°, 43°, and 58°
$400–$500

Chapter 6

Mathematics and Science

CONTENTS

This chapter describes styling practices that relate specifically to mathematical and scientific copy. It is intended for the nonspecialist who is preparing technical matter for general-interest publications; it is not intended to be an exhaustive explanation of all aspects of scientific and technical style. The Bibliography at the end of this book contains listings for style manuals that offer more detailed information about various kinds of technical publishing. General information on the styling of numbers can be found in Chapter 5, "The Treatment of Numbers."

Mathematics

Setting mathematical material in type is expensive, difficult, and time-consuming. It presents two major problems: typesetting the specialized mathematical characters often requires extensive handwork, and the nature of the subject demands absolute accuracy. Authors and editors can maintain accuracy and avoid costly printing errors by writing all mathematical notations legibly, by making subscripts and superscripts clearly evident as such, and by making it clear whether symbols are separated by spaces or closed up. Using a typewriter as much as possible to reproduce these notations helps make them legible; symbols that cannot be typed can be written in by hand. It also helps to leave extra-wide margins around the text and plenty of space above and below expressions that are set off on their own lines as displays. If that space is too small, the large amount of markup that is often required for mathematical copy may obscure the author's intention. For more information on how copy editors mark mathematical copy that is going to a typesetter, see the section on Special Text Elements, beginning on page 313, in Chapter 11, "Production Techniques."

Signs and Symbols

Mathematical copy makes heavy use of specialized characters. Many of these signs and symbols can be provided by a typesetter who specializes in mathematics; less common ones cannot. Before the editing process begins, the author or editor should list all the specialized characters in the manuscript. Through the production manager, the list can then be checked with the typesetter, who will have to acquire or make up any symbols that are not in stock. This is an expensive process. Authors and editors should be aware that available characters can frequently be substituted for costly new ones.

Other symbols—such as the overbar that forms the horizontal extension of the radical sign—can be set readily in some typesetting systems but not in others. When setting the overbar is a problem, a partial radical sign $\sqrt{}$ is often substituted. And even when the full radical sign can be easily set, it may be best not to use it in running text, because the bar could interfere with the line above.

The typesetter is often the final arbiter of what symbols and characters can be used. Characters with multiple diacritical marks (as $\bar{\bar{u}}$ or $\overset{..}{u}$) are often particularly difficult for a typesetter to reproduce precisely. If an author has used marks such as these, the editor may want to ask the author if less complicated equivalents can be substituted.

Commonly used mathematical symbols are found in the Signs and Symbols section at the end of this chapter.

Italic, Roman, and Bold Typefaces

In mathematical copy, the single English letters that represent unknowns and variables are set in italic type, even when they are used in subscripts and superscripts. Letters used to describe geometric figures are also italicized. The e for exponent is italicized (but not the fuller abbreviation *exp*), as is d for derivative and f for function. An underline on handwritten or typewritten copy indicates *italics*. Usually the author does not bother to underline these letters; it is considered the job of the copy editor who marks up the manuscript for the typesetter.

In contrast to single letters, numerals are set in roman type. Also set in roman are the abbreviations for units of measurement and abbreviations such as cos (cosine), csc (cosecant), log (logarithm), sec (secant), sin (sine), tan (tangent), var (variance), and others that are used in mathematical copy.

$$\tan t = -\sqrt{15}$$
$$\sin x \, (2 \cos x + 1) = 0$$
$$\log_a(x^y) = y \log_a x$$

Boldface roman type is usually used for vectors and tensors and in matrix notation. A wavy underline on handwritten or typewritten copy indicates **boldface roman.** However, subscripts, superscripts, and signs of operation that are used with vectors are set in lightface type; for a fuller discussion of vectors and tensors, see pages 139–140.

Structure of Equations

Equations can be either displayed (set on their own lines with extra space above and below them) or placed within the text line. Most publications prefer the displayed presentation, especially if the equation is too large to fit the regular depth of a line. In these cases, extra leading or space must be added to separate that line from the ones above and below. Setting these large equations on the line is difficult, and the effect is often unattractive. A displayed equation is either centered in the space provided for it or indented a fixed amount from the left margin.

$$I(x) = \int_a^x f(t)dt$$
$$2k + 4 = 4k - 5$$
$$Sy = (0.577)S_x - (0.0001333)S_x{}^2$$

Long equations are best handled in a display to avoid an awkward break at the end of a line of text. However, some complicated equations have to be broken even in the displayed form. If such an equation runs over, the break should occur just before an operational sign or, preferably, an equal sign. The runover line can be (1) set flush with the right margin if the runover is long enough to overlap the first line by an inch or so, (2) indented from the right margin if an equation number (as explained on page 136) is used or if necessary to provide visual balance by overlapping the first line, or (3) lined up according to operational or equal signs as a point of orientation, as in the example below. The last alternative is preferred for equations that run more than two lines.

$$
\begin{aligned}
\rho_3 &= \sqrt{(ad + bc)^2 + (ac - bd)^2} \\
&= \sqrt{a^2 + 2abcd + b^2c^2 + a^2c^2 - 2abcd + b^2d^2} \\
&= \sqrt{a^2d^2 + b^2c^2 + a^2c^2 + b^2d^2} \\
&= \sqrt{a^2(c^2 + d^2) + b^2(c^2 + d^2)} \\
&= \sqrt{(a^2 + b^2)(c^2 + d^2)} = \sqrt{a^2 + b^2} \cdot \sqrt{c^2 + d^2}
\end{aligned}
$$

An element such as ρ in the example given above that is shared by several parts of an equation, or by a series of equations, is usually not repeated.

In contrast to displayed equations, equations run in with the text are broken after an operational sign or an equal sign.

If there are no operational signs or signs of relationship (as $=$, $>$, etc.) within a mathematical formula, it should not be divided at all, either on the line or in display. Units of aggregation within parentheses, brackets, or braces should not be split at the end of a line, nor should fractions or radical expressions.

Equations are basically sentences. The signs of relationship represent the verb of the sentence, and an equation may be used as a clause within another sentence. Thus, equations are in some ways capitalized and punctuated like sentences. If the first word of a displayed equation happens to be a full word, it is capitalized; however, the capitalization or lowercasing of letters used as symbols or as variables is not influenced by their position in the equation. The text that precedes a displayed equation is punctuated as required by its own grammatical construction.

The resulting quadratic equation is thus

$$x^2 - 3x - \frac{5}{2} = 0$$

or, after multiplying both sides by 2,

$$2x^2 - 6x - 5 = 0$$

Within the text line, equations are followed by a terminal period when they occur at the end of a sentence. After a displayed equation, however, the use of punctuation is optional. Punctuation can clarify the progression of a complex displayed equation and indicate the end of a sentence.

$$x + y = 9,$$
$$x - y + 3z = 2,$$
$$4y - 3z = 5.$$

However, the use or omission of punctuation should be consistent throughout a publication.

Two equations may be displayed on the same line. Usually they are separated by a two-em space without punctuation.

$$PF = a - f \qquad PF' = a + f$$

A few publications use both a two-em space and a comma to separate equations displayed on the same line.

$$a + 0 = a, \qquad a \cdot 1 = a$$

A space of two ems is used on both sides of the words *and* and *or* when they separate two equations on a line; explanatory words and limiting terms that are used with equations are set off with a space of either one or two ems.

$$(a + b) + c = a + (b + c) \qquad \text{and} \qquad ab = ba$$
$$A = (R^2 - r^2) \quad \text{(for } R\text{)}$$

A sign or symbol used as an appositive directly following a descriptive term is not set off by punctuation unless it is necessary to avoid ambiguity.

Two sets A and B are said to be equivalent if there is a one-to-one correspondence between them.

The symbol $\sqrt[n]{}$ is called the nth radical

Words used to link lines of displayed equations are usually set in roman type, flush left on the same line as the equation they introduce. A series of linked equations is either centered or aligned according to a sign of relationship such as an equal sign. In the following example, the word *therefore* is capitalized because it introduces a new concept that follows a period.

Thus we have the equation:

$$3r^2 \cos^2\theta + 2r^2 \sin^2\theta = 6$$

or

$$r^2 \cos^2\theta + 2r^2(\cos^2\theta + \sin^2\theta) = 6.$$

Therefore

$$r^2 \cos^2\theta + 2r^2 = 6$$

or

$$r^2(\cos^2\theta + 2) = 6.$$

Bits of space are inserted into equations in order to clarify the parts. The spaces are usually the same size or slightly smaller than the word spaces that appear in the text. For example, a word space is usually left before and after operational signs and signs of relationship. (However, when a plus or minus sign is used with a number to denote a positive or negative quantity, as $+3$ or -5, it is closed up.) A space also occurs after a comma used to separate mathematical coordinates, and a thin space (a space that is one fourth of an em in thickness) is inserted around abbreviations for trigonometric functions such as *sin*.

Numbering of Equations

Many mathematical publications assign numbers to displayed equations as a handy means of cross-referencing. Double numeration may be used, in which the chapter number is the first digit and the equation number the second; the two numbers are usually separated by a period. In each chapter the equations begin with number 1. The equation number is placed in parentheses at the right margin of the line on which the equation is displayed, at least an em space from the end of the equation. References to these numbers in the text are also enclosed in parentheses.

If both sides are squared, then

$$2x + 5 = x^2 - 10x + 25 \tag{6.2}$$

Short publications such as journal articles may assign single numbers to displayed equations.

We are left with

$$a_1b_2 - a_2b_1 = 0 \tag{17}$$

Numbering systems are used only with displayed equations that are referred to in the text, not with equations that appear in the running text. Also, when there are only a few equations, they may not be numbered at all.

When an equation takes up several lines, or when a single number refers to a series of equations displayed together, the number is either centered vertically or placed on the last line of the display.

$$\begin{aligned}
a_1x + b_1y + c_1z &= d_1 \\
a_2x + b_2y + c_2 &= d_2 \\
a_3x + b_3y + c_3z &= d_3
\end{aligned} \tag{3.2}$$

$$(3 - j5)(4 + j2) = 12 - j20 + j6 - j^2 10$$
$$= 12 + 10 - j20 + j6 = 22 - j14 \tag{5.7}$$

Subscripts and Superscripts

Single-letter abbreviations used as subscripts and superscripts are set italic. Longer abbreviations, whole words, and numbers are set roman when they are used as subscripts or superscripts. Small type is used for all these forms.

$$C_v \qquad \Phi_m \qquad A_{ij} \qquad k_{max} \qquad P_0P_2$$

Note that the 0 in P_0P_2 in the example above is a subscript zero. The letter *oh* would be italicized.

Complex symbols may have both subscripts and superscripts. The preferred handling of these combinations is to align them vertically.

$$\frac{d^m}{dz^m} \qquad S_{p-1}^v \qquad \Phi_m^k$$

While this styling is preferred, it is not always possible in some typesetting systems. The alternative is to stagger the subscripts and superscripts, with the subscript set before the superscript.

$$H_k^{\ 2} \qquad P_n^{\ m}$$

However, if the superscript symbol is an asterisk, a degree sign, or a prime, or if it consists of three or more characters, then the superscript must be placed directly above the subscript.

$$K_p^* \qquad R_n' \qquad R_b^{2n-1}$$

Alignment of subscript and superscript is also preferable when one of them is complex. But both the staggered and the aligned formats are difficult to set in such cases, and a helpful alternative is to insert parentheses and set the expression in the following manner:

$$(J_{sx+n})^2$$

A complex subscript or superscript becomes more legible when all its elements are closed up; thus, the rule about spacing around operational signs and after commas does not apply to these marks.

Signs of Aggregation

Parentheses, brackets, and braces are used in most kinds of mathematical copy to indicate units contained within larger units. The traditional order, beginning with the innermost element, is parentheses within brackets within braces. If more than three aggregations are required, the parentheses, brackets, and braces are repeated in larger type. These symbols should be large enough to enclose the elements they contain.

$$\{[(\{[(\qquad)]\})]\}$$

$$\iint_A \left[\left(\frac{\partial w}{\partial x}\right) + \left(\frac{\partial w}{\partial y}\right)^2\right] \mathrm{d}x'\mathrm{d}y$$

Other notations such as bars (also called *vinculums*) (as in $a - \overline{b - c} = a - [b - c]$) and angle brackets should not be substituted for the signs of aggregation shown above. These other symbols have specialized meanings of their own, and their use can change the intention of a mathematical expression.

Units of aggregation within parentheses, brackets, or braces should not be split at the end of a line.

Fractions

Writers should be familiar with the different ways to express fractions and the circumstances in which each is used. Fairly short, uncomplicated fractions are good candidates for conversion from the standard *built-up* form to the form with the numerator and the denominator placed on the same line and separated by a virgule /.

$$\frac{\pi r^2 h}{2\pi r} \qquad becomes \qquad r^2h/2\pi r$$

The use of the virgule (also called *solidus, diagonal, slash,* or *shilling mark*) makes possible the setting of fractions within running text and reduces the amount of white space on a page. The virgule is also used to express fractions used as subscripts and superscripts; the result is a fraction that is more compact and easier to set.

$$(p + p')^{\frac{x+y}{z}} \qquad becomes \qquad (p+p')^{(x+y)/z}$$

When a built-up fraction containing an operational sign is converted to the virgule form, parentheses are usually added to indicate that the symbols are to be considered as a unit.

$$\frac{ad + bc}{bd} \qquad becomes \qquad (ad + bc)/bd$$

$$5 - \frac{x + 4}{y} + 18 \qquad becomes \qquad 5 - (x+4)/y + 18$$
$$or \qquad 5 - [(x + 4)/y] + 18$$

If a built-up fraction is followed by a number or by a letter symbol, a sign of aggregation such as parentheses or brackets must be inserted before the fraction can be expressed in virgule form. Signs of aggregation are not used for this purpose when the built-up fraction is preceded by a number or letter symbol.

$$\frac{a}{b}x \qquad becomes \qquad (a/b)x$$

$$x\frac{a}{b} \qquad becomes \qquad xa/b$$

Expressions of Multiplication

Multiplication can be indicated by the multiplication or times sign $\times$, by a centered dot, by signs of aggregation such as parentheses, or by the juxtaposition of characters.

14×7
$(-a) \cdot (+b) = -ab$
$4(8) \quad or \quad (4)(8) \quad$ *but not* $\quad (4)8$

When one of the multipliers is an expression denoting a power of ten, the multiplication sign is conventionally used.

0.595×10^{-2}
$365 \times 3600 = 1.314 \times 10^6$

The multiplication sign is also used at the end of a line (or at the beginning of a runover line) to indicate that the first item on the next line is a part of the multiplication formula that has been broken.

Factorials, on the other hand, are conventionally multiplied with centered dots.

$n! \cdot m! \geq (nm!)$

Ellipses

Material omitted from a mathematical expression is indicated by three spaced points of ellipsis. However, the punctuation that occurs with ellipsis points in mathematical copy differs from that used with ellipsis points in regular copy as described in Chapter 1, "Punctuation." When commas or semicolons are used in an elision within a mathematical expression, they are placed after each mathematical term that precedes an ellipsis, as well as *after* the ellipsis when it is followed by a final term. A space appears after each punctuation mark.

$a_1, a_2, \ldots, a_x \quad$ *but not* $\quad a_1, a_2, \ldots a_x$

When an operational sign is used adjacent to an elision, the sign of operation usually appears both before and after the ellipsis.

$a_1 + a_2 + \ldots + a_x$

Points of ellipsis are often centered on the line after a sign of operation, as in the example given above, and also when they are not accompanied by any marks of punctuation. However, centering the ellipsis points is done purely for the sake of appearance, and the points may be set on the baseline in any context. In running text, they *must* be set on the baseline.

Integral, Summation, and Product Signs

The indices to an integral symbol appear to the right of the symbol. Indices of summation and product limits are set above and below the symbols. However, when these symbols appear in running text, the indices and limits of products may be written to the right as superscripts and subscripts to avoid putting extra space between the lines.

$$\int_a^b f(x)dx = F(b) - F(a)$$

$$s = \sum_{v=1}^{\infty} u_v$$

$$\sin \pi x = \pi x \prod_{k=1}^{\infty} (1-x)$$

Thus we have $s = \sum_{v-1}^{\infty} u_v$

Thus we have $\sin \pi x = \pi x \prod_{K=1}^{\infty} [1 - (x^2/k^2)]$

Arrays

When mathematical elements are arranged in horizontal rows and vertical columns, the arrangement is called an *array*. There are two types of arrays: *determinants* and *matrices*. A determinant is presented as a square array; a matrix may be square or rectangular. Vertical lines set off determinants, while matrices are enclosed within brackets or parentheses. The numbers inside a matrix are called *entries*.

In both types of array, the mathematical elements are either aligned or centered below one another in each column. Labels for the columns or rows are set in smaller type outside the array. If all the entries are numbers, the columns are aligned as in tables, according to the right-most whole digit. If the entries consist of combinations of numbers and letters, they are centered below one another. An em space is used to separate the columns, but when a plus or minus sign occurs before an entry, or a subscript follows it, balance is provided by separating *all* the columns with two-em spaces.

The omission of a column is indicated by a vertical series of three horizontal dots. The omission of a row is indicated either by a horizontal series of three vertical dots or by a continuous horizontal line of dots.

$$\begin{vmatrix} x & y & 1 \\ x_1 & y_1 & 1 \\ x_2 & y_2 & 1 \end{vmatrix} = 0 \qquad \begin{pmatrix} 1 & -2 & 2 & 4 \\ 2 & 5 & -1 & 1 \\ 3 & 6 & -2 & 2 \\ 4 & 2 & 5 & 3 \\ -1 & 3 & 2 & 5 \end{pmatrix} \qquad \begin{bmatrix} a_{11} & a_{12} & \cdots & \cdots & a_{1n} \\ a_{21} & a_{22} & \cdots & \cdots & a_{2n} \\ \cdots & \cdots & \cdots & \cdots & \cdots \\ \cdots & \cdots & \cdots & \cdots & \cdots \\ a_{n1} & a_{n2} & \cdots & \cdots & a_{nn} \end{bmatrix} = (a_{ik})$$

Arrays commonly use up several lines and thus may pose a problem if they occur at the bottom of a page. Complicated arrays can be cast as figures and moved to a part of the page where they will not break. The array can then be referred to in text by its figure number.

Vectors and Tensors

A vector is a quantity that has magnitude and direction. It is usually indicated with boldface type. It is important that vectors be set in a different typeface from other mathematical notation. A wavy line in handwritten or typewritten material indicates **boldface.** Vectors may also be shown by an arrow written above the expression, but the boldface form is much easier to typeset.

$$\mathbf{r} \qquad \mathbf{AE} \qquad \overrightarrow{r} \qquad \overrightarrow{AE} \qquad r \qquad \boldsymbol{AE}$$

Subscripts, superscripts, signs of operation, and other components of vectors are set in lightface type.

$$\mathbf{r}_1 - \mathbf{r}_2 = P_2\,P_1$$
$$\mathbf{c} = \frac{-\mathbf{i} + \mathbf{k}}{\sqrt{2}}$$

However, in the multiplication of vectors, the multiplication sign and the centered dot, which have different meanings in this context, are set bold to match the vectors.

$$\mathbf{b}{\cdot}(\mathbf{a} \times \mathbf{b})$$
$$\mathbf{U} \times (\mathbf{V} + \mathbf{W}) = \mathbf{U} \times \mathbf{V} + \mathbf{U} \times \mathbf{W}$$

A tensor is a generalized vector with more than three components. It is often indicated by **boldface italic** type to distinguish it from a vector. Boldface italic type is indicated by a straight line with a wavy underline below it. Some typesetters use a bold sans serif typeface instead of bold italic; as long as the vectors are set in a typeface with serifs, the two can be distinguished.

$$(\boldsymbol{r} \times \boldsymbol{F})dV = 0$$

Greek Letters

Greek letters are frequently used in mathematical copy. It is a good idea for the author to write out the name of each letter in the margin opposite the first use of the letter, to ensure that the typesetter interprets the symbol correctly. The table below gives the names and shows the forms of the letters of the Greek alphabet.

GREEK ALPHABET

Name	Capital	Lowercase	Name	Capital	Lowercase
alpha	A	α	nu	N	ν
beta	B	β	xi	Ξ	ξ
gamma	Γ	γ	omicron	O	o
delta	Δ	δ or ∂	pi	Π	π
epsilon	E	ε	rho	P	ρ
zeta	Z	ζ	sigma	Σ	σ or ς
eta	H	η	tau	T	τ
theta	Θ or Θ	θ or ϑ	upsilon	Υ	υ
iota	I	ι	phi	Φ	ϕ or φ
kappa	K	κ	chi	X	χ
lambda	Λ	λ	psi	Ψ	ψ
mu	M	μ	omega	Ω	ω

Physical Sciences

Many of the conventions established for the writing of mathematical notations apply also to the physical sciences; still other conventions are unique to this field. This section describes some of the styling conventions that apply specifically to the physical sciences and to the International System of Units.

Astronomy

The International System of Units that is discussed at the end of this section is widely used in astronomy. In addition, astronomers use the equatorial system as a way to define the position of a celestial object. In this system the equatorial coordinates *right ascension* (abbreviated with the lowercase Greek letter α alpha) and *declination* (abbreviated with the lowercase Greek letter δ delta) are analogous to terrestrial longitude and latitude. Right ascension is usually expressed in units of time rather than in degrees of arc, so measurements are given in hours, minutes, and seconds. Declination is given in degrees, minutes, and seconds of arc. Declination is marked positive (+) north of the celestial equator and negative (−) south of it. A declination number that lacks a positive or negative sign is considered positive.

The signs of the zodiac are occasionally used in astronomy as a short-hand method of indicating in which of the 12 zodiacal constellations a celestial object may be found. The section on Signs and Symbols at the end of this chapter contains the names and symbols of the constellations of the zodiac along with a list of other signs and symbols commonly used in astronomy.

For conventions governing the capitalization of the names of planets, stars, and other celestial objects, see paragraph 69 in the section on Proper Nouns, Pronouns, and Adjectives, beginning on page 52, in Chapter 2, "Capitals, Italics, and Quotation Marks."

Chemistry and Physics

A list of signs and symbols that are commonly used in chemistry and physics may be found at the end of this chapter. In addition, a list of technical manuals that will help with styling problems that are not covered in this chapter may be found in the Bibliography.

Names of elements, compounds, and particles The names of chemical elements and compounds are written lowercase. Two-word compounds are written open, without a hyphen.

> glyceraldehyde
> hydrogen chloride
> sodium sulfate

Chemical symbols are one-, two-, or three-letter abbreviations for the names of the chemical elements. The letters are set in roman type without periods, and the first letter is capitalized. Abbreviations for other chemical substances (such as B for base, Me for methyl) are styled in the same manner. The table below gives the names of the chemical elements with their symbols.

Names of subatomic particles and quanta may be written out or their symbols may be used. The symbols are set either roman or italic. The table on page 143 gives the names of subatomic particles and quanta with their symbols.

CHEMICAL ELEMENTS AND THEIR SYMBOLS

Element	Symbol	Element	Symbol	Element	Symbol
actinium	Ac	helium	He	radium	Ra
aluminum	Al	holmium	Ho	radon	Rn
americium	Am	hydrogen	H	rhenium	Re
antimony	Sb	indium	In	rhodium	Rh
argon	Ar	iodine	I	rubidium	Rb
arsenic	As	iridium	Ir	ruthenium	Ru
astatine	At	iron	Fe	samarium	Sm
barium	Ba	krypton	Kr	scandium	Sc
berkelium	Bk	lanthanum	La	selenium	Se
beryllium	Be	lawrencium	Lr	silicon	Si
bismuth	Bi	lead	Pb	silver	Ag
boron	B	lithium	Li	sodium	Na
bromine	Br	lutetium	Lu	strontium	Sr
cadmium	Cd	magnesium	Mg	sulfur	S
calcium	Ca	manganese	Mn	tantalum	Ta
californium	Cf	mendelevium	Md	technetium	Tc
carbon	C	mercury	Hg	tellurium	Te
cerium	Ce	molybdenum	Mo	terbium	Tb
cesium	Cs	neodymium	Nd	thallium	Tl
chlorine	Cl	neon	Ne	thorium	Th
chromium	Cr	neptunium	Np	thulium	Tm
cobalt	Co	nickel	Ni	tin	Sn
copper	Cu	niobium	Nb	titanium	Ti
curium	Cm	nitrogen	N	tungsten	W
dysprosium	Dy	nobelium	No	unnilhexium	Unh
einsteinium	Es	osmium	Os	unnilpentium	Unp
erbium	Er	oxygen	O	unnilquadium	Unq
europium	Eu	palladium	Pd	uranium	U
fermium	Fm	phosphorus	P	vanadium	V
fluorine	F	platinum	Pt	xenon	Xe
francium	Fr	plutonium	Pu	ytterbium	Yb
gadolinium	Gd	polonium	Po	yttrium	Y
gallium	Ga	potassium	K	zinc	Zn
germanium	Ge	praseodymium	Pr	zirconium	Zr
gold	Au	promethium	Pm		
hafnium	Hf	protactinium	Pa		

Symbols for chemical elements and subatomic particles have limited use in running text. Even in technical writing, they tend to be used only if the full name of the element, compound, or particle has been written out at the first appearance of the symbol.

Subscripts and superscripts Four numerical indices are used with chemical symbols. The *mass* number is given as a superscript to the left of the symbol, the *ionic charge* as a superscript to the right. The *atomic number* is given as a subscript on the left, the *number of atoms* of an element in a molecule as a subscript on the right. Superscripts and subscripts are usually aligned vertically; the right-most digit is the basis of alignment in numbers of two digits or more that are set on the left. Indices set on the right are often aligned, but frequently the subscript is set before the superscript.

$$Fe^{3+} \qquad {}^{63}_{29}Cu \qquad {}^{1}_{1}H \qquad {}^{228}_{90}Th \qquad S_2O_3{}^{2-}$$

The mass number is sometimes placed as a superscript to the right of a chemical symbol instead of to the left, especially in nontechnical writing. The left position, however, should be used in equations. Thus, in nontechnical writing C^{14} is often found, whereas in equations ^{14}C is the common form.

In running text, an isotope is specified in full. The name of the element is written out, followed by a space or a hyphen and then the mass number.

carbon 14
carbon-14

The ionic charge, given as a superscript to the right of the chemical symbol, may be either plus $(+)$ or minus $(-)$. A number may precede the charge sign, but the charge sign is never followed by a number.

$$CN^- \qquad\qquad S^{2-} \text{ ions} \qquad\qquad Na^+ \qquad\qquad Zn^{2+} \text{ ions}$$

$$CO_3^{2-} \quad \textit{but not} \quad CO_3^{-2} \qquad O^{2-} \quad \textit{but not} \quad O^{-2}$$

SUBATOMIC PARTICLES AND QUANTA AND THEIR SYMBOLS

Particle or Quantum	Symbol	Particle or Quantum	Symbol
alpha particle	α	nucleon	N
beta particle	β	omega particle	Ω
deuteron	d	photon	γ
electron	e	pion	π
kaon (formerly K-meson)	κ	proton	p
lambda particle	Λ	sigma particle	Σ
muon	μ	triton	t
neutrino	ν	xi particle	Ξ
neutron	n		

In running text, however, the charge sign precedes the number on the line when it is not attached to the chemical symbol.

a -3 charge

Some complex formulas contain two symbols with adjacent right- and left-hand indices. To clarify the structure, a thin space is inserted between the indices.

Spacing When two or more element symbols are combined to represent a chemical compound, no space appears between the symbols or any subscripts, superscripts, brackets, or parentheses within the compound.

$[Co(NH_3)_6]Cl_3$ $C_5H_8O_4NaN$

$Pt(NH_3)_2Cl_2$ Na_2SiO_3

A number that precedes the compound is usually closed up also, but in some publications a thin space is inserted between the number and the compound symbol, especially if needed for clarity. In the compound 25 $O_2(g)$, for example, a space is inserted after the 25 so that the symbol for oxygen (O) is not mistaken for a zero.

2KCl or 2 KCl

$6H_2O$ or 6 H_2O

In chemical expressions each discrete unit is set off by a space. This space may be as large as a word space in the text, but many publications set smaller spaces. A thin space or larger is also used on both sides of connecting signs such as $+$, $-$, $=$, $\rightarrow$, and $\rightleftharpoons$.

$2C_8H_{18}(l) + 25\ O_2(g) \rightarrow 16CO_2(g) + 18H_2O(l)$

$Mg_3N_2 + 6H_2O \rightarrow 3Mg(OH)_2 + 2NH_3$

Marks of punctuation and relationship A period is placed at the end of a sentence that ends with a chemical expression; commas and semicolons are also used in appropriate positions within the sentence. When chemical expressions are not part of a sentence, however, they are unpunctuated.

The arrow $\rightarrow$ means "reaction" or "yields." It is used between the symbol for a reactant and the symbol for a product in nonreversible or nonequilibrium reactions.

$Hg^{2+} + 2Cl^- \rightarrow Hg_2Cl_2(s)$

$2NH_4Cl + Hg_2(NO_3)_2 \rightarrow Hg_2Cl_2(s) + 2NH_4NO_3$

The symbol $\triangle$ signifying heat, or the chemical symbol for or other description of the catalyst involved, may be set close to the arrow. The type used for the description of the catalyst is smaller than that used for the rest of the equation, and any abbreviations or words in the description are lowercased. The reaction arrow may be extended if necessary to accommodate the size of the chemical symbol for the catalyst.

$$2KClO_3 \xrightarrow{\triangle} 2KCl + 3O_2$$

$$C_6H_6 + Br_2 \xrightleftharpoons[50°]{Fe} C_6H_5Br + HBr$$

$$CH_3CH_2CH_2Cl + 2 NH_3 \xrightarrow{\text{sealed tube}} CH_3CH_2CH_2NH_2^+ \ NH_4^+ - Cl^-$$

The arrow ↓ signifying a precipitate and the arrow ↑ signifying a gas are preceded by a thin space.

$$2 AgNO_3 + CaCl_2 \rightarrow Ca(NO_3)_2 + 2 AgCl \downarrow$$
$$H_2SO_3 \rightarrow H_2O + SO_2 \uparrow$$

Two single-barbed arrows ⇌ indicate a reversible reaction. Arrows with two barbs ↔ indicate resonance between two equivalent structures. Spaces are used around both types of arrow.

$$Hemoglobin + O_2 \rightleftharpoons Oxyhemoglobin + H_2O$$
$$CaCO_3(s) \rightleftharpoons CaO(s) + CO_2(g)$$
$$Cu(NH_3)_4^{2+} \rightleftharpoons Cu^{2+} + _4NH_3$$

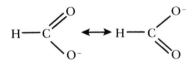

The abbreviations used in thermochemistry for phase states (*aq* aqueous, *g* gas, *l* liquid, *s* solid, and *c* macrocrystalline) are enclosed in parentheses and set next to the formula that they follow, without an intervening space. These abbreviations may be roman or italic.

$$BaO_2(s) \rightarrow BaO(s) + ½O_2(g)$$
$$Na(s) < NaCl(s) < Br_2(l) < Br_2(g) < N_2O_4(g)$$

The oxidation number of an element is shown by Roman numerals enclosed in parentheses. (The Arabic zero is used for zero.) There is no space between the element's name or symbol and the opening parenthesis.

Fe(III)
iron(III) perchlorate
tin(IV) chloride

Brackets are used to designate units of chemical concentration.

$$[H^+] = K_a \times \frac{[HC_2H_3O_2]}{[C_2H_3O_2{}^-]}$$

A valence number attached to a formula requires that the formula be enclosed in brackets.

$$[M(CN)_4]^{2-}$$

A hyphen separates prefixes composed of single letters, numerals, or letter-numeral combinations from the rest of a chemical term. In addition, the following italicized prefixes are followed by a hyphen: *cis, trans, para* (or *p*), *meta* (or *m*), *ortho* (or *o*), *tert* (or *t*), *sec* (or *s*), *e* (for electron), *n* (for neutron), and *p* (for proton).

> *z*-butene
> 4*H*-quinoziline
> α-particles *but* alpha particles
> β-emitters *but* beta emitters
> *cis*-oleic acid

The hyphen is also used to separate units of certain complex terms.

> α-amino-β-(*p*-hydroxyphenyl)propionic acid
> 2-methyl-3-ethylpentane

The hyphen separates locants, which denote the position of an atom or group within a molecule. Locants precede the term they refer to, and they are separated from one another by unspaced commas.

> 6*H*-1,2,5-thiadiazine

In amino acid sequences, hyphens are used to separate the abbreviations.

> Ala-Lys-Pro-Thr-Tyr-Phe-Gly-Arg-Glu-Gly

Segments of amino acid sequences are written with a hyphen at each end of the sequence to indicate that parts are missing.

> -Ser-Leu-Tyr-Glu-
> $\quad\quad\quad\quad\quad |$
> $\quad\quad\quad\quad NH_2$

The centered dot set close to the symbol that it follows indicates an unshared electron in the formula of a free radical.

> $Cl_2 \xrightarrow{\text{UV photon}} 2\ Cl\cdot$
> $CH_3\cdot + HCl$
> $CH_3\cdot + Cl\cdot$

The centered dot that is used to show water of hydration is usually set closed up; a thin space may be inserted on either side. Style varies regarding the weight of this dot: both light and boldface dots are commonly used for this purpose.

> $BaCl_2 \cdot 2H_2O(s) \rightarrow BaCl_2(s) + 2H_2O(g)$

The asterisk may be used as a superscript after the lowercase Greek letters sigma (σ) and pi (π) to indicate high-energy antibonding orbitals, as opposed to lower-energy bonding orbitals, which do not use the asterisk.

> σ*1s

English (but not Greek) letters used as hyphenated prefixes are italicized unless a small capital is indicated in the copy. Number prefixes are not italicized.

$_4H$-quinoziline
D-arabinose
but
2,3-dimethylbutane

Letters used in atomic orbitals are italicized.

a $3d$ orbital
three $2p$ orbitals

In thermodynamics, italicized letters are used to indicate quantities.

$$dS = \frac{Dq}{T}$$
$$dE = Dq - Dw$$
$$T\,dS - Dq\,\pounds\,0$$

Line breaks Chemical symbols, including their subscripts and super-scripts, represent complete units and should not be broken at the end of a line. Similarly, arrows that signify precipitate and gas should be kept with the symbols that precede them and not be separated from them at the end of a line. When chemical equations must be broken, the equation may be split at a horizontal arrow. Most technical journals prefer that the arrow appear at the beginning of the new line; some advocate its position at the end of the first line. If necessary, lines may also be broken at the point where a connecting symbol such as $+$, $-$, or $=$ occurs; the con-necting symbol is usually placed at the beginning of the runover line.

$Zn^{2+} + S^{2-}$
$\rightarrow ZnS(s)$

Modifiers Modifying words used beneath chemical formulas are set in type smaller than that used for the formulas themselves. The first word is capitalized.

Ethylene   Polyethylene

$$H-C\equiv C-H + H_2O \xrightarrow[\text{HgSO}_4]{40\%\,H_2SO_4} [CH_2\!=\!CHOH] \rightarrow CH_3CHO$$

Vinyl alcohol   Acetaldehyde
(not isolable)

Bonds and structural formulas Bonding in linear formulas is shown by a single line without spacing. Multiple bonds are shown by two or more lines without spacing. If the formula is written in the text, however, bond lines are omitted.

$$(N\equiv C—Ag—C\equiv N)^-$$

If a structural formula is incorporated into the text, the central part of the formula is aligned with the text line.

. . . which gives R—C=O

O—H

However, structural formulas that occupy more than two lines of text should be displayed.

Compounds that contain a ring structure made up of one type of atoms are divided into two groups. A small number are called *alicyclic compounds*. The rest of the ring compounds are related to benzene (C_6H_6) or its derivatives and are called *aromatic compounds*. The benzene ring is usually condensed into a simple hexagon when it is used in structural formulas. The circle indicates aromaticity.

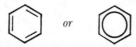

Alicyclic compounds are represented by a regular polygon without the circle that indicates aromaticity.

cyclohexane   cyclopentane

International System of Units (SI)

The International System of Units is also known as SI, from the French name *Système internationale d'unités*. Derived from the metric system of physical units, it was established by the General Conference on Weights and Measures as an international system of units of measurement. There are seven basic units in the system.

Quantity	Unit	Abbreviation
Length	meter	m
Mass	kilogram	kg
Time	second	s
Electric current	ampere	A
Thermodynamic temperature	kelvin	K
Light intensity	candela	cd
Amount of substance	mole	mol

In addition to the seven basic units, the following units of measurement are frequently found in scientific writing: minute (min), day (d), hour (h), and liter (L).

The basic SI units and their abbreviations are written lowercase unless the abbreviation is derived from a proper name, such as *K* for *kelvin*. The abbreviations are set in roman type and do not have periods.

The other units of measurement are derived from these basic units by combination or by the addition of a prefix that denotes multiplication or division. These prefixes are listed in the table below. They represent a power of ten when added to the basic unit. Prefix and basic unit are closed up, whether written in full or abbreviated. The unpunctuated abbreviation represents both singular and plural forms.

m/s meters per second   km kilometer
cm centimeter(s)   mL milliliter(s)
ps picosecond(s)

In the International System, only numbers between 0.1 and 1,000 are used with SI units. Quantities larger than 1,000 or less than 0.1 are expressed by choosing a different unit of measurement. 11,200 meters, for example, is expressed more compactly as 11.2 kilometers. And the product of 365×3600 may be expressed not as 1,314,000 but as 1.314×10^6.

By the use of these special units of measurement and by the use of multiple powers of ten, lengthy numbers can be avoided by scientific writers using the International System. On those occasions when it is necessary to write lengthy numbers, they are not punctuated like numbers in general writing. Each group of three digits is separated not by a comma, but by a space. Digits on both sides of a decimal are thus separated, counting from the decimal point.

23 400 055   15 076.129 300 77

Some writers follow the European practice of using a decimal comma instead of a decimal point. Either styling is acceptable in technical writing.

PREFIXES USED WITH SI UNITS

Factor	Prefix	Symbol	Factor	Prefix	Symbol
10^{18}	exa	E	10^{-1}	deci	d
10^{15}	peta	P	10^{-2}	centi	c
10^{12}	tera	T	10^{-3}	milli	m
10^9	giga	G	10^{-6}	micro	μ
10^6	mega	M	10^{-9}	nano	n
10^3	kilo	k	10^{-12}	pico	p
10^2	hecto	h	10^{-15}	femto	f
10	deka	da	10^{-18}	atto	a

Biology and Medicine

Signs and Symbols

The section on Signs and Symbols at the end of this chapter lists the symbols commonly used in biology and medicine. In this section of the chapter, four kinds of symbols—the degree sign, the percent sign, the virgule, and diacritical marks—are briefly discussed because of their special application to biological and medical writing.

Degree sign Although there is some difference of opinion on this issue, it is generally recommended that the degree sign be included in expressions of temperature except in references to the Kelvin scale.

> 100°F
> 39°C

The use of the degree sign is described in paragraphs 16 and 17 of the section on Specific Styling Conventions, beginning on page 119, in Chapter 5, "The Treatment of Numbers." In that chapter, which is devoted to general, nontechnical writing, a space occurs between the degree sign and the abbreviation F or C (32° F; 0° C). In technical writing, the common practice is either to close up the notation entirely, as in the examples above, or to leave a space between the number and the degree sign (32 °F; 0 °C).

Percent sign When a specific amount is to be expressed, a numeral is used with the sign %. There is no space between the numeral and the percent symbol.

> studied 5.2% of the patients
> found that in 91% of the slides

The percent sign is included with all numerals in a series or unit combination, even if one of the numbers is zero.

> a variation of 0% to 10%

The symbol should never be substituted for the word *percent* or *percentage* without an accompanying number.

> a small percent of the test plants
> a greater percentage of the subjects experienced contraindications

Virgule In formal biological and medical writing, the virgule is substituted for the word *per* only when all three of these circumstances occur: (1) the expression contains units of measurement for time or physical quantities, (2) at least one element in the expression is or is part of a specific numerical quantity, and (3) each element of the pair is either a specific numeral quantity or a specific unit of measurement.

> a hemoglobin level of 16 gm/100 cc
> rats treated with $1W/cm^2$ for 10 min
> amylase test: 60-150 Somogyi units/100 mL

The virgule does not replace *per* if a prepositional phrase occurs between two or more segments of the construction. *Per* is also written out if one segment of the construction contains a series or if the construction does not contain a specific quantity or amount expressed in numbers.

40 units of insulin per day
6, 8, and 10 mg per hour
half a dozen weeks per year
one or two hours per day
about seven times a week

Diacritics The excessive use of diacritics unnecessarily complicates typesetting. To avoid these complications, most American scientific writers now omit diacritics whenever possible. For example, the bolle over the *A* in *Ångstrom* can be omitted without causing confusion, as can the umlaut in terms like *Böttger's* in *Böttger's test* and *Mönckeberg's* in *Mönckeberg's arteriosclerosis.* Acute or grave accent marks, as in *Bergonié's method* and *Lasègue's sign,* can also be dropped. However, there are instances in which a term's meaning may be changed by the omission of a diacritic, as in *atu* versus *atü* in the metric technical system. In cases like this, the diacritical marks should be retained.

Greek Letters

The table on page 140 gives the letters of the Greek alphabet, several of which are used in biological and medical writing. Typical uses of Greek letters include their appearance in units of measure (400μg), in clinical designations (γ-globulin; hemoglobin α chain deficiency), in statistical data ($\Sigma \times B^2 = 2{,}393.82$), in mathematical expressions (πr^2), and in generic drug names and chemical terms (β-amylase; α-methylphenethylamine sulfate).

In a sentence that begins with a Greek letter, it is not necessary to write out the name of the letter. The lowercase Greek form is retained, and the first English word to follow the letter is capitalized.

α, β-Unsaturated carbonyl compounds are . . .

When submitting a manuscript to a publisher, it is helpful to include on a separate sheet a list of all Greek letters used in the manuscript and the number of the page on which each first occurs. This practice will assist the editor and later the typesetter.

Arabic and Roman Numerals

Roman numerals have many specialized uses in formal biological and medical writing, especially in molecular biology and genetics and in established technical and medical terms, such as blood-clotting factors, ECG leads, or designations of cranial nerves.

Blood-clotting factor VII
lead II
the cranial nerves (II, IV, and IX) are . . .

Arabic numerals are also regularly used in biological and medical writing.

Medical writing uses these numerals especially with terms designating blood platelet factors, heart murmurs (to denote their intensity in grades 1 through 6), and with the terms *para, gravida,* and *abortus.* Arabic numbers are regularly used in the names of virus and organism types; however, roman numerals are frequently used for this purpose also.

> platelet factor 3
> gr. i/6 systolic [heart] murmur
> para 1
> gravida 3
> abortus 1
> adenovirus type 2
> B77 avian sarcoma virus RNA subunits
> HTLV–I

Taxonomic nomenclature

Living organisms have been given Latin names composed of a genus or generic name followed by a species or specific name. The combination of the two names is called a *binomial.* Binomials are italicized. The genus name is capitalized; the species name is lowercased. Depending on the structure of the sentence in which they occur, genus and species names may or may not be set off by commas or parentheses.

> Malaria is caused by protozoa of the genus *Plasmodium.*
>
> Everyone recognizes the bamboo-chomping, black-and-white, bearlike giant panda, but few know the long-tailed lesser panda, *Ailurus fulgens.*
>
> Some insects, such as the ladybug *(Hippodamia convergens)* and the mealybug destroyer *(Cryptolaemus montrouzieri),* are beneficial in the garden.

When a binomial occurs within an all-italic passage, it is set in roman type in order to distinguish it.

In botanical literature the species name is often capitalized if it has been derived from a proper name. Capitalization is optional, however, and if this styling is chosen, it should be followed consistently throughout a text.

> *Chionodoxa Luciliae*   *Iris Danfordiae*
> *Schlumbergera Bridgesii*   *Tulipa Kaufmanniana*

Zoological taxonomy, on the other hand, does not follow this convention. Thus, the binomial for the Lady Amherst's pheasant is styled *Chrysolophus amherstiae,* even though the species name is derived from a proper name.

After a binomial has been used once in a running text, the genus name may be abbreviated to its initial letter, uppercased and followed by a period.

> The tiger, *Felis tigris,* does not form lasting family bonds. By contrast the lion, *F. leo,* is a social animal that lives in large permanent family groups.

However, an abbreviation is not used when it is possible for the reader to confuse it with another genus mentioned in the text that begins with the same initial.

Genus names are sometimes followed by the abbreviation *sp.* (plural *spp.*) set in roman type. The abbreviation either refers to some or all of the species within a given genus or indicates that a species cannot be identified or has not yet been named.

> The microscope revealed the presence of *Paramecium* sp.
>
> Monkshood (*Aconitum* spp.) requires a rich but light soil.

Subspecies designations Living organisms all have a genus name and a species name. In addition, they may have a subspecies or subspecific name, also called a *variety* or *race* name. Like the species name, this third name is italicized and lowercased. If the genus and species names have already been given in the text, they can be abbreviated when the subspecies is named.

> The great horned owl, *Bubo virginianus,* is usually thought of as a dark brown bird, but the northern subspecies *B. v. subarcticus* is nearly pure white.

Subspecific names in zoology are styled like the example above. In botany, however, names of subspecies are often introduced by the designation *var.* These designations are always set in roman type.

> *Polygonum bistorta* var. *superbum*
> *Dahlia excelsa* var. *anemonaeflora*
> *Juniperus communis* var. *oblongapendula*

In taxonomic material the name of the first person or persons to propose a species or subspecies name may be given when the Latin name is first used, along with the date of naming. The author's name is sometimes abbreviated. Both the author's name and the date are set in roman type.

> *Homo sapiens* Linnaeus [*or* Linn. *or* L.], 1758

If there has been a change in the genus name, as is sometimes the case, the original author's name is added in parentheses.

> *Ocypus olens* (Muller)

Divisions larger than genus Taxonomic names of divisions larger than the genus (as subfamily, family, suborder, order, subclass, class, subphylum, and phylum) are capitalized and set in roman type. They are treated as plurals unless they are accompanied by a designation of category.

> Chordata (phylum)
> Mammalia (class)
> Carnivora (order)
> Canidae (family)
> Many Carnivora eat vegetable matter as well as flesh.
> The order Carnivora contains a wide range of forms.

Horticultural varieties The names of horticultural varieties or cultivars of plants follow the Latin names. Main words within the name are capitalized, and the names are set in roman and usually placed within single quotation marks.

Artesmisia schmidtiana nana 'Silver Mound'
Hippeastrum striatum 'Fulgidum'
Punica granatum 'Double Dwarf'
Scilla campanulata 'Juliana' or 'King of Whites'

Hybrids Plant and animal hybrids are usually indicated by the sign X meaning "crossed with." A space is left on either side of the X sign. Plant hybrid names may be written in several ways:

X *Tulipa*   (intergeneric)
X *Salix*

Crinum bulbispermum X *C. Moorei*   (interspecific, both species names given)

Garrya X *Thuretii*   (interspecific, a hybrid between two species of the genus *Garrya*, with *Thuretii* a created name for the hybrid)

Animal hybrids are usually expressed as a cross between the two parents, with the male parent listed first:

Bernicla canadensis X *Anser cygnoides*

Viruses Virus names are often given in the vernacular, without a Latin form. Usage is erratic as to styling, so no set formula can be given regarding the capitalization or phrasing of these terms. In general, however, virus names are written lowercase, and most proper nouns within them are capitalized.

human wart virus
vesicular stomatitis virus (serotype Indiana)
mosquito iridescent virus
Rauscher leukemia virus
Sindbis virus
California encephalitis virus
Epstein-Barr virus

Arabic numerals are usually used to designate types of viruses, but Roman numerals are sometimes used instead.

B77 avian sarcoma virus   reovirus type 3
Coxsackievirus B2   HTLV III
adenovirus type 2

One of the major medical dictionaries should be consulted regarding the styling of virus names. A list of titles is given in the Bibliography at the back of this book.

Vernacular forms Many Latin taxonomic names have English counterparts with a simplified spelling. These English names are set in roman type and are lowercased.

Chordata	chordate	Carnivora	carnivore
Mammalia	mammal	Canidae	canid

The styling of plant and animal names in the vernacular does not follow any one set of guidelines. Some ornithological publications routinely capitalize bird names, and animal-breed publications tend to capitalize all breed names. In most general-interest publications, references to breeds are usually capitalized, but references to animals that belong to those breeds are lowercased unless they contain a proper noun as a separate element, in which case the proper noun is capitalized. (For more on this use of capitals, see paragraph 5 in the section on Proper Nouns, Pronouns, and Adjectives, beginning on page 52, in Chapter 2, "Capitals, Italics, and Quotation Marks.")

> In the western states Hereford cattle are raised extensively.
> We saw 12 herefords in the field.

Consulting an unabridged dictionary, such as *Webster's Third New International Dictionary,* can provide further guidance regarding the capitalization of plant and animal names.

Many breed, hybrid, and varietal names are the coinages of their developers. Some of these are registered trademarks or have been patented. The styling of all of these should follow the preference of their developers.

> Bold Leader amaryllis   Golden Harvest trumpet daffodil
> Carey Quinn day lily   Sonata freesia

Nomenclature of Drugs and Diseases in Medical Copy

Nonproprietary drug names may be used in running text, but trade names should be avoided unless a manuscript has a specific reference to a particular drug. American Medical Association publications and some non-AMA journals request that their authors include a separate list of the nonproprietary names as well as the trade names of all drugs referred to in a manuscript. If a proprietary drug name is used, it should be capitalized and placed in parentheses after the first use of the generic name for the drug.

> was tranquilized with chlorpromazine (Thorazine)
> the administration of cholestyramine (Questran)

The names of diseases, signs, symptoms, syndromes, and other medical categories are written lowercase, with the exception of elements that are formed from proper names. These are capitalized.

> Buchwald's atrophy   muscular dystrophy
> Baker's cyst   rheumatoid arthritis
> dengue   Rocher's sign
> Graves' disease   Sanger-Brown ataxia
> foot-and-mouth disease   Wassermann reaction

Note that the names of diseases based upon the Latin names of pathological organisms are written lowercase and roman, even though the name of the organism itself may be capitalized and italicized.

> Canine rickettsiosis is caused by microorganisms of the genus *Rickettsia.*

Consulting one of the major medical dictionaries can help with most styling problems. See the Bibliography for a list of such dictionaries.

Computer Terminology

This section contains a brief discussion of the patterns of capitalization that are unique to computer terminology. The conventions described here apply to the great majority of computer languages. Also in this section is a discussion of some of the styling conventions to follow in reproducing a computer printout in typeset form. This conversion is often necessary because most printouts are not of a quality suitable for photographic reproduction.

Names of Computer Languages, Programs, and Networks

The names of many specific computer languages take the form of acronyms. These acronym letters and other abbreviations are set in roman type, without periods. Usually all letters are capitalized, but sometimes only the initial letter is capitalized.

> APL   BASIC   CP/M   PL/1   RPG II
> ALGOL *or* Algol   COBOL *or* Cobol
> FORTRAN *or* Fortran   Pascal *or* PASCAL

When the names of specific computer languages are written in full, usually the initial letter of each major word is capitalized. General or category names of the languages, such as *algorithmic language* or *problem-oriented language,* are usually lowercased. But some of these general names are the same as specific names. In these cases, the specific name is usually capitalized, the general name not.

> PL/1 is short for Programming Language 1
>   *but*
> a programming language

Names of dialects, versions, or subsets of specific computer languages, particularly if they form words, are usually written lowercase, with only the initial letters of major words capitalized.

> Code and Go FORTRAN
> True BASIC

The specific names of computer software, such as programs, subprograms, systems, packages, routines, and subroutines, are usually written as acronyms in full roman capitals. Less frequently the letters are written with only the initial letter capitalized.

OLTEP   Writing routine   OPUS   SPSS   PERT/TIME

The names of computer time-sharing networks are written with capitalized initial letters.

Compuserve *or* CompuServe
Dialog
Dow Jones News/Retrieval
The Source

Other Acronyms and Abbreviations

Acronyms other than computer-language names are also widely used in computer technology. These are set in roman type, without periods, and usually the letters are all capitalized. Plurals, where needed, are formed by adding a roman lowercase *s*.

ABEND   (abnormal end of task)
FIFO   (first in, first out)
PAM   (pulse amplitude modulation)
PROM   (programmable read-only memory)
RAM   (random access memory)
TSO   (time-sharing option)
new CCDs   (charge-coupled devices)

The styling of abbreviations varies in some instances. *Complementary metal oxide semiconductor,* for example, may be abbreviated CMOS or C-MOS. To find answers to styling problems, you can consult one of the computer dictionaries listed in the Bibliography at the back of this book. The same abbreviation should be used consistently throughout a text.

Styling of Computer Instructions and Other Statements

Computer instructions and specific computer-language terms such as reserved words are usually written in full roman capitals. Plurals are formed by adding a lowercase roman *s*. Instructions may be typeset as full capitals or as small capitals with capitalized initial letters.

BLOCK DATA   REDEFINES
BREAK IN   SIN
COS   TAB   TABs
DVCDN   WAIT macroinstruction
GOSUB GOSUBs   WRU is an inquiry character
GOTO   the statement GOTO 540

Numbers—even those below ten—in computer languages are expressed as figures.

Spacing or its absence can change meanings in many computer languages, so care should be taken to follow exactly the pattern of a computer printout when converting it to typeset form. Generally, a word space appears between each element within a statement.

Statement numbers are 1- to 5-digit numbers used to identify a particular computer statement. Extra space is left between a statement number and the following statement.

    11050 IF A4 > 0 OR F <> 1 THEN GOTO 1505
    11055 PRINT D1$; D0$; D1$; D8$

Operational signs (such as +, −, =, <>, *) should also have a space on each side.

    41   PRINT AT R + 1, C * 7 − 3; R * 25 + C * 6 − 30

When mathematical notation is written in computer languages, the symbols usually take the form of roman capital letters. Typeset versions are also set roman, and they also retain the computer mathematical signs, such as the asterisk that denotes multiplication.

    T2(− 15)   (A * B) − C = 14
    A→B   A/B
    Y = SQRF(A * X ** 2 − 4.0 * W)

Groupings of parentheses are used to show the sequence in which operations should be carried out. In most computer languages brackets are not used at all.

    X70 POKE((PEEK 16396 + 255 * PEEK 16397) + X), A(X)

Asterisks are often used to indicate multiplication and exponential forms. For example, in FORTRAN, C^3 is written as C ** 3.

Binary numbers, no matter how large, do not contain commas.

Load numbers to be added, 11010 and 11101, into registers A and B.

Signs and Symbols

Astronomy

SUN, GREATER PLANETS, ETC.

☉	the sun; Sunday
●, ☾, or ☽	the moon; Monday
●	new moon
☽, ●, ☽,)	first quarter
○ or ⊕	full moon
☾, ●, ☾, (	last quarter
☿	Mercury; Wednesday
♀	Venus; Friday
⊕, ⊖, or ♁	the earth
♂	Mars; Tuesday
♃	Jupiter; Thursday
♄ or ♄	Saturn; Saturday
♁, ♅, or ♅	Uranus

♆, ♆, or ♃	Neptune
♇	Pluto
☄	comet
* or ✱	fixed star

ASPECTS AND NODES

☌	conjuction—indicating that the bodies have the same longitude, or right ascension
☐	quadrature—indicating a difference of 90° in longitude, or right ascension
△	trine—indicating a difference of 120° in longitude, or right ascension

♂ opposition—indicating a difference of 180° in longitude, or right ascension; as, ♂ ♆ ☉ opposition of Neptune to the sun
☊ ascending node
☋ descending node

SIGNS OF THE ZODIAC

♈ Aries

♉ Taurus
♊ Gemini
♋ Cancer
♌ Leo
♍ Virgo
♎ Libra
♏ Scorpio
♐ Sagittarius
♑ Capricorn
♒ Aquarius
♓ Pisces

Biology

× crossed with; hybrid
+ wild type
F_1 offspring of the first generation
F_2 offspring of the second generation
F_3, F_4, F_5 offspring of the third, fourth, fifth, etc., generation

○ an individual, specif., a female—used chiefly in inheritance charts
□ an individual, specif., a male—used chiefly in inheritance charts
♀ female
♂ or ♂ male

Chemistry

+ signifies "plus," "and," "together with," and is used between the symbols of substances brought together for, or produced by, a reaction; placed to the right of a symbol above the line, it signifies a unit charge of positive electricity: Ca^{++} denotes the ion of calcium which carries two positive charges

— signifies a single "bond," or unit of attractive force or affinity, and is used between the symbols of elements or groups which unite to form a compound: H—Cl for HCl, H—O—H, for H_2O; placed to the right of a symbol above the line, it signifies a unit charge of negative electricity: Cl^- denotes a chlorine ion carrying a negative charge; it is used also to indicate the removal of a part from a compound (as $-CO_2$)

· is used: (1) sometimes to indicate a single bond (as H·Cl for H—Cl) or (2) to denote the presence of a single unpaired electron (as H·) or (3) to separate parts of a compound regarded as loosely joined (as $CuSO_4 \cdot 5H_2O$)

◯ or ◎ denotes the benzene ring
= indicates a double bond; placed to the right of a symbol above the line, it signifies two unit charges of negative electricity (as $SO_4 =$, the negative ion of sulfuric acid carrying two negative charges)
≡ signifies a triple bond or a triple negative charge
: is used to indicate an unshared pair of electrons (as $:NH_3$) or sometimes a double bond
⦂ is used sometimes to indicate a triple bond
() marks groups within a compound [as in $C_6H_4(CH_3)_2$, the formula for xylene which contains two methyl groups (CH_3)]
⌐ or ⌐ join attached atoms or groups in structural formulas for cyclic compounds, as that for glucose

⌐——O——⌐
$CH_2OHCH(CHOH)_3CHOH$

= give or form
→ gives, leads to, or is converted to
⇌ forms and is formed from, is in equilibrium with

↓ indicates precipitation of the substance

↑ indicates that the substance passes off as a gas

≡ is equivalent—used in statements to show how much of one substance will react with a given quantity of another so as to leave no excess of either

1-,2, etc. used initially in names, refer-

ring to the positions of substituting groups, attached to the first, etc., of the numbered atoms of the parent compound

²H *also* H² deuterium

³H *also* H³ tritium

R group—used esp. of a univalent hydrocarbon group

X halogen atom

Z atomic number

Flowchart symbols

⊖ TERMINAL. Marks the beginning and the end of the flowchart.

☐ PROCESSING. Indicates the performance of a given task.

▽ MANUAL OPERATION.

◇ DECISION. Indicates a juncture at which a choice must be made.

⊏ ANNOTATION. Connected to the flowchart proper by a dotted line.

○ CONNECTOR. Used to indicate common points in the flow when connecting lines cannot be drawn.

▱ INPUT/OUTPUT. This is the general symbol for input/output. It may be replaced by one of the more specific symbols below.

▱ PUNCHED CARD.

▱ PUNCHED TAPE.

○ MAGNETIC TAPE.

▱ MANUAL INPUT. Usually indicates a keyboard device.

○ DISPLAY OUTPUT. Indicates a video display.

☐ DOCUMENT. Indicates output from a printing device (as a line printer).

α ON-LINE STORAGE. Indicates a mass storage unit (as a drum or disk).

∀ *or* ▽ OFF-LINE STORAGE. Indicates data storage that cannot be accessed directly by a computer.

↑ ← DIRECTION OF FLOW. Arrowheads need not be used when direction of flow is from top to bottom or from left to right.

⌐ COMMUNICATION LINK. Indicates a transfer of data from one location to another (as by a telephone connection).

Mathematics

+ plus; positive ⟨*a* + *b* = *c*⟩—used also to indicate omitted figures or an approximation

− minus; negative

± plus or minus ⟨the square root of $4a^2$ is ±$2a$⟩

× multiplied by; times ⟨6 × 4 = 24⟩—also indicated by placing a dot between the factors ⟨6•4 = 24⟩ or by writing factors other than numerals without signs

÷ *or* : divided by ⟨24 ÷ 6 = 4⟩—also indicated by writing the divisor under the dividend with a line between ⟨$\frac{24}{6}$ = 4⟩ or by writing the divisor

after the dividend with an oblique line between ⟨3/8⟩

= equals ⟨6 + 2 = 8⟩

≠ *or* ⧥ is not equal to

> is greater than ⟨6>5⟩

>> is much greater than

< is less than ⟨3<4⟩

<< is much less than

≧ *or* ≥ is greater than or equal to

≦ *or* ≤ is less than or equal to

≯ is not greater than

≮ is not less than

≈ is approximately equal to

≡ is identical to

∼ equivalent to

≅ is congruent to

∝ varies directly as; is proportional to

:   is to; the ratio of

∴   therefore

...   and so forth $\langle 1,2,3, \ldots \rangle$

∵   since

::   as (in ratios) $\langle 4{:}6{::}2{:}3 \rangle$

∞   infinity

$<$ *or* ⦤   angle; the angle $\langle \angle \text{ ABC} \rangle$

∟   right angle $\langle \llcorner \text{ ABC} \rangle$

⊥   the perpendicular; is perpendicular to $\langle \text{AB} \perp \text{CD} \rangle$

∥   parallel; is parallel to $\langle \text{AB} \parallel \text{CD} \rangle$

⊙ *or* ○   circle

⌒   arc of a circle

△   triangle

☐   square

▭   rectangle

√   root—used without a figure to indicate a square root (as in $\sqrt{4} = 2$) or with an index above the sign to indicate another degree (as in $\sqrt[3]{\ }\,3$, $\sqrt[3]{\ }\,7$); also denoted by a fractional index at the right of a number whose denominator expresses the degree of the root $\langle 3^{1/3} = \sqrt[3]{3} \rangle$

()   parentheses⎫

            ⎪ indicate that the quantities

[]   brackets⎬ enclosed by them are to

            ⎪ be taken

{}   braces⎭ together

—   (above the quantities) vinculum

Δ   the operation of finding the difference between two nearby values of a variable (as y) or of a function (as f) for two values of its independent variable (as x) differing by a small nonzero amount (as h) $\langle \Delta y = y_2 - y_1 \rangle$ $\langle \Delta f(x) = f(x+h) - f(x) \rangle$

∫   integral; integral of $\langle \int 2x\,dx = x^2 + C \rangle$

$\int_b^a$ the integral taken between the values a and b of the variable

∮   contour variable

δ_j^i Kronecker delta

s standard deviation of a sample taken from a population

σ   standard deviation of a population

Σ   sum; summation

$\bar{x}$ arithmetic mean of a sample of a variable x

μ   arithmetic mean of a population

μ_2 *or* σ^2 variance

x^2 chi-square

P the probability of obtaining a result as great as or greater than the observed result in a statistical test if the null hypothesis is true

r correlation coefficient

$E(x)$ expected value of the random variable x

π   pi; the number $3.14159265+$; the ratio of the circumference of a circle to its diameter

Π   product

!   factorial

e *or* ϵ (1) the number $2.7182818+$; the base of the natural system of logarithms (2) the eccentricity of a conic section

i the positive square root of minus one; $\sqrt{-1}$

n an unspecified number (as an exponent) esp. when integral

°   degree $\langle 60° \rangle$

′   minute; foot $\langle 30' \rangle$—used also to distinguish between different values of the same variable or between different variables (as $a\,'$, $a\,''$, $a\,'''$, usually read a prime, a double prime, a triple prime)

″   second; inch $\langle 30'' \rangle$

$^2, ^3$, etc.   —used as exponents placed above and at the right of an expression to indicate that it is raised to a power whose degree is indicated by the figure $\langle a^2$, the square of $a \rangle$

$^{-2}, ^{-3}$, etc.   —used as exponents placed above and at the right of an expression to indicate that the reciprocal of the expression is raised to the power whose degree is indicated by the figure $\langle a^{-2}$ equals $1/a^2 \rangle$

$\sin^{-1}x$ arc sine of x

$\cos^{-1}x$ arc cosine of x

$\tan^{-1}x$ arc tangent of x

$\cot^{-1}x$ arc cotangent of x

$\sec^{-1}x$ arc secant of x

$\text{cosec}^{-1}x$ arc cosecant of x

f function

f^{-1} the inverse of the function f

f' derivative of f
f'' second derivative of f
f^n n^{th} derivative of f
$\frac{df}{dx}$ derivative of f with respect to x
$\frac{\partial f}{\partial f}$ partial derivative of f with respect to x
$|z|$ the absolute value of z
$\oplus$ an operation in a mathematical system (as a group or ring) with $A \oplus B$ indicating the sum of the two elements A and B
$\otimes$ an operation in a mathematical system (as a group or ring) with $A \otimes B$ indicating the product of the two elements A and B

$[x]$ the greatest integer not greater than x
(a,b) the open interval $a<x<b$
$[a,b]$ the closed interval $a \leqq x \leqq b$
$(a,b]$ half-open interval
(a,b) or $\langle a,b \rangle$ ordered pair
$\aleph_0$ aleph-null
ω the ordinal number of the positive integers
$\cup$ union of two sets
$\cap$ intersection of two sets
$\subset$ is included in, is a subset of
$\supset$ contains as a subset
ϵ is an element of
$\notin$ is not an element of
Λ or 0 or ϕ or $\{\}$ empty set, null set

Medicine

$\overline{AA}$, $\overline{A}$, or āā   ana; of each
℞   take—used on prescriptions; prescription; treatment
☠   poison

APOTHECARIES' MEASURES

℥   ounce
f℥   fluidounce
fℨ   fluidram
min or ℔   minim

APOTHECARIES' WEIGHTS

℔   pound
℥   ounce (as ℥ i or ℥ j, one ounce; ℥ ss, half an ounce; ℥ iss or ℥ jss, one ounce and a half; ℥ ij, two ounces)
ʒ   dram
℈   scruple

Physics

α alpha particle
β beta ray
γ gamma; photon; surface tension
ϵ electromotive force; permittivity
η efficiency; viscosity
λ wavelength
μ magnetic moment; micro-, permeability
ν frequency; neutrino
ρ density; resistivity
σ conductivity; cross section; surface tension
ϕ luminous flux; magnetic flux
Ω ohm
a   acceleration
B   magnetic induction; magnetic field
c   speed of light in a vacuum
e   elementary electronic charge

e^- electron
E   energy; electric field; illumination
F   force
G   gravitational constant; conductance; weight
h   Planck's constant
$\hbar$ $h/2\pi$
H   enthalpy
L   inductance
m   mass
n   index of refraction
p   momentum of a particle
S   entropy
T   absolute temperature, period
V   electrical potential; frequency
W   energy
X   power of magnification, reactance
Y   admittance
Z   impedance

Weather

barometer, changes of
╱   Rising, then falling

╱   Rising, then steady; or rising, then rising more slowly

/   Rising steadily, or unsteadily
✓   Falling or steady, then rising; or rising, then rising more quickly
—   Steady, same as 3 hours ago
\\   Falling, then rising, same or lower than 3 hours ago
\\   Falling, then steady; or falling, then falling more slowly
\\   Falling steadily, or unsteadily
\\   Steady or rising, then falling; or falling, then falling more quickly
◎   calm
○   clear
◐   cloudy (partly)
●   cloudy (completely overcast)
+   drifting or blowing snow
,   drizzle
≡   fog
∾   freezing rain

〰 front, cold
〰 front, warm
〰 front, occluded
〰 front, stationary
)(funnel clouds
∞   haze
⬤   hurricane
6   tropical storm
↔   ice needles
•   rain
⁑   rain and snow
⥼   rime
⌇   sandstorm or dust storm
▽   shower(s)
▽̇   shower of rain
⊖   shower of hail
△   sleet
✳   snow
⎏   thunderstorm
⤳   visibility reduced by smoke

Chapter 7

The Treatment of Quotations

CONTENTS

Authors rely on two common conventions to indicate that a passage of prose or poetry is being quoted from another source. Short quotations are most commonly run in with the rest of the text and set off with quotation marks. Longer passages are most commonly indented as separate paragraphs without enclosing quotation marks. These paragraphs are usually referred to as *extracts, excerpts,* or *block quotations.* This chapter tells how authors decide which format to use. It also explains the conventions that apply to the treatment of long quotations set as extracts and specifies the conditions under which authors are allowed to alter the original source.

Most of the information needed to punctuate short run-in passages can be found in Chapter 1, "Punctuation," especially in the section on Quotation Marks, Double, beginning on page 39, but also in the sections on Brackets, Colon, Comma, Ellipsis Points, and Virgule. Information about the capitalization of run-in quotations can be found in the section on Beginnings, starting on page 49, in Chapter 2, "Capitals, Italics, and Quotation Marks."

Choosing between Run-in and Block Quotations

The length of a quotation usually determines whether it is run into the text or set as a block quotation. For prose quotations, length can be assessed in terms of the number of words, the number of typewritten or typeset lines, or the number of sentences in the passage. Authors who consider the number of words in making this decision usually run in quotations of less than 100 words and set off quotations of more than 100 words. Authors who base their decisions on the number of lines in the passage use cutoff points ranging from four to ten lines. When the number of sentences is the criterion, passages of one sentence in length are run in; passages of two or more sentences are set off as extracts, although some authors add the condition that the quotation must also run to at least four lines.

Each of these approaches relies on an arbitrary cutoff, and no matter which approach is used, the writer will want to make exceptions for certain sentences. For instance, writers who want to make a passage read more smoothly may prefer to run in the longer quotations, even if the system they are using would dictate that the quotations be set as extracts. Alternatively, writers who want to emphasize quoted passages to make them easier for the reader to locate will set even short quotations as extracts.

For quotations of poetry, different criteria are used. Full lines of poetry are usually set as extracts, although it is also common to run one or two lines into the text.

Styling Block Quotations

Block quotations are set off from the text that precedes and follows them by a number of devices, including (1) the addition of extra space between the quotation and the text; (2) indenting each line of the quoted matter —on the left only or on both right and left margins; (3) setting the quotation in smaller type; and (4) leaving less space between the lines of quoted material than there is between lines of the main text. Most often some combination of these devices is used, as in the examples below.

typeset passage with extra space between text and quotation, smaller type for the quotation, and each line indented

He took the title for his biography of Henry David Thoreau from a passage in *Walden*, one of Thoreau's most well-known books:

> I long ago lost a hound, a bay horse, and a turtle-dove, and am still on their trail. . . . I have met one or two who had heard the hound, and the tramp of the horse, and even seen the dove disappear behind a cloud, and they seemed as anxious to recover them as if they had lost them themselves.

However, the title *A Hound, a Bay Horse, and a Turtle-dove* probably puzzled some readers.

typewritten passage with less space between lines of the quotation and each line indented

```
He took the title for his biography of Henry David Thoreau

from a passage in Walden, one of Thoreau's most well-known

books:

     I long ago lost a hound, a bay horse, and a turtle-dove, and
     am still on their trail. . . . I have met one or two who had
```

```
heard the hound, and the tramp of the horse, and even seen
the dove disappear behind a cloud, and they seemed as
anxious to recover them as if they had lost them themselves.
```

```
However, the title A Hound, a Bay Horse, and a Turtle-dove
```

```
probably puzzled some readers.
```

Introductory Punctuation, Capitalization, and Indention

Typically, block quotations are preceded by a full sentence ending with a colon, and they begin with a full sentence whose first word is capitalized. However, if the opening words of the quoted passage can be made to flow with the syntax of an incomplete sentence that precedes the quotation, then no punctuation is required to introduce the extract, and the quotation can begin with a lowercase letter. (For an explanation of the conditions under which authors can alter the original capitalization of a quoted passage, see the section on Alterations, Omissions, and Interpolations in this chapter.)

> The chapter begins with a general description of interoffice memorandums:

> > The interoffice memorandum or memo is a means of informal communication within a firm or organization. Its special arrangement replaces the salutation, complimentary close, and written signature of the letter with identifying headings.

> They describe the interoffice memorandum as

> > a means of informal communication within a firm or organization. Its special arrangement replaces the salutation, complimentary close, and written signature of the letter with identifying headings.

If the sentence that precedes the quotation does not introduce the quotation or refer directly to it, the sentence ends in a period.

> As of the end of April she believed that the product had been introduced well and that it stood a good chance of success.

> > Unit sales are strong, revenues are better than forecast, shipments are being made on schedule, and inventory levels are stable.

A block quotation is sometimes introduced by a sentence that includes words or sentence fragments quoted from the same source as the quotation that follows.

> The report spoke of a "sense of direction" and "newfound optimism" in the community.

> > This community is building for its future. New institutions are being created, and existing ones are being strengthened. Civic, cultural, and social events are once again well attended.

When the beginning of a block quotation is also the beginning of a paragraph in the original, the first line of the quotation begins with extra indention.

> The first chapter includes a statement that should be encouraging to secretaries:

> In the past, many secretaries have been placed in positions of responsibility without being delegated enough authority to carry out the responsibility. The current pressures affecting managers have caused them to rethink the secretarial function and to delegate more responsibility and authority to their secretaries.

Quotations that include two or more consecutive paragraphs follow the paragraphing form of the original; each new paragraph is indented.

Quotations within an Extract

If a block quotation itself contains quoted material, that material is enclosed in double quotation marks.

> The authors of the book recommend the following procedures for handling reports:
>
> > The presiding officer will call for the appropriate report from an officer, a board member, a standing committee, or a special committee by saying, "Will the chairperson of the Ways and Means Committee please present the committee's report?" After the report is presented, a motion is heard to accept the report.

Dialogue in a block quotation is enclosed in quotation marks. The beginning of each speech is also marked by extra indention. If a speech runs to more than one paragraph, open quotation marks appear at the beginning of each paragraph of the extract; closing quotation marks appear only at the end of the final paragraph.

> Marion makes her invitation at the end of the first chapter, but Richard's reply is at least somewhat tentative.
>
> > "Would you like to come visiting again on your next vacation?" she asked.
> > "Yes, I would," I replied, "but I don't know when that will be. It's becoming harder and harder for me to find the time to get away.
> > "By the way," I went on, "I want to thank you for introducing me to those people last night."
> > "It was my pleasure," she said.
> > "I really appreciate it."
> > "I do hope you will come again."
> > "I'd like to."

Alterations, Omissions, and Interpolations

Although absolute accuracy is always of first importance when quoting from another source, there are certain kinds of alterations, omissions, and additions that authors and editors are traditionally allowed to make. Most of these alterations occur at the beginning or end of the quotation. The following paragraphs explain the kinds of changes that authors and editors may make and how these changes are indicated. All of the conventions described in this section are illustrated with block quotations; however, the conventions are equally applicable to run-in quotations. Examples of alterations, omissions, and interpolations occurring in run-in quotations can be found in the section on Brackets, beginning on page 5, and in the section on Ellipsis Points, beginning on page 28, in Chapter 1, "Punctuation."

Changing Capital or Lowercase Letters

If the opening words of a quotation act as a sentence within the quotation, the first word is capitalized, even if that word did not begin a sentence in the original version. (In the following example, the full version of the passage being quoted appears in the example on page 167.)

> The authors make exactly this point in the first chapter:
>
> > Many secretaries have been placed in positions of responsibility without being delegated enough authority to carry out the responsibility. The current pressures affecting managers have caused them to rethink the secretarial function and to delegate more responsibility and authority to their secretaries.

In some situations in which meticulous handling of original source material is required, the capital *M* would be placed in square brackets to indicate that it was not capitalized in the original source.

> The authors make exactly this point in the first chapter:
>
> > [M]any secretaries have been placed in positions of responsibility without being delegated enough authority to carry out the responsibility.

When the opening words of a quoted passage are joined syntactically to the sentence that precedes the quotation, the first word is generally not capitalized, even if it was capitalized in the original version. A few writers, however, retain the capital letter of the original in these circumstances. (Once again, the full version of the passage quoted below appears on page 167.)

> The author of this chapter knows full well that
>
> > in the past, many secretaries have been placed in positions of responsibility without being delegated enough authority to carry out the responsibility. The current pressures affecting managers have caused them to rethink the secretarial function and to delegate more responsibility to their secretaries.

Omissions at the Beginning or End of a Quotation

If an omission is made from the beginning of a quotation, no ellipsis points are required. However, style varies somewhat on this point, and some writers will use ellipsis points for this kind of omission, although usually only in very formal contexts.

> They describe an interoffice memorandum as
>
> > . . . a means of informal communication within a firm or organization. Its special arrangement replaces the salutation, complimentary close, and written signature of the letter with identifying headings.
>
> *but more commonly*
>
> They describe an interoffice memorandum as

a means of informal communication within a firm or organization. Its special arrangement replaces the salutation, complimentary close, and written signature of the letter with identifying headings.

A quoted passage that is cut off before a period in the original may be concluded with a period and a set of three ellipsis points to show that the last part of the original sentence was omitted. Any original punctuation at the end of the quotation—with the exception of question marks and exclamation points, which are discussed in the next paragraph—may then be dropped. In the example given below, the quoted passage ended with a comma in the original version. In the extract, the first of the four periods at the end of the passage marks the end of the sentence; the periods that follow are ellipsis points that indicate the omission of material.

> The book offers this advice about overseas calls:
>
>> Give the Overseas Operator the same information that you would give to the regular Long-distance Operator. There may be a delay, but it is possible to call practically every telephone in the world by this method. Direct dialing is also available to many countries. . . .

If the final sentence in the original version ends in an exclamation point or a question mark, that mark of punctuation is retained and is preceded by three ellipsis points. In the example given below, words that immediately precede the question mark in the original version are omitted.

> The authors recommend that secretaries take the following steps to improve their working environment:
>
>> You could think of ways to improve the flow of paperwork: Where do backlogs occur, for example, and where and why do most errors occur? Can you design a new rubber stamp or sticker to help speed the flow of paper? Are there ways to reduce interruptions to your work . . . ?

Omissions within Quotations

Omission of a full paragraph   If a full paragraph or more is omitted from a block quotation, the omission is indicated by ellipsis points at the end of the paragraph that comes before the omission. In the example that follows, the quoted passage includes text from two different paragraphs in the original version and omits entirely an intervening paragraph.

> The chapter offers the following advice regarding preconference preparations:
>
>> After the cutoff date for preregistration, and usually one week before the meeting, the rooming list of conference participants should be sent to the conference manager. . . .
>>
>> Whenever possible, the conference name tags or badges should be prepared ahead of time and arranged in a system that will facilitate easy distribution. These items are often included in the conference packets. All convention- or conference-related materials should be assembled in packets for the participants. These items include the convention program, appropriate brochures, relevant reports, minutes, and other materials.

Omission at the beginning of a paragraph   If text is omitted from the beginning of any paragraph other than the first paragraph of the extract, the omission is marked by three ellipsis points at the beginning of the paragraph from which the omission has been made. Regular paragraph indention precedes the ellipsis points. The example that follows shows how the preceding example would look if the writer doing the quoting decided to omit the first two sentences of the final paragraph.

> The chapter offers the following advice regarding preconference preparations:
>
> > After the cutoff date for preregistration, and usually one week before the meeting, the rooming list of conference participants should be sent to the conference manager. . . .
> > . . . All convention- or conference-related materials should be assembled in packets for the participants. These items include the convention program, appropriate brochures, relevant reports, minutes, and other materials.

Omission within a sentence   Omissions from quoted material that fall within a sentence are indicated by three ellipsis points.

> The chapter offers the following advice regarding preconference preparations:
>
> > Whenever possible, the conference name tags should be . . . arranged in a system that will facilitate easy distribution.

Punctuation used in the original that falls on either side of the ellipsis points is often omitted; however, it may be retained, especially if such retention helps clarify the meaning or structure of the sentence.

> The chapter offers the following advice regarding preconference preparations:
>
> > After the cutoff date for preregistration . . . the rooming list of conference participants should be sent to the conference manager. . . .
> >   Whenever possible, . . . badges should be prepared ahead of time and arranged in a system that will facilitate easy distribution.
> >
> > *or*
> >
> > After the cutoff date . . . , the rooming list of conference participants should be sent to the conference manager. . . .

Omission of a full sentence   If an omission comprises an entire sentence or the beginning or end of a sentence within a paragraph, the end punctuation preceding or following the omission is retained and followed by three periods.

> The chapter offers the following advice regarding preconference preparations:
>
> > Whenever possible, conference name tags or badges should be prepared ahead of time and arranged in a system that will facilitate easy distribution. . . . All convention- or conference-related materials should be assembled in packets. . . . These items include the convention program, appropriate brochures, relevant reports, minutes, and other materials.

On page 164 we presented the following description of how authors choose between block and run-in formats for prose quotations:

> The length of a quotation usually determines whether it is run into the text or set as a block quotation. . . . Length can be assessed in terms of the number of words, the number of typewritten or typeset pages, or the number of sentences in the passage.

The capitalization of the word *Length* in the second example is generally acceptable, although in some situations in which meticulous handling of original source material is required, the capital *L* would be placed in square brackets. For an example of this use of square brackets, see the second example on page 168.

Other Minor Alterations

Archaic spelling and punctuation   Archaic spellings and styles of punctuation should be preserved in direct quotations if they do not interfere with a reader's comprehension. If they occur frequently in a quotation, the author may wish to modernize them. An explanation to this effect should be placed in the text, in a note, or in a general statement within the preface if such modernizing has been done throughout the work. On the other hand, obvious typographical errors in modern works may be corrected without explanation.

Insertions   Sometimes an author wishes to insert into a quotation a brief explanation, clarification, summary of omitted material, or correction. These insertions (also called *interpolations*) are enclosed in square brackets. This use of brackets is explained and illustrated in the section on Brackets, beginning on page 5, in Chapter 1, "Punctuation."

Italics added   Words that were not italicized in the original version of a text may be italicized in the quoted passage in order to give emphasis to a particular word or phrase if the author informs the reader of the change. Any of several notations may be used. The notation may appear in the quoted passage, following the italicized portion, or at the end of the passage.

In works that include footnotes or other kinds of source notes, the notation may be set as a footnote or added to a source note. Common examples of notations are "italics mine," "emphasis added," and "italics added."

> The first chapter includes a statement that should be encouraging to secretaries:
>
> > In the past, many secretaries have been placed in positions of responsibility *without being delegated enough authority to carry out the responsibility.* The current pressures affecting managers have caused them to rethink the secretarial function and to delegate more responsibility and authority to their secretaries. [Italics mine.]
>
> The chapter offers the following advice regarding preconference preparations:

> Whenever possible, conference name tags or badges should be prepared ahead of time and arranged in a system for early distribution. These items are often included in the conference packets. *All convention- or conference-related materials should be assembled in packets for the participants.* [Emphasis added.] These items include the convention program, appropriate brochures, relevant reports, minutes, and other materials.

If the note is placed at the end of the passage, parentheses may be used in place of brackets.

Footnote or endnote reference symbols or numbers are usually omitted from short quotations. In their place, authors often insert their own references.

Quoting Verse

The major difference between quotations of prose and poetry is that lines of poetry keep their identity as separate lines when set as extracts and also when run in with the text. When more than one line is run in, the poetic lines are separated by a virgule. When poetic lines are set as extracts, the lines are divided exactly as in the original.

> When Gerard Manley Hopkins wrote that "Nothing is so beautiful as spring— / When weeds, in wheels, shoot long and lovely and lush," he probably had my yard in mind.

> The experience was one that reminded them of the wisdom of Pope's observation:
>
> > A little learning is a dang'rous thing;
> > Drink deep, or taste not the Pierian spring:
> > There shallow draughts intoxicate the brain,
> > And drinking largely sobers us again.

Style varies regarding spacing around the virgule. Some authors and publishers put no space on either side; others prefer a word space on each side. The virgule is sometimes omitted when each line of the original begins with a capital letter and the quotation contains no other capitals. Up to three or four lines of poetry are sometimes run in if they are closely integrated with the text. However, quotations of as few as two lines of poetry are commonly set off from the text as extracts.

> It was a fatalistic view of life that seemed to say, as James Payn did, "I never had a piece of toast / Particularly long and wide; / But fell upon the sanded floor, / And always on the buttered side."

> Some lines from Wordsworth seemed to express their attitude:
>
> > Bliss was it in that dawn to be alive,
> > But to be young was very heaven!

Horizontal Spacing

In typeset material, poetry quoted as an extract is usually arranged so that the longest line is centered on the page and the first word of all other flush-left lines align above or below the first word of the longest line. If the poem includes varied line lengths and indention, the alignment in the original version should be preserved. In typewritten material, authors will frequently choose a uniform indention for all lines that are flush left in the original version rather than center each poetry extract separately. Authors using this approach still indent lines that are not flush left in such a way as to preserve the alignment in the original.

Consider these stanzas from Edgar Allen Poe, the first from "Annabel Lee," the second from "The Bells."

> She was a child and I was a child,
>   In this Kingdom by the sea,
> But we loved with a love that was more than love—
>   I and my Annabel Lee—
> With a love that the wingèd seraphs of Heaven
>   Coveted her and me.

> Hear the sledges with the bells—
>   Silver bells!
> What a world of merriment their melody foretells!
>   How they tinkle, tinkle, tinkle,
>   In the icy air of night!
> While the Stars that oversprinkle
> All the heavens seem to twinkle
>   With a crystalline delight;
>   Keeping time, time, time,
>   In a sort of Runic rhyme
> To the tintinnabulation that so musically wells
>   From the bells, bells, bells, bells,
>   Bells, bells, bells—
> From the jingling and the tinkling of the bells.

If the quotation does not start at the beginning of the line, the alignment in the quotation should still follow the original.

He praised her with words taken from Shelley:

> Wit and sense,
> Virtue and human knowledge, all that might
> Make this dull world a business of delight,

For an explanation of how to style poetry quotations that do not end in a period, see page 175.)

Sometimes the lines of a poem are too long to center. In these cases, the quotation may be set using a standard indention; runover lines are indented further.

They were asked to comment on the following lines by Walt Whitman:

> You flagg'd walks of the cities! you strong curbs at the edges!

You ferries! you planks and posts of wharves! you
     timber-lined sides! you distant ships!
You rows of houses! you window-pierc'd façades! you roofs!
You porches and entrances! you copings and iron guards!
You windows whose transparent shells might expose so much!
You doors and ascending steps! you arches!
You gray stones of interminable pavements! You trodden crossings!
From all that had touch'd you I believe you have imparted to yourselves and now
     impart the same secretly to me,
From the living and the dead you have peopled your impassive surfaces, and the
     spirits thereof would be evident and amicable with me

Quotation Marks in Poetry

If a quotation mark occurs at the beginning of a line of poetry, it should
be aligned with the first letter of other lines. In a speech that extends over
several lines, quotation marks are placed at the beginning of the speech
and at the beginning of each stanza within the speech as well as at its
conclusion.

They based their comments on the following lines from Matthew Arnold's
"Stanzas from the Grande Chartreuse":

O children, what do ye reply? —
"Action and pleasure, will ye roam
Through these secluded dells to cry
And call us? — but too late ye come!
Too late for us your call ye blow,
Whose bent was taken long ago.

"Long since we pace this shadowed nave,
We watch those yellow tapers shine,
Emblems of hope over the grave,
In the high altar's depth divine;
The organ carries to our ear
Its accents of another sphere.

"Fenced early in this cloistral round
Of reverie, of shade, of prayer,
How should we grow in other ground?
How can we flower in foreign air?
—Pass, banners, pass, and bugles, cease;
And leave our desert to its peace!"

Omissions from Poetry

When a full line or several consecutive lines of poetry are omitted from
a quotation, the omission is indicated by a line of spaced points. The lines
of points extend the length of the preceding line or of the missing line.

Whitman's attitude on the subject is revealed in these lines from "When I
Heard the Learned Astronomer":

When I heard the learned astronomer,
. . . .
How soon unaccountable I became tired and sick,
Til rising and gliding out I wandered off by myself,

> In the mystical moist night-air, and from time to time,
> Looked up in perfect silence at the stars.

Style varies regarding the treatment of poetry quotations that do not end in a period. Sometimes authors indicate an omission with ellipsis points, sometimes they prefer not to use ellipsis points but rather to reproduce the text exactly as it appeared in the original version.

> Whitman's attitude on the subject is revealed in these lines from "When I Heard the Learned Astronomer":
>
> > When I heard the learned astronomer,
> > . . . .
> > How soon unaccountable I became tired and sick, . . .

or

> Whitman's attitude on the subject is revealed in these lines from "When I Heard the Learned Astronomer":
>
> > When I heard the learned astronomer,
> > . . . .
> > How soon unaccountable I became tired and sick,

Attribution of Sources

The ways in which authors acknowledge the sources of quotations vary with the kind of publication they are writing for and the kind of system that they are using to document sources of information throughout the work. In some cases, simply including the author's name is sufficient; in other cases, full bibliographical information is required, including the name of the publisher of the work quoted, the date of publication, and the number of the page on which the original passage can be found. The following paragraphs describe some of the alternative methods that are available to authors. For more on the details of styling such documentation, see Chapter 8, "Notes and Documentation of Sources."

In Works without Notes or a Bibliography

In works that do not include footnotes, endnotes, or a bibliography, authors often include all necessary information in the body of the text preceding the quotation.

> Levin summarizes these points in an article entitled "The Office in the Electronic Age" on page 46 of the March, 1982, issue of *The Office*:
>
> > The quality of work in general, whether involving electronic equipment or not, is based on the manager's knowing the responsibilities of each worker, careful assignment of tasks, effective written and oral communication, and periodic evaluation and modification of procedures.

An alternative method used in books that do not include notes or a bibliography is to run in all bibliographical information in a parenthetical note that follows the quotation. If the quotation is a run-in quotation the note comes between the closing quotation mark and the terminal punctuation of the sentence. If the quotation is set as an extract, the note follows the terminal punctuation.

> Levin makes the same points when she says, "The quality of work in general, whether involving electronic office equipment or not, is based on the manager's knowing the responsibilities of each worker, careful assignment of tasks, effective written and oral communication, and periodic evaluation and modification of procedures" ("The Office in the Electronic Age," *The Office*, March 1982, 46).

> Levin has summarized these points as follows:

>> The quality of work in general, whether involving electronic office equipment or not, is based on the manager's knowing the responsibilities of each worker, careful assignment of tasks, effective written and oral communication, and periodic evaluation and modification of procedures. ("The Office in the Electronic Age," *The Office*, March 1982, 46)

In each of these examples, it is assumed that the author's full name has already been given in the text and therefore does not need to be repeated.

In Works with Footnotes or Endnotes

In works that include footnotes or endnotes, the source of a quotation can be indicated by a raised reference number or reference mark that is placed at the end of the quoted passage after any terminal punctuation. For a full description of how to style footnotes and endnotes, see the section on Footnotes and Endnotes, beginning on page 180, in Chapter 8, "Notes and Documentation of Sources."

> Levin makes the same point when she says, "The quality of work in general, whether involving electronic office equipment or not, is based on the manager's knowing the responsibilities of each worker, careful assignment of tasks, effective written and oral communication, and periodic evaluation and modification of procedures."[17]

> Levin has summarized these points as follows:

>> The quality of work in general, whether involving electronic office equipment or not, is based on the manager's knowing the responsibilities of each worker, careful assignment of tasks, effective written and oral communication, and periodic evaluation and modification of procedures.[17]

If a work with footnotes and endnotes includes more than one quotation from the same source, reference to full bibliographical information is required only at the first quotation. The usual practice is to include an explanation with the footnote to the first quotation that all subsequent references to that work in the text are from the same source. Having done that, one needs only to mention the page number at subsequent references.

> Levin makes the same point when she says, "The quality of work in general, whether involving electronic office equipment or not, is based on the

manager's knowing the responsibilities of each worker, careful assignment of tasks, effective written and oral communication, and periodic evaluation and modification of procedures" (p. 46).

Levin has summarized these points as follows:

> The quality of work in general, whether involving electronic office equipment or not, is based on the manager's knowing the responsibilities of each worker, careful assignment of tasks, effective written and oral communication, and periodic evaluation and modification of procedures. (p. 46)

In a Work with Parenthetical References

In a work utilizing parenthetical references to provide bibliographical information, the parenthetical reference is either included in the sentence that precedes the quotation or placed after the quotation, as were the page references in the preceding examples. Note that these references are placed before the terminal punctuation of a run-in quotation, but after the terminal punctuation of an extract. For more on the placement of parenthetical references, see the section on Parenthetical References, beginning on page 192, in Chapter 8, "Notes and Documentation of Sources."

In Other Contexts

In a context in which only the author's name or the author's name and the title of the work quoted are required, the attribution can be placed on its own line following the quotation. The attribution is usually set flush right and either enclosed in parentheses or preceded by an em dash. In a variation on this arrangement, the attribution may be run in with the quotation and either enclosed in parentheses or preceded by a dash.

> I went to the woods because I wished to live deliberately, to front only the essential fact of life, and see if I could not learn what it had to teach, and not, when I came to die, discover that I had not lived.
> —Henry David Thoreau, *Walden*

> That things always collapse into the *status quo ante* three weeks after a drive is over, everybody knows and apparently expects. . . . And yet many managements fail to draw the obvious conclusion. . . .
> (Peter F. Drucker)

> Winter lies too long in country towns; hangs on until it is stale and shabby, old and sullen. —Willa Cather, *My Ántonia*

When an attribution line follows a passage of poetry, the line may be set flush right, or it may be centered on the longest line in the quotation, or it may be indented a standard distance from the right margin.

> If this belief from heaven be sent,
> If such be Nature's holy plan,
> Have I not reason to lament
> What Man has made of Man?
> —William Wordsworth, "Lines Written in Early Spring"

The sun descending in the west,
The evening star does shine;
The birds are silent in their nest,
And I must seek for mine.
    —William Blake, "Night"

Happy the man whose wish and care
  A few paternal acres bound,
Content to breathe his native air
  In his own ground.
               —Alexander Pope, "Ode on Solitude"

Chapter 8

Notes and Documentation of Sources

CONTENTS

Writers and editors often need to provide readers with information that they do not wish to make part of their main text. This type of information is usually included in a note, which may take the form of a footnote at the bottom of a page, an endnote at the end of a chapter or at the end of a work, or a note in parentheses. A principal reason for using notes is to document the source of a quotation or a piece of information. In addition, authors use footnotes and endnotes to offer additional information and commentary and sometimes to provide cross-references.

Authors and editors use various methods to indicate the source of a given quotation or piece of information. In works related to the social and natural sciences, writers have relied on a system of parenthetical references within the text that refer readers to a list of sources at the end of the work or one of its divisions. In works related to the humanities, the footnote form has traditionally been preferred. In recent years, however, the footnote form has become slightly less popular, as some style books have urged writers in the humanities to adopt parenthetical references. For more on the reasons why writers are being encouraged to avoid footnotes and endnotes, see the section on Footnotes and Endnotes that follows.

Despite these urgings, footnotes and endnotes are still widely used, and this chapter describes both the footnote or endnote system and the system of parenthetical references. For both of these systems, the examples in this chapter illustrate ways of styling references that are generally acceptable when writing for most kinds of publications. However, writers and editors should be aware that many professions and academic disciplines have developed their own systems for documenting sources, and some of these systems differ from the stylings illustrated in this chapter. Professions and disciplines that have developed their own systems usually rely on a published style manual that describes the system. A list of some of these style manuals can be found in the Bibliography at the end of this book.

Footnotes and Endnotes

A footnote or an endnote keys full bibliographical information about a source, including author, title, place of publication, publisher, date, and page number, to a specific text passage making use of that source. The text passage is marked with a number, and all such notes are set aside from the rest of the text. Notes that appear at the bottom of the page are called *footnotes*. Notes that appear at the end of the chapter or at the end of an entire work are called *endnotes*.

Some recently published style manuals have discouraged the use of footnotes and endnotes for providing readers with bibliographical information about sources. Among the obvious difficulties with footnotes is that they are troublesome for typists to type and expensive for typesetters to set. The problem is that it is necessary to reserve sufficient space at the bottom of each page to allow for the notes that go with the text on that page. While the last note on a page may go over to the next page, each note should begin on the same page on which its number appears in the text. If there are many notes on a page, the result can be an unattractive page with more space given to footnotes than to text. And in some cases, there may be no way to get each footnote to begin on the same page as its text reference without rewriting some portion of the main text or the footnote or both.

The disadvantage of endnotes is less a matter of difficulty and cost for the author, typist, or typesetter than of inconvenience for the reader. When reading a book with endnotes, the reader has to flip back and forth in the book from the main text to the notes. This can be especially frustrating when the note contains no more than a page reference to a work already cited.

The use of parenthetical references to document sources does not guarantee that writers and readers will be saved entirely from these disadvantages. However, it does usually result in fewer footnotes or endnotes, and it does allow authors to treat notes that provide strictly bibliographical information—the details of which readers are often willing to do without—differently from notes that provide commentary, cross-references, or additional information. For more on the styling of parenthetical references, see the section on Parenthetical References in this chapter.

Placement of the Elements

Footnotes and endnotes to a text are indicated by unpunctuated Arabic superior numbers (or reference symbols, discussed later in this section) placed immediately after the quotation or information with no intervening space. The number is usually placed at the end of a sentence or clause, or at some other natural break in the sentence when the reference material is not a quotation. The number follows all marks of punctuation except the dash. If a terminal quotation mark appears (as at the end of a short quotation that is included in the running text), the numeral is placed outside the final quotation mark with no space intervening (see the sample on page 182). The numbering may be consecutive throughout the work or, as in the case of book-length works, it may begin again with each new chapter. Footnotes to tables and illustrations are numbered separately, as described in Chapter 9, "Illustrations and Tables."

Footnote numbers like 7a and 7b, which usually result from last-minute revisions in the manuscript, are to be avoided, even if it means renumbering all the notes in the copy.

The text of the note itself is introduced with the applicable Arabic numeral or reference symbol. The numeral may be a superior numeral, unpunctuated and separated from the first word of the footnote by one space, or it may be set on the line and followed by a period and one or two spaces. The latter styling has become more popular recently and is much easier to type.

traditional styling
[7] Ibid., p. 223.

newer styling
7. Ibid., p. 223.

The indention of footnote and endnote text varies according to individual preference. Indenting the first line of the footnote to a paragraph indent with runover lines returning to flush left (as shown on pages 184 and 186) is probably the most common styling. However, the flush-left styling and the flush-and-hang styling, in which the first line is set flush left and succeeding lines are indented, are also common. The following examples reproduce the first three footnotes on page 184. In these examples, the reference number is set on the line in the flush-left styling and is raised in the flush-and-hang styling; however, either of the positions for reference numbers may be used with any of the indention styles.

flush left
1. Jennie Mason, *Introduction to Word Processing* (Indianapolis: Bobbs-Merrill, 1981), p. 55.
2. John E. Warriner and Francis Griffith, *English Grammar and Composition* (New York: Harcourt Brace Jovanovich, 1977), p. 208.
3. Ruth I. Anderson et al., *The Administrative Secretary: Resource* (New York: McGraw-Hill, 1970), p. 357.

flush and hang
[1] Jennie Mason, *Introduction to Word Processing* (Indianapolis: Bobbs-Merrill, 1981), p. 55.

According to Lesikar, if a "quoted passage is four lines or less in length, it is typed with the report text and is distinguished from the normal text by quotation marks."[17] However, a different procedure is used for longer quotations:

> But if a longer quotation (five lines or more) is used, the conventional practice is to set it in from both left and right margins (about five spaces) but without quotation marks. . . . The quoted passage is further distinguished from the report writer's work by single spacing. . . .[18]

A series of usually three periods called ellipsis is used to indicate omissions of material from a passage.[19]

Footnotes may be placed "at the bottom of the page . . . separated from the text by a horizontal line. If a line is used, it is typed a single space below the text and followed by one blank line."[20] Lesikar prefers the separation line to be one and one-half or two inches.[21] Generally, typewriting textbooks state that a two-inch line is adequate (20 pica strokes; 24 elite strokes). The line is constructed by striking the underscore key.

From a typing standpoint, reserve three lines of blank typing space per footnote at the bottom of the page.

17. Report Writing for Business (Homewood, Ill.: Richard D. Irwin, Inc., 1981), p. 187.

18. Ibid.

19. Ibid., p. 188.

20. Ruth I. Anderson et al., The Administrative Secretary: Resource (New York: McGraw-Hill Book Company, 1970), p. 391.

21. Lesikar, op. cit., p. 189.

Figure 8.1. A typewritten page with footnotes

 ² John E. Warriner and Francis Griffith, *English Grammar and Composition* (New York: Harcourt Brace Jovanovich, 1977), p. 208.

 ³ Ruth I. Anderson et al., *The Administrative Secretary: Resource* (New York: McGraw-Hill, 1970), p. 357.

In typewritten publications, the notes themselves are usually single-spaced, but double spacing is used between notes. When a manuscript is being typed prior to typesetting, however, the notes should be double-spaced internally with triple spacing between the notes. In typeset material, footnotes and endnotes are usually set in type that is one or two points smaller than the text type. Extra space may or may not be placed between the notes according to individual preference.

When endnotes rather than footnotes are being used, all of the notes are gathered together in a single list (as shown on page 184) either at the end of a chapter or other section or at the end of an entire work. When a book uses a single note section at the end of the entire work, the section is usually divided with chapter headings to indicate where the notes of a particular chapter begin and end. An endnote may be styled in any of the ways that a footnote is styled.

Content and Styling for First References

Both footnotes and endnotes provide full bibliographical information for a source the first time it is cited; however, in subsequent references, this information is provided in an abbreviated manner. The following paragraphs describe the content and style used for first references. Subsequent references are discussed later in this section. Examples of the stylings described in this section are shown on pages 184 and 186. (The content and style for entries in bibliographies and lists of references are given in the section on Bibliographies and Lists of References later in this chapter.)

Books A footnote or endnote that refers to a book contains as many of the following elements as are relevant. Examples of each of the elements described below can be found in the references on page 184.

1. *Author's name* In footnotes and endnotes, the author's first name comes first and the last name after. If there are more than three authors, the first author's name is followed by the phrase *et al.,* which is an abbreviation for the phrase *et alii* or *et aliae,* meaning "and others." (For examples of notes describing books with multiple authors, see notes 2, 3, and 7 on page 184.) If a publication is issued by a group or organization and no individual is mentioned on the title page, the name of the group or organization may be used in place of an author's name; in this case, the group or organization is thought of as being the corporate author. (For an example of a note describing a work with a corporate author, see note 8 on page 184.) In footnotes and endnotes, the author's name is followed by a comma.

NOTES

1. Jennie Mason, *Introduction to Word Processing* (Indianapolis: Bobbs-Merrill, 1981), p. 55.

2. John E. Warriner and Francis Griffith, *English Grammar and Composition* (New York: Harcourt Brace Jovanovich, 1977), p. 208.

3. Ruth I. Anderson et al., *The Administrative Secretary: Resource* (New York: McGraw-Hill, 1970), p. 357.

4. Simone de Beauvoir, *The Second Sex,* trans. and ed. H. M. Parshley (New York: Alfred A. Knopf, 1953), p. 600.

5. Alfred H. Markwardt, *American English,* ed. J. L. Dillard (New York: Oxford University Press, 1980), p. 94.

6. Martha L. Manheimer, *Style Manual: A Guide for the Preparation of Reports and Dissertations,* Books in Library and Information Science, vol. 5 (New York: Marcel Dekker, 1973), p. 14.

7. Charles T. Brushaw, Gerald J. Alred, and Walter E. Oliu, *Handbook of Technical Writing,* 2d ed. (New York: St. Martins Press, 1982), pp. 182–184.

8. National Micrographics Association, *An Introduction to Micrographics,* rev. ed. (Silver Spring, Md.: National Micrographics Association, 1980), p. 42.

9. *The World Almanac and Book of Facts* (New York: Newspaper Enterprises Association, Inc., 1985), p. 310.

10. *Rules for Alphabetical Filing as Standardized by ARMA* (Prairie Village, Kans.: Association of Records Managers and Administrators, 1981), p. 14.

11. Peggy F. Bradbury, ed., *Transcriber's Guide to Medical Terminology* (New Hyde Park, N.Y.: Medical Examination Publishing Co., 1973), p. 446.

12. Kemp Malone, "The Phonemes of Current English," *Studies for William A. Read,* ed. Nathaniel M. Caffee and Thomas A. Kirby (Baton Rouge: Louisiana State University Press, 1940), p. 133–165.

13. Robert Chambers, *Cyclopaedia of English Literature,* 2 vols. (New York: World Publishing House, 1875), vol. 1, p. 45.

Figure 8.2. A page of endnotes illustrating footnote and endnote style for references to books

2. *Title of the work* The title is underlined in typewritten manuscript and italicized in type. Each word of the title is capitalized except for articles and short prepositions other than the first word. In cases in which no author's name is used in the note, the title comes first. This is commonly the styling for well-known reference books and for publications that have corporate authors but are more likely to be known by their titles. (For examples of notes in which the title comes first, see notes 9 and 10 on page 184.)

3. *Portion of the book* If a reference is to one portion of a book (as an essay within a collection), the name of the portion should be included. The titles of chapters within nonfiction works by a single author are usually not part of a footnote reference. The titles of parts of books, such as short poems, short stories, and essays, are enclosed in quotation marks. (For an example of a reference to a work within a collection, see note 12 on page 184.)

4. *Editor, compiler, or translator* The name of an editor, compiler, or translator is preceded by the abbreviation *ed., comp.,* or *trans.* or some combination of them joined by *and.* The abbreviation is separated from the title that precedes it by a comma. (For examples of notes describing a book with a translator or editor, see notes 4, 5, and 12 on page 184.) If there is no author mentioned on the title page of the book, the name of the editor, compiler, or translator is placed first in the note, followed by the abbreviation *ed., comp.,* or *trans.* (For an example of a note in which the editor's name comes first, see note 11 on page 184.)

5. *Name of the series* If a book is part of a series, the name of the series should be included. If the book corresponds to a specific volume in that series, the volume number is also included. The volume number is separated from the title by a comma. The name of the series is separated from the title of the volume by a comma and is capitalized as a title, but it is not underlined or italicized. (For an example of a note describing a book that is part of a series, see note 6 on page 184.)

6. *Edition* If a work is other than the first edition, the number or the nature of the edition should be indicated. (For examples of notes describing books that are not first editions, see notes 7 and 8 on page 184.)

7. *Volume number* If a work has more than one volume, the total number of volumes is given after the title and edition data. In addition, the number of the particular volume cited should precede the page number. In traditional footnote styling, a *vol.* or *vols.* precedes the volume number, but many authors now omit these abbreviations. (For an example of a note referring to a multivolume work, see note 13 on page 184.)

8. *Publishing data* The city of publication, the name of the publisher, and the year of publication should all be included. These items are usually placed within parentheses; a colon separates the city from the pub-

---

NOTES

1. John Heil, "Seeing is Believing," *American Philosophical Quarterly* 19 (1982): 229–239.

2. Donald K. Ourecky, "Cane and Bush Fruits," *Plants & Gardens* 27, No. 3 (Autumn 1971): pp. 13–15.

3. Xan Smiley, "Misunderstanding Africa," *Atlantic* (Sept. 1982): pp. 70–79.

4. Shiva Naipaul, "A Trinidad Childhood," *New Yorker* (17 Sept. 1984): pp. 63–64.

5. Gail Pitts, "Money Funds Holding Own," *Morning Union* [Springfield, Mass.] (Aug. 23, 1982): p. 6.

6. Jeremy C. Rosenberg, "Letters," *Advertising Age* (7 June, 1982): p. M–1.

7. M. O. Vassell, rev. of *Applied Charged Particle Optics,* ed. A. Septier, *American Scientist* 70 (1982): 229.

8. Joyce A. Velasquez, "The Format of Formal Reports," report prepared for the Southern Engineering Company, Johnson City, Miss. (May 29, 1985).

9. Clive Johnson, letter to Elizabeth O'Hara, 9 Nov. 1916, Johnson Collection, item 5298, California State Historical Society, San Marino, Calif.

Figures 8.3. Sample notes showing footnote and endnote styling for references to periodicals and unpublished sources

lisher's name. Names of states may be abbreviated, but not names of cities. A comma separates the publisher's name from the year of issue.

9. *Page number* The number of the page on which the quotation or piece of information can be found should be included. In traditional footnote styling a *p.* or *pp.* precedes the page number or numbers; however, many authors now omit those abbreviations.

Periodicals A footnote or endnote describing an article in a periodical should include all of the following information that is relevant. Examples of each of the elements described below can be found in the sample references on this page.

1. *Author's name* The author's name is treated in the same way as described above for a reference to a book. The names of writers of letters to a periodical and contributors of signed book reviews are

treated like names of authors. (For examples of references to a letter and to a signed review, see notes 6 and 7 in the sample above.)

2. *Title of the article* The title of the article is enclosed in quotation marks. The words of the title are capitalized as in a book title. The title of the article is followed by a comma that is placed inside the quotation marks.

3. *Name of the periodical* The name of the periodical is treated in the way described above for the title of a book.

4. *Volume and number of the periodical* If a periodical uses both volume and number designations to identify an issue, both should be used. If a periodical uses some other system for identifying issues (as the month and year of issue), that system should be used. Note 1 on page 186 illustrates a reference to a periodical in which pages are numbered consecutively through a volume, and therefore only a volume number is required. Note 2 illustrates a reference to a periodical that uses a seasonal designation as well as volume and number designations for each issue, and which paginates each issue independently of the volume. Note 3 illustrates a reference to a monthly magazine. Most monthly magazines have a volume and number designation somewhere in them, but they are more commonly referred to by month and year.

5. *Issue date* Periodicals variously use months, days, and years to identify issues. The date is written in whatever form the periodical uses, but the names of the months may be abbreviated.

6. *Page number* The number of the page on which the quotation or piece of information can be found is included. The varying use and omission of the abbreviation *p.* or *pp.* as described above for books hold true for references to periodicals as well. One situation in which the abbreviation is almost always dropped occurs when the reference is to a volume number and page number only. In that case, the volume number and page number are separated by a colon, and neither is identified with an abbreviation. Notes 1 and 7 on page 186 illustrate this styling.

   NOTE: In making the decision of whether or not to include the abbreviation, writers and editors should keep in mind the needs of their readers. If most of the readers are well acquainted with footnote style, the abbreviation can be safely dropped. However, if a significant number of the readers of a text are unfamiliar with footnote styling, including the identifying abbreviation will help lessen the chances of confusion.

Unpublished materials A footnote referring to a work that is unpublished should include as many of the following elements as are known or are relevant. The elements described below are illustrated in notes 8 and 9 on page 186.

1. *Author's name* The author's name is treated in the same way as described above for a book.

2. *Title of the work* The title is enclosed in quotation marks and capitalized like a book title.
3. *The nature of the material* The reference should include a description of the document (as "letter" or "dissertation").
4. *Date* Include the date of the material if it is known.
5. *Folio number or other identification number* Include whatever kind of identification number is conventionally used with the material.
6. *Geographical location of the material* Include the name of the institution where the materials can be found and the city where the institution is located.

Style and Content for Subsequent References

There are two systems that are currently used to refer to a source that has already been cited. One makes use of a shortened footnote styling; the other uses Latin abbreviations. Both systems are described below.

Shortened footnotes When the same source is cited repeatedly with intervening footnotes, shortened footnotes may be used as space-saving devices. The following styling is generally acceptable for most publications.

1. If the author's name occurs in the running text, it need not be repeated in footnote references to the work after the first one.

    first reference
      1. Albert H. Marckwardt, *American English* (New York: Oxford University Press, 1980), p. 94.

    repeated reference
      2. *American English,* p. 95.

2. If the author's name does not appear in the running text prior to a repeated reference, either of the following stylings may be used. The styling of footnote 3 should be followed if more than one work by the same author is cited within the text.

    repeated reference
      3. Marckwardt, *American English,* p. 95.
        or
      4. Marckwardt, p. 95.

3. In repeated references to books by more than one author, the authors' names may be shortened. The styling of footnote 6 should be followed if more than one work by the same authors is cited within the text.

    first reference
      5. De Witt T. Starnes and Gertrude E. Noyes, *The English Dictionary from Cawdrey to Johnson 1604–1775* (Chapel Hill: University of North Carolina Press, 1946), p. 120.

repeated reference
6. Starnes and Noyes, *The English Dictionary from Cawdrey to Johnson 1604–1775*, p. 126.
or
7. Starnes and Noyes, p. 126.

4. A long title may be shortened if it has already been given in full in an earlier footnote.
8. Starnes and Noyes, *The English Dictionary*, p. 126.

5. A shortened reference to an article in a periodical that has been cited earlier should include the author's last name; the title of the article, which can be shortened if it is a long one, and if no similar title by the same author is being cited; and the page number.
9. Goldman, "Warren G. Harding," p. 45.

Latin abbreviations While the simplified and shortened footnote stylings described above have gained wide currency, some writers still prefer to use the traditional Latin abbreviations *ibid., loc. cit.,* and *op. cit.* as space-savers in repeated references to sources cited earlier. Current usage indicates that these abbreviations need no longer be typed with underscoring or italicized in type; however, some writers still prefer this traditional styling. When a page reference follows one of these abbreviations, it may or may not be set off with a comma.
10. Ibid. pp. 95–98.
or
11. Ibid., pp. 95–98.

These Latin abbreviations are capitalized when they appear at the beginning of a footnote or endnote, but not otherwise.
The abbreviation *ibid.* (for *ibidem,* "in the same place") is used when the writer is referring to the work cited in the immediately preceding footnote. The abbreviation may be used several times in succession.

first reference
12. Simone de Beauvoir, *The Second Sex,* trans. and ed. H. M. Parshley (New York: Alfred A. Knopf, 1953), p. 600.

repeated reference (immediately following note 12)
13. Ibid., p. 609.

repeated reference (immediately following note 13)
14. Ibid.

When *ibid.* is used without a page number, it indicates that the same page of the same source is being cited as in the footnote immediately preceding. Thus, note 14 above cites page 609 of *The Second Sex.*

The abbreviations *loc. cit.* (for *loco citato,* "in the place cited") and *op. cit.* (for *opere citato,* "in the work cited") may be used only in conjunction with the author's name, which may occur in the running text or at the beginning of the first reference. When the writer cites a book or periodical, its complete title should be included the first time it is referred to in a footnote. In subsequent references, *loc. cit.* or *op. cit.* with or without page numbers may be substituted for the title, depending on the type of citation.

The difference between *loc. cit.* and *op. cit.* is that *loc. cit.* is used only when referring to the same page or pages of the same source cited earlier with footnotes intervening, while *op. cit.* is used to refer to a source cited earlier but not to the same page or pages of that source.

first reference

15. De Witt T. Starnes and Gertrude E. Noyes, *The English Dictionary from Cawdrey to Johnson 1604–1775* (Chapel Hill: University of North Carolina Press, 1946), pp. 119–133.

repeated reference (with other footnotes intervening)

18. Starnes and Noyes, loc. cit.
21. Starnes and Noyes, loc. cit., p. 119.

The note without a page number indicates that pages 119–133 are being cited again.

Examples of the use of *op. cit.* are as follows:

first reference

22. Albert H. Marckwardt, *American English* (New York: Oxford University Press, 1980), p. 94.

repeated reference

24. Marckwardt, op. cit., p. 98.

The title of the work rather than the Latin abbreviation should be used if the writer is using material from more than one work by the same author.

Nonbibliographical Footnotes and Endnotes

Nonbibliographical notes provide additional information, commentary, or cross-references that the author does not want to include in the main text. They are keyed to the text in the same way as bibliographical notes. In texts in which bibliographical notes are keyed with superior numerals, nonbibliographical notes are included in the same sequence, as in the examples below. In some cases, authors will use numbered endnotes for bibliographical notes and footnotes keyed with reference marks for nonbibliographical notes; however, this system is not very common.

1. Lyon Richardson, *A History of Early American Magazines* (New York: Thomas Nelson and Sons, 1931), p. 8.
2. Total average circulation per issue of magazines reporting to the Bu-

reau of Circulation rose from 96.8 million in 1939 to 147.8 million in 1945.

3. For a particularly compelling account of this episode, see James P. Wood, *Magazines in the United States* (New York: The Ronald Press Company, 1949), pp. 92–108.

4. Richardson, op. cit., p. 42.

5. For more details, see Appendix.

Texts that rely on parenthetical references for bibliographical notes can still include footnotes or endnotes for other notes. When a nonbibliographical note mentions the name of a book or article that is not the source of a quotation or piece of information in the text, footnote styling is used to describe the reference.

In some publications, there are certain nonbibliographical notes that are not keyed to the text with any kind of symbol. These include notes that an editor places at the beginning of each part of a collection of works by different authors and that identify each author. They also include notes that an author uses to acknowledge those who gave assistance or contributed to the writing of the work. One reason that these notes are not keyed is that the only logical place to put the reference mark (described below) or number would be following the title of the work or the name of the author (both of which are often set in a larger distinctive type style), and some editors and designers are reluctant to use footnote symbols in this position. These unnumbered notes are conventionally placed in the footnote position on the first page.

Reference Marks

In texts that have only a limited number of footnotes or endnotes, writers sometimes substitute reference marks for reference numbers. The traditional footnote reference symbols are listed below in the order in which they are usually used.

* asterisk
† dagger
‡ double dagger
§ section mark
‖ parallels
¶ paragraph mark
# number sign

The sequence of these symbols can begin anew with each page or with each chapter. If more than seven notes are needed in a sequence, the reference marks are doubled, as **, ††, etc.; however, if such a large number of footnotes is needed, reference numbers rather than reference symbols should probably be used. A common alternative to using the full set of symbols when only a few footnotes are needed is to use an asterisk for the first note, a double asterisk for the second, and so on without using the dagger or other marks. A variation on this that works for up to four footnotes in a sequence is to use the asterisk and dagger in the following order:*, **, †, ††.

Parenthetical References

The system of parenthetical references is an extension of the system of shortened footnotes used for subsequent references that was explained in the preceding section. Like the shortened footnote, the parenthetical reference includes very abbreviated bibliographical information (typically the name of the author followed by a page number but sometimes just a page number), and it refers readers to a fuller bibliographical description elsewhere in the work. However, unlike shortened footnotes, parenthetical references are enclosed in parentheses and included in the main body of the text, thus removing the need for bibliographical footnotes and endnotes. And parenthetical references are used for all references, not just subsequent references, because they refer the reader not to an earlier reference but to a list of references that is found at the end of the article, chapter, or book. A list of references is simply a bibliography, and details regarding its content and styling are presented in the section on Bibliographies and Lists of References, later in this chapter. For purposes of convenience a sample list of references is included on the next page, and all parenthetical references in this section refer to it.

Parenthetical formats have the advantage of providing essential and useful information within the text, without providing so much information that reading the text is impeded. They can help the reader decide whether to turn to the list of references for further information.

The practice of using parenthetical references originated in the social and natural sciences; however, its adoption for writing in the humanities, and for all general writing that includes numerous bibliographical references, is being encouraged more and more. In general, most systems of parenthetical references are similar, but details of styling do exist among the systems used by various academic disciplines and professional organizations. The style manuals listed in the Bibliography at the end of this book provide details for styling bibliographies in a number of special fields. The examples in this section of the book are styled in accordance with the precepts of the *MLA Handbook for Writers of Research Papers,* second edition, to which readers of this book are referred for more details regarding parenthetical references. A discussion of two different parenthetical reference systems that are used in the sciences follows at the end of this section.

Placement of the Reference

Parenthetical references are placed immediately after the quotation or piece of information whose source they refer to. The sample on page 194 reproduces the text of the sample on page 182 and shows how the same text would appear using parenthetical references instead of footnotes. Note especially that sentence punctuation (that is, punctuation not associated with a quotation) is placed after the reference. This means that pe-

---

List of References

Anderson, Ruth I., et al. *The Administrative Secretary: Resource.* New York: McGraw-Hill, 1970.

"Aristotle." *Webster's New Biographical Dictionary.* Springfield, Mass.: Merriam-Webster Inc., 1983.

Brushaw, Charles T., Gerald J. Alred, and Walter E. Oliu. *Handbook of Technical Writing.* 2d ed. New York: St. Martin's Press, 1982.

Chambers, Robert. *Cyclopaedia of English Literature.* 2 vols. New York: World Publishing House, 1875.

Lesikar, Raymond V. *Report Writing For Business.* Homewood, Ill.: Richard D. Irwin, Inc., 1981.

National Micrographics Association. *An Introduction to Micrographics.* Rev. ed. Silver Spring, Md.: National Micrographics Association, 1980.

Rules for Alphabetical Filing as Standardized by ARMA. Prairie Village, Kans.: Association of Record Managers and Administrators, 1981.

Figure 8.4. A sample list of references

riods and commas are placed outside of quotation marks and that run-in quoted sentences that end in an omission are styled with three spaced ellipsis points before the reference and a terminal period closed-up after the reference. If the final sentence of the extract quotation on page 194 had been set as a run-in quotation, it would appear as follows:

> Lesikar says, "The quoted passage is further distinguished from the report writer's work by single spacing . . ." (187).

Content and Style of Parenthetical References

The content and style are determined by two factors: (1) the style and content of the first element of the entry in the list of references to which it refers and (2) the bibliographical information that is included in the text around it.

These general principles are illustrated in the example on page 194. For instance, in the third paragraph, the parenthetical reference "(Anderson et al. 391)" is given because, in the list of references, the full reference to this source begins "Anderson, Ruth I., et al."

The way that bibliographical information in the text determines the styling of the parenthetical reference is illustrated in the first sentence of the first paragraph. The parenthetical reference "(187)" is sufficient, be-

According to Lesikar, if a "quoted passage is four lines or less in length, it is typed with the report text and is distinguished from the normal text by quotation marks" (187). However, a different procedure is used for longer quotations:

> But if a longer quotation (five lines or more) is used, the conventional practice is to set it in from both left and right margins (about five spaces) but without quotation marks. . . . The quoted passage is further distinguished from the report writer's work by single spacing. . . . (187)

A series of usually three periods called ellipsis is used to indicate omissions of material from a passage (Lesikar 188).

Footnotes may be placed "at the bottom of the page . . . separated from the text by a horizontal line. If a line is used, it is typed a single space below the text and followed by one blank line" (Anderson et al. 391). Lesikar prefers the separation line to be one and one-half or two inches (189). Generally, typewriting textbooks state that a two-inch line is adequate (20 pica strokes; 24 elite strokes). The line is constructed by striking the underscore key.

From a typing standpoint, reserve three lines of blank typing space per footnote at the bottom of the page.

The first line of a footnote is indented from one to six (but usually two or five) spaces from the left margin, depending on the writer's preference or the style manual being followed. The footnote may be introduced with the applicable superscript Arabic numeral, unpunctuated and separated from the first letter of the author's first name by one space; or it may be introduced by the

Figure 8.5. A typewritten page with parenthetical references

cause it is clear that Lesikar is the author of the source that is being quoted. In the second paragraph, the full parenthetical reference "(Lesikar 188)" is required because it is not clear from the sentence who is the source of the information being provided.

Sometimes a reference is supported by citations to two separate sources; the two citations are enclosed in the same parentheses but are separated by a semicolon, as "(Lesikar 189; Anderson et al. 390)." Lengthy parenthetical references should be avoided because they interrupt the flow of text. Authors can avoid unwieldy parenthetical references by incorporating as much of the bibliographical information within the text as can be smoothly absorbed.

Matching the list of references The name in a parenthetical reference must correspond to a name that begins an entry in the list of references. In general, the last name of the author is usually sufficient within a parenthetical reference, as it was in the case of the references to Lesikar's book in the sample on page 194. However, if there had been another author with the last name Lesikar in the list of references, it would have been necessary to include both first and last name, as "(Lesikar, Raymond, 188)." Alternatively, if the list of references had included two different books both of which were by Raymond Lesikar, it would have been necessary to include both the author's name and the book's title (which may be shortened) in the parenthetical reference, as "(Lesikar, *Report Writing* 188)." The following paragraphs explain some other special cases.

1. *A work with two or three authors* The list of references on page 193 includes an entry for a book by Charles T. Brushaw, Gerald J. Alred, and Walter E. Oliu. A parenthetical reference to that work would take the following form:

   (Brushaw, Alred, and Oliu 182–184)

2. *A work with more than three authors* A work with more than three authors is listed in the list of references under the name of the first author, followed by the phrase *et al.* The reference to Anderson et al. in the third paragraph of the sample on page 194 illustrates this style.

3. *A work by a corporate author* The list of references on page 193 includes an entry in which National Micrographics Association is given as the author. A parenthetical reference to that work would also use National Micrographics Association as its author, although the name may be abbreviated.

   (National Micrographics 42)

   or

   (Natl. Micrographics 42)

4. *A work listed by its title* The list of references on page 193 includes an entry for a book *Rules for Alphabetical Filing as Standardized by ARMA.*

A parenthetical reference to that work should also refer to it by its title, which may be shortened for convenience.

(*Rules for Alphabetical Filing* 14)

  or

(*Rules* 14)

Locators Usually the only locator that is required in a parenthetical reference is a page number. However, sometimes additional or alternate information is needed to help the reader find the original source. The following paragraphs describe some of these special situations. Note that in all cases no punctuation separates the author's name or the title from the locator and that no abbreviation is used to identify the nature of the locator unless confusion would result from its omission (but see the note following paragraph 1 below).

1. *A multivolume work* The list of references on page 193 includes a reference to Robert Chambers's two-volume *Cyclopaedia of English Literature*. A reference to that work would have to include a volume designation as well as a page number. The volume number and the page number are separated by an unspaced colon.

    (Chambers 1:45)

    NOTE: If an entire volume of a multivolume work is being referred to, the abbreviation *vol.* is used to make it clear that the number is a volume number and not a page number.

    (Chambers, vol. 1)

2. *A reference book* A reference to an entry in a reference book often begins with the name of the entry being cited, as in the entry for "Aristotle" on page 193. A parenthetic reference need only mention the name of the entry, as no page number is included in the list of references. The name of the reference book should be mentioned in the text preceding such a reference; otherwise, the reader must consult the list of references to know what source is being cited.

    ("Aristotle")

3. *Literary works* Parenthetical references to literary works often include references to stanzas, lines, verses, chapters, books, parts, and the like. This is often very useful to readers trying to find a particular passage, because they may be using an edition of the work whose pagination differs from that of the edition used by the author of the note. For more on giving references to literary works, see the section on Special Cases later in this chapter.

References to unpublished sources Parenthetical references are also used to cite unpublished sources that are not listed in a bibliography, such as letters to the author or telephone interviews. The following information should be included: the name of the person providing the information, the type of source, and the date, as "(Paul Roberts, letter to the author, Sept. 1984)." Any of these elements may be omitted from the parenthetical reference if included in the text.

Parenthetical Reference Systems Used in the Sciences

Two other systems of parenthetical citation that are used mostly in the social and natural sciences are the author-date system (also called the name-year system) and the number system.

Author-date system   In the author-date system the parenthetical reference contains the author's last name and the date of publication with no intervening punctuation. A third element, a page number, is optional. If the author's name is mentioned in the introductory text, only the date and possibly the page number are needed within the parentheses. By referring to the list of references, the reader can find complete bibliographical information about the work. However, lists of references written in connection with the author-date system must also follow the scientific styling of placing the date after the author's name in each entry.

A book or article by two or more authors would be represented by the following stylings:

> (Martin and Zim 1951)
> (Martin, Zim, and Nelson 1951)
> (Martin et al. 1951)

A corporate author name or a title may be substituted when there are no individual authors. An editor's last name may also be substituted, but the name is not followed by the abbreviation *ed.*

A page number or other number indicating a division of the work is often added to the date with a comma (a colon in some stylings) between date and page numbers. For citations to the short articles so prevalent in the scientific literature, page numbers are unnecessary, but for books page references are certainly helpful to the reader.

> (Martin et al. 1951, 147–149) *or* (Martin et al. 1951:147–149)

Volumes are indicated by Arabic numerals. Thus, "(1.147–149)" denotes volume 1, pages 147–149.

More than one work by the same author can be readily shown with the listing of a second date that follows the first with a comma between them, as "(Martin et al. 1951, 1958)." Two or more separate citations can also be included within one parenthesis if they are separated by a semicolon.

More than one work published in the same year by the same author can be indicated by adding an *a, b,* or *c* to the date. The same letters should be added to the dates in the entries in the list of references.

> (Martin and Zim 1952a)

Number system In the number system, the parenthetical references consist only of numerals that are keyed to numbered entries in a list of references. Sometimes the numerals are italicized to show that they represent a title. In most variations on this system, a comma and a page number may follow the key numeral, as "(*3*,259)."

A list of references developed in connection with this system is usually arranged not in alphabetical order but in order of the first citation of each entry in the text, since this arrangement is easier for the reader who wants to locate an entry on the list. Also, the year is usually written toward the end of the entry; it does not need to appear as the second element as it would in the author-date system. Since the list is not alphabetized, it is unnecessary to use hanging indention.

The number system is not widely used. Although it takes up less space in the text, it can be no more satisfying to the reader than the system of footnote reference numbers. Furthermore, it is difficult for the editor and author to make last-minute revisions in the text where repositioning of the numbers might be involved.

Bibliographies and Lists of References

A bibliography differs from a list of references in that it lists all of the works that a writer has found relevant in writing the text. A list of references, on the other hand, includes only those works that are specifically mentioned in the text or from which a particular quotation or piece of information was taken. In all other respects, however, bibliographies and lists of references are quite similar. They both appear at the end of an article, chapter, or book, where they list sources of information that are relevant to the text. They differ from a section of bibliographical endnotes in that their entries are arranged alphabetically (as in the sample on page 193), and they use different patterns of indention, punctuation, and capitalization, as explained in the paragraphs that follow. Bibliographies and lists of references are punctuated and capitalized in the same way, and hereafter in this chapter, references to bibliographies should be understood to be inclusive of lists of references as well.

Additional detail regarding the styling of bibliographical entries is provided in the following paragraphs. For each of the kinds of entries that are described below, two examples are given. The first example is in a style used in the humanities, which is also the style used in most general writing and the style that is familiar to most writers. The second example is in a style that is representative of the social and natural sciences.

In general, bibliographical stylings used in the sciences differ from those used in general writing in that (1) the author's first and middle names are expressed with initials only, (2) the date, which is important in scientific writings, is often placed near the beginning instead of at the end of the entry, (3) less capitalization is used, (4) titles of articles are not enclosed in quotation marks, (5) book titles are not underlined or italicized, (6) dates are usually written as day-month-year, which results in less punctuation, and (7) more abbreviations are used. In content, however, the two stylings are much the same, and both rely on periods to separate each element of the bibliographical entry.

The examples used in this section by no means exhaust the possible variations on these two basic stylings. Different combinations of the styles illustrated here, as well as other alternatives, are found in print. Several of these variations are recommended by various professional organizations and academic disciplines within the social and natural sciences. The entries in this section that illustrate scientific style are based on the style described in the *CBE Style Manual,* fifth edition, published by the Council of Biology Editors. (NOTE: Some entries in this section may differ somewhat from preferred CBE style. Writers who need to style their bibliographies in strict accordance with CBE style should consult that manual.) Other style manuals that give details of bibliographical styling used in specialized fields within the social and natural sciences are listed in the Bibliography at the back of this book.

Books

Style and content of entries A bibliographical entry that refers to a book includes as many of the following elements as are relevant. The order of elements listed here is the order in which they appear in entries written in the styling of the humanities. Each of these elements is illustrated in the examples that begin on page 201.

1. *Author's name* The author's name or authors' names come first, whether the author is a single individual, or a group of individuals, or an organization. Names of coauthors are arranged in the order in which they are found on the title page. A work without an author but with an editor is styled with the editor's name first, followed by a comma and *ed.* (see paragraph 4 below). The name of the first author is inverted so that the surname comes first and can be alphabetized. In bibliographies that follow the style of the humanities, the author's name is written as it appears on the title page. In many stylings used in the social and natural sciences, the last name and first two initials are always used, regardless of how the author's name is printed on the title page. This is the style followed in this section for examples of bibliographical entries in the social and natural sciences; however, authors should remember that some confusion can result if more than one writer in the relevant subject area has the same initials and last name. The best way to avoid this difficulty is to include first names whenever there is a chance of confusion.

In the humanities and in some stylings in the social and natural sciences, if there are more than three authors the first author's name is followed by *et al.*, which is an abbreviation for the Latin phrase *et alii* or *et aliae,* meaning "and others." In other stylings, the names of all the authors are included.

2. *Title of the work* In the humanities, the title is underlined in typewritten manuscript and italicized in type. In the social and natural sciences, the title may follow this styling or it may be left without underlining or italicization. Capitalization is either headline-style (that is, all words are capitalized except for internal articles and prepositions) or sentence-style (that is, only the first word and proper nouns and adjectives are capitalized). In the humanities, headline-style capitalization is used; in the social and natural sciences, both styles of capitalization are used. The titles of references in the sciences that appear as examples in this chapter are unitalicized and use sentence-style capitalization. Another difference between the two stylings is that titles in the humanities include any subtitles, whereas subtitles are often omitted in bibliographies for the sciences. Subtitles are italicized and capitalized to match the styling of the titles that precede them.

3. *Portion of the book* Some bibliography entries cite only one portion of a book, as an essay within a collection or an article within a symposium. For these entries, the name of that portion is given first as a title. It is either italicized or enclosed in quotation marks, depending on its nature, or it is left alone as in stylings for the sciences. The title of the book is given next. The titles of chapters within nonfiction works by a single author are usually not included in the entry.

4. *Editor, compiler, or translator* In entries for books that have an author, the name of an editor, compiler, or translator comes after the title and is preceded or followed by the abbreviation *ed., comp.,* or *trans.* or some combination of these. If no author is listed, the name of the editor, compiler, or translator is placed first in the entry—styled like an author's name but followed by a comma and the lowercase abbreviation *ed., comp.,* or *trans.*

5. *Edition* If a book is other than the first edition, the number (as "2d ed." or "1986 ed.") or other description of the edition is written after the title. If the edition is identified by a word instead of a numeral, the first letter in that word is capitalized, as "Rev. ed."

6. *Volume number or number of volumes* In a bibliography entry that cites a multivolume work, the total number of volumes in that work is written before the publication information as, for example, "9 vols." There is no need to cite the volumes actually used, since this information will be in a note or in a parenthetical reference. On the other hand, if only one volume of a multivolume work was consulted, that volume alone is listed as an entry, so that the text references need cite only page numbers, not volume numbers as well.

7. *Name of the series* If the book is part of a series, the name of the series

should be included, as well as the book or volume number if the book represents a specific numbered volume in that series. The series name is not italicized.

8. *Publication data* The city of publication (with the state abbreviation if the city is not well known), the name of the publisher, and the year of publication of the particular edition used—together these form the grouping called the publication data. A colon usually follows the city name, a comma follows the name of the publisher, and a period after the date ends the bibliographical entry if the styling is that used in the humanities. In stylings used in the sciences, the date often appears after the author's name.

All of this information comes from the title page and the copyright page. If the title page lists more than one city, only the first is mentioned in the bibliography. Some books are published under a special imprint name, which is usually printed on the title page above the publisher's name. In a bibliographical entry, the imprint name is joined to the publisher's name with a hyphen, as *Golden Press-Western Publishing Co.* Short forms of publisher's names are often used in bibliographies. This usage is acceptable if consistently applied. Also the word *and* and the ampersand are equally acceptable within a publisher's name if they are used consistently.

For a multivolume work that is published over a period of several years, inclusive numbers are given for those years. The phrase *in press* is substituted for the date in works that are about to be published.

9. *Locators* Page numbers are added to book entries in a bibliography only when the entry cites a portion of a book such as a story or essay in an anthology or an article in a collection. If that portion is in a volume of a multivolume work, both volume and page number are given.

Examples The following examples illustrate how each of the elements described above is styled in a number of different situations. In each case, the first example illustrates a typical style in the humanities and general publications; the second illustrates a representative style used in the social and natural sciences.

1. *Book with a single author*

   Chapman, R. F. *The Insects.* New York: American Elsevier, 1969.

   Chapman, R. F. 1969. The insects. New York: American Elsevier.

2. *Book with two or three authors*

   Starnes, De Witt T., and Gertrude E. Noyes. *The English Dictionary from Cawdrey to Johnson 1604–1775.* Chapel Hill: University of North Carolina Press, 1946.

   Starnes, D. T.; Noyes, G. E. 1946. The English dictionary from Cawdrey to Johnson 1604–1775. Chapel Hill: University of North Carolina Press.

3. *Book with more than three authors*

> Allee, W. C., et al. *Principles of Animal Ecology*. Philadelphia: W. B. Saunders Co., 1949.
>
> Allee, W. C.; Emerson, A. E.; Park, O.; Park, S.; Schmidt, K. D. 1949. Principles of animal ecology. Philadelphia: W. B. Saunders Co.

4. *Book with a corporate author*

> National Micrographics Association. *An Introduction to Micrographics*. Rev. ed. Silver Spring, Md.: National Micrographics Association, 1980.
>
> National Micrographics Association. 1980. An introduction to micrographics. Rev. ed. Silver Spring, Md.: National Micrographics Association.

5. *Book without an author listed*

> *The World Almanac & Book of Facts*. New York: Newspaper Enterprises Association, Inc., 1985.
>
> The world almanac & book of facts. 1985. New York: Newspaper Enterprises Association.

6. *Book with editor listed and no author*

> Bradbury, Peggy F., ed. *Transcriber's Guide to Medical Terminology*. New Hyde Park, N.Y.: Medical Examination Publishing Co., 1973.
>
> Bradbury, P. F., editor. 1973. Transcriber's guide to medical terminology. New Hyde Park, N.Y.: Medical Examination Publishing Co.

7. *Book with author and editor-translator*

> Beauvoir, Simone de. *The Second Sex*. Trans. and ed. H. M. Parshley. New York: Alfred A. Knopf, 1953.
>
> Beauvoir, S. 1953. The second sex. Parshley, H. M., translator and editor. New York: Alfred A. Knopf.

8. *Multivolume book*

> Farrand, John Jr., ed. *The Audubon Society Master Guide to Birding*. 3 vols. New York: Alfred A. Knopf, 1983.
>
> Farrand, J. Jr., editor. 1983. The Audubon Society master guide to birding. New York: Alfred A. Knopf, 3 vol.

9. *Multivolume book only one volume of which was consulted*

> Chambers, Robert. Vol. 1 of *Cyclopaedia of English Literature*. 2 vols. New York: World Publishing House, 1875.
>
> Chambers, R. 1875. Cyclopaedia of English literature. Vol. 1. New York: World Publishing House.

10. *Portion of a book*

> Malone, Kemp. "The Phonemes of Current English." *Studies for William A. Read*. Ed. Nathaniel M. Caffee and Thomas A. Kirby. Baton Rouge: Louisiana State University Press, 1940. pp. 133–165.

Malone, K. 1940. The phonemes of current English. In: Caffee, N. M.; Kirby, T. A., eds. Studies for William A. Read. Baton Rouge: Louisiana State University Press: p. 133–165.

11. *Book in a series*

Manheimer, Martha L. *Style Manual: A Guide for the Preparation of Reports and Dissertations.* Vol. 5 of Books in Library and Information Science. New York: Marcel Dekker, 1973.

Manheimer, M. L. 1973. Style manual. New York: Marcel Dekker. (Books in library and information science; vol. 5.)

Articles in Journals or Other Periodicals

Style and Content of Entries A bibliography entry for an article in a journal or other periodical or in a newspaper includes as many of the following elements as are relevant. Examples of each of these elements can be found in the reference samples beginning on page 204. The elements are listed here in the order in which they appear in entries styled on the humanities pattern.

1. *Author's name* The author's name is written as it appears on the printed page and is styled in the way described above for an entry that refers to a book. Names of people who write letters to a periodical or who contribute signed reviews are treated like names of authors.
2. *Title of the article* The title of the article is written in full as it appears in the printed article. In most bibliography stylings used in the humanities, the title and subtitle are enclosed in quotation marks (with a period before the closing quotation mark) and capitalized headline-style. Titles of articles styled for use in the social and natural sciences tend to omit the quotation marks, use sentence-style capitalization, and omit subtitles.
3. *Name of the periodical* The name of the periodical is treated in the same way as described above for a book: underlined to indicate italics in bibliographies for the humanities but not italicized in bibliographies for the sciences. However, unlike book titles, periodical titles are fully capitalized in bibliographies in both the humanities and the sciences. In addition, there are special principles for the styling of periodical names in both categories. One is the omission of an initial article. Whereas the initial article is included in a book title but ignored in alphabetizing, the initial article of a journal title is dropped completely. Another is the use of abbreviations for journal titles of more than one word. These abbreviations are widely used in technical writing. Each discipline has its own set of abbreviations for the journals that tend to be used in that discipline. For general writing, however, these titles are written in full for the reader's convenience, and the examples that follow show journal titles in unabbreviated form. Journal titles that begin with the words *Transactions, Proceedings,* and *An-*

nals are often reversed for the purpose of alphabetizing so that these words come last.

Names of newspapers are treated as they appear on the masthead, except that initial articles are omitted. Also, a place name is added in brackets after the newspaper's name if it is necessary to distinguish that particular paper.

4. *Volume and number of the periodical* This information comes after the name of the periodical and identifies the particular issue cited. An issue that is identified by both volume and number should be identified in that way in a bibliography entry, as "3(2):25–37" for volume 3, number 2, pages 25–37. If the issue is identified in some other manner, as by a full date, that method is used in the bibliography entry. Issue numbers are not commonly used, however, unless the issue is paginated independently of the volume as a whole and the number is needed to identify the issue. Examples 1 and 5 below illustrate entries for a periodical in which pages are numbered consecutively through a volume and which therefore needs only a volume number. If the volume number corresponds to a particular year, as in the examples, the year in parentheses follows the volume number—but not, of course, in the scientific stylings, where the year is placed after the author's name.

Example 2 on page 205 illustrates a reference to a periodical that uses a seasonal designation in addition to a volume and number designation; the pages in this issue are numbered independently of the volume as a whole. Example 3 illustrates a popular monthly magazine, issues of which are commonly referred to by date rather than by volume or issue number. Newspapers are always identified by date.

5. *Issue date* Periodicals issued daily, weekly, monthly, and bimonthly are usually designated by date of issue. The date follows the unpunctuated day-month-year order (27 May 1984) rather than the punctuated month-day-year order (May 27, 1984). Names of months that are spelled with more than four letters are usually abbreviated.

6. *Page numbers* Inclusive pages for the whole article are written at the end of the entry. For newspaper entries, it may be necessary to add a section number or edition identification number as well, as "p. B6." Articles that are continued on later pages are styled thus: "38–41, 159–160." The use of the abbreviations *p.* or *pp.* in bibliographies is the same as it is in footnotes (see page 187).

Examples The following examples illustrate how each of the elements described above is styled in a number of different situations. The first example of each group illustrates a style used in the humanities and in general publications; the second illustrates a style used in the social and natural sciences.

1. *Article in journal with continuous pagination of volume*

   Heil, John. "Seeing is Believing." *American Philosophical Quarterly* 19 (1982): 229–239.

Heil, J. 1982. Seeing is believing. American Philosophical Quarterly 19:229–239.

2. *Article in journal that paginates each issue separately*

Ourecky, Donald K. "Cane and Bush Fruits." *Plants & Gardens* 27, No. 3 (Autumn 1971): pp. 13–15.
Ourecky, D. K. 1971. Cane and bush fruits. Plants & Gardens 27(3):13–15.

3. *Articles in periodicals issued by date*

Smiley, Xan. "Misunderstanding Africa." *Atlantic*, Sept. 1982, pp. 70–79.
Smiley, X. 1982. Misunderstanding Africa. Atlantic, Sept.:70–79.

Rosenberg, Jeremy C. "Letters." *Advertising Age*, 7 June 1982, p. M–1.
Rosenberg, J. C. 1982. Letters. Advertising Age, 7 June: M–1.

4. *Article in newspaper*

Pitts, Gail. "Money Funds Holding Own." *Morning Union* [Springfield, Mass.], 23 Aug. 1982, p. 6.
Pitts, G. 1982. Money funds holding own. Morning Union [Springfield, Mass.] 23 Aug.:6.

5. *Signed review*

Vassell, M. O. Rev. of *Applied Charge Particle Optics*, ed. A. Septier. *American Scientist* 70 (1982): 229.
Vassell, M. O. 1982. Rev. of A. Septier, ed., Applied charge particle optics. American Scientist 70:229.

6. *Anonymous article*

"Education at Home: A Showdown in Texas." *Newsweek*, 25 March 1985, p. 87.
Anonymous. 1985. Education at home. Newsweek 25 March:87.

Unpublished Materials

Bibliography entries for unpublished materials include as many of the following elements as are known or are relevant.

1. *Author's name* The author's name is treated in the same way as described above for a book.
2. *Title of the work* If there is an official title, it is copied as it appears on the work. It is enclosed in quotation marks and capitalized like a book title in a bibliography using a styling from the humanities. If the work has no official title, a descriptive title is used, as in example 2 below, but it is not enclosed in quotation marks.
3. *The nature of the material* The entry should include a description of the document, such as "letter to the author" or "doctoral dissertation." For works without official author or title, this element is the first part of the entry.

4. *Date* The date must be included if it is known. If the date is known but is not written on the document, it is enclosed in brackets.
5. *Name of collection and identification number* Whatever information is necessary to completely identify the document is included.
6. *Geographical location* The name of the institution and the city where the materials can be located are often listed last in this kind of bibliographical entry.

Examples

1. *Unpublished report*

   Velasquez, Joyce A. "The Format of Formal Reports." Report prepared for the Southern Engineering Company. Johnson City, Miss., May 29, 1985.

   Velasquez, J. A. 1985. The format of formal reports. Report prepared for the Southern Engineering Company. 29 May. Johnson City, Miss.

2. *Letter in a collection*

   Johnson, Clive. Letter to Elizabeth O'Hara. 9 Nov. 1916. Johnson Collection, item 5298. California State Historical Society, San Marino, Calif.

   Johnson, C. 1916. Letter to Elizabeth O'Hara. 9 Nov. Located at California State Historical Society, San Marino, Calif.

Format of a Bibliography

Bibliographies are always typed beginning on a new page. Most are alphabetically arranged and indented flush-and-hang to set off the alphabetical sequence. Initial articles that are included in a title that begins an entry are ignored in determining the alphabetical order. All the entries are usually listed together in a single alphabetical arrangement, whether the first word is an author's surname or the title of an anonymous work. It is possible to divide a bibliography into categories by date of publication or by subject matter, but such divisions are not recommended unless the single-list form proves unmanageable. For rules of alphabetizing, see pages 273–275 in Chapter 10, "Indexes."

More than one work by an author After the first listing of an entry by an author or group of coauthors who have more than one work listed in the bibliography, that person's name is replaced in succeeding, adjacent entries by a dash. In typewritten bibliographies, the dash is usually represented by three typed hyphens. The author is not usually expected to type this dash or its equivalent in hyphens; instead, the editor substitutes the dash for the author's names as needed on the copyedited page. The dash is followed by a period, just as a name would be, or by a comma and an abbreviation such as *ed.*

The dash substitutes for the author's full name (or the full names of the set of coauthors) but no more. Thus, the dash may be used only when the names are exactly the same in adjacent entries. For example, if an entry for a work by Kemp Malone is followed by an entry for a work coauthored by Malone and someone else, the second entry would be spelled out. But if Malone and his coauthor wrote more than one book together, the dash would be used to replace both names in the second reference. A work by a single author precedes a work by that author and another; and works edited by an author usually follow works written by the same person.

In the general bibliographical stylings, the various works by a single author or group of coauthors are arranged alphabetically by title. In bibliographies in the social and natural sciences, however, where the date appears after the author's name, these multiple entries are arranged by date of publication. Occasionally an author publishes more than one article during a year. In these cases, the work is identified by a letter (often italicized) that follows the year. Thus, an author's works may be listed as 1977, 1979a, 1979b, 1980, and so on.

Headings Depending on their scope as explained at the beginning of this section, bibliographies may be headed *Bibliography* or *List of References*. Writings in the sciences often list bibliographical entries under the heading *Literature Cited*. If this heading is used, then only "literature"—that is, published works—and only works actually cited can be included on the list. Unpublished works that are referred to in the text must carry information such as the author's name and the title and where the work can be located, as well as the word *unpublished,* within the text or within parentheses. To avoid having to refer to an unwieldy number of unpublished works in the text, the author or editor may head the reference list *References Cited,* which allows the inclusion of unpublished works. Works in press are usually listed under *Literature Cited* heads even though they are not yet published. In lieu of the date, the entry contains the phrase *in press.*

Annotated bibliographies Annotated bibliographies are those in which the entries are written as for a regular bibliography but are then followed by a sentence or paragraph of description. Annotated bibliographies are designed to lead the reader to the most useful works for further study. Comments may be added to all or just some of the entries. The descriptive part may be run in with the bibliographical entry, or it may be set off typographically by lines of space, indention, italics, or smaller type.

Special Cases

Lists of references frequently contain items that do not fit neatly into any of the categories described in the previous sections of this chapter. Some are printed items like government publications, others are nonprint items. These special references are styled, as far as possible, in formats similar to those used for the published and unpublished works described and illustrated in the previous sections. They are arranged and punctuated in a way that corresponds to whatever styling has been chosen for the publication's notes, parenthetical references, and bibliography entries.

In the following paragraphs there are several references to the styling of titles in quotation marks or italics. These statements refer only to the documentation styles used in the humanities and in general-purpose writing. As was pointed out in the preceding section, titles have no special styling in the documentation formats used in the social and natural sciences. Also the date of publication, which occurs near the end of the references discussed here, is set after the author's name in the bibliographical stylings used in the sciences.

Nonprint Sources

Many sources in the following categories are often not cited in bibliographies and lists of references. When they are not, however, full documentation should be supplied within the text or in a note.

Personal communications The name of the person who supplied information in a personal communication is listed first in this kind of reference; the name is styled like an author's name. A descriptive word or phrase (like *personal communication* or *telephone interview*) follows, unitalicized and without quotation marks. The place, if applicable, and date of the communication are also given. This type of source is rarely included in a list of references. In scientific publications a form like the following is often found as a parenthetical reference: "(J. Scott, pers. comm. 1985)."

Speeches Lectures and other addresses are listed with the speaker's name first, then the title of the speech in quotation marks (or a descriptive term if the speech has no title), the name of the meeting or sponsoring organization or the occasion, then the place and date.

Radio and television programs The title of the program is usually listed first and is underlined or italicized. However, if the program is an episode of a multipart series, the episode title is placed in quotation marks and the name of the series follows without underlining or italics. If the reference in the text is to a particular performer, composer, or other person, that person's name may be listed before the title. Following the title are the names of the network, the local station and city (in a bibliography entry these two are separated by a comma not a period), and the date of the broadcast. Depending on its relevance, additional information may be given after the title, such as the names of the performers, the composer, or the director.

Sound recordings, films, and videotapes Sound recordings, films and filmscripts, and videotapes are usually documented according to their titles. If the name of a particular writer, composer, or performer is stressed in the text, and especially if the source is a recording, that person's name may be listed first. The italicized title is usually followed by whatever names are needed to identify the work, such as writers, performers, and others. Some programs may need to be further identified by a descriptive term like *filmstrip, slide program,* or *videocassette.* The director's name follows, preceded by the abbreviation *dir.* Finally, the name of the distributor, the year, the catalog number, and other information is added as needed to complete the identification of the work. The following example illustrates a bibliography entry for a recording.

> Brahms, Johannes. *A German Requiem (Ein deutsches Requiem),* Op. 45. Cond. Erich Leinsdorf. Boston Symphony Orchestra. RCA, LSC-7054, 1969.

Works of art References to works of art include the artist's name, which is styled like an author's name, an italicized title, the name of the proprietary institution, and the city.

Computer software References to computer software contain the following elements: the name of the program's writer, if known; the title of the program, which is italicized; the descriptive term *computer software*; the name and location of the distributor; and the year of publication. Additional information, such as the machines or the operating systems the software is designed for, may be added at the end of the note or bibliographical entry.

Microforms Materials in microform are documented in whatever styling is appropriate for their contents—as periodical articles, unpublished reports, etc.—except that to the end of the note or the bibliography entry is added a term that describes the form (as *microfiche*) and also the name and location of the commercial service that supplied the form. However, regular published material that has been microfilmed and preserved in a library is cited as if the actual works had been handled, and there is no mention of the microform process.

Material from an information service Sources from an information service are documented like books, articles, reports, and other printed materials, but at the end of the note or bibliography entry is added the name of the service, its location, and any identification numbers for the material.

Government Publications

If a publication by a government agency has a named author, that name may go first in a note or bibliography entry. Most government publications, however, are authored by an agency. The name of the government (as United States, Montana, or Chicago) often comes first, then the name of the department if applicable, then the name of the specific agency responsible for the publication. These names are not abbreviated when they precede the title of the work.

Next is the title, italicized like a book title and further identified as needed by series or publication numbers or by whatever format the agency uses to identify the work. As with other kinds of documentation, publication data is also included. Most U.S. government publications are published by the Government Printing Office, which is usually referred to in notes and bibliographies as *GPO*. References to congressional documents usually omit the GPO publication data, because it is understood. Standardized abbreviations are often used in these references, but names may also be spelled out, especially in writings for the general public.

> United States. Department of Labor. Employment and Training Administration. *Dictionary of Occupational Titles.* 4th ed. Washington: GPO, 1977.

Congressional documents are often attributed first to the "U.S. Congress" in notes and bibliography entries but not in parenthetical references. The name of the appropriate house follows (the short forms *House* and *Senate* are used), and then the name of the committee, if applicable. The document title is listed next in the reference, followed by the number and session of Congress. The year is listed next, then the number or other description of the document. The *Congressional Record* needs to be identified only by date and page number, as in the following bibliography entry:

> *Congressional Record.* 96th Cong., 2d sess., 1976. Vol. 5, pt. 7, pp. 13–27.

Bills in Congress are identified in a special way. *H.R.* is the conventional abbreviation for the House of Representatives in this case, and *S.* for the Senate. Thus, bills are referred to as "H.R. 93" or "S. 120." In citations to congressional reports, however, the House is abbreviated *H.* (as in "H. Rept. 1303"), while a Senate report would be styled "S. Rept. 671." In each case, the number and session of the congress follow the document title.

Laws and constitutions References to laws and constitutions are documented in notes and bibliography entries unless full information is provided in the text. These citations are not italicized. In legal writing, a large number of standard abbreviations is used, but in most writing for a general audience the abbreviations are limited to those which can be readily understood by the public. Roman numerals are traditionally used to denote certain sections of constitutions, as shown in the first two examples below.

> U.S. Constitution, Amendment XIII.
>
> Indiana Constitution, Art. III, sec. 2, cl. 4.
>
> Trade Agreements Act, Public Law 96–39, sec. 32, 96th Cong., 1st sess., July 26, 1979.
>
> 90 Stat. 1113 (1976).

The fourth reference in the list above is an example of the abbreviated form that is typical of legal citations. It is also typical in that the volume number comes *before* the name of a multivolume work. The reference points to a statute that is found in volume 90 of the *U.S. Statutes at Large* beginning on page 1113. Inclusive numbers are not used in legal references. The examples below illustrate a reference to a federal statute that has been codified in the *U.S. Code* and that can be found in volume 28, section 17 of that work, together with its supplement.

> 28 U.S.C. sec. 17. (1964).
> 28 U.S.C. sec. 17 (1964), as amended (Supp. II, 1966).

Regulations of the federal government also conform to official citation form. Like codified statutes, regulations codified in the *Code of Federal Regulations* or the *Federal Register* are identified first by volume number, then by section or page number and date.

> 33 C.F.R. sec. 403.2 (1980).
> 43 Fed. Reg. 54221 (1978).

Court Cases

Titles of court cases are italicized within the text, whether they involve two opposing parties (as *Surner* v. *Kellogg*) or whether they have titles like *In re Watson* or *In the matter of John Watson*. When these cases are listed in a bibliography, however, they are not italicized. The *v.* (for versus) within a case title is usually set roman in printed matter, but on a typewritten page the underscore is usually extended throughout the case title. A citation to a court case gives the name of the case, the number, title, and page of the volume in which it is recorded, and the date.

> *A Minor* v. *State*, 85 Nev. 323, 454 P. 2d 895 (1969).

The example above refers the reader to two sources in one reference: volume 85 of *Nevada Reports* on page 323, and also volume 454 of the second series of the *Pacific Reporter,* on page 895. Frequently the name of the court that decided the case is listed before the date.

Literary Works

Since literary works are printed in so many different editions, each of which is paginated differently, documentation of such works as poems, stories, plays, and novels does not always involve page numbers. Instead, reference is frequently made to the divisions of the work, such as chapter, book, part, act, scene, or line. Page numbers are referred to, however, in prose works if the edition used is clearly identified in a list of references or in a note; but in poetry and verse plays, where each line has a number, documentation refers to lines rather than to pages.

In cases where the author wishes to lead the reader to a particular chapter or part of a work of prose, the page number may be given in a reference, followed by a semicolon and the appropriate location, as "22; ch. 2" or "433; pt. 7."

Numerals alone, without accompanying terms like *chapter, verse, act, scene,* or *line,* are used in footnotes and endnotes and especially in parenthetical references, where they take up little space. Numerals are used wherever they can be easily understood without accompanying words or abbreviations. Frequently two numerals are used together, one that indicates a large division of the work and another that indicates a smaller division, as "4.122" for book 4, line 122. The two numerals are separated by a period or sometimes by a comma. Some stylings use capital and lowercase Roman numerals to denote the act and scene of a play, as "*Hamlet* III.ii" for act 3, scene 2; but the Arabic form 3.2 is also found, as in "*Hamlet* 3.2."

A single numeral is generally not used in a reference without an identifying word or abbreviation because it could be confusing. Thus, parenthetical references such as the following should include an identifying term: (*Hamlet,* Act 3) and ("The Waste Land," part 4). The abbreviations for line and lines (*l.* and *ll.*) should be used with great care, since they are easily confused with the numbers 1 and 11.

The Bible

Biblical references are not usually listed in a bibliography unless a particular version or edition is specified in the text. A text reference includes the name of the book, which is not italicized and which is often abbreviated, followed by Arabic numerals representing chapter and verse. Chapter and verse numerals are traditionally separated by a colon, but a period is a common alternative. A book with two or more parts is styled with an Arabic numeral before the name of the book, as "2 Chron. 2:18." Page numbers are never used to refer to biblical material.

Chapter 9

Tables and Illustrations

CONTENTS

Tables and illustrations are graphic devices for presenting information in a clearer, more orderly, and more concise form than can be accomplished by textual explanation alone. Tables present information by arranging data into vertical columns and horizontal rows. Illustrations can take the form of photographs, drawings, maps, charts, and graphs. Because they differ so much from ordinary text in structure and appearance, they are styled, designed, and even typed in ways that are often quite different from ordinary text. This chapter presents information about designing, styling, editing, and preparing copy for tables and illustrations. For information about the production steps involved with tables and illustrations, such as marking, cropping, or screening illustrations or inserting typeset tables into page proofs, see Chapter 11, "Production Techniques."

The Author's Role in Preparing Tables

Tables are expensive to set in type and can cause layout problems; therefore, they should be avoided whenever the data can be presented clearly and concisely in the regular text. If the table is needed, it should be referred to in the accompanying text, and the reference should precede the table. If there are several tables, they are usually referred to by number. An alternative is to use phrasing like "the table below," "the following table," or "the table on the opposite page." Text references may be inserted within parentheses, as "(see Table 3)," or they may be incorporated into a sentence, as: "The results of the survey, as shown in Table 3, indicate that . . ."

Authors who are preparing tables for magazine or journal articles should ask for a copy of the publication's styling requirements, as these requirements often vary. Tables published in books usually need only to be styled consistently with other tables in the same book, but the author should check with the publisher to find out if there are restrictions such as a maximum allowable size.

Generally authors should try to keep in mind the following guidelines for the construction of tables:

1. Aim for simplicity in order to keep typesetting costs down and to increase readability. A series of short, related tables is often more useful than one long, complex table. Use brief, simple phrasing.
2. Be consistent. For example, place only one type of information beneath each column head in a statistical table and be sure that the type of data listed is logically consistent with the column head. If the table consists of words, make each item under a column head similar in grammatical construction. Aim for consistency in terminology, abbreviations, and format within a series of related tables.
3. Aim for compactness. If the resulting table can be kept simple, consider the possibility of combining two tables, especially if each has an identical column of figures.
4. Aim for clarity. Choose headings judiciously. Consider adding an extra column of percentages next to a column of figures if the percentages would make the raw numbers more meaningful—or vice versa. Remember that figures are easier to compare when arranged vertically rather than horizontally.
5. Aim for maximum readability. Columns should look as even as possible. Tables should avoid large white spaces that make it difficult for the reader to make visual connections between items in a row. Enough space should be kept, of course, between columns and groups of rows to ensure visibility and order. Tables that are extremely long may be made more readable by inserting a horizontal line of space (or a thin rule) after every fifth entry or so.

The Parts of a Table

The parts of a table and the conventions regarding the arrangement of those parts are explained in this section of the chapter. Anyone who prepares a table can safely follow these conventions. However, styling options are numerous, and frequently the author has a wide choice regarding such things as centered or aligned headings, style and size of type, forms of capitalization, the handling of runover lines, and the use of indention and parentheses.

Most of the table parts that are explained in this section are included in and labeled on Table 1 on page 216.

The Table Caption

Style manuals differ in their use of the word *caption* in connection with tables. As used in this book, the term *table caption* refers to the title, identification number, or both that are used to identify a table.

A table caption is conventionally positioned above the table. It may be centered or set flush against the left margin of the page or, if the table is indented, aligned at the left side of the table. Table captions are frequently set in boldface type and sometimes in italic. In a few cases, tables have no captions at all. These tables are usually small ones that are inserted in the text with only a brief textual introduction.

Identification number   As mentioned above, every table should be cited at least once in the text, either by number or in a phrase. Tables are usually not numbered in works that contain only a single table or widely scattered tables or in works where their position can be easily described and found. In technical and scientific works, however, tables are commonly identified by number. Numbered tables are always sequenced in the order in which they are first mentioned in the text. Arabic numbers (as *Table 4*) are nearly universal, although the older use of Roman numerals (as *Table IV*) is sometimes found. Combinations of numbers and letters (as *Table 5a* or *Table 5b*) are usually avoided.

Tables should generally be numbered separately from illustrations, including charts and graphs. In a few publications they are combined in the same numbering sequence, usually with the word *exhibit* (as *Exhibit 3*) in the captions of both tabular and illustrative material. This practice has certain advantages when a work contains a very large number of tables, graphs, and charts and therefore two separate numbering systems might confuse the reader. But the advantages are offset by the fact that tables and illustrations are handled separately at all stages of production up to the final proofs. A separate numbering system for each group is a good protection against mix-ups.

Tables within a text are also numbered separately from any tables in an appendix. Appendix tables are commonly identified as *Table A–2* (second table of Appendix A), *Table B–1* (first table of Appendix B), and so on.

Tables may be numbered consecutively throughout a book, or they may be numbered anew with each chapter. In the latter system a form such as *Table 2.1* or *Table 2–1* would be used to indicate the first table of Chapter 2, *Table 3.4* or *Table 3–4* to indicate the fourth table of Chapter 3, and so on. Chapter-by-chapter enumeration is recommended (1) when the chapters are written by different authors, as in a symposium or the proceedings of a conference; (2) when the book itself is arranged by chapter and section number; and (3) when there are numerous tables, as in a technical publication.

Text references to numbered tables are usually capitalized (as "For a summary of the results, see Table 3"), but some publishers prefer the lowercase styling *table 3*. Even when lowercased in the text, the identification is always capitalized within the caption. Otherwise, the styling and

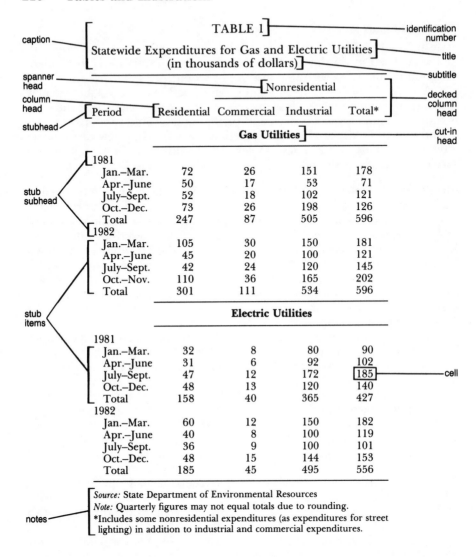

position of the identification number is quite variable. It may be set flush left on a line by itself with the title directly below it, or the number and title may be centered on separate lines. The number may be on the same line with the title, in which case it is usually followed by a punctuation mark—a period or dash, or sometimes both—to separate it from the title. When set on a separate line, the word *table* is usually all in capitals or in capitals and small capitals (as TABLE 3 or TABLE 3). When run in with the title, its style often matches that of the title.

Title   The title of a table should be descriptive yet brief and direct, usually no more than one phrase, clause, or sentence in length. Articles are usually omitted, as are unnecessary phrases like "summary of." Any extra information can be included in the column heads, a subtitle, a headnote, a footnote, or the text. Complicated explanations should be provided as headnotes or general footnotes (a full discussion of footnotes in tables begins on page 231). The title, when not a full sentence, should be a noun or a noun phrase, such as "Operating Expense of Maintenance Truck" or "Estimated One-Day Energy Requirements." A period may follow the caption, but is usually omitted unless the title forms a full sentence.

Headline-style capitalization—in which the initial letters of all words except coordinating conjunctions, articles, and short prepositions are capitalized—is the most common styling for table titles. Sentence-style capitalization—in which only the first word and proper nouns are capitalized—is also used and is considered more modern. For printed tables, either is preferable to an all-capitalized title, which is space-consuming and hard to read. The use of capitals and small capitals (as SUMMARY OF RESULTS) is widespread and is also acceptable, though today it is considered a bit formal and old-fashioned.

When long titles run over into a second line, short runover lines should be avoided. The first line of the title need not spread all the way to the right margin; some words may be cut off and added to the runover line so that the lengths of the two lines closely match, with the first line being slightly longer. It is also better for the line to break at a point where a natural break in thought occurs. Runovers of centered titles are always centered below the first line; runovers in titles set on the left margin may be flush left or indented.

Subtitles The caption may include a subtitle whose purpose is to provide an explanation of the sort usually provided in footnotes but important enough to be set above the table. Subtitles explain briefly certain elements of the table such as abbreviations, units of measurements, how the data were obtained, or limitations in the data. A very common example of a subtitle is the phrase *In Thousands,* which allows the author to eliminate the extra zeroes in a table in which all the figures end in two or more zeroes. Another common example is the indication of the number of individuals in a group when that number applies to percentages listed in the columns of the table, as $N = 532$. Other examples of subtitles:

    in percentages
    Based on latest fiscal data
    1980 = 1
    1980 = 100%
    for the year ended Dec. 31, 1983

These explanatory subtitles must pertain to the whole table, not just to certain columns. If explanation of specific items is required, a footnote is placed below the table.

Although subtitles sometimes appear in a type different from that of the title, as in Table 2 on page 219, they are frequently set off in parentheses instead, especially when run in with the title. Subtitles may be lowercased, or they may be capitalized headline-style or sentence-style. They are most commonly placed on a separate line below the title, although they may also be run in with the title when enclosed in parentheses. Like titles, subtitles usually do not end in a period.

If the caption is very short, the information usually found in a subtitle may be placed within the title itself as, for example:

> Table 1. World Sales in Thousands of Dollars
> Table 2. U.S. Fiber Consumption (millions of pounds) and Prices
>   (dollars per pound)

The Headnote

A headnote serves the same purpose as a subtitle; that is, it provides an explanation that is important enough to be set above the table. In general, any explanation that takes the form of one or more full sentences is referred to as a headnote. Like subtitles, headnotes may begin on the same line with the title, or they may begin a new line. Like footnotes, headnotes may be set in type smaller than that used in the body of the table.

The Stub

The leftmost column of a table is the stub. It usually lists independent variables, or the items that are under consideration. Information about each of these items is listed in the columns to the right. A heading over the stub (called a *stubhead*) is not always necessary. For example, the word *Year* may be omitted over a stub consisting of a list of years. When stubheads are used, they are usually set flush left, even if the other column heads are centered, and they should always be brief.

The items within a stub, if capitalized, are capitalized sentence-style. They are not numbered as a list except in those rare instances when the itemized lines are referred to by number in the text discussion of the table. In these cases, an Arabic number enclosed in parentheses precedes each item. Like other columns in a table, the stub should contain items that are logically and grammatically similar.

Sometimes, if there is room, explanatory notations are included with a stub item instead of being set as a footnote. These notations—often units of measurement (as *in dollars*) or other explanations (as *at end of year*)—are set in lowercase letters to the right of the stub item and are usually enclosed in parentheses.

An unavoidably long stub line may have to run over to a second line to prevent the stub column from becoming too wide. Runover lines are usually indented one em space (about two character spaces). However, if the stub also contains indented items that are grouped under subheads, as described below, any runovers should be indented one em more than the greatest indention used with subhead groupings.

Special attention must be paid to horizontal alignment when stub items run over to a second line, because it is essential that the items align with information about them in the other columns. The general rule is to

Table 2
Letter Placement Table
Three Sizes of Stationery

Lines in Letter Body	Words in Letter Body	Number of Blank Lines between Date and Inside Address*	Typewriter Marginal Stops Elite/Pica	Length of Typing Line	
				Inches	Spaces Elite/Pica
Half-sheet Stationery: Assume Letterhead takes 7 vertical lines. (Baronial—center No. 33 for Elite; No. 28 for Pica)					
9–10	60–66	7	15–60/10–50	4	48/40
11–12	67–73	6	15–60/10–50	4	48/40
13–14	74–80	5	15–60/10–50	4	48/40
15–16	81–87	4	15–60/10–50	4	48/40
17–18	88–94	3	15–60/10–50	4	48/40
19–20	95–100	2	15–60/10–50	4	48/40
Executive-size Stationery: Assume Letterhead takes 8 lines. (Monarch—center No. 43, Elite; No. 36, Pica)					
13–14	95–115	8	15–75/10–60	5	60/50
15–16	116–135	7	15–75/10–60	5	60/50
17–18	136–155	6	15–75/10–60	5	60/50
19–20	156–175	5	15–75/10–60	5	60/50
Full-size Stationery: Assume Letterhead takes 9 lines. (Standard—center No. 51, Elite; No. 42, Pica)					
3–5	under 100	7–12	25–75/22–62	4	48/40
6–10	100–200	4–8	20–80/17–67	5	60/50
11–14	175–200	7	15–87/12–72	6	72/60
15–18	201–225	6	15–87/12–72	6	72/60
19–22	226–250	5	15–87/12–72	6	72/60
23–26	251–275	4	15–87/12–72	6	72/60
27–30	276–300**	3	15–87/12–72	6	72/60

*Assume that the date is typed three lines below the last line of the letterhead on all letters.
**Letters consisting of more than 300 words should be two-page letters

align the stub runover line with the items in the corresponding columns. However, if both the stub and at least one of the corresponding column items have runovers, the first lines of each item should align to form the row.

Leaders (a full discussion of which begins on page 230) are sometimes used to connect items in the stub with information in other columns across the row. Leaders are useful when there is a wide space between the columns, or when stub items are of widely varying lengths, making it difficult for the eye to connect the data that go together.

Stub subheads Stub items frequently fall into categories that are grouped under stub subheads. In most cases the stub subhead simply labels the grouping; there is no data in the row extending across the table from the stub subhead, as in the following example:

	Amount ($000)	Percent of sales
Standard cost of goods sold:		
Prime costs	860,000	40
Factory overhead	740,000	35
Total standard cost	1,600,000	75

Sometimes, however, the subhead acts as a total or subtotal itself and requires the addition of data in the columns across the row:

Standard cost of goods sold	**1,600,000**	**75**
Prime costs	860,000	40
Factory overhead	740,000	35

A variety of methods is used to make these stub groupings accessible to the reader. Subheads may be set in italic or boldface type or in a larger size of type. They may be centered over the pertinent part of the stub or set at the left margin. Frequently a line of horizontal space just above the subhead separates each grouping. Stub subheads that are set flush left may be followed by a colon, as in the first example above, or by no mark of punctuation, as in the second example.

Subheads usually result in one or more levels of indention, because indention is the conventional way to indicate levels of subordination. Items listed below a subhead that is flush left are usually indented one em. If there are two levels of subheads, the second-level subheads are indented an em space, and the items listed under them are indented an additional em. Very complicated stubs may have even more than two levels of subheads. In these cases the different levels must be distinguished as clearly as possible, and indention can be supplemented by other devices. For example, first-level subheads can be centered over the stub and second-level subheads flush against the left margin. Or all heads can be set flush left but distinguished by different typefaces such as bold, italic, or small capitals.

Another solution to the formatting of stubs that have two or more levels of subordination is to use *cut-in headings,* also called *table spanners,* for the highest-level heads. These headings are set on a horizontal space that cuts across the full width of the table and are often set off by rules that also extend across the stub and body of the table. The effect is to create a major division within the table, as if two or more tables were combined in one, with two or more separate stubs under a single set of column heads. Examples of table spanners may be found in Tables 1 and 2; in the former these heads are centered across the table; in the latter they are set flush left.

Column Heads

Column heads are single words or concise phrases that categorize the data listed in the vertical columns below them. Except for the stubhead, which is optional, column heads must appear over all columns of a table. Column subheads and other special types of headings called *spanner heads* may be added as a table's complexity increases.

A column head is usually a noun or brief noun phrase. The column head should not be much wider than the widest items in the column beneath it, although with a column of figures achieving this result may be difficult. There should also be at least two characters of space between the widest parts of adjacent headings. The usual way to narrow the space taken by the column head is by setting one or more runover lines. This adds a little length to the table but can reduce its width considerably.

Column heads are frequently set in roman type with headline-style capitalization, though modern styling often favors sentence-style capitalization. Boldface type is also commonly used. Any abbreviations, figures, or symbols used in column heads should match the styling used in the body of the table. A period never follows a column head.

A major consideration in the styling of tables is whether to center the column heads or to align them at the left or right with all the items in the column. If the table's caption is centered above the table, the column heads are usually centered too. If the caption is flush left, the column heads may be aligned at the left. One alternative is to align the stubhead on the left while centering all other heads over their columns. Another alternative is to align headings on the left over all word columns but on the right over figure columns. The reason for doing this is that columns of figures usually are right-aligned to begin with. Tables that are ruled so that the column heads appear within boxes look best with headings centered vertically and horizontally within the box.

When column heads are aligned right or left, so are runovers and subheads. When heads are centered, any runover lines and subheads are also centered. Centered column heads look best when the top line is the longest. This inverted-pyramid effect is pleasing but not so important that it should result in the dividing of short words to achieve it. Only long words should be divided within a column heading.

The vertical space allowed to all the column heads in a table depends on the number of lines in the longest column head. When the heads each have a different number of lines, the designer must decide how to align these varying column heads horizontally. Horizontal alignment is not always a consideration with centered column heads, because they may be centered within the vertical space allowed as well as within the horizontal space. On the other hand, flush-styled column heads and centered heads with different line lengths generally align according to the last line of the heading especially if the table is unruled.

It is traditional for a horizontal rule to be drawn across the table, below the lowermost line of column heads. Some publications, however, prefer unruled tables in which the careful use of spacing and type styles substitutes for the obvious borderlines that rules provide.

Column heads should be set on the horizontal if at all possible. Sometimes, to save space, they are set on their side so that they run up instead of across. A combination of horizontal and vertical column heads in one table is also acceptable, but the stubhead should never be set vertically. Vertical column heads are generally set flush at their left, and they are used most frequently over narrow columns of figures. Vertical rules may have to be added to separate these heads from other column heads.

Column subhead A subhead set below a column head explains something about the data in the column below. Its most frequent use is to state the unit of measurement that applies to the data, and its purpose is to avoid having to repeat the unit quantity for each item in the column. For example, the subhead *$1000* means that the dollar sign and three ciphers are omitted from all the items in that column. The figure 450 in that column would thus represent the sum of $450,000. Other examples of common subheads include the following:

$mil   *meaning*   figures represent millions of dollars
000   *meaning*   add 000 to each figure
$ *meaning*   figures represent dollars
%   *meaning*   figures represent percentages
thousands of dollars
millions
in miles

Subheads are usually distinguished from column heads by being set on a separate line. They may be enclosed in parentheses, and sometimes italic type is used. Or, if the heads are all-capitalized, the subheads may be capital-and-lowercase. They may also be set below a horizontal rule but directly above the first column item in order to distinguish them from column heads.

Subheads that are very brief may be run in with the column head. These may be enclosed in parentheses, separated only by a comma (as *weight, ounces*), or expressed as a prepositional phrase (as *Production in tons*).

A subhead explanation may apply to more than one column head by being spread across both columns, as the following example:

1983   1984
(thousands of dollars)

Like stubs, columns are occasionally numbered or lettered strictly for the convenience of discussion in the text, where reference is made to the identifying symbols. If this is necessary, the column letters or numbers should be enclosed in parentheses either below or above the column heads and separated from them by a line of space. A set of such reference letters or numbers should always align horizontally.

Decked column heads *Decked heads* are used to categorize certain groupings of columns and to avoid repeating words in column heads. Decked heads consist of (1) an inclusive *spanner head* which is set on top and which spans the width of the two or more subordinate column heads beneath it, and (2) the individual column heads below the spanner head. Each column head covers only one column, while a spanner head covers two or more columns.

	Temperature (C)	
two-column spanner head	Mean	Range

	Year Ended Oct. 31		
three-column spanner head	1985	1984	1983

	Dissolved oxygen (ppm)			
			Mean saturation (%)	Saturation range (%)
four-column spanner head with subheads	Mean	Range		

Spanner heads may be separated from their subordinate column heads by a line of space, a rule, or a distinctive typeface. A very common styling, illustrated above and in Tables 1 and 2, is a rule drawn below the spanner head exactly the width of all the affected columns beneath it. This rule makes it clear that the column heads are subdivisions of the spanner head. Another common way to set off the spanner head is to set it in a different typeface. In a table with vertical and horizontal rules, the rule below the spanner head forms the top of the boxes in which the subordinate column heads are enclosed.

Columns

The meaning of a column depends on the column head above it; that head, therefore, must apply logically to each item in the column. In certain circumstances the column head may have no meaningful application to a particular item in the stub. When this situation occurs, there should be no information at the point where that stub row intersects with the column. That intersection (often called a *cell*) is left blank—or the abbreviation *N/A, N.A.,* or *n.a.,* meaning *not applicable,* is written in—to indicate that the data do not apply in this particular case. On the other hand, the use of a centered em dash or three or more ellipsis points in the cell conventionally means "data not available." It is sometimes important to make the distinction between *not applicable* and *not available,* although not all tables do; in some, ellipsis points are used for both circumstances. If a distinction is desired, the writer may wish to explain the chosen symbols in a general footnote to the table. Of course, when quantities are being tabulated and the quantity that applies in a particular instance is a zero, a zero is written in the cell. The set of ellipsis points may be a full column wide or as small as three points only.

Some tables increase their data-holding capacity by adding extra information to items in a column instead of adding another column. The last column of Table 2 effectively combines two columns, for example. The added information may be set in parentheses just below the item or a bit to the right of it. A common use of this device is to add the raw numbers that go with a list of percentages, but if this procedure is followed, a general footnote must be added to explain it. Another way to include raw numbers is to set a separate column next to the percentages. Alternatively the information maybe in a headnote, a subhead, or a general footnote.

Words in columns are never capitalized headline-style; word columns are capitalized sentence-style or not at all. If the column head or the table caption mention such things as units of measurement, these units are not repeated within the columns.

Alignment To be readable, the columns of a table have to be precisely aligned, vertically and horizontally. The reader should be able to see at a glance that a particular stub item goes with a particular column item, or that a column item belongs under a particular column head.

Horizontal alignment is extremely important. Stub items should always align with the row they govern; care should be taken with any runover lines in the stub or any stub subheads that require a horizontal line of space across the whole table. As a rule, the last runover line of a stub item is the one that aligns with the corresponding items in the other columns. However, if the column entries themselves have runovers, horizontal alignment should proceed along the first lines of both stub entry and column items.

Vertical alignment is also important. Items are seldom centered within a column. Words in a column, for example, are nearly always flush against the left edge of the column. And figures are nearly always aligned vertically: at the right edge of the column by their last digit if they are whole numbers, by the rightmost whole digit if they include fractions, and by decimal point if they are decimal numbers. The centering of a column of figures is visually unappealing and makes comparison of the figures difficult. If, however, the figure column consists of extremely dissimilar items, centering them is acceptable if the visual effect is good.

Vertical alignment may also be based on recurring symbols such as dollar signs or percent signs, or on the initial letters of certain words. The choice is normally based on whatever looks most orderly, and more than one basis for vertical alignment may be chosen to achieve this order. For example, in the column below the figures align according to the rightmost full digit, the center dash, and also the dollar sign:

$576–$1,200
$480–$1,000
$400–$ 850

Dollar amounts To save space in columns that contain dollar amounts, decimal points and zeroes are omitted when the columns contain only whole-dollar amounts. However, if one of the amounts in the column contains a cents figure, the decimal points and zeroes must be added to the whole-dollar amounts.

$100	$100.00
95	95.25
125	125.00

In a vertical column consisting only of dollar amounts, the dollar sign is usually placed only in the following positions: (1) next to the first item, (2) next to the total amount if there is one, and (3) next to the first item following any break in the column such as a subheading, a subtotal, or a horizontal rule. If some of the items in the column are not dollar amounts, the dollar sign must be repeated as needed. For instance, if some amounts are measured in foreign currency, or if a word such as *negligible* is substituted for the figure, then the dollar sign is repeated before each dollar amount in the column, and the dollar signs need not be aligned. Dollar signs should also be repeated with all dollar amounts listed in a table stub.

Dollar signs align vertically down the column; this means that before positioning the dollar sign beside the top number, the author or typist must determine the largest amount in the column, which will be the total if there is one. Exceptions to the general rule that dollar signs align occur (1) when not every item in the column is a dollar amount, or (2) when the column contains inclusive figures that consist of two dollar amounts. In the second case it is the internal connecting symbols, not the dollar signs or the figures, that determine the alignment of the column.

$7–9	$10 to $50
$102–123	$50 to $150
$24–30	$150 to $200
$1,014–1,178	

Decimals Decimal places should not be carried farther than is necessary. While it is true that rounded-off numbers are less exact, they usually provide enough data for valid comparisons, and in fact they make the determination of many patterns much easier. As a general rule, decimal fractions are carried to the same number of places in every figure within a column by the addition of zeroes. This is not always practicable, however, in a column consisting of decimals carried to more than two places. Tables showing the atomic weight of chemical elements, for instance, dispense with the extra zeroes—some of which would extend four decimal places—because they would be distracting.

The conventional rules for listing decimal numbers are illustrated in the following examples and explained in the numbered paragraphs that follow:

3.85	5.43	3.8	0.4
18.00	0.20	18.0	.6
12.50	0.60	12.5	.6782
7.00	8.81	7.0	.3
		0.9	

1. When some numbers in a column are carried one or two places to the right of the decimal point, the others should add one or two zeroes as necessary so that the numbers extend equally to the right edge of the column.
2. In columns consisting of both whole numbers with decimal fractions and decimal fractions less than a whole number, a zero is usually added to the unit column on the left of each decimal fraction. But if all items in the column are decimal fractions less than a whole number, the placing of a zero to the left of the decimal point is optional.
3. If the first number in a column or below a rule, subhead, or other break in a column is a decimal fraction only, it is always a good idea to add a zero to the left of its decimal point.
4. A zero that is used alone in a column of money or other decimal figures is usually aligned in the unit column without a decimal point, although in some tables the zero amount appears as *0.0* or even as a zero centered in the column.

67.2	67.2	67.2
54.3	54.3	54.3
0	0.0	0
56.0	56.0	56.0

Decimal points are the basis of vertical alignment in columns where they appear except where the numbers represent different units of measure. Any such mixture of figures—as a mix of decimals and fractions, or a combination of disparate measures such as feet and pounds, or a list in which some figures contain parenthetical matter and others do not—usually aligns at the left or the right.

Other types of figure columns The use of other symbols and abbreviations in columns of figures may be summarized as follows:

Percentages Percent signs are not necessary in columns of figures if *percentage* is indicated in the column head or subhead. However, if space is available, the percent sign is often repeated with each number for clarity even when it is not needed.

Inclusive numbers Inclusive figures such as *20–25* or *20 to 25* are aligned on the internal hyphen or en dash or on the word *to* when such numbers comprise the whole column. See, for example, Table 3 on page 227.

Parentheses When some but not all of the items in a column are enclosed in parentheses, the figures usually align on the right with the closing parenthesis falling in the space between the columns.

Mathematics signs Plus or minus signs that appear at the left of a set of figures do not affect the vertical alignment of those figures. The symbols themselves may be aligned, but more often they are set directly against the figures so that they cannot be mistaken for anything other than mathematics signs.

$$-8$$
$$-18$$
$$-4$$

TABLE 3

THE BEAUFORT SCALE

BEAUFORT NUMBER	NAME	MILES PER HOUR	DESCRIPTION
0	calm	less than 1	calm; smoke rises vertically
1	light air	1–3	direction of wind shown by smoke but not by wind vanes
2	light breeze	4–7	wind felt on face; leaves rustle; ordinary vane moved by wind
3	gentle breeze	8–12	leaves and small twigs in constant motion; wind extends light flag
4	moderate breeze	13–18	raises dust and loose paper; small branches are moved
5	fresh breeze	19–24	small trees in leaf begin to sway; crested wavelets form on inland waters
6	strong breeze	25–31	large branches in motion; telegraph wires whistle; umbrellas used with difficulty
7	moderate gale (*or* near gale)	32–38	whole trees in motion; inconvenience in walking against wind
8	fresh gale (*or* gale)	39–46	breaks twigs off trees; generally impedes progress
9	strong gale	47–54	slight structural damage occurs; chimney pots and slates removed
10	whole gale (*or* storm)	55–63	trees uprooted; considerable structural damage occurs
11	storm (*or* violent storm)	64–72	very rarely experienced; accompanied by widespread damage
12	hurricane*	73–136	devastation occurs

*The U.S. uses 74 statute mph as the speed criterion for hurricane.

A plus or minus sign that follows a figure also does not affect the alignment of the figures but falls in the space between the columns.

Words in figure columns Although columns consisting entirely of words usually align on the left, columns with combinations of figures and words may align on the right or on the left, or they may be centered.

Symbols and Roman numerals Any symbols or Roman numerals within a column of figures align on the right with the figures. A column consisting only of Roman numerals aligns at the left.

Fractions When tabulating a column of whole numbers that have fractions, one should align the whole numbers on the right but their fractions on the left. A whole number without a fraction is thus followed by a blank space.

Price Range
7⅜– 3
4⅞–22¾
9⅛– 6¼
12 – 7¾
14¾– 6⅛
9⅞– 5¾

However, if a column contains different values of numbers—such as mixed decimals and fractions—all numbers should be right-aligned.

Dates In order to align a column of dates—month, day, and year—extra space may have to be inserted, as shown in the following examples.

May 27, 1892	Sept	27
Mar 8, 1901	Oct	3
Oct 12, 1904	Nov	13

There are cases, however, when the decision to center the dates in the column may be preferable:

| 1898 |
| 1899 |
| 1899–1900 |
| 1901–2 |

A column of dates that forms a stub may be handled differently. The abbreviation for the month may extend into the left margin to provide more white space and better visibility:

Oct	10
	20
	31
Nov	10
	20
	30

Totals The word *total,* when used in a table, appears most often at the foot of the stub and the total figures in one or more of the columns to the right of the stub. The word may be omitted if the figures are obviously totals. *Total* is typically capitalized and indented much farther right than any other item in the stub, although it may align with other stub subheads. Grand totals are usually indented even further than subtotals.

Total numbers should be highly visible. Some publications set them in boldface. More often, the numbers are set off with a line of space above and below, or with a rule above and perhaps a double underscore below. These rules and underscores are set the full width of the total figure, including the dollar sign or any other symbol used with the figure. In a column of figures containing breaks where groups of figures are added or subtracted, double rules may be used above a grand total and also to mark other major breaks in arithmetic.

Totals in a column consisting of percentages that add up to 100 percent are optional. If the numbers do not add up to 100 percent, an exact total percentage should be given and a general footnote such as "Percentages do not equal 100 because of rounding" should be written to explain the apparent discrepancy.

Columns of words Most tables present quantitative data in columns of figures. But many tables—and some parts of figure tables—consist of words in tabular format. Tables such as these are called *word tables,* or *reading tables,* and they are intended to be read like text. For this reason they use abbreviations sparingly and should not be so compactly phrased as to be less than easily intelligible. On the other hand, these tables differ from text in that articles are often omitted and numbers are not spelled out.

Word tables look best when they are simple, with brief entries and no rules. Runover lines are usually indented, as in Table 3, unless rules or lines of space serve to separate one item from another.

The alignment of word tables depends upon a number of factors. If the items are brief—say a word or two, with a few or no runover lines—a centered styling may look best. Long items with runover lines look best when aligned at the left side of the column. Horizontal alignment of word columns usually proceeds according to the top line of any items that have runovers.

Rules

Rules can improve the appearance of tabular matter, but their chief use is functional. They clarify the parts of a table by separating densely packed columns or rows of figures and by filling the space in tables whose parts are too widely separated. However, the use of rules within tabular matter—especially the use of vertical rules—has decreased in many publications to the point where rules are now frequently avoided altogether, being replaced by the judicious use of horizontal and vertical spaces. An author submitting a table for publication should not ink or type rules within a table. Whether and where to place rules is a decision best left to the editor, although the author may lightly pencil in certain rules to guide the editor's decision. For a table that is being typewritten in its final form, however, rules are easy to draw and may be used as needed. Both horizontal and vertical rules may be made with the typewriter or drawn separately with ruler and black ink. The use and placement of rules should be determined before any typing begins.

Tables with horizontal rules conventionally use only three full-width rules: one below the caption and above the column heads, one below the column heads, and one below the table and often above any footnotes. The rule below the column heads is often omitted. In addition to these, internal horizontal rules of varying width may be used, as well as external rules that separate table from text. Rules set below spanner heads, for example, are continuous rules set exactly the width of the columns they cover with space on either side. Similarly, the rules set above total amounts are exactly as wide as the totals. Other full-width rules may mark cut-in heads or may divide a long table into more readable sections.

Vertical rules Vertical rules are sometimes used to separate columns and column heads, especially in crowded statistical tables. But they are relatively expensive to set in type and seldom worth the distinctions they provide. Many publications avoid their use entirely. As long as enough space is provided between columns, there is usually no need for them. Vertical rules are often used, however, in typewritten tables because they are easy to draw in. They are also common in doubled tables (a full discussion of which begins on page 239). For those occasions when the use of vertical rules is justified, the columns—but not necessarily each column item—should be centered between the rules, and cut-in heads should be enclosed in a horizontal space that extends across the table and interrupts any vertical rules.

Leaders

Leaders are periods, or sometimes hyphens or dashes, set in a row that provides a horizontal connection between the columns of a table. They usually connect only the stub and the first column of a table, and are used only when the columns are set so far apart that the eye would have trouble connecting the data without the visual aid of the line of leaders. Since they tend to clutter a table, they should not be used routinely. Certain conventions govern the use of leaders:

1. Leaders are spaced. That is, a space should appear between each point in the row and also before the first point and after the last point.
2. When leaders follow stub items, the longest stub line must be followed by at least one point, which must be spaced so that it does not look like a period.
3. Rows of leaders align vertically.
4. Leaders connect the last line of any stub runover with its corresponding column items, unless one of those column items also contains runover lines, in which case the leaders connect the first lines of stub and column item.
5. Leaders are sometimes omitted from the first and last rows of a table, as these lines can almost always be easily read without them.
6. In some stylings, all leaders end shortly after the longest stub line and do not extend fully to the next column, leaving a column of white space between leaders and the first column. The effect is to make the stub items appear to be of equal length when they are not.

Braces

Braces provide a means of enclosing certain items in a column to indicate a category. Braces are rarely used in tables, however, because of the difficulty and expense of properly setting them. When used, they should be positioned carefully so as to enclose all of the pertinent items, including any runover lines.

Ditto Marks

Ditto marks (or the abbreviation *do.*) are avoided in tabular matter because of the difficulty of absorbing their meaning. If used, they appear in the regular columns and never in the stub. Alternatives to ditto marks are to repeat the information in each column or to include it in the column head.

Footnotes

Tables are frequently footnoted to provide explanations that, if included in the table proper, would make it unwieldy. Footnotes to tables include general notes, sometimes unnumbered, that acknowledge a source or explain such things as the meaning of abbreviations or the limitations of the data, and specific notes, always indicated by a number or other reference mark, that explain specific items in a column.

Footnotes are positioned just below the table and are usually set in type smaller than that of the table. Unnumbered general notes are best grouped together as a paragraph under the single heading *Notes*. They may also be listed separately, each headed by the word *Note* and separated by a thin line of space. Footnotes may begin flush against the left margin or they may be indented like a paragraph. Runover lines are flush left, or they are indented so that they align below the first word of the footnote instead of below the footnote symbol or the introductory word *Note* or *Source*. A period terminates every note.

The author often has a choice of whether to include certain data in the table itself or in footnotes. Sometimes a column or row of the table that has very few variables may be taken out of the table and the information supplied in a couple of footnotes. In an effort to keep captions and column heads simple, the author may add explanatory footnotes. On the other hand, to avoid a table with too many notes, the author may add data to column heads or add a new column of data.

Table footnotes are always kept separate from text footnotes and are numbered independently of them. If the text page on which a table appears also has footnotes, the two sets of notes are separated, either by lines of text or by a rule about an inch long set across from the left margin. Text footnotes appear at the bottom of the page, below this rule, and table footnotes are placed above the rule. It is a good idea to further distinguish text and table footnotes by using different footnote symbols for each. For example, if the text uses superior numbers for footnote symbols, the table may use superior letters or other types of reference marks.

The three major types of footnotes are source notes, other general notes, and specific notes.

Source notes Often the first note below the table is a source note. Such a note is required when the table is reprinted from another source or when the author has created a new table using data derived from another source. Reprinting tables and using material from other sources often involves more than just writing the proper form of footnote, however. For copyrighted material, the author must ask for and receive written permission in order to use another person's or another publication's material. Credit should be given to the original author and, if the material is copyrighted, separately to the copyright holder.

The introductory heading to source notes (as *Source:* or *Note:*) are frequently italicized. The form that the note takes matches the bibliographic style used elsewhere in the work. Depending on the type of source used, there are three basic ways to acknowledge a source in a footnote.

1. Acknowledge the source of data used in a table compiled by the author. Permission from the original source is required unless it is public property. The footnote is commonly introduced by the word *Source* or *Sources* followed by a colon or period, or it is introduced by phrases such as "Data from . . ." or "Adapted with permission from . . ."

   Adapted from Full Name of Author, *Title of Book,* 3d ed. City: Publisher, year, p. 000.

2. Acknowledge the source of the actual table or any section of it. Permission from the source is required unless it is public property. The pages on which the original table was published must be included. This type of footnote is introduced by the word *Source* or *Note* and usually includes the word *permission.*

   Note: Reprinted, by permission of the publisher, from Name of Author, "Title of Article," *Title of Periodical* 00 (year): 000.

   Table 3 is reproduced with permission from . . .

   Source: Author's Full Name, *Title of Book,* 3d ed. City: Publisher, year, 000. Reprinted with permission.

3. Acknowledge the source of a copyrighted table. The author must not only get written permission but must also determine any further requirements. The copyright holder may demand that the permission note be worded in a specific way, for example, or in a minimum size of type. Two common forms are illustrated here:

   Source: "Title of Article" by Author's Full Name, year, *Title of Journal,* 00, p. 000. Copyright 1900 by Name of Copyright Holder. Reprinted by permission.

   NOTE: Reprinted, by permission, from Author's Full Name, ed. *Title of Book* (City: Publisher's Name, year), p. 000. © 1900 by Publisher's Name.

Source notes do not always appear as footnotes. Sometimes they are set as headnotes below the caption and above the table. This is a more prominent position which may be required by some copyright holders.

Other general notes General notes explain information pertaining to the table as a whole, such as the reliability of the data, how the data were obtained, and the meaning of any nonstandard abbreviations or symbols used throughout the table. These notes are often introduced by the word *Note* and they are often unnumbered. If a table has more than one general note, they should be run together in a paragraph, headed *Notes,* just below the table, because paragraphs of notes are easier to read than lists. A single note might be placed as a headnote below the caption, if it is important enough.

Specific notes Specific footnotes are those introduced by superior symbols, often called *reference marks,* that correspond to marks that follow specific items in a column or column head. (Specific footnotes are usually not used on a caption.) Each specific note may begin on a separate line, or the notes may run together like general notes, each one separated from the other by a space of about two ems. Sometimes long footnotes are set to run the full width of the table, while short footnotes for the same table are set together on a single line in order to save space.

Reference marks The symbols used to mark specific footnotes are often superior numbers, but if numbers are used in the text to signal textual footnotes, tables should use a different kind of symbol. Some stylebooks prescribe superior letters anyway, because of the chance that a superior number used with tabular data might be mistaken for a mathematics exponent sign. If some tables consist of figures and others of words, the decision may be made to use superior letters with figure tables and superior numbers with word tables. Letters used as footnote reference marks are lowercase, not capital letters. If there is any chance that a superior number or letter might confuse the reader, the traditional footnote symbols, listed below in the order in which they are used, may be used throughout the table instead.

*	asterisk
†	dagger
‡	double dagger
§	section mark
‖	parallels
¶	paragraph mark
#	number sign

If more than seven notes are needed for one table, the reference marks are simply doubled, as **, ††, etc. On the other hand, if such a large number of footnotes is needed, one should probably rely on superior numbers or letters instead, as a courtesy to the reader, who is probably not familiar with the order of these traditional marks. A very common modern alternative when only a few footnotes are needed in a table is to use first a single asterisk, then a double asterisk, and so on without resorting to the dagger and other marks. This alternative—illustrated in Table 2—is especially useful in typewritten tables, where the asterisk and number sign are the only traditional footnote reference marks readily available. A variation on this alternative that works for up to four footnotes is to use the asterisk and the dagger in the following order: *, **, †, ††.

Each table has its own set of general and specific notes. Each set of specific footnotes for a table begins with a superior *1, a,* or asterisk. It is best to sequence the footnote symbols in reading order: row by row, from left to right, starting with the top row. Any reference mark may be used more than once within a table; in fact, it is common for a single footnote to explain more than one item.

Reference marks are positioned, without a space, directly *after* the pertinent figure or word in the table, not before it. Footnote reference symbols are not included in any consideration of alignment; they hang in the space between columns. It is not uncommon for a tabular item to be marked by two reference marks, to guide the reader to two separate footnotes. In these cases, the reference symbols are separated by a small comma, as 405[a, c] or 405[1, 3].

Reference marks that precede the actual footnotes are handled differently. Each specific footnote is signaled by a superior reference symbol that matches one of the footnote symbols in the table. The reference mark is usually set with a space between it and the beginning of the note, but the space may be omitted.

[1] Data for October unavailable.
[1]Data for October unavailable.

In printed matter, the footnote letter or number is usually set as shown in the examples above. In typewritten tables, however, even when superior symbols are found in the actual table, the footnotes themselves may be introduced with regular numbers or letters set on the baseline and followed by a period and a space, as in the following example.

NOTES:

a. $n = 25$.
b. Plus accrued and unpaid dividends, if any.

Even in printed matter, footnote reference marks may not always be set as superior figures or letters. Many publications today prefer to use symbols that are more easily typed. Thus reference marks may also be found as small letters in parentheses set on the base line or even as capital letters that immediately follow a figure. If any of these nontraditional reference marks are used, care must be taken that the reader understands them to be footnote symbols.

Still another usage is found often in annual reports where tables may be followed by a lengthy series of explanatory notes. In these, "Note 1" may appear in parentheses after a stub item or below a column head. The corresponding explanation is introduced in the footnote section with the head "Note 1." These reference symbols can be used only with stub items and column heads, where there is room to fit them in; footnotes to specific items in the table must be handled in the traditional way.

Typing Tables

Tables in a manuscript submitted for publication are typed on pages separate from the rest of the manuscript, one table to a page. The pages are not numbered with the manuscript. Each table is numbered, however, either with a permanent number that becomes part of the caption or with a temporary number whose function is to prevent mix-ups during the editorial and production processes. Only the briefest of tables, usually only about four lines long and two columns wide, may be typed along with the text.

The reason for this procedure is that there may not be room enough on the printed page to fit the whole table below a specified line of text. The author therefore separates manuscript text and tables but at the same time marks, in the margin of the manuscript, the appropriate point where the tables should go. The margin notation, which denotes the table by number, might be "Insert Table 3 here." (Some journals prefer that the body of the manuscript be interrupted with lines of space and a notation such as "Table 3 goes here" centered in the space.) Conversely, a notation with each table should indicate the manuscript page that it goes with.

Tables for Typeset Publications

Tables typed for publication are each begun on a separate page and are properly identified. A good way to identify a table is to type in the upper right corner of the page the table number, the author's name, a short title of the work in which the table is to appear, and the corresponding manuscript page number.

Tables are typed in a form similar to the final printed form except that the typewritten form is always double-spaced. The only exceptions to double spacing are the single spacing of runover lines in column heads and in items within a column. Even footnotes should be double-spaced. If the author specifies a table with horizontal rules, the typist should use normal double spacing, then draw a horizontal rule within the line of space. These rules should be drawn in pencil in case the editor decides to eliminate them.

The word *Table* with an identifying Arabic numeral (as *Table 4*), if used, is typed two or more lines above the table and is followed by a title for the table. All tabular data must be correctly aligned. The author tells the typist whether to center the columns and headings or whether to align them on the left, on the right, or at some midpoint such as a decimal point. The most common problem for the typist is estimating the width of a table and making it fit the width of the page. Column width is usually determined by the longest word or figure in that column or in the column head, although words in long column heads are usually continued as runover lines to reduce the width of the heading. In addition, ample space (usually three characters or more of space) should be allowed between columns. The author should advise the typist on how to handle tables that are too wide for the page. The suggestions listed on pages 237–238 may be helpful, or the typist may type the table sideways. A table typed across an 11-inch page will usually fit vertically on a printed page when the table is set in small type.

Very long tables that must be continued on another page are discussed on pages 239–240.

Tables in Typewritten Reports

Tables in a report that is typewritten in its final form, instead of being set in type, require a special care. First of all, the typist must estimate and plan both the actual width and length of the table to determine whether it can fit the page. If the table is too long to fit at the point where the author specifies, it is better to move the whole table to the next page than to divide it lengthwise. If the table is too wide, it may be typed broadside to fit. Extra-large tables are sometimes photographically reduced for inclusion in typewritten reports. The table is typed on a large sheet of paper, reduced to the desired size, then pasted in place on a page of the proper size. To estimate the table's width, the typist counts the number of characters and blank spaces within the longest item in each column (or column head if it is longer) and adds two characters of space (three or more if possible) between each column. Lines within column heads may run over as necessary to narrow the width of the column. There should be equal space between columns. In estimating the vertical linage, one includes any blank lines that will go between title and table, above footnotes, or within the table itself. Subtracting the estimated vertical linage of the table from the available lines on the page (usually six lines to each vertical inch) will give the total top and bottom margin available, which should be split equally or with extra space going to the bottom margin.

Tables that are typewritten in their final form instead of being typeset are usually single-spaced, with double spacing between major parts. Leaving one and a half spaces between lines is also frequently done, and it works well. Double spacing is useful in a table with columns that are few and are separated by large amounts of white space, because the extra horizontal space created by double spacing balances the extra space between the vertical columns. A double-spaced table should have extra space between its major parts, however, such as between the caption and the table itself.

At least three blank lines of space should be left at the top and bottom of a table if it has text above and below it. If possible, there should also be five character spaces or more of extra margin inside the regular margins to set off the table.

Centering of titles and column heads is often discouraged in typewritten tables because of the extra time it takes. If a centered styling is chosen, it must be adhered to precisely; noticeably off-center headings detract from the appearance of the table.

Without the options made available by the use of italic and boldface type, typewritten tables use underlining generously to mark major parts. A very common styling is to type the caption all in capital letters and the column heads in capital and lowercase letters, headline-style, and to underscore both.

Alternative Table Construction

Ideally, a table is designed to fit a single page. If an author or editor discovers that a table is too large to fit its page, there are several courses to follow. First the author or editor can look for ways to reduce the size of the table through the steps outlined in the section below. If none of those steps works, an alternative table construction, such as a broadside table or doubled, parallel, or continued tables, may have to be used.

Determining Table Size

If an author or editor suspects that a table is too large to fit the page, the first step should be to determine as precisely as possible the table's size. The depth of the table is measured by a line count that includes the caption, the table (including all column-head runovers and other runover lines), all footnotes, all blank lines between the parts of the table, and any horizontal rules (which count as one blank line). Width is measured by counting the number of characters and spaces in the widest part of the stub and of each column (or column head, whichever is wider) plus two characters or more of space to go in each margin between columns. Any indented lines in the stub will add two extra characters of space to that line.

A typewriter character count may be converted to a count of typeset characters to provide an estimate of the size of a printed table. Since most tables are printed in eight-point type, and since most eight-point typefaces allow three characters per pica, one can estimate the table's width by multiplying the width of the type page (which is measured in picas) by three to produce the equivalent number of typewritten characters. Thus, a book page that measures 30 picas across would allow approximately 30 × 3 or 90 typewritten characters per line.

Reducing the Size of the Table

Before considering an alternative table design for a table that will not fit the page, the author or editor should first attempt to decrease the size of the table. If the table is too wide for the page, the following steps may help solve the problem.

1. Examine carefully the column heads and the stub. Could the phrases be briefer without loss of meaning?
2. Break column heads and set them on more than one line to save space; divide words if necessary to achieve even runovers.

3. Decrease the width of the stub by breaking long stub items into two or more shorter lines.
4. Consider whether a factor common to all the items in a column can be incorporated into the column head, thus reducing the width of items in the column.
5. Use a footnote to indicate any variable that might pertain to only a few of the items in a column.
6. Use abbreviations and symbols. A column head, for example, might be written as these three lines:

> 12 Mos.
> Ended
> 6/30/84

Only standard, easily recognized abbreviations should be used in tables, because too much condensing of information can discourage readers. Any nonstandard abbreviation or symbol must be explained in a general footnote to each table in which it is used. For example, the letters *P, R,* and *E* could appear next to certain figures in the table and be explained in a general footnote of this sort:

NOTE: *R* (revised), *P* (preliminary), *E* (estimate).

The meaning of *standard* and *nonstandard* varies, of course, depending upon the background of the intended reader. For example, in a table showing stock market information for a particular company there is no need to indicate that *Div. per Share* and *P/E Ratio* mean *dividends per share* and *price/earnings* ratio. Likewise, any abbreviation that is explained in the caption or a column head need not be footnoted. An equally important principle is that any abbreviation occurring in a table should be consistently abbreviated throughout that table and any other table in the series.

Broadside Tables

Large tables that are broader than they are long may be set broadside in some publications. Such tables should be set on a lefthand page if possible for easier reading. The caption is set as usual over the top of the table, so that it runs vertically along the left side of the page, and the table itself also reads across from the bottom of the page to the top. If the table is shorter than the page is wide, it is centered on the page.

Broadside tables that begin on the lefthand page and are continued down onto the righthand page should be set so that the inside margins are flush; that is, the table on the left page comes all the way down to the right margin, while on the right page the table is continued exactly at the left margin. This procedure minimizes the white space that breaks the table in two. A continued broadside table is rarely begun on the righthand page and continued on the next lefthand page unless the table is several pages long. When broadside tables are set to be continued from a left to a right page, there is no need to repeat the column heads or stub subheads, but if the table runs over to the next lefthand page, column heads and stub subheads, if applicable, are repeated. A more detailed discussion of continued tables appears below.

Doubled Tables

Some tables are so long and narrow that they may be doubled up; that is, the table is divided into two (or three or more) sections which are run side by side below the caption. Column heads plus any subheads that describe units of measurement are repeated over each section. The column heads for each section must be identical and also must align. If the table happens to be divided within a stub category that has a subhead, that subhead must be repeated over whatever item begins the second half of the table.

Rules are often used in doubled tables to distinguish the two halves: either a thin vertical rule between the two sections, or easier-to-set, horizontal rules below the column heads but broken by a space between the two halves of the table.

The opposite may be done with a table that is very wide but not deep. It may be divided in two (column heads along with the columns) and the second half set below the first half. In this case, it is the stub items that are repeated in the second half.

Parallel Tables

Parallel tables are very wide tables spread across two pages. A short caption may be set on the lefthand page only, but usually the caption and any headnotes are centered over the table with a break between the two pages. No words should be divided at the break. At the point where the table divides, both caption and table body should be flush against the inside margins so that the two parts are close together. If a spanner head or cut-in head should continue across the page it should be repeated on the new page, followed by the word *continued* or its abbreviation. Parallel tables work best when wide margins are left on either side. If the last column is too far from the stub, the table may be too wide to be easily absorbed.

Footnote symbols used in parallel tables are sequenced from left to right, horizontally across both pages, just as the table is read. The footnotes to a parallel table start on the lefthand page and continue to the righthand page; the number of footnote lines on each page should be equal. However, if there are no reference marks at all on the lefthand page, all notes begin on the righthand page.

Continued Tables

Continued tables, also called divided tables, are those which involve the turning of a page or more to complete their reading. They are never more than two pages wide, but they may be several pages long because of numerous stub items. The continued portions of such tables must be very carefully marked by the author in the manuscript version of the table. The following suggestions are designed to aid in this effort.

1. It is helpful, especially in the typewritten manuscript table, to type, in parentheses, *table continued* at the bottom of each page where needed.

Similarly, the top of each new page should give the table number and the word *continued* (or *cont.*) in parentheses.

2. Column heads and column subheads are repeated on each new page.
3. If the new page begins with an indented stub item, the subhead over that item should be repeated, followed by the word *continued* or *cont.* on the same line.

General notes that appear as headnotes below the caption are not repeated in continued tables unless essential for understanding the table. General notes that appear as footnotes are always set at the foot of the first page of the table (or at the foot of a two-page spread if the table is both parallel and continued); these are not repeated on the new page, nor are any specific footnotes that refer to column heads. Specific notes are most useful when positioned on the page where the reference mark first appears. However, when a specific footnote refers to items on more than one page (as when a superior number is repeated in several places throughout the table), the author has three choices. (1) The original footnote may be repeated on each new page which contains the reference mark. (2) To save space, the references on the new pages may say something like, "See footnote 3, page 987." (3) With very long tables one may place all the specific footnotes at the end of the table. If the last choice is made, at the foot of each page on which the table appears there should be a general note directing the reader to the "footnotes at end of table, p. 989."

The Author's Role in Preparing Illustrations

If a published work is to include illustrations, the author is often asked to submit either rough drafts or finished, camera-ready artwork to the publisher. This chapter discusses ways in which illustrations are handled by the author when finished artwork is required. Details regarding the production aspects of preparing illustrations for publication are discussed in Chapter 11, "Production Techniques." However, by way of introduction, authors should understand that illustrations, unlike tables, usually cannot be set in type. Instead, the original artwork is photographed (and often photographically reduced to a specified size) before being positioned, along with the accompanying type, on the page to be printed. Some typesetting companies do have some computerized graphics abilities, so that some illustrations can be handled just like tables; however, these capabilities are still quite limited, and the author should not assume that his or her artwork can be handled in that way. Illustrations are expensive and time-consuming to prepare for publication, and they always require close communication among the author, artist, editor, designer, and typesetter.

Preparing Illustrations

Illustrations should never be drawn on a manuscript. Like tables, they are always prepared on separate sheets, a separate one for each figure. The location of each figure is marked on the manuscript, however, usually in the margin but sometimes in a space across the manuscript with the notation "Insert Figure 4 here" or a similar instruction.

Captions and legends that accompany illustrations are treated altogether differently from table captions. Whereas a table caption is typed above the table, captions for figures are typed together on a separate sheet of paper, usually headed *List of Captions* or *Figure Captions and Legends*. The reason for this is that captions and legends for illustrations are typeset. They are not considered part of the artwork because they are positioned outside the figure area. Since they are handled separately from the illustrations during the editorial and production processes, they must be typed separately from the illustrations and from the manuscript. Like the manuscript, the list of captions is typed double-spaced. An identification number appears with each caption or legend on this sheet, even if it will not appear in the final printing. A temporary number is usually circled to prevent its being mistakenly typeset.

The illustration itself is also identified with a temporary or permanent number. To further ensure against misidentification, the figure should also be marked with the last name of the author, a short form of the caption, and the page number of the manuscript where the figure should be inserted. It is also a good idea, if the figure might cause confusion as to its proper position, to write TOP at the top margin of the figure or at the top of the back.

Picture identification is usually written lightly on the back of an illustration in a soft lead or grease pencil that will not create indentions on the front side. Even then, one should write close to the margin to prevent any creases or dark marks from showing through to the figure on the front. Ballpoint pens should definitely not be used, because they nearly always create such creases. Identification may be written on the front only if the margins are very large.

Handling Illustrations

The author should keep all finished artwork—even figures that are awaiting the addition of typeset labels—in an envelope. This envelope should contain stiff cardboard and it should be large enough to protect the unfolded illustrations. Artwork is handled in this way to prevent scratches, tears, creases, dirt spots, and other flaws that could show up when the figure is reproduced. Artwork should never be stapled. The use of paper clips is also discouraged unless the illustration is thoroughly protected from creases on both sides by extra thicknesses of paper.

Finished artwork, especially photographs, should be further protected by being placed between cardboards, perhaps with a tissue over the front. A tissue overlay is useful for pointing out flaws in the art that need to be retouched or corrected. The figure identification may also be written in the lower margin of such an overlay, which allows the artwork and the identification to be seen in one glance. These tissues are usually taped near the top margin on the back and folded over the length of the illustration in front.

Kinds of Illustrations

Publishers make a clear distinction between *line art* and *continuous-tone art* (or *halftone art*). The distinction is important because the two types print by completely different processes of photography. The simplest and least expensive is the reproduction of line art or line copy. Line art is any material that can be reproduced in black and white only—that is, simple lines and areas of black on a white background. Continuous-tone art consists of figures that contain not only black and white but also varying shades of gray. Photographs, wash drawings, paintings—even shaded bar graphs—are examples.

Line Art

Line drawings, bar and line graphs, diagrams, charts, and maps are best prepared by a professional graphic artist. Figures that are drafted and submitted in rough form by the author are usually redrawn by the artist and then shown to the author for approval. The author must determine early in the planning of a text whether the publisher requires the submission of finished artwork or will provide the services of an artist to work from the author's rough drafts.

Stencils and press-on patterns can help the nonprofessional create figures for a publication that does not require the product of a professional graphic artist. One can also purchase *transfer letters* which rub off onto the paper when placed face down and rubbed with a flat tool. *Stick-on letters* may be preferable for the beginner. These are taken off the sheet, placed face up on the drawing paper, and smoothed down very tightly. Stick-on letters can be lifted off and repositioned if necessary, while a mistake with transfer letters must be erased. Both transfer and stick-on letters are purchased in sheets that contain complete sets of letters and numbers in a particular font. Other symbols—circles, heavy lines, etc.—are also available. For more ambitious artwork, there are *clip books* available with camera-ready line illustrations that can be cut out and placed on the final art pasteup.

Figures are usually drawn to a scale up to twice as large as the proposed final print and then reduced to fit the page during the photographic process. The larger size makes the artist's job easier, and reduction minimizes any flaws in the artwork. On the other hand, reducing the figure may make certain details difficult to discern. Thus, the lines of a figure should be simple and clean with a minimum of detail.

Line drawings The graphic artist preparing line drawings generally uses black india ink on smooth, glossy, heavy white drawing paper of high quality in order to achieve the best contrast. High-contrast art reproduces well and provides sharp detail. Lesser-quality black-on-white artwork, such as that in photocopies, does not reproduce well because it lacks the sharp contrast. The effect of shading can be achieved in line art by the use of patterns of lines or dots within certain areas. Such patterns may even be purchased ready-made on pressure-sensitive paper, cut into shape, and placed on the areas where "shading" is desired.

Charts Charts are essentially labelled boxes connected by lines. They can be used effectively to show simple hierarchies, sequences of steps in a process, or relationships between the parts of a whole. Flowcharts and organization charts are common examples. Charts are also effective for diagramming the various parts of a working system. Explanatory labels and legends (discussed on pages 247–250) are essential elements of any chart.

Maps Maps, which should always be prepared by a professional, are accompanied by legends, labels, or keys that may (1) identify the important parts of the map, (2) indicate the location of the mapped area, (3) show compass direction, and (4) indicate the scale. Additional labels may explain the map's purpose or offer other information. Arrows are useful, too, for pointing to areas of focus. It is important not to overdecorate a map with detail, especially if it is to be reduced.

Graphs Graphs are useful for conveying numerical data and for showing relationships between sets of data, such as comparisons and percentages. Graph lines should always be clean and uncluttered. Information should be arranged logically and consistently; units of measurement, for example, should never be arbitrarily switched within a graph. The most commonly used graphs are pie charts and line and bar graphs.

Pie charts One of the simplest and most visually arresting graphs is the so-called pie chart, which marks sections of a circle to show the proportional parts of a whole in percentages, finite numbers, or both. The size of each section is determined by converting these numbers to the appropriate number of degrees within a 360-degree circle and measuring the arcs with a compass. The best pie charts are those with fewest sections: more than six sections tend to make a chart too complex. Pie charts are traditionally read clockwise from 12 o'clock, with the largest section first and the smallest section last, but other arrangements may be more logical in a particular case. If color is available, the sections may be further highlighted; or the highlighting can be done by shading, with the largest section lightest, for example, and the smallest section darkest. Depending upon the size of the chart and the lettering, labels that identify the parts may be placed inside each section or outside the circle.

Bar graphs Simple bar graphs, like the one illustrated on page 244, can supply a great deal of information in a compact space. Like pie charts, they can provide proportional comparisons with visual impact, but the bar form allows the addition of more complex information. For example, a large number of bars, each representing the measurement of an object or process, may be used. Or each bar in the graph may be subdivided to show different kinds of data, as measurements for two contrasting years, within each bar. Or the data may be presented in groups of multiple bars,

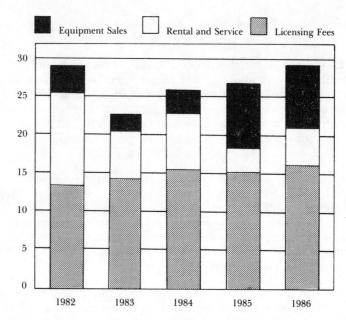

Figure 9.1. Annual Revenues (in millions)

each bar representing a unit to be compared with the others in the group. The distinctions between the parts of these multiple graphs may be shown by color or shading. Bars may be either horizontal or vertical; within a vertical graph they may even run downward to indicate losses or other negative numbers.

Bar graphs can be prepared without the help of a professional artist by sticking strips of press-on tape on graph paper. The bars may be drawn or taped on regular graph paper (the lines of which will show up when the figure is photographed) or on graph paper with blue lines that will not photograph. Units of measurement should appear on a grid at regular intervals alongside the bars, and the final measurement that each bar represents may also be shown in a label within or near the bar.

With a vertical bar chart, the independent variables—the things being measured with a bar—are listed across the bottom of the chart on the horizontal axis, while the units of measurement are shown along the side in grids going upward in sequence along the vertical axis. A horizontal bar chart, on the other hand, lists the independent variables at the left. The bars extend across the chart from left to right, with units of measurement indicated at regular intervals below. Frequently the number of words needed to explain the variables or the units of measurement will determine the direction of the chart. If space allows, some of the labels may be placed within the bars, especially if they are horizontal bars or very wide vertical bars.

Line graphs Like bar graphs, line graphs may be plotted on graph paper with blue lines that will not show when photographed, or regular graph paper with black or brown lines may be used. Line graphs are excellent for depicting a continuous process, such as a change over a period of time. Each axis should be labeled clearly: the vertical axis with the range of measurements and the horizontal with the units of time involved. A line graph showing the rise and fall of interest rates, for example, would have the vertical axis marked, from bottom to top, with numbers representing percentages, while the horizontal axis would be marked with months or years. Similarly, a line graph showing the rise and fall of stock prices would have the vertical axis marked, from bottom to top, with index prices and the horizontal axis marked with months or years.

The vertical axis is usually about two-thirds the length of the horizontal axis. Grid marks indicate units of measurement at regular intervals. The graph should be roughed out before the final form is chosen; if the intervals along the vertical axis are too large in relation to the intervals on the horizontal axis, for example, the line across the graph will not accurately reflect the situation. One should look carefully at the proposed line and its movements: if they exaggerate or minimize the actual changes that took place, the grid marks should be repositioned. The scale of the grid marks must be appropriate to the process that is being described.

The numbers along the vertical axis should begin with the lowest number that is relevant to the graph. In many cases this will be zero, but it doesn't have to be zero. For instance, the vertical axis in a graph showing the movement of the Dow Jones Industrial Average since 1970 could begin with 575. Another way to handle a vertical axis in which there is a large unused space is to put a break in the vertical axis (usually with a double slash mark) that indicates a series of missing numbers.

Line graphs provide additional data when they display more than one line for the comparison of two processes. For example, both earnings and dividends per share of a common stock can be shown in two lines on a single graph with a vertical axis marked in dollar amounts. To prevent difficulty of reading, no more than four or five lines should be on a graph, and the lines should be spaced widely enough to be legible, especially if the figure is being reduced for reproduction. Each line should be clearly identified with a label or key. If there are only two lines, one may be dotted or dashed to distinguish it from a continuous line, but a grouping of solid and discontinuous lines can be difficult to read. It is usually preferable to label each line with a symbol that readily identifies it.

The labels along each axis must be carefully positioned for ease of reading. Any labels that are needed to mark grid points or other points in the graph, or to identify individual lines if there are several lines on the graph, should be set horizontally if possible. Numbers should always be written horizontally, but words and phrases may occasionally have to be set sideways.

Continuous-Tone Art

Photographs and other figures that contain shades of gray are more expensive to produce than line art, because they have to be shot first through a screen that breaks up the image into hundreds of tiny dots of black and white that fool the eye into seeing shades of gray. The resulting image, called a *halftone*, is then reshot for printing with the text.

Any photograph submitted for publication should be a glossy, unretouched black-and-white print with sharp detail and high contrast. It should not be cropped or mounted by the author; that is a job for the editor or artist. Color photographs may be submitted, but since color reproduction is tricky, it is a good idea to have on hand a black-and-white print made from a color negative. Because of the complicated process by which it is reproduced, continuous-tone art is expensive to print. The author must be certain that any illustration of this kind is worth the extra expense before submitting it for publication.

The Parts of an Illustration

Identification Number

Illustrations are often identified by number within a book or article. Numbering is optional, especially when illustrations are few or when they consist of photographs or other pictures that do not have to be studied along with a textual explanation. On the other hand, charts and graphs that illustrate technical works are nearly always identified by number.

The usual mode of identification is to use the word *figure* followed by an Arabic numeral (in some stylings a letter is used if the illustrations are not numerous). The figure number generally appears in the caption above or below the illustration, and it also appears in the manuscript reference to the figure. Like unnumbered tables, unnumbered figures are referred to in text by page number or by phrases like "the figure below" or "the opposite figure." In some publications, figures and tables are numbered together as *Exhibit 1, Exhibit 2,* and so on.

Even when it is decided not to number the illustrations in a work, each one must still be assigned a temporary number for identification throughout the editing and production processes.

As with tables, there are two methods of numbering figures: either consecutively through the book as a whole in the order mentioned in the text, or chapter by chapter. Chapter-by-chapter enumeration is common in technical works which contain many graphs and other figures. Double enumeration may also be used. With this system, each figure has two numbers, the first representing the chapter and the second the number of the figure within the chapter, as *Figure 5–3* for the third figure in Chapter 5. Figures are usually numbered this way in books with chapters by different authors and in books that organize and index their material by chapter and section numbers. A dash or period may be used to separate the two numbers, as *Figure 5–3* or *Figure 5.3.*

All figures are usually numbered together with no distinction made between photographs and other kinds of artwork. An exception frequently occurs, however, with maps, which may be numbered in a separate series as *Map 1, Map 2,* etc. Plates, which are printed separately and tipped in later, are also numbered separately from figures: *Plate 1, Plate 2.*

Each figure should be identified with a whole number, not with a combination like *3a* or *3b.* An illustration may be divided into parts labeled *a* and *b,* but the whole illustration is known by one number only. Identification numbers are followed by periods only if a caption or legend is run in on the same line. The word *figure* is capitalized and usually spelled in full, although it may also be abbreviated when run in with a caption or legend. On a line by itself without a caption, however, it is almost never abbreviated.

In the text, a reference to an illustration may or may not be set off in parentheses. Within parentheses, brackets, or footnotes the word *figure* may be abbreviated to *Fig.,* but only when followed by a number, as *(See Fig. 4).* For text references to an illustration, some publications prefer the lowercase *figure 4,* but in most cases the word is capitalized, thus making it consistent with the styling of the identification number at the illustration.

The Caption

The caption of an illustration is its identification. A caption consists of an optional identification number and a title or headline. Most often, the number and the title appear on the same line, separated by an em dash or a period and space.

Captions are generally brief—usually a substantive phrase, such as "Increase in Weight of Boys from Birth to Year Eighteen" or "Variation in Unit Cost of Production with Size of Plant." A caption for a graph often includes a subtitle that further describes the data (as "after discounting inflation") or indicates the type of measurement used. Many of the styling decisions regarding the caption are the editor's concern, but the author can make choices such as whether the caption will end with a period if it is not a full sentence (most phrasal captions do not end with a period unless run in with a following legend) and whether captions will be fully capitalized or capitalized headline-style or sentence-style (headline style capitalization is most common).

The Legend

A caption identifies an illustration; a legend explains it. The word *legend,* unfortunately, is used in different ways by different people, including publishers. In this work, *legend* refers to the remarks that follow the figure identification number or caption and that explain the purpose of the figure, identify its elements, offer historical or other background information, or in any other way help the reader to understand the illustration. Legends are sometimes quite lengthy and may even break into paragraphs, although most publishers prefer single-paragraph legends. If a very detailed explanation of a figure is required, it probably belongs in the text.

Author and editor have a variety of choices as to the phrasing, position, and typeface of legends. They are frequently complete sentences that end with periods. Sometimes they are incomplete phrases, in which case they may or may not end with a period. In many of today's publications, the identification number, caption, and legend are run together, as in the following example:

> Fig. 2. Cell and its Organelles as Seen with an Electron Microscope. *A*, nucleolus; *B*, nucleus; *C*, cytoplasm; *D*, mitochondrion; *E*, Golgi apparatus.

Identifying the parts of an illustration When sections of a figure or people in a photograph are being identified, the explanations should lead from left to right and from top to bottom. To identify people in rows, it is conventional to begin a legend with an introductory phrase or sentence describing the purpose of the picture. Then the individuals are introduced with a phrase such as *Top row, from left*, or *left to right*. If there are many names, each row's listing should begin a new paragraph. Rows are usually described as *top* or *back row, center row*, and *bottom* or *front row*.

When only a few people are shown in a photograph, it is best to identify them through a description of their actions and to minimize the use of words like *left* and *right*. The major actor in the scene is identified first, as "Signing the contract for the XYZ Project is Frank Smith." Other people in the scene are identified by their actions, by traditional signals such as *above left* or *below right*, or by the processes of elimination or contrast. If it is necessary for a particular person to be described further, as with a long business title, that title should be given in a separate sentence after the first sentence.

When possible, the parts of a figure should be identified without resort to the use of matching symbols such as *a, b, c*, and so on. It is preferable to use traditional pointers like *above left, clockwise from left, at center*, etc., to refer to specific areas of a figure, if these phrases can be used without ambiguity and if they number six or fewer. These phrases are usually placed before the name of the part identified. They are lowercase, usually italic, and sometimes enclosed in parentheses.

> Figure 4. Gypsy Moth. *Above left*, egg mass; *above right*, second instar; *below left*, fifth instar; *center*, pupa; *below right*, adult female Gypsy Moth. *Left to right:* egg mass, larva, pupa, adult male, adult female

Symbols and keys When these traditional phrases are inadequate to explain the parts of a complex figure, identifying symbols—usually letters or numbers—may be used in a legend to refer to corresponding symbols that appear in the illustration. In these cases, the symbols in the key of the legend should match the symbols within the figure as closely as possible. The letter *A*, for example, if capitalized in the figure should be capitalized in the legend and also in any reference to the figure in the text. It is important for terminology to agree wherever possible. Any revision made to a symbol in the text reference, legend, or illustration must be checked against the others to maintain consistency. Letters used for identification purposes are not followed by periods, and they are more often lowercased than capitalized.

> Fig. 5. Cotton: *a,* flowering branch; *b,* fruit, unopened; *c,* fruit, partly opened
>
> Cotton: *(a)* flowering branch, *(b)* fruit, unopened, *(c)* fruit, partly opened
>
> Figure 5—Cotton. *A,* flowering branch; *B,* fruit, unopened; *C,* fruit, partly opened.

These letters are conventionally italicized in legends and in text, though not necessarily within the figures themselves.

A key that appears in a legend may be set in paragraph form like the examples above, or it may be set as a list, especially if there are many symbols to be explained.

A symbol or abbreviation that appears in more than one figure should be explained in each figure's legend. But if there are so many symbols that the legend for each illustration would be too long, a common symbol key may be prepared for a grouping of similar figures. The legend accompanying each figure, however, should state exactly where the key to the symbols can be found—e.g., "For explanation of abbreviations, see key to Figure 1." Also, the key should be visible without the reader having to turn the page.

Labels

A label is any word, lettering, or other symbol that is part of an illustration. It generally identifies a particular part of the figure. The words inside the boxes of an organizational chart are labels, as are the words and numbers that denote the coordinates on the axes of a graph. Labels should be positioned close to the part of the figure that they identify. Enough space should be allowed between letters or numbers for them to be legible when they are reduced in size. They should be large enough, sharp and clear, and of uniform blackness.

Lowercase words and phrases are more readable as labels than are all-capitalized words and phrases. All-capitalized labels may be used, however, especially when it is necessary to distinguish different categories of labels through differences in capitalization styles or other differences in typeface.

Lettering of this sort is never typewritten directly on the illustration. It is applied in one of three ways: (1) Labels may be lettered or drawn by a graphic artist, or they may be applied by the artist or author directly on the illustration with letter stencils or transfer or stick-on letters. (2) Labels may be typeset separately on white, glossy paper as camera-ready copy, then cut out and pasted in position on the final artwork, which has been reduced to paper size. (3) Labels may be typeset separately as camera-ready copy, cut out and pasted in position on the illustration, then photographically reduced along with the rest of the illustration. The last process, however, is seldom used because the typeset portions lose contrast when reduced. Since the handling of typeset labels is usually the editor's responsibility, it is discussed on page 339 of Chapter 11.

The Credit Line

Any illustration reproduced from another source should include a statement acknowledging that source and, if the source is copyrighted, stating that permission has been granted to use or adapt the illustration. This acknowledgment may appear as a separate credit line or in the legend or as a footnote. Another way to acknowledge sources occurs when all or most of the figures in a work come from a single source. In these cases, the credit may be given in the book's preface or on a special page of acknowledgments. A different method, often used when there are numerous illustrations from several sources, is to list all credits together on pages in the front or the back of the book.

Credit lines take many forms; usually the author or editor chooses a single form to be used with all illustrations derived from any outside source. However, if a copyright holder specifies that a particular form is to be used with an illustration, that form must be used, even if it is inconsistent with other credit lines in the same work.

Figures that are drawn by the author do not normally require credit lines, but if necessary to ensure that credit will not be given to another source, a credit line may say simply, *Illustration by the author.* Similarly it is not necessary to credit a figure drawn for hire by an artist, although, as a courtesy, the artist may be credited with an acknowledgment at the figure, such as *Map by Mary Kennedy,* or in the preface. And there is no obligation to credit illustrations from the public domain; however, even if an illustration is in the public domain, it is a courtesy to the original source and an aid to the reader to acknowledge the source. In all other cases, the author must obtain written permission to reproduce or adapt a photograph or other illustration previously published.

For the reproduction of charts and graphs taken from outside sources, one usually requests permission from the publisher. However, for illustrations which may be considered artistic and in which the artist may have a proprietary interest—photographs and drawings, for example—permission should be obtained not only from the publisher but sometimes also from the artist.

Illustrations are often freely donated by companies and institutions for the purpose of one-time reproduction. In credit lines for these figures, it is conventional to use the word *courtesy,* as in these common examples:

Photographs by Frank Smith, courtesy of XYZ Museum
Photograph courtesy of XYZ Company
Courtesy XYZ Company
Courtesy of the XYZ Library, New York

The conventional position for a brief credit line is immediately below or alongside of the illustration. It is usually set in small type without a terminal period. Sometimes it is italicized. Simple credit lines may include only the name of the artist or photographer, preceded by *courtesy (of)* if use of the illustration was provided without fee; or credit may be given to a donor institution (its name preceded by the copyright symbol © if applicable) or to a picture agency.

A lengthy acknowledgment is frequently set at the end of the legend, where it is sometimes enclosed in parentheses or set in italic type; brief credit lines may also appear in this position.

... (Reprinted, with permission, from Name of Author, Title, p. 00. © 1900 by XYZ Publishers.)
... Photo by Frank Smith

Acknowledgments may also appear as footnotes:

NOTE: The data in this figure are from "Title of Article" by Name of Author, 1900, *Title of Journal* 0, 00. Copyright 1900 by Name of Copyright Holder. Reprinted by permission. [*or* Adapted by permission.]

Figures designed by the author using materials from another source may be credited in the legend as follows (the latter two examples indicate sources that are further described in a bibliography):

Source: U.S. Department of Agriculture
Data from Author, *Title* (Place: Publisher, 1900), Table 10
Adapted from Last Name of Author 1900, Table 10
Redrawn from Last Name of Author, *Title*, Fig. 4

Credit lines for sources that gave permission to reprint their materials usually include the word *permission:*

Reprinted, by permission, from Author, *Title*, p. 00.

Credit lines acknowledging copyrighted sources must mention the copyright:

© XYZ Museum 1972

Reprinted, by permission, from Author, *Title*, p. 00. Photograph by Photographer's Name. Copyright 1900 by Name of University.

Full bibliographic information is included in a credit line where applicable unless a bibliography elsewhere in the book lists the source, in which case a short form is acceptable.

Footnotes

Footnotes are not often used with illustrations, but occasionally they are necessary to expand upon a complex legend, and sometimes they are used to acknowledge a source. Like footnotes to tables, figure footnotes are set in very small type and separated from text footnotes by the use of different reference symbols. Like table notes, they appear below the figure, not at the foot of the page.

Chapter 10

Indexes

CONTENTS

An index is a list of key words and phrases that makes information accessible by pointing to all the specific places in a book, pamphlet, or report where pertinent information occurs. Not all publications include indexes. Indexes are usually not present, for instance, in corporate annual reports, in books arranged alphabetically (such as glossaries or directories), or in books and pamphlets short enough to allow readers to find information by leafing through. However, most published works of nonfiction include an index of one sort or another. This chapter describes the various types of index that are in use today, the parts of those indexes, and how to go about writing, editing, designing, typing, and solving problems associated with indexes.

A full description of the parts of an index is presented later in this chapter. For now it is enough that readers of this chapter understand that an index consists of alphabetically arranged main entries, each of which usually consists of a main heading together with its page references and any cross-references that go with the main heading. Each main entry may be followed by subentries, sub-subentries, or sometimes even sub-sub-subentries. Each subentry consists of a subheading with its page references and any cross-references associated with the subheading. A complete entry, then, is any main entry with all of its subentries and cross-references. In some cases, an entry consists of a cross-reference alone.

Types of Indexes

Before an indexer can begin work on an index, he or she must know what kind of index the book is to have. Specifically, indexers need to know (1) whether the index is to be composed entirely of main entries or whether it can have subentries, (2) whether there is to be a single index or multiple indexes, and (3) whether the index should have an indented or paragraph-style format. These types of indexes are described in the following paragraphs.

Simple Indexes

The simplest kind of index is one composed entirely of main entries, with no subentries. The main entry typically consists simply of a main heading and one or more page references. This type of index, sometimes called a *simple index,* is suitable for short, uncomplicated treatments of a subject. However, most publications calling for an index require a more complex index, complete with subentries, sub-subentries, and sometimes even sub-sub-subentries.

Single and Multiple Indexes

A *single index* that combines all kinds of entries is appropriate for most publications; however, some books are best served by *multiple indexes.* Some biographical and historical works, for instance, contain a separate index of personal names in addition to their regular subject index. Some books about law contain a separate index of legal citations, often called a *table of cases.* Other works may lend themselves to other types of separate indexes—medical terms, first lines of poems, place names, etc.—depending on the subject of the book being indexed.

Multiple indexes are not common, however, and they should be considered only when (1) the index is lengthy to begin with, (2) a large percentage of the total index consists of the special entries under consideration, and (3) it would be a real service to the reader to provide more than one index.

Indented and Paragraph-Style Indexes

If any of the entries in an index is broken down into subentries, the indexer must decide which of two formats to use to arrange the subentries: the *indented* (also called *entry-a-line*) styling or the *paragraph* (also called *run-on* or *run-in*) styling.

In an indented index, each new main entry, subentry, and sub-subentry begins on a new line. The paragraph index, by contrast, runs all subentries in to form a single paragraph headed by the main entry. Examples of each styling are shown below. For a discussion of how to punctuate each styling, see pages 269–270.

indented styling	*paragraph styling*

Questionnaires by mail, 205–210
  accuracy, 207–209
  anonymity of, 313
  costs, 232–234
  sampling, 210–218
    collecting data from, 212–216
    selecting the sample, 211
  speed, 234–236
	Questionnaires by mail, 205–210;
	  accuracy, 207–209; anonymity of,
	  313; costs, 232–234; sampling,
	  210–218, collecting data from,
	  212–216, selecting the sample,
	  211; speed, 234–236

Indented indexes are by far the more common, especially in complex works such as reference books. One advantage of the indented styling is that it lends itself much more easily to the use of sub-subentries. Another advantage is that the reader can find a topic by scanning down the vertical column. As the preceding examples show, it is more difficult to find a particular alphabetical subentry in the middle of a long paragraph.

Paragraph styling, however, is favored by some publishers because it uses space more economically. Moreover, as long as each entry has only a few subentries and no sub-subentries, it is not hard to locate a desired topic. Paragraph indexes are frequently found in histories and biographies, especially where the order of certain subentries might be chronological instead of alphabetical.

In some cases indexers find it desirable to insert an occasional sub-subentry into a paragraph-style index. Several ways to handle this special problem have been developed. One method is to use a comma instead of the usual semicolon to separate sub-subentries within a subentry, as illustrated in the example above, "Questionnaires by mail." The difficulty with this solution is that the reader cannot readily see the relationship between the parts of the entry. A few publications employ a combination of paragraph and indented styles in those rare cases where a sub-subentry is needed in a paragraph index. The following is an example of such a compromise format that might appear in an otherwise all-paragraph index:

Questionnaires by mail, 205–210
—accuracy, 207–209
—anonymity of, 313
—costs, 232–234
—sampling, 210–218; collecting data
    from, 212–216; selecting the sam-
    ple, 211
—speed, 234–236

Note that each subentry in the example begins on a separate line, preceded by a one-em dash set flush left. Sub-subentries are run in with the appropriate subentry, and all runover lines are aligned with the first word of each subentry.

Compromise formats like these make demands on the reader, and some can be very confusing. For this reason, an indexer faced with inserting sub-subentries in a paragraph-style index should seriously consider switching to an indented index.

The Parts of an Index

The principal parts of an index are the main headings, the subheadings, the locators, and the cross-references. Each of these parts is described in full in the following paragraphs.

Main Headings

A main heading should always be a noun or noun phrase, the first word of which is the key word—that is, the word the reader is likely to think of when consulting the index. The natural syntax of a phrase may have to be adjusted in order to get the key word in initial position, but that is expected in an index. A comma is used to mark any inversion of natural order.

natural order	*index order—key word first*
personalized exercise program	exercise program, personalized
indented index	index, indented
disadvantages of photocopying	photocopying, disadvantages of
history of the Society of Jesus	Society of Jesus, history of

Indexers try to avoid unnecessary inversions, however, and try to keep closely related words of a heading together. For instance, the heading "descriptive words and phrases" is inverted as "words and phrases, descriptive," not "words, descriptive, and phrases."

Adjectives and grammatically similar words cannot function by themselves as main headings, although they may function as subheadings. When part of a heading, modifiers generally follow the key word, which is usually a noun. Sometimes, however, the key word is an adjective that is the first word of a phrase that is so familiar that the reader will naturally search for the adjective in the index. Examples include *terrestrial habitats, social groups, random pairs, civil rights,* and *hot springs.* These adjective-plus-noun compounds are usually not inverted for indexing. Noun-plus-noun compounds present the same situation, and they are usually not inverted either. Examples include *exercise program, fuel crisis, life zone, tax law, reference works, sand trap, water power,* and *photo finish.*

There are cases in which the decision whether to invert the natural order of a compound could go either way. In these cases, two separate entries may be made, one in natural order and one in inverted order. The indexer should put the full entry at whatever term seems most likely to be consulted and a cross-reference to it at the other entry.

Subheadings

Subheadings are used to make information easier to find and to keep main headings from being followed by long, discouraging lists of page numbers, as shown in the example below:

entry with subheadings	*entry without subheadings*
Minutes, 571, 573–579, 600	Minutes, 202, 205, 355, 388
capitalization in, 202, 205	410, 419, 571, 573–579, 600
certification of, 576	
corporate, 410, 419	
paper quality, 388	
resolutions, 576	
shorthand notes and, 355	
typing of, 576–579	

If the subject warrants it and if an indented styling has been chosen, an indexer may go one step further and break subjects down into three levels—main entry, subentry, and sub-subentry. A fourth-level entry (with sub-sub-subheadings) is usually avoided, however, as unnecessarily complex. If such minute divisions appear to be needed, the need can often be met through careful rephrasing, as:

sub-subheading:	animals, domestic
sub-sub-subheadings:	cats
	dogs
sub-subheadings:	cats, domestic
	dogs, domestic

There should always be a logical relationship between heading and subheading, and frequently a grammatical relationship as well. A grammatical relationship means that the heading and subheading can be combined to make a meaningful phrase:

index order	*natural order*
Minutes	
certification of	certification of minutes
corporate	corporate minutes
shorthand notes and	shorthand notes and minutes
typing of	typing of minutes

There are many cases, however, where a purely logical relationship will suffice. For example, the subheading *resolutions* under the main heading *Minutes* is sufficient, since a resolution may be a component of a set of minutes.

Subheadings, like main headings, are typically indexed alphabetically by the most important word. But the arrangement of subheadings may differ from that of main headings in two important ways. First, the key word—the one used to determine alphabetic order—does not necessarily come first in a subheading. For clarity, a subheading may begin with a preposition or conjunction that helps show the precise relationship between that subheading and the main heading; however, these initial prepositions and conjunctions are disregarded when the subheadings are alphabetized.

> Numerals, 215–218, 281
>   in addresses, 198
>   at beginning of sentence, 215
>   in dates, 215, 394
>   enumerations, 215
>   ordinals, 217, 218
>   punctuation with, 221, 223–224, 229
>   and symbols, 218

Many indexers try to phrase subheadings so that these words appear at the end of the key word rather than at the beginning, as in the earlier example under *Minutes*. The advantage of this approach is that alphabetic order is more apparent. Some indexers delete these words altogether, making alphabetic order easy to recognize, but at the same time making it hard for the index user to understand what the headings mean.

A second major difference between the arrangement of main headings and subheadings is that while main headings are always listed alphabetically, subheadings may on occasion be listed chronologically, or in some other sensible sequence. Such formats are found most commonly in histories and biographies where a series of dates or other numbers is appropriate. A series of Chinese dynasties, for example, might be listed chronologically. Such an arrangement usually occurs in only a few pertinent entries within an otherwise alphabetically ordered index.

Locators

Without locators, or page references, index headings are useless. The term *locator* is used here because not all references are to page numbers; some are to other kinds of divisions in a book, such as chapter, section, sub-section, and paragraph (as 8.22.3b), depending on how the work is organized. Locators are separated by commas, and they are always in numerical sequence from lowest to highest.

Inclusive page numbers A few indexers give only the first page number of a discussion that may continue past that page. This practice is easy for the indexer but misleading to the reader. Inclusive page numbers are needed to tell the reader exactly where the discussion of a topic is begun, interrupted, resumed, and ended. For example, the sequence 212–216, 219–220, 222 tells the reader that a lengthy discussion of the topic in question occurs on pages 212–216, with briefer mentions later on. If the first interruption in this discussion had been minor and very brief, the indexer would have written the locators as follows: 212–220, 222. When a discussion of a topic is continuous from, say, page 24 to page 25, the indexer writes 24–25. If there are two separate, discontinuous references to the topic on these pages, the indexer writes 24, 25.

There are two ways to style inclusive numbers. One is to give all numbers in full, as 232–234, 504–506. The other is to elide them, as 232–34, 504–6. Elided numbers are commonly used because they save space, but the indexer must understand the principles of their use and adhere consistently to those principles. The most commonly used style for the elision of inclusive numbers is based on the following rules:

1. Never elide inclusive numbers that have only two digits: 33–37, *not* 33–7.
2. Never elide inclusive numbers when the first number ends in 00: 100–108, *not* 100–08 *and not* 100–8.
3. In other numbers, omit *only* the hundreds digit from the higher number: 232–34, *not* 232–4.
4. Where the next-to-last digit of both numbers is zero, write only one digit for the higher number: 103–4, *not* 103–04.

Locators for extended discussions In some cases, an indexer may wish to alert the reader to the fact that a particularly lengthy discussion is spread out with irregular mentions for several pages past the major discussion. In cases like these some indexers prefer not to list the entry's locators in the usual way, as "Corrosion, 55–61, 62, 64, 67, 68, 75, 77." Instead, they write the entry "Corrosion, 55–77 *passim*" (a Latin word meaning "here and there"). *Passim* does not give the reader as much information as does a list of actual page numbers; consequently, it should be used only in exceptional circumstances.

One occasionally sees indexes that rely on *ff* (an abbreviation for *folios*, meaning leaves or pages of a book) following a page number to indicate a continuing, but interrupted or less important, discussion of a subject. A much more helpful method, however, from the reader's point of view, is to give inclusive page numbers for a general discussion in the main entry, then a list of subheadings with their specific locators, which may or may not be part of the inclusive numbers in the main entry:

> Trade, international, 530–540
> > Chamber of Commerce, 537, 549
> > Commerce Department, 533–535
> > Export Development Offices, 533–534
> > Export-Import Bank, 537–538
> > financing exports, 537–539

Locators for nontext references Nontext materials such as tables, charts, diagrams, photographs, maps, and other illustrations are sometimes identified as such in the index, especially if they appear on a different page from the pertinent text. One way to identify illustrations is to print in italic or boldface type any numbers that locate such material. Indexers using this method need to add a note at the beginning of the index to explain the procedure. They should also keep in mind that italic numbers are sometimes hard to distinguish from roman numbers when they are printed together. A more common method is for the locator numbers to be preceded by an identifying term such as *map, table, illus.,* or *illustration* printed in italic. These special locators may be positioned at the end of the regular numbers:

> Coupons, 25–26, 53, 78–80, *illus.* 54

or, the more common practice, in sequence with other locators:

> Venezuela, 204–209, *map* 210, 335, 376

A few indexers prefer to list illustrations as separate subheadings to make them more obvious:

> Woodpecker, 119, 302
> > downy, 44, 125
> > holes, 165
> > pileated, 45
> > > illustrated, 46
> > white-headed, 126

Footnotes that merely document a bibliographic source are never indexed. But footnotes that supply explanations or additional information may be indexed with the abbreviation *n* (for *note*) added to the page number, as *22n*. (If the footnote is on the same page with similar information that is being indexed anyway, the footnote reference is unnecessary.) There is more than one acceptable styling for footnote locators; however, using an unpunctuated, roman *n* will facilitate typing and typesetting and reduce clutter on the page.

Numbered footnotes are handled differently. Any reference to an endnote (a footnote appearing at the back of a chapter or book instead of at the foot of the page) must include not only the page number but the footnote number as well. A reference to one of several numbered footnotes at the bottom of a page may or may not include the footnote number, depending on the indexer's judgment. Whenever a footnote is identified by number, one of the following forms is used:

reference to one footnote (as for page 22,   22n.3
  note 3)

reference to more than one footnote (as   22nn. 2, 4
  for page 22, notes 2 and 4)

Some indexers like to make the footnote reference clearer by enclosing it in parentheses, as 22 (n.3) or 22 (nn. 2,4). This styling is acceptable, but it adds keystrokes.

Cross-References

Cross-references help index users to find subjects they might otherwise miss when looking for a topic under a key word that differs from the one the indexer has chosen. Whether to make cross-references, and in what form to make them, requires careful thought on the part of the indexer, who will need to determine enough cross-references to guide the reader, but not so many as to overload the index and insult the reader's intelligence.

There are two kinds of cross-references, *see* and *see also*. A *see* reference looks like this:

Bill of Rights. *See* Constitution, U.S.

The example above tells the reader that all information on the Bill of Rights is supplied at the other entry, *Constitution, U.S.*

There are many reasons for adding *see* references to guide the reader to the appropriate entry. It is done (1) to refer the reader from a popular term to an official term (as "FDA. *See* Food and Drug Administration, U.S."); (2) to refer the reader from an author's pseudonym to his or her real name (as "Parley, Peter. *See* Goodrich, Samuel G."); (3) to refer the reader from a woman's married name to her maiden or professional name (as "Bonynge, Mrs. Richard. *See* Sutherland, Joan"); (4) to refer the reader from the defendant's to the plaintiff's name in a citation of case law (as "Smith, Colby Corp. v. *See* Colby Corp. v. Smith"); (5) to refer the reader to an alternate form of a corporate name (as "Mark D. Bancroft and Sons, Inc. *See* Bancroft, Mark D. and Sons, Inc."); or (6) in any other instance when an entry is alphabetized at some place other than where the reader might expect it.

Experienced indexers know that sometimes it is better to make a double entry rather than a *see* reference. They do this when a heading has no subheadings and very few locators:

Bill of Rights. *See* Constitution, U.S.	Bill of Rights, 56–58
Constitution, U.S., 56–58	Constitution, U.S., 56–58

Each form takes about the same amount of space, yet the second will save a little time for the reader who happens to look first under *Bill of Rights*. If the entry *Constitution, U.S.* contained subheadings or a long list of locators, the cross-reference method in the first example would be preferable.

A second type of cross-reference is the *see also* reference, illustrated here:

Evaluation, 154–156, 303, 305. *See also* Rating systems	Professionals, career, 245–251. *See also* Managers; Middle management

This kind of cross-reference usually comes at the end of a particular entry or subentry. It directs the reader to additional information on a closely related subject.

For details regarding the styling of entries, see pages 269–271.

Steps in Preparing an Index

The procedures for preparing an index, though painstaking in practice, are simple in outline: First, you mark page proofs, then you transfer this information to index cards. After editing and sorting the cards and adding cross-reference cards, you alphabetize the lot. Finally, you type the index manuscript from the cards and have the manuscript marked up for typesetting. The materials required are also simple: a thousand or more index cards, a file box, card-file dividers, plenty of table space, and a typewriter with copy paper.

Markup of Page Proofs

The indexer works from page proofs—the stage of production at which page numbers are first assigned to a work. It is inefficient to work from earlier unpaged galley proofs, because so much time will have to be spent later, looking for the same material on the page proofs and copying the page numbers. In addition, there is always the chance that the galleys will be heavily edited, requiring time-consuming revision of the index. The only time that working from galleys is efficient is when a work is to be indexed according to locators other than page numbers.

Before marking the page proofs, it is a good idea to read through the whole work. One need not read for close understanding at this point; scanning is enough to give some idea of the scope, purpose, and terminology of the book. The next step is to reread the work and mark the page proofs, chapter by chapter.

Handling errors As you are reading you may discover errors on the printed page. Remember that the page proofs you are working with are probably an unproofread set and that someone else is probably correcting a duplicate set at the same time. You may want to ask the editor or author, whomever you are working with, beforehand if you should send a list of typographical and other obvious errors that you might find during your reading for the index. Other errors that are less obvious require careful handling, because a basic rule of indexing is to record material exactly as the author has recorded it, unusual spellings and all. If you have doubts, you should check with the editor or the author.

You might wish to ask the author for some pre-arranged assistance too. For example, if the material is unfamiliar, you could ask the author to underline key words on the proofs before giving them to you, or even write words in the margins. You may want to set up a system for querying the author about doubtful passages too.

What to mark on page proofs First, the indexer must understand that there are certain nontext parts of a book that should not be indexed. These include prefaces, glossaries, bibliographies, chapter summaries, questions at the end of chapters, and any footnotes that merely give a source.

Nontext material that may be indexed if it is useful to the reader includes the following: (1) information within an introduction; (2) bibliographical references within the text; (3) tables and charts, but not separate items within them; (4) appendices if they contain important material that is not in the text; (5) footnotes and other notes if they are informative and not merely documentary; and (6) maps and other illustrations.

As you read, it is important to keep the index user in mind by asking yourself, Is this information likely to be looked up? If so, under what word? If there is more than one possible key word, what related words and phrases should be noted in the margin? Look for significant nouns. Proper nouns are the most obvious, but you should resist the temptation to index those that merely provide background information. Pay special attention to such things as definitions (all of which should be indexed) and any unusual terminology.

How to mark proofs As you read underline or circle key words and phrases. In the margins, write additional key words that summarize the information; add synonyms and related phrases for the terms you have

←Paper→   XR Stationery

All About Paper   **137**

of

Good-quality paper is an essential element in the production of attractive, effective letters. Paper with rag content is considerably more expensive than sulfite bonds. Nevertheless, many business firms use rag-content paper because it suggests the merit and stature of the company. Since the cost of paper has been estimated at less than five percent of the total cost of the average business letter, it is easy to understand why some companies consider high-quality paper to be worth the added expense—at least for certain types of correspondence.

When one assesses paper quality, one should ask these questions: *Stationery—*

1. Will the paper withstand corrections and erasures without pitting, buckling, or tearing?
2. Will the paper accept even and clear typed characters?
3. Will the paper permit smooth written signatures?
4. Will the paper perform well with carbons and in copying machines?
5. Will the paper withstand storage and repeated handling and will its color wear well over a long time?
6. Will the paper fold easily without cracking or rippling?
7. Will the paper hold typeset letterhead without bleed-through?

An important characteristic of paper is its fiber direction or grain. When selecting paper, one should ensure that the grain will be parallel to the direction of the typewritten lines, thus providing a smooth surface for clear and even characters, an easy erasing or correcting surface, and a smooth fit of paper against the typewriter platen. Every sheet of paper has what is called a felt side: this is the top side of the paper from which a watermark may be read, and it is on this side of the sheet that the letterhead should be printed or engraved.   *of paper*

of paper

The weight of the paper must also be considered when ordering stationery supplies. Basis weight, also called substance number, is the weight in pounds of a ream of paper cut to a basic size. Basis 24 is heaviest for stationery; basis 13 is lightest. The table below illustrates various paper weights according to their specific uses in the office.

Weights of Paper for Specific Business Correspondence Applications

Application: letter papers and envelopes	Basis Weight: letter papers and envelopes
Standard (*i.e., corporate correspondence*)	24 *or* 20
Executive	24 *or* 20
Airmail (*for overseas correspondence*)	13
Branch-office *or* salesmen's stationery	20 *or* 16
Form letters	20 *or* 24
Continuation sheets	match basis weight of first sheet
Half-sheets	24 *or* 20

The paper used for carbon copies is lighter in weight and is available as inexpensive manifold paper, a stronger and more expensive onionskin, or a lightweight letterhead with the word COPY printed on it.   *paper*

Stationery— Continuation sheets, although blank, must match the letterhead sheet in color, basis weight, texture, size, and quality. Envelopes should match both the first and
Stationery and— continuation sheets. Therefore, these materials should be ordered along with the letterhead to ensure a good match.

Letterhead and continuation sheets as well as envelopes should be stored in their boxes to prevent soiling. A small supply of these materials may be kept in the typist's stationery drawer, but they should be arranged carefully so as not to become damaged over time.   *Stationery, storage of*

Paper, storage of

Figure 10.1. A page proof marked for indexing

underlined. During this marking process you may decide that a particular word will be a main heading or a subheading. Use a symbol to indicate which it will be. A dash or colon after the word is a good way to indicate a main heading; a dash or colon before the word can indicate a potential subheading. If you underline a proposed subheading in the text, write the heading in the margin if you think you might know what it will be. Also, indicate potential inversions by inserting a diagonal line (virgule) at the point of inversion.

Suggestions for the Phrasing of Headings

The discussion of headings and subheadings on pages 256–258 emphasized the importance of nouns and noun phrases for main headings, how to use modifiers with main headings and subheadings, and the use of inversion to get the key words to the front of a phrase. Along with these general considerations, the indexer should also keep the following in mind:

1. Stick as closely as possible to the author's phrasing, spelling, and use of capitals, italics, quotation marks, and accents. If the author of a booklet on job-hunting uses the optional accent marks in *résumé*, so does the indexer.
2. Choose judiciously a particular form of the key word (as singular or plural) so that all references to that topic will occur under that form. The plural form (as *Paragraphs* and *References* in the examples that follow) is usually suitable for both singular and plural references, but the singular form (as *Creeper*) is best for some cases.
3. Be concise. Avoid unnecessary prepositions like *concerning* and *regarding* in subheadings. Retain only those words that clarify the meaning or the relation of main heading and subheading. Examples:

   no connecting words needed for clarity

   Paragraphs
      development and strategy
      form paragraphs
      indention

   connecting words needed for clarity

   Paragraphs
      conjunctions and
      in correspondence
      in legal documents
      omission of
      of quoted material

   In the first example above, the relationship is purely logical, so no connecting words are needed. In the second example that relationship is reinforced by a grammatical relationship; one can combine headings to read "omission of paragraphs" or "paragraphs of quoted material."
4. If two different topics require identical headings because they are homonyms, make separate cards and separate entries for each head-

ing, but identify each heading with a modifier or other explanatory word or short phrase that will appear in the final index. Examples:

Creeper (bird), 224   References, employment, 145–147
Creeper (plant), 361–362   References, in manuscript, 222–226

Preparation of Note Cards

Although note cards may be prepared chapter by chapter as you finish marking the page proofs, it is usually best to wait until all proofs in the grouping you have been given are read and marked. Having closely examined a large portion of the work will give you a perspective that may help determine the best headings for the individual parts.

Professional indexers sometimes use slips of paper of a uniform size, because they are cheaper and take less room than cards. However, for a beginning indexer, cards are a much better choice; they are more durable, easier to handle, and less likely to be misplaced. You will need many cards—from less than a thousand to three thousand or more, depending on the size of the book and the complexity of its index.

Cards may be handwritten or typed; indexers choose the method best suited to their skills and work habits. It should be remembered, however, that typewritten numbers are less likely to be misread than handwritten numbers.

There are seven basic steps to the preparation of note cards, each of which is explained below:

1. *Transfer entries from page proof to card.* Write the key word first, followed by any applicable modifiers. In doing this, an unalterable rule is to make a separate card for each reference. Each card will hold one heading (or subheading) and one locator. Do not attempt to enter subheadings under a heading on the same card in order to be economical, or because you are certain they will appear that way in the final index. It is a very simple task to group individual cards together later on, but it will be frustrating to try to separate lists already compiled on one card.
2. *Add one locator to each card.* Note where a particular reference ends; check the next page to see if the discussion continues so that locator numbers (they may be inclusive numbers) will be precise. Make a separate card for each reference to a particular heading. For example, two separate cards would be necessary to record references to "Eurail Pass, purchase of" on pages 25 and 28 of a work. If you list more than one locator under a heading on a card, you may later find the need to subdivide that heading or consolidate it with a similar heading, and it will be difficult then to regroup the list of locators.
3. *Write notations on cards.* These notations should further identify the topic. For example, they might key a prospective subheading back to its prospective heading. In this case, you might write the heading above the subheading already on the card, or you might list proposed subheadings under a main heading. These notations should be cir-

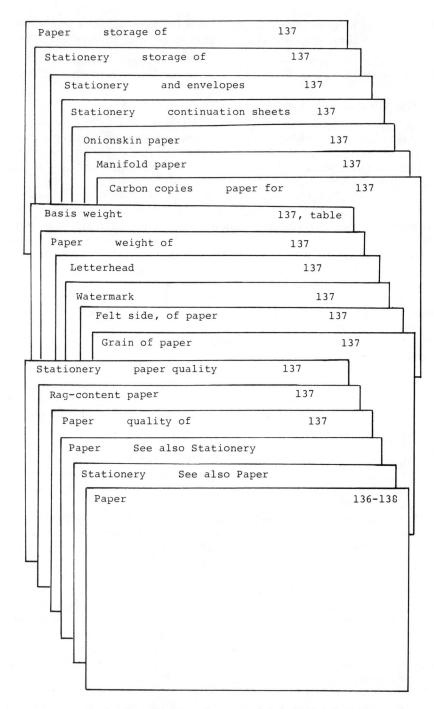

Figure 10.2. Cards made from the marked page in figure 10.1

cled, however, or a line should be drawn through them to indicate that they are not to be copied onto the final index manuscript. Their function is only to aid your subsequent sorting job. After writing each card, double-check the information before filing the card. Check the spelling of proper nouns and scientific or technical terms. Check the accuracy of locator numbers. It will be much more difficult to confirm these numbers later.

4. *Make cross-reference cards.* Make a separate card for each cross-reference. Consider adding *see* references that direct a reader to this topic; consider adding *see also* references that direct the reader to related topics elsewhere in the index.

5. *Edit the cards.* It is at this point that final decisions are made about phrasing and the relative significance of headings. Ideally editing should be done only after all note cards have been completed, because only then does the indexer have a full understanding of the work. However, because of the time pressures under which they work, indexers usually edit the cards for each grouping of chapters as they are received. Begin with the first chapter of page proofs and reread each card to make sure the information is accurate. Is the material significant enough to index? Do the headings and subheadings make sense? Are they headings the reader is likely to look up? Are locator numbers correct? Are all cross-references necessary? Are additional ones needed? Are all cross-references that you have considered still valid, or should they be revised in view of your previous editing? Do your cross-references copy precisely the phrasing of the relevant headings elsewhere in the index?

6. *Sort the cards.* Group all cards together that have the same heading, with locators in numerical order. Group all identical subheadings together behind their main heading, each subheading with its particular locators in order. Position cross-reference cards in proper order within the entry. During this process, watch for and eliminate any duplication. You may consider consolidating some subheadings if you see a large number of closely related ones with only one or two locators each. Conversely, a subheading with a very large number of locators might be broken down into sub-subheadings. You may also wish to break a broad topic down into two separate headings, if the topic has a very large number of subheadings. The heading *Photocopying,* for instance, could be divided into *Photocopies* and *Photocopy process,* each with its appropriate subheadings.

7. *Mark cards for typing.* The final step in editing cards is to prepare them for the typist. Be sure that the main entries you have written above any subentries are circled or crossed out so the typist does not copy them. Also delete any duplicated subheadings so that the typist will not repeat a subheading before each of its locators. You will also have to mark the cards for proper punctuation, capitalization, and levels of indention. Details regarding these three aspects of styling the index are presented in the next section below.

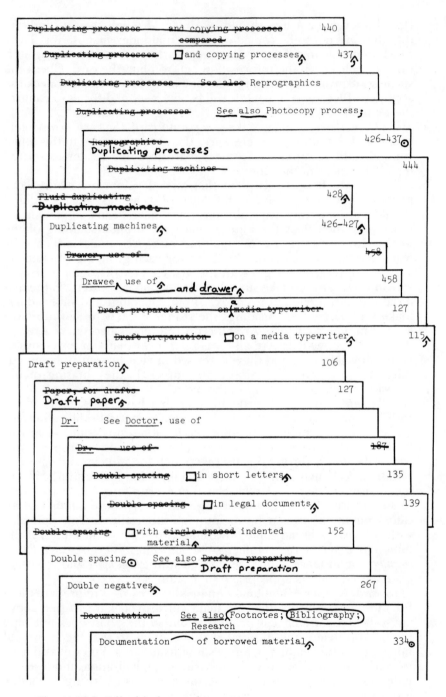

Figure 10.3. Edited index cards

Styling of Entries

In order to prevent index users from becoming distracted or puzzled by apparent inconsistencies in the appearance of entries, index users rely on style rules to determine the punctuation, capitalization, and indention of entries. The following paragraphs present general rules of styling that apply to most kinds of entries. Aspects of styling specific to cross-references are discussed on pages 271–273. Styling of some particularly problematic kinds of entries is discussed in the section on Special Indexing Problems, later in this chapter.

Punctuation Both indented and paragraph-style indexes make use of commas, periods, and semicolons. The comma, the most common mark, is used (1) to mark an inverted phrase in a heading so that the key word comes first; (2) to separate each heading or subheading from its locators; and (3) to separate locator numbers within an entry from one another. Periods are used only to terminate certain abbreviations and to separate an entry from a cross-reference that follows it, as "Shrimp, ghost. *See* Sand beach, marine life"; they are never used to mark the end of an entry. (Some indexers prefer to use a comma or dash to set off cross-references.) Semicolons are used to separate the parts of a multiple cross-reference, as "Water. *See also* Dew point; Humidity; Oceans; Rain."

An indented index uses fewer punctuation marks than a paragraph index, since indention itself serves to separate the parts of an entry. The most common form of indented index styling, illustrated below, uses no punctuation other than that described above for use with all indexes.

Bankruptcy law	Bankruptcy law, 4, 10, 23–26
forms, 356, 358	forms, 356, 358
judges, 11	judges, 11
referees and receivers, 19	referees and receivers, 19

A less common styling places a colon after a heading when it has no locators of its own but does have subheadings with locators:

Exposures:
 filters and, 33–35
 how determined, 36–38
 time:
  interiors, 44–45, 58
  with microscope, 100–102
  for stars, 122

Occasionally one finds an indented index that attempts to save space by running in the first subentry on the same line with the main heading and indenting the remaining subentries, as in the example below. The heading, which has no locators of its own in these cases, is followed by a colon.

Waves: longitudinal, 99
 seismic, 94–96
 sound, 96
 surface, 90

One problem with this format, however, is that it is often difficult to determine the actual relationship between the headings.

A paragraph index uses punctuation marks to separate the main entry from its subentries and also to separate subentries from one another. The mark used to separate subentries is the semicolon. The choice of punctuation mark to follow the main heading depends on whether the heading has its own locator numbers distinct from the numbers attached to the subheadings. If the main heading has no locators, a colon separates it from the first subheading:

> Mineral deposits: coal, 55–57; formation of, 17, 23–26; petroleum, 126–130

If the main heading has both locators and subheadings, the following punctuation is used:

> Mineral deposits, 20–28, 199; coal, 55–57; formation of, 17, 23–26; petroleum, 126–130

If there are no subentries in a paragraph index, the punctuation is the same as in an indented index: Mineral deposits, 20–28, 199.

Capitalization The initial letters of main headings may be either capital or lowercase. Capitalized main headings, with lowercase subheadings, are by far the most common styling, and the distinction they help create between the two levels of heading is useful. Some indexers, however, elect to lowercase all headings (except, of course, proper nouns and adjectives), thus making the typing and the typesetting easier.

Certain main headings should always be lowercased, even when they are main entries in an index which capitalizes its main entries. For example, the particles in proper names that are indexed by a lowercase particle are not capitalized: *de Gaulle, Charles* (for more on styling personal names, see page 276–279). Also, any abbreviation that is normally printed in lowercase letters keeps its typical form as a main entry, as *f-stop* or *pH measurement.* If in doubt as to whether a word should be capitalized, one should follow the styling used by the author. However, a heading should never be capitalized simply because it happens to be capitalized as a chapter or section heading in the text.

Indention All indexes are set with hanging indention; that is, the first line of each complete entry is flush left, while all other lines of the entry are indented to some degree. Hanging indention is used because alphabetical listings are more readily scanned when the key word is thus set off.

With paragraph indexes, indention decisions are simple. The main entry begins flush left, and all runover lines in that entry are indented the same degree. With an indented index, however, there may be several levels of indention, each of which indicates a specific relationship between the parts of the entry.

On the printed page the usual measure of indention is one em. Thus, for an indented index the main entry is flush left, subentries are indented one em, and sub-subentries are indented two ems, as in the first example below. Runover lines for all entries—main entries as well as all subentries—are indented in the same degree, which is usually one em more than the largest subheading indention.

indented (3 levels of indention)

Telephone communications, 10–12, 34–35, 61, 255–260
  local calls, 255
  long-distance calls, 256–260, 267–269
    bill-to-third-party calls, 257
    collect calls, 257
    credit card calls, 258–259
  PBX systems, 34–35, 48

paragraph (1 level of indention)

Telephone communications, 10–12, 34–35, 61, 255–260; bill-to-third-party calls, 257; collect calls, 257; credit card calls, 258–259; local calls, 255; long-distance calls, 256–260, 267–269; PBX systems, 34–35, 48

In an index with only one level of subentry, main entries would be set flush left, subentries would be indented one em, and all runover lines would be indented two ems.

Styling Cross-References

The first principle in cross-reference styling is that the cross-references should match exactly the phrasing, capitalization, and punctuation of the heading or subheading they refer to. Only in rare cases when the heading is exceptionally long should it be shortened in a cross-reference. A second principle is that multiple *see also* references are always listed in alphabetical order and separated by semicolons: "*See also* Library; Reference works; Research." Third, cross-references are not terminated by periods, even though they read like sentences.

Fourth, as a general rule, *see* and *see also* are italicized. An exception may occur when the heading referred to is already italicized (as a book title or a species name in Latin). In these cases *see* and *see also* are frequently set roman to distinguish them from the italicized headings.

Fifth, the initial *s* in *see* or *see also* is capitalized (1) when it begins a new line, as *see also* does in some indented indexes, or (2) when it is separated from the preceding part of the entry by a period. Whenever a cross-reference is enclosed in run-in parentheses (as in many paragraph indexes) or preceded by a mark of punctuation other than a period (as in a few indexes), the *s* is lowercased.

Sometimes the indexer may wish to direct the reader to other headings that are too numerous to mention. In these cases, general cross-reference instructions are given, normally in italics:

Herbs, wild, 560–567. *See also specific herbs*

Government, state, 134, 136–137. *See also* Governors; *names of individual states*

Cross-reference to a subentry Some cross-references direct the reader not to a main entry but to a subentry. There are two conventional ways to handle these. One is to use the term *see under* or *see also under*, followed by the heading under which the subheading may be found.

> Syrinx. *See under* Sound production

The reader is thus directed to an unnamed subentry under the main entry *Sound production*. The second method is to direct the reader not only to the main heading but to the specific subheading as well. This is done by giving the main heading, followed by a colon (or comma) and the subheading in question, as:

> Syrinx. *See* Sound production: in syrinx

As with any *see* reference, a double entry may be substituted if conditions allow: if the locators for *syrinx* were limited to one or two, they could be entered after the main heading *Syrinx* instead of resorting to the more complicated cross-reference.

Cross-reference styles for indented and paragraph indexes The position and punctuation of cross-references depend on two factors. One is whether the cross-reference is attached to a main entry or a subentry. The other is whether the index is indented or in paragraph style.

In all indexes, indented or paragraph, a *see* reference is run in with its heading or subheading. There is greater variety, however, in the position of *see also* references. In most indented indexes, a *see also* reference is run in with its entry.

> Monetary policy, 122–125, 244
>   Federal Reserve System and,
>   *See* Federal Reserve System
>   Great Depression and, 412–414
>   recession of 1907 and, 34, 35–37.
>   *See also* Knickerbocker Trust
>   Company
>
> Taxes, 233–252. *See also* Tax
>   collection systems
>   federal estate tax, 233–237
>   life estate, tax consequences
>   of. *See* Life estate
>   state inheritance tax, 240–
>   246

An alternate styling for *see also* references in indented indexes is to set the cross-reference as a separate subheading, always the last one in any list. A *see also* reference from a main heading is set as a subheading; a cross-reference from a subheading is set as a sub-subheading. Indexers who follow this styling frequently enclose these cross-references in parentheses:

> Trustees, 54–56, 75–80
>   college, 433, 467
>   as guardians, 77–80
>   (*See also under* Banks)
>
> Homes, 35–40
>   heating of, 236–237
>   remodeling of, 298–302
>   (*See also* Contractors;
>   Home sales)

Cross-references in paragraph-style indexes require special punctuation to help distinguish them from other elements in the paragraph. While a *see* reference is always positioned immediately after the heading it applies to, and while a *see also* reference that applies to a subheading is positioned immediately after that subentry, there are alternatives for the position of *see also* references that pertain to the main heading. These cross-references may appear either at the end of the main entry or at the end of the complete entry:

Tundra (*see also* Alpine ecosystem; Arctic ecosystem): biotic community, 225–227; soils, 221–222; and taiga, 220

Tundra: biotic community, 225–227; soils, 221–222; and taiga, 220. *See also* Alpine ecosystem; Arctic ecosystem

The traditional and most typical position of a *see also* reference is at the end of the complete paragraph entry. The argument for placing it there is that the additional information should not distract the reader from the main body of information.

Cross-references that apply to a subheading are always positioned just after the subentry in paragraph indexes as well as indented ones. In a paragraph index, they are enclosed in parentheses to distinguish them from preceding and following elements and, if they refer to the last subheading in the entry, to prevent confusion with any cross-reference that applies to the main entry.

Territory: boundaries, 22–25; breeding and nonbreeding, 25–29; functions of, 20–21; maintenance of, 26–27 (*see also* Chickadee, territorial behavior of). *See also* Aggression; Breeding

In the example, the first cross-reference relates to the subtopic of territorial maintenance, the second to the main topic of territory. Note that cross-references within parentheses in a paragraph index require a lowercase *s,* since they are not preceded by a period and do not begin a new line.

Alphabetizing the Cards

When you are ready to alphabetize, you will need plenty of space. A common method of sorting is to reserve space on a table for each letter of the alphabet, then to sort all the cards onto piles A, B, C, and so on. Put these cards in a file box sectioned by letters of the alphabet so that they stay in order; then take out one letter section at a time and alphabetize the cards within that group. You may wish to reserve space on the table again for Ab, Ac, Ad, and so on. After all letter sections are individually alphabetized and refiled, you are ready to recheck alphabetic order and do any last-minute editing or markup for the typist.

Alphabetic systems There are two basic ways to alphabetize. One is the word-by-word system, in which one alphabetizes by the first solid word of a phrase. Under this system, if two headings have identical first words, then the second word is considered, then the third, and so on up to the

first comma, colon, or period. The word-by-word system is the one familiar to many file clerks, who are taught that "nothing comes before something." That is, a group of letters followed by a space is filed before any
identical group of letters followed immediately by additional letters, a hyphen, or an apostrophe.

word-by-word order

High Top Fire Tower	Capital gains
Highlands Audubon Society	Capital stock
Highways, maintenance of	Capitalism
	Capitals, list of states and
New York	Carbon monoxide
Newfoundland	Carbonic anhydrase

The other system is the letter-by-letter system, or dictionary styling,
so called because it is commonly used in dictionaries. In this system, every
letter is considered in sequence up to the first comma, period, or colon;
any intervening word spaces are ignored.

letter-by-letter order

Civil Aeronautics Board	National Insurance Act of 1911
Civilian Conservation Corps	Nationalization of industries
Civil War	National Labor Relations Board

The letter-by-letter system tends to make alphabetizing a little easier
for the indexer, while the word-by-word system can be easier for the
reader because it groups identical single words together. But the differences are minor, and either system can, at times, result in an awkward-
looking series.

word by word	*letter by letter*
East African Common Market	East African Common Market
East India Company	"Eastern banking establishment"
"Eastern banking establishment"	Eastern Europe
Eastern Europe	East India Company
Eastman Kodak	Eastman Kodak
Bank Holding Company Act	Bankers in government
Bank of America	Bankers Trust
Bankers in government	Bank Holding Company Act
Bankers Trust	Bank of America

Both alphabetic systems are in wide use in the indexing of books.
The word-by-word system is slightly more common; however, either styling is acceptable. It is very important to follow whichever system is chosen
with consistency.

General rules for alphabetizing Certain principles that apply to both alphabetic systems are outlined here. For additional information on the al-

phabetic order of proper nouns, titles, abbreviations, numerals, and other special terms, see the next section of this chapter.

1. Quotation marks, apostrophes, and accent marks are ignored in alphabetizing. Hyphens that link elements of a compound (such as *Pan-African*) or elements of a unit modifier (such as *bill-to-third-party* calls) are also disregarded, and the linked elements are considered as a single unit.

word by word	*letter by letter*
Film clips	Flower pictures
Film jam	"f" number
Film-advance lever	Focal length
Film-frame counter	Focal-plane shutters

2. Words that precede a comma, colon, or period are alphabetized before any identical words followed by additional words with no intervening punctuation.

Capital, convertibles as source of
Capital, cost of
Capital budgeting
Capital expenditures

3. The indexer should ignore any introductory article, conjunction, or preposition in a subheading and alphabetize only by the key word that follows. (See, for example, the entry for *Numerals,* illustrated on page 257.)
4. Words that are spelled alike but that have different meanings are sorted according to the following order: (1) name of a person, (2) name of a place, (3) common noun, (4) title of a work. Examples:

Cleveland, Grover	Lévis, Quebec	civil disobedience
Cleveland, Ohio	Levis (jeans)	*Civil Disobedience* (Thoreau)

Identical headings that are distinguished by parenthetical explanations are indexed according to the words in parentheses; the order may be alphabetical or chronological:

references (employment)	Grey, Sir George (1799–1882)
references (manuscript)	Grey, Sir George (1812–1898)

Special Indexing Problems

Some kinds of entries tend frequently to pose problems regarding styling, alphabetizing, and other aspects of indexing. The kinds of entries discussed in this section are (1) personal names, (2) place names, (3) titles, (4) abbreviations, (5) numerals, and (6) legal citations.

Personal Names

Most personal names are easily indexed: the surname comes first, followed by a comma and the given name. But some foreign names, especially those beginning with articles or other prefixes, and names with titles attached require the indexer to understand and follow certain conventions. The most important of these are listed here.

1. Names of persons should be indexed in the form in which they are most familiarly known, even if the author of the book being indexed uses a short or different form.

2. A person's name may have to be indexed in more than one place. Authors who write under a pseudonym, for instance, should be indexed under their real names, even if the real name is less well-known. There should also be an entry at the pseudonym that refers the reader to the real name. A double entry is also appropriate. Similarly, a married woman who is widely known by her maiden or professional name is indexed under that name with a cross-reference from her married name. If she is more widely known by her married name, the maiden name should be the cross-reference. In either case the other form of her name is sometimes supplied as an aid to the reader.

O'Keeffe, Georgia (Mrs. Alfred Stieglitz)
Stieglitz, Mrs. Alfred. *See* O'Keeffe, Georgia

Godwin, Mary Wollstonecraft. *See* Shelley, Mary Wollstonecraft
Shelley, Mary Wollstonecraft (née Mary Wollstonecraft Godwin)

3. Any information, such as a title, brief modifier, or dates, that might help the reader identify a person listed in the index should be added in parentheses:

Charles II (King of Great Britain)
Charles III (King of France)
Charles III (King of Spain)

Baker, Josephine (entertainer)
Baker, Sara Josephine (physician)

4. Compound surnames in English, with or without hyphens, are indexed according to the individual's preference or, if that is unknown, the most familiar usage. The desired form may be found in the text. It is always a good idea to cross-reference the less familiar form of the name or make a double entry:

cross-reference

Douglas-Home. *See* Home
Home, Sir Alec Douglas-

double entry

Evert Lloyd, Christine
Lloyd, Christine Evert

5. Names of Christian saints are indexed under their given name (as Peter, Saint). The word *Saint* is always spelled in full. Modern-day saints are indexed under the family name, and it may be necessary at times to add parenthetical identification.

Cabrini, Saint Frances Xavier (Mother Cabrini).

6. Personal-name suffixes such as *Jr., II, III,* and *IV* follow the given name, as "Markey, James III" or "Markey, Mrs. James F. Sr."

7. Titles of honor such as *Dame, Lady, Lord,* and *Sir* that precede personal names are retained in an index but ignored in alphabetizing. The same is true for clerical titles that precede a personal name:

Grey, Sir George   Smith, Rev. James S.
Grey, Lady Jane   Smith, Msgr. James T.

8. Courtesy titles—*Mr., Mrs., Miss, Ms., M., Mme.,* and *Mlle.*— are deleted from indexed names unless (1) a married woman is indexed under her husband's name, as "Roosevelt, Mrs. Franklin D. (Eleanor)," or (2) the courtesy title is in the title of a work, as *Mr. Smith Goes to Washington.*

9. Academic titles that precede a name and degrees that follow a name are deleted from indexed personal names.

10. For someone who holds a title of nobility, it is best to use the name by which that person is most familiarly known. Cross-references and double entries are commonly used to index such names:

Edward VIII
Windsor, Duke of. *See* Edward VIII

11. Popes, monarchs, and immediate members of royal families are indexed by their official given name if that is the most familiar designation:

Charles, Prince of Wales
Charles XII, King of Sweden
Clement VIII, Pope (1592–1605)
Elizabeth II, Queen of England

12. When the name of a monarch, saint, or pope is identical to the family name of another person listed in the index, the order is as follows: monarch, saint, or pope, then the family name, then other nouns:

John XXIII, Pope
John, Augustus
John Birch Society

13. Personal names that begin with particles (articles, prepositions, or other prefixes) can be difficult to alphabetize. A general rule is that English and American names derived from foreign languages are indexed with the prefix first, uninverted. Likewise, any foreign name that is already familiar in this country is indexed with the prefix first:

D'Avenant, Sir William   de Beauvoir, Simone
La Guardia, Fiorello H.   de Gaulle, Charles
Van Allen, James A.   Van Gogh, Vincent

Other, less familiar, foreign names should be alphabetized according to the customs of the country and its language. Details of some of these customs are explained in the next section below.

Foreign names When in doubt about the form of any name—its spelling, capitalization, or whether to invert the particle or other element—the indexer should check the author's treatment of the name in the text or consult a standard reference source such as *Webster's New Biographical Dictionary*. Cross-references and double entries should also be made as needed.

French and Belgian surnames beginning with the preposition *de* are inverted when indexed, while those with the article *la* keep their natural order:

> Coster, Charles de
> La Salle, Antoine de
> La Tour, Georges de

Spanish surnames retain forms of the preposition *de* in indexes (de la Madrid Hurtado, Miguel), and so do Dutch names (De Vries, Hugo). However, the prepositions *von* and *van* in Dutch and German names are inverted (Bismarck, Otto von).

Spanish surnames, frequently compound in form, are usually indexed under the first element of the compound, the father's family name: *Lopez Portillo, José; Santos-Dumont, Alberto*. However, many Spanish names do not fit this category. For example, some surnames are single, not compound; other Spanish speakers use two given names and only one surname (as *Monge, Luis Alberto*). Other complicating factors are that one element of the compound may itself be compound (as *de la Madrid Hurtado, Miguel*) and that *y* sometimes joins the two parts of the compound surname (as *Ortega y Gasset, José*).

The first syllable of a Chinese name is usually the family name, under which the name is indexed; thus it is not necessary to invert traditional Chinese names. However, some modern Chinese invert their names in accordance with Western practice, and these names should be inverted in an index. The way in which the author handles the name should give you a clue. Vietnamese names are similar to Chinese names and should be indexed by the family name with no inversion. However, a cross-reference should be made from any other form that might have become familiar in the West: "Diem, Ngo Dinh. *See* Ngo Dinh Diem."

The traditional order of Japanese names is family name plus given name, with no inversion required for indexing. This form should be used when indexing historical Japanese names. Modern names, however, may be inverted like Western names, with a comma separating the parts. On the other hand, since some modern Japanese prefer the traditional order, the indexer should carefully note how the author handles these names.

Alphabetizing personal names The following principles will help you determine alphabetic order when indexing personal names.

1. Names with contractions (as O'Neill or D'Angelo) are alphabetized as if they were solid words.
2. Names that begin with *Mc, Mac,* or *M'* may be alphabetized in one of two ways. The most common method is to list the names under the

assumption that all are spelled *Mac*, though each name retains its actual spelling. Another method is to alphabetize those names letter by letter as they are spelled.

3. Personal names that begin with *Saint, St., Sainte,* or *Ste.* are always alphabetized as if they were spelled in full, though they may keep their abbreviated form if that is their actual spelling. These compound names are also alphabetized as if they were a single word, even in the word-by-word alphabetic system:

Sager, Ruth
Saint-Andre, Andre Jeanbon
St. Denis, Ruth
Sainte-Beuve, Charles-Augustin
St. Johns, Adela Rogers
Salmon, Lucy Maynard

4. Initials in an inverted personal name precede spelled-out names beginning with that initial:

Smith, J.C.
Smith, J.M.
Smith, J. Morris
Smith, James E.

Place Names

Place names are indexed by the form that appears in the text. Any alternate forms that are common or that are mentioned by the author should be cross-referenced. Many place names need to be further identified geographically, as *Springfield, Mo.; Washington (state); Washita River (Okla.),* or *Andover (Maine) COMSAT Station.*

Choosing the key word is not always easy. Generally, the key word is the name of the geographical place and not a generic word like *lake* or *mount:*

Good Hope, Cape of	Fundy, Bay of
Lookout Mountain	Rushmore, Mount
Michigan, University of	Salton Sea

However, there are a few place names composed of generic word plus specific name that are not inverted, because they form a compound whose parts are thought of as a unit. These names may be indexed by the generic word:

Cape Cod
Lac du Flambeau
Lake of the Ozarks

Some place names begin with articles. Anglicized names beginning with *the* are alphabetized under the key word, as *Hague, The.* For foreign-language place names that begin with articles, the usual practice is to retain the article in initial position and alphabetize according to that article:

El Alamein	Las Vegas
El Paso	Le Mans

Names of cities and towns are never inverted in an index. Thus, towns named for geographical or manmade features always keep their natural order when indexed: *Mount Airy, N.C.; Lake Bluff, Ill.; Fort Wayne, Ind.*

Titles

The titles of works, when indexed, are italicized or enclosed in quotation marks just as they are in a text. Any internal punctuation marks are disregarded for alphabetizing purposes. When titles of books, periodicals, poems, plays, articles, or works of art are indexed, they keep their natural order; they are never inverted in order to position a key word first. An exception occurs, however, with main-heading titles that begin with an article. In the main headings of most indexes, initial articles are moved to the end of the title, preceded by a comma (as *People's Almanac, The*). Some indexers prefer to keep the article in original position (as *A Field Guide to the Insects*), but even when this styling is chosen, the article is ignored in alphabetizing.

It is only the initial article that may be inverted; initial prepositions, no matter how small, stay in place and determine alphabetic order. *Of Human Bondage,* for example, is indexed under *O*.

The indexer must be careful to distinguish main headings from subheadings, because subheading titles in an index keep their initial articles in normal position. Like main headings, however, they are always alphabetized according to the first word that follows the article. An index of first lines, as in a poetry collection, is an exception. Here initial articles in first lines are kept in natural order and determine the alphabetic order.

Newspapers in English should be indexed under the name of the city of publication, as *Chicago Tribune; Springfield* (Mass.) *Daily News,* even if the name of the city is not part of the actual title. An exception is made for those papers not associated with any place of publication, as *U.S.A. Today.*

Foreign titles, like English titles, are alphabetized by the first main word following any initial article. But if there is a chance that the reader might not recognize the article for what it is, the indexer should cross-reference the title with the article first:

> *Esprit des Lois, L'* (Montesquieu)
> *L'Esprit des Lois.* See *Esprit des*
>   *Lois, L'*

As with other entries, it may help the reader in some cases to add information to a title that pinpoints its identity. For example, it is a common practice to list, in parentheses, the author's last name at the end of a title, as *No More Parades* (Ford). Other examples of added information include:

> *Flowers of Evil, The (Les Fleurs*
>   *du Mal;* Baudelaire)
> *Life* magazine
> *Times* (London)

Any work of art may be indexed as a main entry by its title with the artist's name in parentheses. Alternatively, it may be listed as a subheading under the author's name. In this case, if only one or a few works are indexed under the author's name, they should be combined alphabetically with all other subheadings. If, however, there are a great number of works listed among the subheadings, for clarity they may be grouped together at the end of the author entry under the subheading *works*.

Titles of works are never indexed if they appear only in reference notes.

Abbreviations

Indexes make minimal use of abbreviations because fully spelled words, though taking up valuable space, are a better aid to the reader. However, if the abbreviation is very common, and especially if it is an acronym and the author uses it in the text, the indexer should make an entry for the abbreviation. A common abbreviation may be indexed this way: "NATO (North Atlantic Treaty Organization), 576–581." A cross-reference might then read: "North Atlantic Treaty Organization. *See* NATO." On the other hand, a less familiar abbreviation should be indexed by its spelled-out form, with a cross-reference at the abbreviation: "U.A.E. *See* United Arab Emirates (U.A.E.)."

Abbreviations that are acceptable without cross-reference to the fully spelled form include (1) familiar abbreviations whose fully spelled forms are very lengthy (as AFL-CIO); (2) a few geographical terms such as *U.S.* and *U.S.S.R.* that are discussed below; and (3) short forms of state and province names when they are used to identify places within that state or province—but not when the larger unit itself is the entry:

British Columbia	Vancouver, B.C.
Kansas	Manhattan, Kans.

With the exception of *U.S.* and *U.S.S.R.* discussed below, acronyms and other abbreviations are alphabetized letter by letter. Any added parenthetical term is disregarded in considering alphabetical order.

Advertising Age	Associated Press	K (potassium)
AFL-CIO	AT&T (American	K^2 (Himalayan mountain)
Africa	Telephone and	K ration
	Telegraph Company)	
	Atlantic Institute	

It is acceptable for *United States* to be abbreviated *U.S.* in an index, but it should be alphabetized as if it were spelled *United States*. Likewise, the abbreviation *U.S.S.R.*, which may be used in an index heading, is alphabetized as if spelled *Union of Soviet Socialist Republics*. These are the only countries whose names may legitimately be abbreviated in index headings.

Abbreviations are more commonly used in scientific and technical works than in general texts. Consequently, they appear frequently in the indexes to such works.

Numerals

When numerals are used as index headings, they are alphabetized as if they were spelled out. The British horse race 2,000 Guineas, for example, and the insecticide 2,4-D would both be entered in the *T* section of the index. 19th century would be listed under *N,* as if spelled out *nineteenth century.* Only when a series of headings is intentionally listed in numerical sequence is regular alphabetic order suspended:

> Overdue notices, form of
> first notice
> second notice
> final notice

Numerical prefixes that are attached to chemical terms are ignored in alphabetizing. Thus, the following term would be indexed under the letter *P:* 6-phosphogluconic acid.

Legal Citations

Citations to law cases should always be indexed under the names of both adversaries, through the use of either cross-reference or double entry. When the United States is a party to the action, it should be abbreviated U.S.

cross-reference	*double entry*
Marston v. U.S., 25, 36–38, 40, 57, 233, 244, 302 U.S., Marston v. *See* Marston v. U.S.	Marston v. U.S., 25 U.S., Marston v., 25

Some case citations begin with phrases such as *Ex parte, Ex rel., In re,* and so on. These citations should be inverted so that the names of the parties to the action are the key words.

> Jones, Clyde M., Estate of, 133
> Jones, Smith v., In re, 48
> Smith v. Jones, In re, 48

Typing the Index Manuscript

The index manuscript is typed from the information on the note cards. Before typing, the indexer should have positive answers to these questions: Are the cards thoroughly edited and in consistent alphabetic order? Have all cross-references been checked for accuracy and form? Are locator numbers in sequence? Have all design considerations—including indention levels, capitalization, punctuation, and special typefaces—been

INDEX 29

Documentation of borrowed material, 334.

    See <u>also</u> Bibliography; Footnotes;

    Research

Double negatives, 267

Double spacing. See <u>also</u> Draft preparation

  with indented material, 152

  in legal documents, 139

  in short letters, 135

<u>Dr.</u> See <u>Doctor</u>, use of

Draft paper, 127

Draft preparation, 106

  on a media typewriter, 115, 127

<u>Drawee</u> and <u>drawer</u>, use of, 458

Duplicating machines, 426-427, 428, 444

Duplicating processes, 426-437. See <u>also</u>

    Photocopy process; Reprographics

  and copying processes, 437, 440

Duty on goods. See Customs

Dye transfer process, 437

E-COM (Electric Computer Originated

    Mail), 486

<u>Economist, The</u>, 529

EDP (electronic data processing), 447

Editing, 2, 4, 5, 8, 11

  of conference materials, 55

Figure 10.4. A page of an index manuscript based in part on the edited cards illustrated in figure 10.3

determined and marked on the cards? If any special typefaces are being used—such as boldface type for main headings that refer to a major discussion of a topic—has a note been written that explains for the user what the typeface indicates?

To type an index manuscript that is going to be typeset, you should set wide margins. The number of characters in the typewritten line should approximate the total number of characters that can fill the width of the printed column. The manuscript should be typed in only one column, as a single-column, wide-margin format facilitates the editor's marking of the manuscript and estimating its length.

Center the word *Index* at the top of the page. If there is a need for an explanatory note, type the note below the title. Set the typewriter for double spacing, since all lines—whether within or between entries—will be typed double-spaced. Allow extra space, however—perhaps four lines—between sections of the alphabet. Be sure that you understand how deep to indent runover lines. Remember that two spaces on the keyboard represent one em of indention. Number all pages. If it has been decided how to mark entries that are continued from one page to another, use that form where needed at the top of a new page. Alternate ways of styling such entries are presented on page 285.

If the index will not be sent to a printer—that is, if the typewritten copy is the final index, as for a typewritten report—spacing requirements differ. The index may be typed in one column across the page, or it may be typed in two columns separated by a vertical column of space about two characters in width down the middle of the page. Both columns should have equal maximum length, and the right column should begin slightly to the right of center. A two-column format results in a better-looking index, but a single column is certainly easier to type and is acceptable, especially with paragraph-style entries.

For this kind of index, set the typewriter for single spacing. Single-space each entry, but double-space between complete entries. Add extra space between sections of the alphabet.

Index headings should never be typed at the left side of the page and locators at the right, connected by leader dots, as for a table of contents. Such a format is extremely difficult to type and to read.

For a multiple index you will need to type a separate heading (such as "Index of Pharmaceutical Terms") above each index. These indexes may begin on a new page or they may be typed below the end of the regular index if space allows. An index of first lines is formatted differently from other indexes; because of the length of the headings, it is usually printed in a single column.

The typewritten index should be proofread carefully against the note cards. Special attention should be given to locator numbers and to any locators or entries that might have been inadvertently skipped. A copy of the index should be made and kept, along with the page proofs and cards, until the index is printed in its final form.

Marking Up and Typesetting the Index

The typewritten index is still not ready for typesetting until a copy editor has properly marked it up for the typesetter and checked it all over one more time.

Markup

In order to do the manuscript markup the editor must have complete information regarding the basic page design (the size of the type to be used and the number of columns to be set per page), whether right-hand margins are justified, what kind of end-of-line hyphenation is allowed, what size dash to use, how much indention to use, and how to treat entries that are continued from one column to another.

Basic page design Indexes are usually set in two columns per page and in type that is two sizes smaller than the size used in the text; however, before committing to this design, the editor should know how heavily the book was indexed and how many pages have been allotted for the index. The design described above will probably work well if the indexer took, on average, between six and ten references per page and if the desired length of the index is between two and five percent of the total pages in the book. If there are five or fewer references per book page, the index will be on the short end of this range; if there are a dozen or more references per page, the index may be even more than five percent of the total book length.

Some indexes have three columns per page, and a very large book may have a four-column index. Multiple-column indexes are an efficient use of space, especially for indented indexes with their many short lines of headings and subheadings. In addition, if the index is set as more than two columns, the type is usually made smaller than it would be in a two-column design.

Right-hand margins Most indexes use a ragged-right style rather than a justified right margin. The problem with a justified right margin is that because of the narrow column widths, lines of type would frequently have to be very crowded or very widely spaced in order to come out justified.

End-of-line hyphenation Many editors disallow word breaks because of the difficulty they may cause the reader; others do allow breaks so that more characters fill each line. Some editors allow breaks only in very long words which, if not broken, would leave an unsightly white space on the line.

Dashes Most publications use an en dash (about halfway between a hyphen and an em dash in length) within inclusive numbers, such as 131–132.

Indention The general rules regarding indention have already been explained on pages 254–255 and on 270–271. However, at this point the editor may decide that indention takes up too much space. If the columns are very narrow, for instance, and the index is an indented one with sub-subentries, it will mean a one-em indention for subentries, two ems for sub-subentries, and 3 ems for all runover lines. To make better use of this space, the editor may decide against using an extra level of indention for runovers, and instead align runovers with the sub-subentries. An alternative to this choice is to mark indentions not in ems, but in ens, which take half the space of ems.

Continued entries Some notation should appear on the typeset pages to help the reader make the transition when an entry breaks at the bottom of the last column on the right-hand page and continues at the top of the next left-hand page. The usual method is to repeat the heading in the new column, followed by the word *continued* (or *cont.* or *contd.* or *cont'd*) in italics or parentheses. Many variations of this notation are in use; a very common form, *cont.*, is recommended because it is least difficult to type. The heading and notation are placed together on the first line of the new column in an indented index, above the new subentry. In a paragraph index they precede and are run in with the new subentry. Some index editors like to use a *continued* notation over an entry carried from the bottom of the left-hand page to the top of the next right-hand page, but this procedure is not necessary.

Instructions for the typesetter On the front page of the index, the editor identifies the book by author and title and gives the typesetter general instructions: (1) on what page of the book the index will begin; (2) the style and size of type to be used; (3) how many columns each page will have, the exact width per column, and the amount of space between columns; (4) how many lines per page; (5) whether right-hand margins are to be justified or ragged; (6) the type of dash to use with inclusive numbers; (7) the measure of indention for runover lines and also for subentries and sub-subentries of indented indexes; and (8) how to treat entries that are continued from one column to another. Most editors reinforce these written instructions for indention by writing the proper number of em-quads within the indention spaces on the first page.

Final Copy Check

Before sending the index to the typesetter, the copy editor reads the whole index one more time to check it for consistency of style and logic of arrangement. During this reading, the following tasks are attended to: (1) pages are checked to see that they are numbered in proper order; (2) words to be set in italic or boldface type are checked to be sure that they are so marked; (3) the precise amount of blank space between letter divisions is indicated; (4) any *continued* notations that refer to the typewritten version are marked for deletion so that they will not be set.

Proofreading

After receiving page proofs of the final index, the editor carefully proof-reads the typeset pages against the marked-up typescript. Page numbers and transitions from column to column are closely checked, especially those transitions from page to page where the *continued* notation is used.

The editor must also watch for any bad breaks between lines, as described on 284, which are objectionable for esthetic reasons. Any alphabetical division that begins at the bottom of a column should have at least two lines of entry below it; if that is not possible, the editor will have to begin the new alphabetical section at the top of the next column. Also, a single line should never appear at the top of a column followed by any line of space, nor should a line consisting of only one or two locators be allowed to head a column. The editor fixes these breaks by moving certain lines from column to column, by adding or deleting lines, by adding extra space where space already exists, by making all columns on facing pages one line shorter or longer than on other pages, or by a combination of these methods. These copyediting techniques are discussed and illustrated in Chapter 11.

Chapter 11

Production Techniques

CONTENTS

The term *production* is an editorial term that refers to the processes by which a publication is produced: from the completion of the manuscript to the making of the plates from which the pages will be printed. During production, the author's copy is edited to increase its accuracy and readability and is marked up in such a way that it can be readily typeset. The typeset copy is proofread, fitted on pages along with any illustrations or other material that could not be set in type, and reproduced as film negatives. The negatives are used to make the printing plates, which lay down ink on paper on a printing press.

Depending upon the size of the publishing house, editorial production may be handled by a large staff of specialists or by a single person. Large book publishers employ staffs of acquisitions editors, general editors, copy editors, production editors, fact-checkers, designers, proofreaders, and artists. On the other hand, a small company publication may require only one editor to handle all production tasks. In this chapter, the tasks are somewhat arbitrarily allocated to an *editor* (who has overall charge of getting the author's manuscript into copy that the typesetter can interpret), a *designer* (who makes decisions about typography, layout, and the physical appearance of the publication), and a *proofreader* (who checks any newly typeset proofs against the copy from which type was set). In actual situations, any one of these jobs may be handled by two or more specialists, or all of them may be managed by only one person.

Overview of the Process

The production process usually encompasses all or most of the steps listed below. Each of these steps is discussed either in this chapter or in

Chapter 12, "Design and Typography," or in Chapter 13, "Composition, Printing, and Binding."

1. The author submits a manuscript.
2. The manuscript—also called *typescript* or *copy*—is read by at least one editor, who makes corrections and other revisions.
3. The revised manuscript may be sent to the author at this point for approval or the answering of queries.
4. The designer chooses typography and page format.
5. The editor may ask the typesetter for *sample pages* of the copy to see how the designer's choices actually look in print. Sample pages should include examples of all kinds of copy that will appear in the book, including headings, figure captions, tables, and running heads, to ensure that the various kinds of type look good together on the page.
6. The manuscript is typemarked according to the designer's specifications.
7. The edited and marked-up manuscript is sent to a typesetter, or *compositor,* who sets it according to the editor's instructions.
8. The typesetter returns at least two sets of proofs, usually in the form of galleys.
9. The editor may send a set of galley proofs to the author, who makes corrections and returns the galleys to the editor.
10. A proofreader corrects the galley proofs and carries any other corrections from the author to a *master galley proof,* which is returned to the typesetter.
11. Material for illustrations, having been made camera-ready, is sent to the typesetter.
12. The typesetter makes the corrections indicated on the master galley by resetting parts of the copy.
13. Page layouts, or *dummies,* are made by the designer or by the typesetter.
14. The compositor makes up page proofs by combining the typeset material from the galleys with any illustrations; these proofs are sent to the publisher.
15. The editor either approves the pages or asks for revised pages; no page receives final approval until the editor has seen an acceptable proof of it.
16. The compositor sends high-quality prints (called *repro proofs*) or film (usually photographic negatives) of the final pages to a printer, who uses these materials to make the printing plates. (The compositor and the printer may be the same, but in most cases the two jobs are divided.)

These steps may become complex, especially when there is a large amount of artwork or when the copy is divided into chapters or sections that go through each stage at a different time. It helps the editor to keep a chart of all the steps involved in a particular project and to check off each stage as it is completed for each chapter or section.

Scheduling is extremely important. Compositors' jobs and printers' presses are scheduled to take advantage of the machinery every possible working minute. If a publishing staff fails to meet a deadline, its work may be put off for several weeks while the compositor or printer handles other previously scheduled jobs. Thus, the handling of manuscript and proof has to be carefully scheduled so that deadlines can be met without sacrificing the quality of the editing or proofreading.

To an ever-increasing degree, many of the production steps described in this chapter are handled electronically, through the use of word processors, text-editing systems, and computerized typesetting systems. The range of possibilities that an author or editor may encounter in terms of kinds of equipment, combinations of equipment, and capabilities of equipment is virtually unlimited. Rather than try to describe a range of possibilities that is subject to constant change, this chapter focuses on describing the basic steps that are used in the handling of paper copy. The point is that, with very few exceptions, no piece of electronic equipment can eliminate any of these steps; rather this equipment simply does electronically, and hence faster and usually more easily, what was once done manually. Therefore, the first step in understanding electronic editing is to understand the basic steps that have traditionally been part of the production process.

The Manuscript: Format and Castoff

A large part of the production process focuses on the author's manuscript, and much of this chapter is concerned with the editor's marking of the manuscript. However, before this editing process can begin, the manuscript needs to be typed neatly and in a format that will make the editing process easier. In addition to editing the manuscript and marking it for typesetting, editors also need to know how many typeset pages or lines a manuscript will require. Editors make this calculation by means of a process known as *castoff*, which is described in this section of the chapter.

Manuscript Format

Manuscript preparation begins when the author's manuscript is typed. By specifying a particular format, the editor can be assured of receiving copy in a form that is easily edited. Copy should be typed clearly, without strikeovers, on good-quality paper that can be handled frequently without damage. Erasable paper is not recommended, because it smudges when handled. Copy should be typed on one side of the page only, because inserts written on the back of the page are easily overlooked.

Authors who are submitting a manuscript that is actually a printout from a word processor should keep in mind that some publishers will not accept manuscripts printed by a dot-matrix printer. All pages of the manuscript should be of the same size, preferably a standard size such as 8-½ by 11 inches. Even so-called reprint copy made from tear sheets, or photocopied matter that is being used as extracts, should be taped to paper of that size.

Double spacing is also required. Even tables, footnotes, and bibliographies are double-spaced. This interlinear space, plus margins of at least one inch at top and bottom as well as both sides, allow the copy editor to mark corrections and specifications legibly.

The editor may also require the author to have the pages typed with the same number of lines on each full page and with a prescribed typewriter width setting, and to have all typing done on either a pica or elite machine. These considerations make it easier for the editor to estimate the length of the manuscript.

The author may also be asked to submit a second copy of the manuscript, which is filed for reference or which is used during production. Two people may work on copy simultaneously to save time; for example, one may verify the content while another copyedits. But this division of labor can be disadvantageous, because there can be only one master copy and eventually the marks from one copy will have to be carried to the other.

Castoff

Castoff is the publisher's term for the counting of the number of characters in a manuscript so that the number of printed pages can be estimated. Castoff calculations are an important step in production: magazine designers need to know how many pages may be allotted to a particular article; book publishers need to know how much paper to order for a particular book; and typesetters need to know the approximate length of a book so that they can schedule the job and estimate their costs.

The editor determines the average line length, in inches, and multiplies that by the number of characters per inch (10 for pica typewriters, 12 for elite) to obtain the character count per line. The average line length, in characters, is then multiplied by the number of lines on the page to obtain the total number of characters per typewritten page.

The character counts produced by these calculations are then converted to an estimate of the number of lines of printed copy. First, the editor consults the typesetter's type book, which, in addition to showing how each style of type will look, gives its number of characters per pica. Different typefaces have different character counts, and the count of the font that is chosen will be specified in the type book. (This number will represent an average, of course, because type is proportionally spaced; that is, characters like lowercase *l*'s and *t*'s take less space than capital *M*'s and *W*'s.)

Next, the number of characters per pica in the chosen typeface is multiplied by the number of picas in the line length that has been chosen for the job. This gives the average number of characters in each printed line. Finally, the number of characters per printed line is multiplied by the desired number of lines on the printed page to find the total number of characters that can be printed on a typical page of the type and design chosen.

At this point, the editor returns to the total number of characters in the manuscript that was found in the first castoff calculation. That number is divided by the number of characters per printed page. The result is the number of pages that will be needed when the manuscript is converted to the chosen style of type.

When making the final estimate, the editor must also consider the fact that headings will take up extra lines, so any extra lines of space that will occur between sections or above or below headings should be added to the total. Also, each chapter of a book should be estimated separately because of the space that is usually left at the end of a chapter when the next chapter begins a new page. Half pages are always counted as full pages; half lines, as at the end of paragraphs, are always counted as full lines. Another complication occurs when some parts of a book are set in a different size of type, as in a book with many examples or extracts. Separate counts should be made of the number of lines for each type size and the two counts totaled afterward. The illustrations must also be considered. The space taken by any artwork or tables, including the space above and below, should be measured and added separately into the total page count.

It is important, when estimating the size of a book, to have already determined such matters as the type page and trim size, typeface and type size—all discussed in Chapter 12, "Design and Typography." These matters—as well as the determination of how many extra pages are needed for front and back matter—will have an important effect on the estimation of both size and costs.

Knowing the final length of the printed work will also allow the editor to make any adjustments if the number of pages is for some reason unacceptable. A manuscript that is too short, for example, may be printed in a typeface that allows more characters per pica, or with more space between the lines; or margins may be set wider. A manuscript that is too long may be edited down, or different adjustments may be made such as the setting of smaller margins, the choice of a type with narrow characters, or the use of less space between the lines.

Copyediting the Manuscript

Copyediting is important because it is usually the last full reading of a manuscript before it is set in type. Revisions in manuscript are cheap; they take but a moment of the author's or editor's time. But mistakes in typeset copy are expensive to correct. Thus, the more closely the manuscript is read, the less expensive the project will be. Typesetters are supposed to "follow copy," mistakes and all; and although many will automatically correct obvious typing errors, they should never be expected to do so.

Basic Tasks

Specific duties of the copy editor can include any or all of the tasks described in the following paragraphs.

1. *Style the manuscript.* The changes that a copy editor makes are usually "mechanical" or stylistic—changes in punctuation, the use of capital letters, abbreviations, numbers, hyphens, etc.—so that the style of the text adheres to the particular style chosen by the publisher or by the editor. Consistency is a major goal. There are so many variations of style in standard use that inconsistencies appear even in the best writing. Removing these inconsistencies so that they do not detract from the writer's purpose is usually the copy editor's principal job.

2. *Rewrite parts of the manuscript only when necessary.* Rewriting the author's prose where its intention is unclear or its style awkward is a responsibility that is handled judiciously. It is all too easy to change the author's meaning inadvertently. A query to the author may be preferable to an editor's attempt to rewrite on the basis of possibly imperfect understanding.

3. *Rearrange the content as needed.* Words, sentences, paragraphs, or whole sections may have to be transposed and sequences renumbered. Certain text matter might be better relegated to a note or an appendix, and vice versa. It is often best to consult with the author before undertaking these kinds of changes.

4. *Verify the data.* Fact-checking is an important part of the production process; some publishers employ people who do nothing but check facts. Quotations should be verified and revised as necessary to match their sources. Bibliographical references should be checked. Dates and the spelling of proper names should be looked up in reference books.

5. *Look for trademarks.* Brand names like Xerox and Vaseline should be spelled and capitalized precisely. Where appropriate, generic names can be substituted for these brand names.

6. *Look for examples of sexual bias.* Rewrite the copy to remove such bias if you have permission to do so from the publisher or author.

7. *Query the author.* Ask for clarification or for approval of revisions you have made.

8. *Make a style sheet.* For suggestions on how to prepare and maintain a style sheet, see pages 297–301 below.

9. *Typemark the manuscript.* Add all of the marks and notations that the compositor will need in order to typeset the text in accordance with the designer's specifications. Markup of copy is discussed in detail in the section on Manuscript Markup, beginning on page 368, in Chapter 12, "Design and Typography."

10. *Review all tables.* The tables may need to be revised to conform to accepted standards of tabular format and to make them all consistent in their styling. For details, see Chapter 9, "Tables and Illustrations," and pages 336–338 in this chapter.

11. *Handle the artwork.* Illustrations should be designed according to the discussion in Chapter 9 and taken through the production steps that are described on pages 338–342 of this chapter.

12. *Add, delete, or otherwise revise headings.* Headings should be edited so that they accurately describe the material that follows them and so that their styling is consistent. Headings are discussed further on page 315.

13. *Check all cross-references.* Verify the author's cross-references and add new ones if necessary. Phrase the cross-references according to the suggestions on page 313.

14. *Examine the table of contents.* The headings there should match those on the manuscript.

15. *Check all sequences.* All numerical lists, all alphabetically arranged items such as bibliographies and glossaries, as well as all sequences of table or figure numbers must be in order.

16. *Check for possible instances of copyright violation, libel, or other potential legal problems.* Ensure that the author has obtained permission to reproduce copyrighted materials.

17. *Renumber the pages if needed.* Page numbers are written on all copy except tables and illustrations, which follow a different numbering system. The numbering of tables is discussed on pages 213–216 in Chapter 9, "Tables and Illustrations," and on pages 337–338 in this chapter.

18. *Create and typemark running heads.* Keep in mind that the style and content of running heads may be different for recto and verso pages. For more on styling running heads, see the section on Other Design Elements, beginning on page 365, in Chapter 12, "Design and Typography."

19. *Make a list of special characters in the copy.* This list should include the number of the manuscript page on which each character first appears. Two copies of this list are needed, one for the typesetter and one for the files.

20. *Keep on good terms with the typesetter.* To accomplish this goal, an editor should see that all instructions are coherent, resist the temptation to make unnecessary changes in copy (especially in galleys and pages), and meet all deadlines. Some knowledge of what a typesetter can and cannot do, of how expensive composition processes are, and of how much time each process takes is also useful so that procedures can stay within the time limits and budgets of both parties.

Because of these various duties, the copy editor usually reads a manuscript twice—more if it is complex or poorly written—at least once for content and again for details such as errors in punctuation and for the verification of such things as the spelling of proper names. It is usually more efficient to copyedit similar things—tables, footnotes, captions, and the like—together. In this way the editor will be more likely to notice inconsistencies and will be more alert for ways to style similar items consistently. In most cases the editor corrects the errors, but sometimes a query to the author is in order.

In some publishing houses, the edited manuscript is sent to the author for approval before being typeset. The author is usually instructed to make his or her revisions with a colored pencil or pen. The author is sent either the master manuscript or a photocopy of it. If the author is sent the master manuscript, a photocopy of it should be made first, in case it is lost in transit. If a photocopy is sent, any revisions made by the author on the photocopy will have to be carefully copied, or *carried,* to the master manuscript.

How to Mark a Manuscript

There are certain conventions, symbols, and codes used and understood by editors and typesetters. Most of these are described and illustrated in this chapter, beginning on page 303. In addition, special instructions have to be written in from time to time, and these should be concise, precise, and legible.

Conciseness is essential because of the limited space on which the copy editor works—margins and interlinear spaces. Corrections are made on the manuscript as close to the normal reading order as possible, because the compositor reads the manuscript through in sequence and must be allowed to find additions and revisions without having to search for them. Normally, the right margin is reserved for notations concerning revisions, the left margin for the typography codes described in Chapter 12. However, a heavily revised manuscript may require notations in both margins in addition to the space between the lines.

All instructions to the compositor are circled to distinguish them from actual revisions. Special notes often begin with the abbreviation "Comp:" to call attention to them. Margin notes should not be written so close to the edge of the paper that they will fail to duplicate in a photocopier.

Should the editor use pen or pencil? Beginners understandably prefer pencil, but a bright-colored, fine-point pen is preferable, because it is easier for the compositor to read and it does not smudge. Colored pens and pencils are necessary if more than one person handles the copy; each should mark the copy with a color that identifies that person. To ensure neatness, the editor's mistakes should not be crossed out but rather whited out or erased with ink eraser or strips of white tape. Mistakes made by the author, however, should never be erased but only crossed out; the author's original should always be visible behind the deletion marks.

Additions to the Text

Brief additions to the text may be written in between the lines of the manuscript or in the margins, as explained later in this section. Lengthy additions, however, should be typed on a separate page of the same size as the manuscript—never on a slip of paper stapled or taped to the manuscript page. The insertion is typed double space and to the same width as the rest of the manuscript copy. It should be clearly identified, too. A typical identification is a note at the top of the page: "Insert 24A. Insert as shown on msp 24." Then, on manuscript page 24, a caret is drawn at the point of insertion, and this instruction is written in the margin: "Insert 24A." Both instructions are circled to ensure that they are not mistakenly set in type.

To ensure that the compositor knows whether the insert should be run in or set as a separate paragraph, the identification and the instructions may be more explicit; for example, "Insert 24A; insert as shown on msp 24; run in" and "Run in insert 24A here"; or the instructions could tell the compositor to "set as new paragraph." Several brief inserts can be typed on one extra page if they are all to be inserted on the same manuscript page and if each is clearly identified as Insert A, Insert B, and so forth. However, this method of inserting additions is advisable only if the number of such inserts is small and manageable.

An alternative, which results in copy much easier for the typesetter to handle, is the cut-and-paste method. Additions are typed on separate pages as described above, and the pieces of copy are cut and pasted or taped in proper sequence on pages of the same size as the rest of the manuscript. This method adds extra pages to the manuscript, which will have to be repaginated.

Special care must be taken to insert the additions properly and also to revise punctuation. All too often copy editors, concentrating on the content of the addition, fail to position it properly in the copy.

Pagination

Manuscript page numbers are checked so that the compositor is not left to wonder about a missing or repeated page number. Page numbers should be complete, in sequence, and positioned near the upper right corner, where they will be readily seen by all who handle the manuscript.

Any pages inserted after the typing of the manuscript should be identified with a letter following the number of the preceding page. Pages 4a and 4b would thus fall between pages 4 and 5. In addition, on the bottom of the preceding page, the instruction "Go to pages 4a nd 4b" or "Page 4a follows" should be written (and circled) so the compositor will know what to expect. For added clarity, one may also write at the top of page 4a, "follows page 4." If the manuscript fills up with numerous *a* and *b* pages, one should renumber the manuscript entirely, taking care to delete any notations such as "Page 4a follows."

Indicating deleted pages is simpler. If pages 15 and 16 are deleted, for example, one simply adds a hyphen plus 16 to the number on page

14 so that it reads: 14-16. This tells the compositor to expect page 17 to follow page 14.

Special Symbols

Any symbol that does not appear on a typewriter keyboard should be *called for* in the margin of the copy the first time that it appears on a page. For example, if the author has written > in a table, the copy editor calls attention to and clarifies the symbol by writing and circling "greater than" in the margin. Similarly, any odd spellings or stylings that are intentional but that the compositor might misread or be tempted to "correct" should also be noted: either by placing stet points (usually in the form of four or more dots written in below the word or words) or by writing a note in the margin to "follow copy." When there might be confusion between a zero and a capital *O*, or between the numeral 1 and the letter *l*, the copy editor should write in the margins *zero, Arabic 1, cap oh,* or *ell.*

Editors should know the names of special symbols, including the Greek alphabet, diacritics, and basic mathematical symbols, so that they can call for them by name in the margin when the symbols appear in the text. Also, on going through a manuscript for the first time, the copy editor makes a list of all these uncommon symbols. Often the author is asked to supply this list instead. This list, which consists of a drawing of the symbol, its name, the size and face of type desired, and the manuscript page on which it first appears, is given to the compositor. It is sent even before the manuscript is sent, because the compositor may not have these symbols in the particular font chosen and may have to order them specially or arrange to set them in a different size of type that is already on hand in the shop.

The Style Sheet

Copy editors work with a style sheet. There are two basic kinds. One, representing the publisher's house style, is a predetermined list of styling decisions which the publisher may give to the editor along with the manuscript. Some publishers even issue their own full-fledged style manuals. The other kind of style sheet is created by the copy editor while reading the manuscript. On these blank pages the editor keeps track of how to handle all words and phrases that have alternate forms. In addition, note is made of formatting and typography decisions. The form that is recorded on the style sheet represents the final decision of the editor, whether it is based on the author's original styling or the editor's preference or the publisher's style sheet.

Everything that might have an alternate form is written on the style sheet because inconsistencies may appear unexpectedly on later pages, forcing the editor to go back to look for the earlier form. Throughout the readings of the manuscript, the editor will both develop the style sheet and consult it. Until the final reading is finished, the style sheet is not finished. Words that have alternate spellings (*acknowledgement* or *acknowledgment*) or alternate forms of capitalization or hyphenation are automati-

ABCD	EFGHIJ	KLMNO
benefitted (4)	headwind (6)	mid=1950s (6)
Atlantic coast (5)	flood plain (7)	Nearctic zone (7)
anticyclonic (5)	funneling (8)	non=breeding (12)
crosswind (6)	field data	midday (13)
buildup (n) (8)	sheet (43)	midpoint (24)
advisor (23)	inter=individual	Midwest (25)
acknowledgment (27)	spacing (44)	M.S. thesis (38)
data base (28)	interspecific (46)	non=motorized
airflow (36)		glider (42)
bird cage (41)		ms. (manuscript) (47)
air speed (42)		

PQRST	UVWXYZ	Numbers
re=enter (3)	Wrangel $\frac{1}{N}$ St. Elias	one fourth (n)
take=off (6)	National Park (7)	ten, 11
sizeable (7)		1,000
setup (8)		1980s
shoreline (15)		1970$\frac{1}{N}$77
reappear (27)		2d, 3d
subadult (42)	**Abbreviations**	6° C
tail feather (43)	mph (5)	23 July 1968
postdoctoral (47)	P.O. Box (7)	
prefrontal (50)	EST (12)	**Capitals**
	e.g. (22)	the Cooper River delta
	WSW (tables) (23)	the east coast
	St. Louis (but Fort	New York state
	Worth) (25,27)	among + between l.c.
	Spell out state and	in titles
	nation names except	seasons of year l.c.
	in addresses (MA,CT)	
	and tables (Mass.,	
	Conn.)	

Figure 11.1. An editor's style sheet

cally included. Words that are often but not always italicized (e.g. or *e.g.*) or that may or may not have diacritical marks (*fiance* or *fiancé*) are included. When the author spells a word inconsistently, the copy editor usually chooses the form that appears most frequently on the copy, but the editor always feels free to correct nonstandard words and phrases.

To make a style sheet, the editor divides a few blank pages into categories such as Numbers and Dates, Lists, Extracts, Footnotes, Abbreviations, Tables, Illustrations and Captions, Headings, and so forth. Additional pages are assembled on which individual words and phrases will be listed in approximate alphabetical order. Examples of problematical stylings are listed on these pages as the manuscript is read. The editor may wish to add manuscript page numbers to certain items on the chance that he or she will need to go back and make styling changes on the basis of stylings encountered later in the text.

All variations on one styling decision need not be listed; a single notation may indicate that similar cases are to be handled in the same manner. For example, the notation "west-northwest (text)—WNW (tables)" tells the reader that other directions are to be styled in the same way.

The notations should also be brief. A single word, "résumé," in the alphabetical listing of particular words and phrases indicates that all instances of that word include the acute accent marks. Similarly, instead of writing the sentence "Decades have no apostrophe before the final *s*," the simple term "1980s" could be listed in the Numbers section. This means that all such forms—*1970s*, etc.—are styled in the same way, without the optional apostrophe. Also, a single sample number like "5,200" on the style sheet can indicate that all four-digit numbers use the optional comma.

When the style sheet is finished—after the last reading of the copy—it is put in final alphabetical order and typed. At this point the entries are checked for clarity, and further descriptive details, such as the abbreviations for parts of speech, are added where appropriate. From now on, the style sheet may be copied and used by the compositor, the author, and the proofreader.

The following alphabetically ordered listing contains suggestions about the kinds of things that may be included on a style sheet.

Abbreviations Every abbreviation on the copy should be taken note of, checked in an abbreviations dictionary for accuracy, and written in its desired form on the style sheet. Attention should be paid to the use of capital letters (some abbreviations are traditionally set in small capitals), punctuation, and spacing. See Chapter 4 for a full discussion of abbreviation styling.

Bibliography Sample listings should be recorded in this section that represent all variations encountered in the copy. The bibliographic form chosen should be one of the standard forms discussed in Chapter 8, "Notes and Documentation of Sources."

Capitalization The capitalization of individual words is indicated by putting those words in the main alphabetical listing in either a capitalized or lowercase form.

Cross-references The style sheet should specify the styling of cross-references. Will they refer to page numbers or to chapter titles, for example? Will the word *page* be abbreviated?

Dates The chosen styling may be indicated with one or two examples, as follows: "26 September 1972" or "September 26, 1972"; "September 1972" or "September, 1972." If abbreviations of months are acceptable in certain instances, those instances should be specified. For example, "Sept. 26, Sept. 1972 (tables only)."

Definitions Some books set off definitions (or sometimes words that are followed by glosses) within running text by printing them in italic or boldface type. The style sheet should tell how to handle these.

Footnotes The style sheet contains samples of footnotes in every variation. It shows such choices as whether *ibid.* is italic or roman and how to style footnote reference symbols.

Foreign words The editor decides if foreign words will be generally italicized or not. Specific words are written on the main alphabetical list, either underlined to indicate italics or typed regularly (for emphasis, with the word *roman* in parentheses next to them).

Hyphenation of compound words Compound words will comprise a good part of the main alphabetical section of the style sheet, since many compounds have open, hyphenated, and closed-up forms. It is sometimes helpful to distinguish between a phrase used as a compound noun and an identical phrase used an an adjective. The distinction may be made simply by writing the initial for the part of speech next to the appropriate term:

> low pressure (n)
> low-pressure system

Illustrations The style sheet should either record a few sample captions or state such specifications as the use of capitals, punctuation, and typography in captions, legends, and any labels within the artwork. Variations are discussed in the section on The Parts of an Illustration, beginning on page 214, in Chapter 9, "Tables and Illustrations."

Lists Specifications for setting lists need to be added to the style sheet if they are not already on the designer's list of type specifications. The styling of lists within running text is a matter not usually considered by designers, so the copy editor has to choose whether items are numbered or lettered, whether the numbers are enclosed in parentheses, and whether they are set roman or italic. A different set of rules has to be devised for displayed lists. The style sheet states whether items in displayed lists are listed by number or letter, what punctuation and spacing appears around each letter or number, and how far the item is indented. Special problems that can occur in the editing of lists are discussed further on page 314.

Numbers The style sheet shows the cutoff point for numbers appearing as numerals or as words. This can be done by writing, in the section on numbers, a shorthand notation such as the following: ten, 11. This reminds the editor that all numbers up to and including ten are spelled out, while all numbers beyond ten are expressed in digits. A rule can also be stated as a sentence, for example: "All numbers are digits except when they begin a sentence."

If the copy contains fractions within the text, the style sheet states whether they are to be spelled out or set as fractions; and, if set as fractions, whether they are solidus fractions (as 3/4) or as case or piece fractions (as ¾ or $\frac{3}{4}$) that fit on a line of text. (For more on case and piece fractions, see page 320.) More complex types of fractions are usually set on their own separate lines, because they do not fit easily on a line of text. A style sheet guide to fractions might be written this way: "one-half, one-fourth, three-fourths (in running text). All fractions with units smaller than tenths in running text set solidus."

Other questions to resolve and record on the style sheet might include the styling of ordinals (second, 2nd, or 2d) and the handling of inclusive figures and dates. For example, should the copy read 1978–80 or 1978–1980? 395–97 or 395–397? How about dollar figures: five cents or 5¢? two million dollars or $2 million? These and many other options are discussed in Chapter 5, "The Treatment of Numbers."

Punctuation The style sheet records all stylings for which there are alternatives. If it is decided to place a comma before the *and* at the end of a series, write "series comma." If it is decided to capitalize a full sentence following a colon, the following might be written: ": Full sentence, : phrase" to show that a phrase following a colon is lowercased.

Spelling One source—a good general dictionary—should be chosen for the checking of spelling. For proper names, an encyclopedia or biographical or geographical dictionary is usually the best source to use. All proper nouns are recorded on the style sheet.

Tables Variations in the styling of tables are described in the section on The Parts of a Table, beginning on page 214, in Chapter 9, "Tables and Illustrations." The style sheet states such things as how column heads are to be capitalized, whether they should be set in bold, italic, or roman type, and whether they are centered over the column or aligned in another way. Consistency in the use of rules and the styling and position of table numbers, titles, captions, and source notes is important, and the style sheet will probably describe these specifications in detail.

Copyright and Acknowledgment of Sources

One of an editor's most important responsibilities is to remain alert to the possibility of copyright violations, libel, and other invasions of a person's right to privacy. These should be brought to the author's attention. All too frequently an editor finds that an author has been careless in quoting or acknowledging an original source. In those cases the author may be tactfully queried, "Author: please supply source."

Interpretations of the 1978 U.S. copyright law have not been fully standardized, but in general an editor should know that all printed material in the *public domain* can be reproduced without permission, though the source should always be acknowledged. Material in the public domain includes, but is not limited to, works published before the twentieth century and also public records and federal or state government publications. In addition, the copyright law allows *fair use* of small amounts of copyrighted material for the purposes of criticism and comment in scholarship. This is a complicated area of law, however. For extended discussion of copyright law the reader is referred to the works listed in the Bibliography at the back of this book.

While reading a manuscript, the editor should keep a list of every item that is credited or that might need to be credited to a source. The entries on this list would include the following information, which should be requested from the author if not available:

1. Title and author of the source
2. Year of publication
3. Name of publisher and copyright holder (These may be different.)
4. Page on which the source originally appeared
5. Whether permission to reprint is needed and has been obtained
6. Fee required, if any
7. Name and address of the person representing the copyright holder
8. Whether the author has permission to adapt the original if requested

Some of this information may be found in a credit line or source note supplied by the author. But much of it will be found in a copy of the permissions correspondence that the publisher usually asks the author to submit along with the manuscript.

Permission to reprint It is important to begin the process of obtaining permission to reprint early. Many publishers are notoriously slow to respond to such requests and may have to be prodded by follow-up letters. The letter of request should supply full information about the source to be reproduced: title, author, year of publication and copyright; an exact description of the part to be quoted or reprinted, including page number or figure or table number and the total number of lines or pages involved. In addition, the copyright holder needs to know about the work in which the source will be reproduced: name of author and publisher, proposed title, approximate date of publication, type of publication, the number of copies to be printed, and the market. The letter should also tell the copyright holder whether the material is to be adapted in any way, as is common with reprinted illustrations and tables, and show precisely how it will be changed.

A letter of approval from the copyright holder will specify certain conditions which must be strictly adhered to. The conditions might include a fee, the number of copies to be sent to the copyright holder, or the precise wording and position of the credit line.

All material taken from another source, with or without permission, should be acknowledged—in running text, in footnotes, or on special acknowledgment pages. Source notes for tables and credit lines for artwork are discussed on pages 231–232 and 250–251 in Chapter 9, "Tables and Illustrations." If the copyright holders permit, credit lines may be grouped together on a single page headed "Acknowledgments" or on the copyright page of the book (which is usually on the back of the title page), under a heading such as "Grateful acknowledgment is made for the use of the following material."

Copyediting Marks

The following section describes the use of copyediting marks to indicate certain kinds of elements in and changes to a text. Many of these uses are illustrated in the example of a copyedited passage on page 304. The marks themselves are the same as the proofreaders' marks listed on page 327.

Additions to the text There are several ways to add passages to a manuscript that is already typed, depending upon the length of the addition and how easily it can be marked for insertion. The symbol commonly used to indicate an addition is a caret placed at the point of insertion; the addition is written over the caret and above the line.

If a character is added in mid-word, only a caret is needed below the inserted character. However, if a character is added to the beginning or end of a word, a close-up sign should be added to the character above the caret to ensure that the typesetter knows that the character should be set closed-up. When a word or phrase is crossed out, the replacement word or phrase may be simply written above the deleted passage, without a caret to point to it. Any large group of added words should be enclosed in a brace so that the typesetter can readily find the beginning and ending of the new phrase.

A very large insertion that will not fit easily between the lines may be written in the margin, with a line drawn from the words to a caret that marks the point of insertion. Any additions within the margin must be written horizontally. The typesetter must never be expected to turn the page in order to read any passage. If the margin is crowded with other notations, the editor must write the insertion so that it is readily seen as a single passage. This may be accomplished by enclosing it partly in a box or brace or by connecting the lines with connecting arrows.

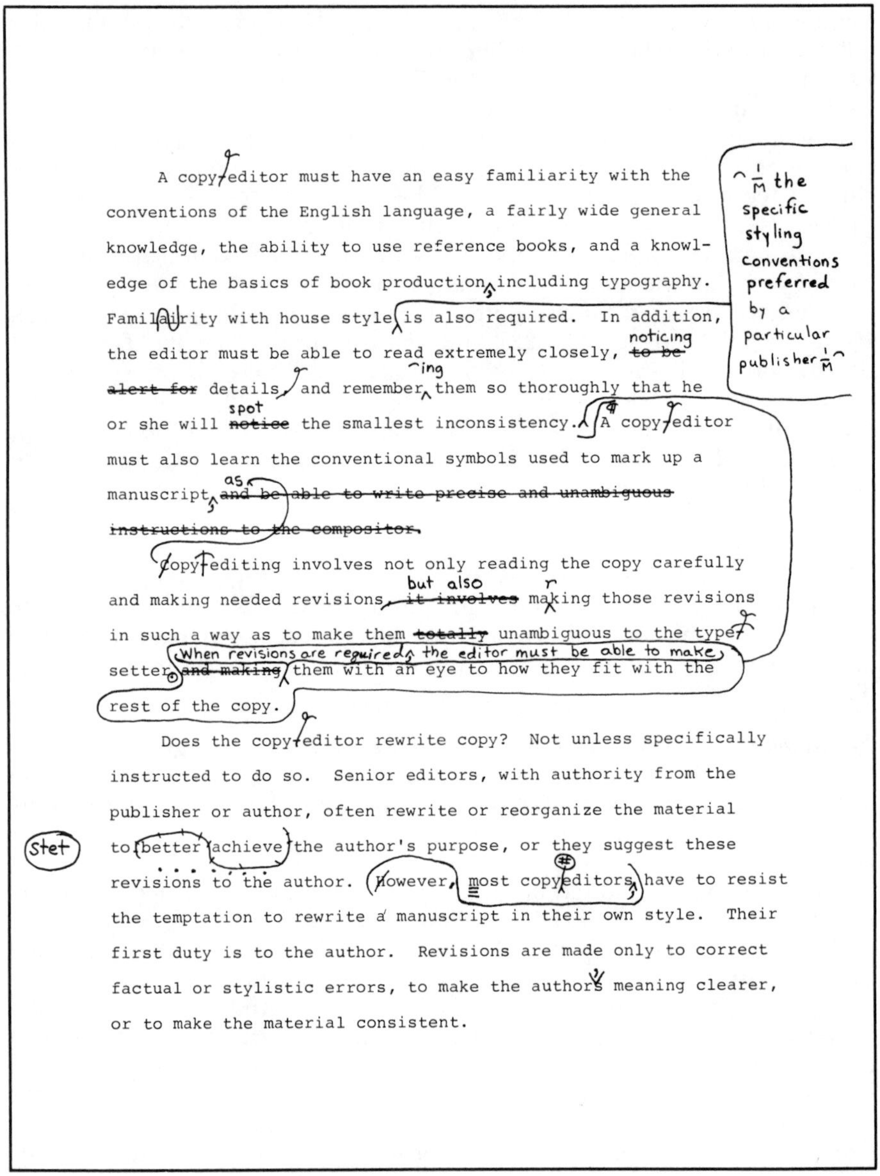

A copy editor must have an easy familiarity with the conventions of the English language, a fairly wide general knowledge, the ability to use reference books, and a knowledge of the basics of book production, including typography. Familiarity with house style is also required. In addition, the editor must be able to read extremely closely, ~~to be~~ noticing ~~alert for~~ details, and remembering them so thoroughly that he or she will ~~notice~~ spot the smallest inconsistency. A copy editor must also learn the conventional symbols used to mark up a manuscript, as ~~and be able to write precise and unambiguous instructions to the compositor.~~

Copyediting involves not only reading the copy carefully and making needed revisions, but also ~~it involves~~ making those revisions in such a way as to make them ~~totally~~ unambiguous to the typesetter. When revisions are required, the editor must be able to make ~~and making~~ them with an eye to how they fit with the rest of the copy.

Does the copy editor rewrite copy? Not unless specifically instructed to do so. Senior editors, with authority from the publisher or author, often rewrite or reorganize the material to better achieve the author's purpose, or they suggest these revisions to the author. However, most copy editors have to resist the temptation to rewrite a manuscript in their own style. Their first duty is to the author. Revisions are made only to correct factual or stylistic errors, to make the author's meaning clearer, or to make the material consistent.

[Marginal insert: the specific styling conventions preferred by a particular publisher]

Figure 11.2   A copyedited page

Any insertion that is too long to fit in the margin should be typed on a separate sheet, as explained on page 296.

Deletions There are three ways to delete material in a manuscript. One is for the editor to simply draw a heavy line through the unwanted copy. The line must be heavy and confident, drawn straight through the copy so that it cannot be mistaken for an underscore. The editor must also take care to begin and end the crossout bar precisely so that no characters or punctuation marks are missed and also so that extra characters are not mistakenly deleted.

The second method is to use the delete sign shown on page 327. This symbol may be used to delete a single character or, when it is appended to a heavy line, to delete larger amounts of copy. The symbol may also be used when the editor wishes to cut a large section such as a whole paragraph. Rather than drawing bars through every line in the paragraph, the editor draws a box around the paragraph, makes a large X within the box, and appends a delete sign to its side in the margin. The advantage of this method is that it makes it instantly clear to the compositor that the whole section can be skipped.

A single character may also be crossed out with a vertical line without an attached delete sign loop. This is done mostly when the delete sign might interfere with an accompanying mark such as a close-up sign.

To delete an underscore, one obviously cannot use a crossout line. Instead, the editor adds a delete mark to the end of the underscore. It is more difficult to delete only part of an underscore, but it can be done. Divide the underscore with vertical lines and place delete marks only on the appropriate sections of the line. If the copy is crowded, it may be preferable to write *ital* or *rom* in the margin, circle the pertinent sections of the underscored material, and draw an arrow between those sections and the margin notation.

The editor's job is to make the compositor's job easy. Thus, to prevent the compositor's having to search the copy to see where deletions begin and end, the editor should add close-up signs, run-in signs, or arrows to guide the compositor from one part of the copy to another. This is especially important when the copy is heavily marked up. The editor should also help by rewriting single words and punctuation marks in their new positions instead of expecting the compositor to search for small pieces of copy in a maze of deletions. One should always rewrite punctuation marks so that they appear immediately after the word they follow.

Close-up A close-up sign indicates a deletion of space. It is used to turn two or more separate words into a single word. Used at the end of a line, it tells the compositor to join this word to the first word of the following line. The symbol is frequently combined with the deletion of a hyphen to instruct the typesetter to set a closed-up word rather than two separate words or one hyphenated word.

stone⌢walled   water⌢fall

A large close-up sign is used in combination with a crossout bar to guide the compositor from the beginning of a deletion to its end. The close-up sign includes both a bottom and a top arc, but one of these alone suffices, especially if there are other markings on the copy that may interfere.

Capitals, small capitals, and lowercase letters Capital letters are marked by three underscores. These are drawn below lowercase letters to indicate a change to capitals, or below capital letters when needed for clarity. Clearly typed capital letters should be left alone, but any handwritten capitals that might be mistaken for lowercase should be reinforced with triple underscoring.

The lowercase symbol, a slash mark through a letter going down from right to left, is used to change a typewritten capital letter and also to ensure that a handwritten lowercase letter is not mistaken for a capital. To change a lengthy phrase to lowercase when it is typed all in capitals, the editor need only slash the first letter of each word. To ensure that the compositor sees the mark, the top of the slash can be extended as a horizontal line across the top of all the other letters in the word.

Small capitals look like capital letters but have less height. They are frequently used to set certain abbreviations, such as A.D. and B.C. Their chief use, however, is in headings and captions, where they are often set with initial capital letters. To call for small capitals, the editor draws a double underscore below typewritten capital or lowercase letters. A combination of three and two underscores is drawn to indicate a combination of capitals and small capitals.

In addition to the symbols, editors use abbreviations such as *cap, lc, sm caps,* and *cap/sc* to call for specific styles of capitalization when writing in margins of copy. For more on these types of abbreviations, see the section on Manuscript Markup, beginning on page 368, in Chapter 12, "Design and Typography."

Space The space symbol instructs the typesetter to insert a *word space,* which is the amount of spacing that appears between all the words on a particular line. To separate two words that were inadvertently closed up on the copy, the editor draws a vertical line between them. It is not necessary to add the space symbol above the line, but it may be added. Sometimes the editor instructs the compositor to add a *thin space,* which is smaller than a word space and which is used on either side of operational signs in mathematics and in other special cases. Usually a vertical line is drawn where the space is desired and a note circled in the margin, "Insert thin #." In certain circumstances, the editor may ask the compositor to insert thin spaces between the letters of all the words in an all-capitalized heading and extra word space between the words of the heading. This process is called *letterspacing*. To achieve it, the editor writes in the margin, "Comp: letterspace this heading." Occasionally an editor or proofreader calls for a *hair space*, which is smaller than a regular thin space. A hair space, barely obvious, is often inserted between two characters that might cause confusion when closed up entirely, as a single quotation mark set next to a double quotation mark. For an explanation of other units of measure used for describing spaces, see the section on Spacing and Measuring Type, beginning on page 346, in Chapter 12, "Design and Typography."

Italic and roman type   Italic type is indicated by a single underscore. If it is necessary to mark the same copy for capital letters, four separate underscores are drawn. For lengthy italic copy, it is neater to write and circle *ital* in the margin and circle or point out the passage so that the compositor can see clearly where it begins and ends. Roman type is not ordinarily marked with special notations. However, the editor should write *rom* in the margin to mark a change from a large block of italic type such as an extract.

When one is marking already-printed copy, such as a tear sheet taped to a copy page, there is no need to underscore words that are already italicized. If any italic copy is to be changed to roman, however, one should underscore the italicized word and write *rom* in the margin directly opposite the word.

For more on italic and roman type, see pages 345–346 in Chapter 12, "Design and Typography."

Boldface   Boldface is a dark, heavy type used sometimes for emphasis and frequently for headings. Design specifications usually determine in advance what words will be set bold, but the editor reminds the compositor by marking the copy. To tell the compositor to set a word or passage in boldface type, the editor draws a wavy underscore below the relevant copy, including its punctuation. If the copy is more than a line long, the abbreviation *bf* may be circled in the margin and the copy clearly pointed out with a brace and an arrow.

To correct copy already marked for boldface that should not be so marked, the editor circles the affected words and in the margin writes *lf* (lightface). This abbreviation is written carefully because a handwritten *lf* can easily be mistaken for a *bf*.

Boldface italic type (abbreviated *bold ital*) is indicated by a straight underscore with a wavy underscore below it. Since not every font has this rarely used typeface, however, one should check with the typesetter first before designing a page that requires the use of bold italic letters or numbers.

For more on boldface type, see pages 345–346 in Chapter 12, "Design and Typography."

Punctuation marks An editor may add or delete marks of punctuation or change them to different marks of punctuation.

Period The copy editor's mark to denote a period, a point enclosed in a small circle, is used only when needed for legibility—when the compositor might miss the period because it is handwritten or otherwise obscured—and also when changing a comma to a period. To make this change, the editor circles the typed comma; the typesetter will know that it has become a period.

Comma Legible commas need no further markup. Commas that are not clear—those inserted next to a deletion, for example—are flagged by a caret drawn over the comma.

Semicolon The semicolon also is signaled by the placing of a caret over it whenever it is felt that it might not be legible. The editor can also change a comma to a semicolon by adding a point over the comma and a caret over the point. To change a semicolon to a comma, the editor simply draws a caret over the comma in such a way that it obscures the point of the semicolon. To change a colon to a semicolon, a tail is drawn on the lower point and a caret drawn over the newly made semicolon.

Colon A small circle or oval is drawn around a colon if it needs clarification, or if it has been changed from a period by drawing in the second point. A semicolon can be changed to a colon by superimposing two heavy dots over the semicolon so that the tail of the lower part of the semicolon is obscured.

Parentheses Parentheses should be inserted carefully. They should be slightly oversize but should still look like parentheses. Some copy editors draw one or two tiny horizontal slashes through each handwritten parenthesis to ensure its identity. Parentheses are set in the same type as the copy surrounding them. Thus, if the material within parentheses is italicized and the surrounding copy is roman, the parentheses would also be set roman and thus would not be underscored.

Brackets Brackets should always be drawn in by the editor unless the brackets on the copy were produced by an authentic bracket key on the typewriter. If the typist made brackets from a combination of slashes and underscores, the editor draws over them so that they look like square brackets.

Ellipsis points Ellipsis points, except for those used as periods following a sentence, should be spaced. In the margin, the editor may call for the insertion of thin spaces between the points if they are typed closed up on the copy. Ellipsis points in mathematical copy are often raised off of the base line instead of being positioned on it. To typemark these, the editor places a caret above and an inverted caret below each point or writes "center points" in the margin.

Quotation marks An inverted caret flags quotation marks only when they might be misread, as when they form part of a handwritten insertion. Combinations of single and double quotation marks might confuse the typesetter, so it is helpful to describe in the margin what is intended. The easiest way to do this is to write and circle "single" in the margin, with a line and arrows pointing to the single quotation marks. Typesetters usually insert a hair space between double and single quotation marks, but editors often ask for the space to ensure that it is set.

Most—but not all—typefaces distinguish between apostrophes and single quotation marks. If there is any possibility of misinterpretation, the compositor should be told which to set in a particular case.

Dashes The em dash, which is typewritten usually as two hyphens or one hyphen with a space on both sides, is marked for the typesetter with a numeral 1 over the typewritten hyphen or hyphens and a capital M below it. To call for dashes longer than one em, the editor writes a larger number over the hyphens. For example, the dash that represents the repetition of an author's name in a bibliography is marked as a three-em dash, with the numeral 3 above and a capital M below the hyphen.

In print, the em dash is usually closed up—that is, it is printed with no space on either side. It is unnecessary for the editor to add close-up marks to an em dash unless the hyphens in the copy are spaced.

The en dash is represented in typewritten copy by a hyphen. Thus, the copy must be marked to distinguish en dashes from hyphens. This is done by writing a numeral 1 above the typewritten hyphen and a capital N below it. If en dashes are not so marked, the typesetter will probably set them all as hyphens.

All handwritten copy containing dashes should be marked to identify the kind of dash desired.

Hyphen The hyphen, the shortest dash, is used to divide words at the end of a line and to form some compound words. The double hyphen is an editorial mark that is made by adding a second line below a typewritten or handwritten hyphen. The double hyphen is used by editors to make it clear that a hyphen is being asked for. Any hyphen within a handwritten insertion should be doubled.

Editors also use the double hyphen when the hyphen within a compound word corresponds with a word break at the end of a line. They mark the double hyphen to ensure that the compositor will not drop the hyphen within the compound when the line breaks differently. Conversely, any end-of-line hyphen that denotes a syllabic break in a word and that might mistakenly be retained by the compositor should be marked for deletion with a vertical line and a close-up mark to show that it connects with the first word of the next line. If there is an end-of-line hyphen to be deleted without closing up the word, the hyphen is crossed with a vertical line and a space symbol is added to indicate that the compound should not be closed.

Some editors mark all end-of-line hyphens for retention or deletion, but usually it is necessary only to mark those hyphens that might be mistakenly deleted or retained because they occur in words that could reasonably be spelled with or without the hyphen.

A handwritten double hyphen is also used to tell a typesetter to insert a hyphen.

Transposition sign The transposition sign—a line curving over one element and under another—is used to indicate transposition of characters, words, phrases, or sentences. Often the transposition symbol on the copy is reinforced by the abbreviation *tr* written and circled in the margin.

A variation of the symbol is used to indicate transposition of more than two elements. The copy editor's marks in the example below, for instance, tell the typesetter to leave the middle word and transpose the other two.

When the material to be transposed is typed on more than one line, the conventional symbol is unwieldy. In these cases, the editor usually circles one of the elements and shows its new position with a line and a caret or arrow. Very complicated transpositions should probably be rewritten by the editor, at least in part, so as not to force the compositor to follow a series of complex arrows and lines.

To delete punctuation during a transposition, one may simply draw the curved line in such a way that it covers and obscures the punctuation mark. All transpositions must be marked with great care and double-checked because it is easy to make a mistake. Punctuation marks are often overlooked in this kind of editing; they frequently have to be rewritten.

Run in The run-in sign—a line with curved ends that leads the reader's eye from one part of the copy to another—is used to connect copy typed on two separate lines so that the compositor will automatically run one right after the other.

Stet *Stet*, a Latin word meaning "let it stand," is used to restore words mistakenly crossed out on the copy. The editor places a series of heavy dots below the deleted material and writes *stet* in the margin to ensure that the compositor notices the dots. Or, if the crossout bar has obscured the original, the editor may prefer to erase the crossout bar and place stet points below the word without a note in the margin.

Spell-out sign To indicate to the compositor that a number is to be spelled out or an abbreviation to be spelled in full, the editor simply circles the short form on the copy. Sometimes *sp* is also written and circled in the margin. However, this can be done only when the intended change is unambiguous. The numeral 3, for example, would pose no problem when circled on the copy; the compositor will set *three*. But what about the circled fraction 1/2? Will the compositor know whether to set *one half* or *one-half*? It is the same with abbreviations. When the abbreviation in *Springfield, Vt.,* is circled, the compositor will unhesitatingly substitute *Vermont.* But the typesetter cannot be expected to know what you want when you circle obscure or ambiguous abbreviations such as *pt.* Often it is better for the editor to cross out the abbreviation and write its replacement above the line. Alternatively, the abbreviation may be circled on the copy and the full word written in the margin if interlinear additions are already crowding the copy.

The spell-out sign may also be used to indicate the reverse, but only in circumstances where the author's intention is absolutely clear. The word *ten,* circled on the copy, would thus automatically tell the compositor to set the numeral 10.

Alignment Proper alignment is usually more of a concern for proofreaders than for editors, but an editor may have to instruct the typesetter concerning alignment of tables and other columns or lists. Usually general instructions are written on the page, such as "Align stubhead left with stub items" or "Align all figure columns right," but alignment symbols may also be drawn on the copy. To indicate vertical alignment, for example, a pair of vertical parallel lines is drawn against the sides of the two or more lines of copy that should be aligned.

Diacritics and other special symbols Authors frequently fail to add diacritical marks to foreign words because their typewriters have no keys to print these marks. The editor must add these by hand, after checking the spelling of the word in an appropriate dictionary. It also helps the compositor either to write and circle in the margin, next to the line, the name of the diacritic or to rewrite the word in the margin with diacritics made obvious. Some commonly used diacritics and their names are listed here:

´	(é)	acute accent	˘	(ŭ)	breve
`	(è)	grave accent	ˇ	(č)	haček
^	(ô)	circumflex	¨	(oö)	diaeresis
˜	(ñ)	tilde	¸	(ç)	cedilla
¯	(ō)	macron			

Typists often use the typewriter's apostrophe to indicate a number of similar symbols that are not found on the keyboard but that are distinguished in a printer's type font: the prime sign, the minute sign, and the symbols for feet, as well as acute and grave accents. The editor names the symbol in the margin, circles the notation, and draws an arrow to the copy to identify it for the compositor.

Subscript and superscript The editor places a caret over any subscripts in handwritten copy or copy that is hard to read. An inverted caret is placed below any superscript (as footnote numbers) in handwritten copy or other copy where these marks might be misread.

Indention and paragraphs Manuscript copy is marked to tell the compositor whether lines should be set flush left, indented on the left, or indented on both sides, as well as the specific amount of indention measured in ems. Most publications contain paragraphs whose first lines are indented and whose remaining lines are flush left. Variations on this arrangement are described on page 368 in Chapter 12, "Design and Typography."

When paragraph divisions are clear in the manuscript, the editor does not need to mark them further. However, when the starting point of a paragraph is obscure, or when the editor wants to put a new paragraph break in mid-line, the paragraph symbol should be added next to the first word of the new paragraph. If the paragraph break does not occur at the beginning of the line, a line-break symbol, illustrated below, may be inserted to mark the point where the new paragraph begins. The line-break symbol is also used frequently in math copy. Any time that this sign is used, the editor must see to it that the compositor understands—either from the general design specifications or from a particular instruction—whether the new line will be indented or flush left.

```
Last line of one paragraph. | The first line of the next.
```

If an editor wants to change an indented paragraph so that it is set against the left margin, as often occurs with new paragraphs that follow an illustration or other display, the flush-left symbol is used. For added clarity, the symbol can be reinforced with the abbreviation *fl l* circled in the margin. The flush-right symbol is rarely used, except to mark math copy or to reposition a credit line. The flush-right symbol may also be clarified by a note in the margin telling the compositor whether the word in question should be set flush with the right margin (*fl rt*) or flush with some particular part of the copy.

When the editor needs to mark a specific amount of indention for an item not covered by the general design specification, *em quads* are used. These symbols are placed just to the side of the line to be indented; they tell the typesetter how much indention to use. The em quad, a small square, indicates one em of space. A number written within the quad indicates a multiple of an em space, so that an em quad enclosing the numeral 3 tells the compositor to set a three-em space. Alternatively, the editor may draw in multiple quads, one for each space requested. Spaces larger than two ems are usually measured in picas but may also be measured in ems.

An en space, symbolized by an em quad with a diagonal line drawn through it, is used mainly to indicate the amount of space between the period that follows a numeral and the first item on a numbered list. It is rarely used to indicate indention.

Em and en quads are usually drawn only at the beginning of an indented section to familiarize the compositor with the desired format. They do not need to be used opposite every indented line.

Design Specifications

Many of the marks that go onto a manuscript are design specifications. They are put on the manuscript to tell the typesetter about the size and style of type to use, the width of the margins, the length and spacing of lines, and other typographical and design specifications. Often these marks are put on the manuscript by the designer after the copy editor has finished the copyediting. However, in some cases this marking up of the manuscript, also known as *type speccing,* is done by the editor. For more on the marking up of manuscripts, see the section on Manuscript Markup, beginning on page 368, in Chapter 12, "Design and Typography."

Special Text Elements

In addition to the running text of which most prose pieces are principally composed, there are special text elements such as cross-references, extracts, lists, and footnotes with which authors and editors must be concerned. This section describes marking and styling considerations related to these elements.

Cross-References

While reading the manuscript, the copy editor is aware of the need to insert cross-references where there are none and to check those already in the manuscript. Cross-references should be rephrased if necessary so that they are accurate and stylistically consistent. Styling directions should be included on the editor's style sheet, and they should address such matters as whether the words *chapter* and *section* are capitalized and whether the word *page* is abbreviated. Page numbers are always given in digits, while chapter and section numbers may be spelled out if desired.

Where the author refers to another page of the manuscript, the editor changes the number to 000 so that the manuscript page number will not be typeset. 000 alerts the proofreader, editor, and compositor to the fact that, later on when pages are made up, the appropriate cross-reference page numbers will have to be added. The editor may also wish to write *X-R* in the margin (circled, of course) to ensure that every 000 is found and changed to the proper page number. In addition, the original manuscript page number is usually written in the margin of the copy to facilitate finding the new position of the original cross-reference. The proofreader is responsible for carrying all of these notations to the margins of the galleys.

There is a less time-consuming and less expensive way to handle cross-references. The editor may simply choose to phrase all cross-references so that they refer to chapter or section numbers or titles, thus avoiding any mention of page numbers and any need to add the correct page numbers in later stages of production.

Extracts

The designer of the publication usually supplies specifications for all extracted and displayed material, including the amount of space above and below each extract, the size of type, and the amount of indention. Extracts are often indented and set in type slightly smaller than that of the main text. The copy editor marks all extracts to distinguish them from the regular text. If the specifications are coded in advance, the editor may simply draw a brace around the proposed extract on the side margin and write, "Comp: Set as Ext." If the specifications are imprecise or if it is helpful to repeat them, the editor specifies the amount of space above and below the extract. This space may be requested in points, as, for example, "20 pts b/b above, 24 b/b below," which tells the typesetter to allow 20 points of space between the base line of the first line of the extract and the base line of the line of text above it; and 24 points of space between the base line of the last line of the extract and the base line of the first line of text below it. An alternative is to ask for one line of space, two lines, or a half line by writing the notation in between the lines, if there is room, or in the margin.

For more explanation and examples of quotations set as extracts, see Chapter 7, "The Treatment of Quotations."

Lists

If the copy contains more than one list, design specifications need to include instructions on how to set up lists so that they are styled consistently. The specifications would state whether lists are to be indented like paragraphs or flush left, and they would specify how much space to put around the introductory letters or numbers and above and below lists, how to indent runover lines, and whether extra leading is required between the items on a list when some of the items have runover lines. Lists may be numbered or unnumbered; unnumbered items may or may not be flagged by bullets. If the specifications supply this detailed information, the copy editor needs only to note in the margin, "Set as list; see specs."

The editor checks all lists for alignment. Columns of numbers should align at the right and along periods or decimal points. If a numbered list contains more than nine items, the editor writes an instruction in the margin, "Clear for ten." This tells the compositor not to set numbers one through nine flush left but to leave enough space so that number nine will align over the zero in ten.

Lists with runover lines should be marked to look as even as possible when set. Runovers are usually set flush below the first word of the item, not below the number or letter that identifies the item.

The editor may wish to change an author's run-in series to a displayed list. This is done by inserting line-break symbols. But it is also important to change the series so that it is appropriately styled for display. This often entails deleting the *and* before the final item on the list, deleting any commas or semicolons between the items, and adding initial capital letters to each item. If the run-in list includes parenthetical numerals, they should probably be changed to numerals with periods, which are more appropriate for a displayed list. Above all, the copyedited paragraph should be read carefully to ensure that it will be printed exactly as intended. The continuing copy also needs to be studied: Will the compositor know whether to begin the rest of the copy below the new display flush left or indented? If not, it must be marked for one or the other.

Similar care is taken when changing an author's displayed list to run-in form. In addition to the run-in symbols that connect each separate line, the editor needs to add the proper punctuation after each item, delete or change the numbering, and change capitalization as needed.

Columns

Copy that is to be set in columns within the text should be marked so that it is set in one column only on the galley proofs. The editor may write in the margin, "Run single column in galleys." The precise makeup of the columns will then be determined on page proofs. It is important to do this because the list may have to be broken up and set on two pages and the columns entirely redistributed among the two pages.

Headings

Any long piece of nonfiction benefits from the addition of headings to mark the major divisions. Headings help the reader understand the material, and they facilitate finding certain passages. The author should be asked to type appropriate headings in the manuscript and should also be advised how to type them if the design of the headings has already been determined. If heading style has not been determined, the author should be asked to type each heading on a line by itself, so that there is room to style them and to make other revisions.

The editor examines each heading to see that it accurately and concisely summarizes the material below it. The editor also compares headings and subheadings, making sure that typeface, style, and position are consistent for all headings and subheadings of the same level throughout the book. In addition, the logical connection of subordinated headings and parallel headings is studied and the headings changed if necessary. The editor should always consider the relation of a heading to the immediately following text; the text should never depend on any words in the heading for an antecedent. If the author has inserted footnote reference symbols within a heading, they should usually be removed and handled in some other way.

Headings are usually nouns or concise noun phrases, though newspaper and magazine headings, which often describe actions, may use a phrase or sentence with a verb as a heading.

The styling and designing of headings is discussed in the section on Manuscript Markup, beginning on page 368, in Chapter 12, "Design and Typography."

Notes

For the formatting of notes and reference lists, the editor should be familiar with the various stylings that are discussed in Chapter 7, "Notes and Documentation of Sources," and should recognize the styling that the author has chosen.

A major decision is whether notes will be set as footnotes or endnotes. If the author has typed reference information as footnotes, and endnotes are required by the publisher, the editor must (1) mark in the margin next to each footnote or set of footnotes: "Set all footnotes together at end of chapter" (or article or book), (2) renumber the notes if necessary so that all the notes in a chapter are numbered sequentially, and (3) at the end of the chapter (or article or book) create a new head called Notes and write the notation, "Insert footnotes 1–00 here."

Likewise, if the author has typed endnotes when footnotes are desired instead, the editor (1) writes a notation such as the following in the margins of the manuscript pages at the points where each note corresponds to the text: "Footnote 7 here from msp 90," and (2) in the margin opposite each endnote writes the appropriate manuscript page number, as "Take footnote 7 to msp 12."

A distinction is sometimes made between reference notes, which can be styled as footnotes or endnotes, and explanatory or descriptive notes, which are usually placed at the bottom of a page. The editor's job is made easier, in either case, if the typist has been instructed to type all notes on pages separate from the text.

Part of the editor's job is to consider the appropriateness of the footnotes and to transfer material from the notes to the text or vice versa where needed. The author's permission is desirable for this type of change. Finally, the editor checks the position of all reference symbols in the text and removes them from improper positions such as chapter titles. Footnote symbols in mathematical copy and numerical tables are examined closely, because a footnote number or letter in those contexts might be mistaken for an exponent or other symbol. A different system may be used to denote the references, as described on page 191 in Chapter 8, "Notes and Documentation of Sources." Alternatively, the symbol may be moved to a word instead of a figure.

Markup of notes Footnote reference symbols that appear in the text are always marked as superscripts. The typesetter's attention is also called to all footnote reference symbols by means of a circled notation in the margin such as "footnote 7" or "ftn 7." Footnotes should always be keyed in the margin so that whatever type specifications apply may be readily followed by the typesetter.

The footnotes themselves are usually set in type smaller than that of the text; six- to eight-point type is common, and sometimes no leading is inserted between the lines. The typesetter can be instructed to insert a thin space between a word or punctuation mark and the reference symbol that follows it in the text or precedes it at the beginning of the note. This instruction usually appears only with the first footnote of each chapter and also in the general instructions. Some typesetters automatically insert this space.

The design specifications will determine whether notes are preceded by superscript symbols or by numbers set on the line. The specs should also state the length of any rule extending partway across the page and separating notes from text, the amount of space above and below this rule, and the amount of space between each note.

The following checklist may help the editor determine whether reference material is ready for typesetting:

1. Is the sequence in order, and do reference symbols in the text correspond to the reference symbols that introduce the notes?
2. Do explanatory notes make better sense as notes or should they be moved to the running text or to an appendix?
3. Is the data within the notes complete?
4. Is the chosen format a standard one and is it applied consistently? (Check for such matters as punctuation, the handling of page and volume numbers, and the styling of publishers' names.)
5. Are short forms of notes used where possible?
6. Will the typesetter be able to find the notes easily and know exactly where they are to be set?
7. Are the notes marked up so that the typesetter will know exactly what type to use and how to position it?

Bibliography

In copyediting bibliographies and other reference lists, the editor will have to (1) check alphabetical order, (2) compare footnote and bibliography references to see that they correspond, and (3) add entries that the author has overlooked, especially those mentioned in the text. In general, the editor sees to it that the copy consistently follows whatever styling the author has chosen.

Some of the minor changes that an editor is allowed to make in the content of the bibliography are the following:

1. Publishers' names are frequently shortened in bibliographies. For example, instead of *John Wiley and Sons*, the short form *Wiley* or *John Wiley* may be used if it is used consistently.
2. Books are often published under the old name of the current publisher, and mergers sometimes affect the publisher currently handling a book published under an obsolete name. It may be helpful to the reader to use the current publisher's name, since one purpose of a bibliography is to direct readers to sources they might wish to search.
3. Long journal titles may be subjected to a standard abbreviated form. Such forms are commonly used in scientific reference lists.

Sometimes an editor is required to style an annotated bibliography. The descriptive part of this kind of bibliography is sometimes set in italic type or in smaller type. It may be run in with the entry or set as a separate paragraph. As a separate paragraph, it may be set as an indented block paragraph, or it may use the hanging-indention format, with its first line indented and all runover lines further indented.

Like notes, bibliographies are marked or keyed to tell the typesetter what type to use. General specifications are written at the top of the page, and very little special typemarking is usually required, although some bibliographies are typemarked to set off the author's name in a different style, such as capitals and small capitals. If the author has not used flush-and-hang indention, a note to the typesetter should specify the proper indention. Also, the dash that is used to indicate the repetition of an author's name is usually marked as a three-em dash, as described on page 206. The dash is followed by a period and a space.

Mathematical Copy

Style rules regarding mathematical copy are described in Chapter 6, "Mathematics and Science." This section focuses on the mechanics of marking mathematical copy for the typesetter.

Any mathematical copy in a manuscript must be carefully read and carefully typemarked. A copy editor does not have to understand mathematics in order to edit it, but a familiarity with the conventions of writing mathematical expressions is essential.

In editing technical material, the editor first checks the author's list of symbols that may require special characters for typesetting. If the author has failed to supply the list, the responsibility falls to the editor. The compositor will need the list as soon as possible, because all the required symbols may not be immediately available in the typeface chosen for the project, and the compositor may have to order them, make them up, or substitute similar symbols.

Unless the copy is difficult to interpret, the editor need not complicate it further with a clutter of typemarking symbols. In most cases the editor can simply write a few general rules at the top of the page, chapter, or article and thereafter typemark only the first few instances of each rule. For example, if the typesetter is instructed to italicize all unknowns in an algebraic expression, the editor need only underline the letters of the first equation or so. On the other hand, symbols and abbreviations like the following should all be underlined because the typesetter may not be intimately familiar with mathematical conventions:

1. Subscripts and superscripts
2. The letter e for exponent (but not the abbreviation *exp*), d for derivative, and f for function
3. Single-letter prefixes to certain chemical terms
4. Certain combining forms such as *meta-* or *m-*, *ortho-* or *o-*, *para-* or *p-*, when attached to chemical terms

5. Parentheses within an italic context. Parentheses in mathematical copy may be italic or roman; they match the style of the surrounding text, not the style of the elements enclosed within parentheses.

Inverted carets need not be drawn below all superscripts nor carets over all subscripts if the copy is clear. Carets should always be used, however, with copy that is unclear or with any multiple subscript or superscript. The following examples show how to draw variations on the caret with these multiple forms.

A subscript carrying a superscript is marked

A superscript carrying a subscript is marked

A superscript carrying a superscript is marked

A subscript carrying a subscript is marked

Vectors should be marked for setting in boldface type, and any arrow that has been drawn over a vector should be deleted. Center dots and multiplication signs between two vectors, as well as special brackets or parentheses around vectors, should also be marked with the wavy underline that indicates boldface.

Several kinds of editing problems can occur in the choice between displayed expressions and mathematical expressions set in running text. For example, sometimes an author types an equation in the text that should be displayed. Then the editor inserts line-break or new-line symbols on both sides of the equation. These lines tell the typesetter to display the enclosed material. The compositor is also told in a margin note (unless it is obvious from the general specifications) how the display should be positioned: flush left, centered, or indented a specified amount. In addition, the editor may have to delete a period or otherwise revise the punctuation. Occasionally the editor uses run-in connecting lines to change a display to a position within the running text. In this case, too, the punctuation may have to be revised.

Math copy positioned in the running text must be made up of symbols small enough to fit the type line. Compositors should not be expected to set extra space above and below a particular line just to accommodate an equation or formula that contains a complicated fraction—although they will when asked to. As illustrated earlier in this chapter, some fractions can be set in solidus form to reduce their height. Thus, the built-up fraction

$$\frac{4(a-b)}{(c+d)}$$

becomes $4(a-b)/(c+d)$. However, the author should be allowed to approve any such editorial change.

Simple fractions are often set on the line as *case fractions* or as *piece fractions*. In the case or piece form the numerator is set on a line above the denominator, but the numbers are small enough so that the whole fraction will fit a type line, much as the fractions on some typewriter keys. An editor may request a change from built-up to case or piece, so that a fraction fits in the running text. A case or piece fraction, however, should consist only of a simple numerator and denominator. The built-up fraction illustrated above would not be set in case form because of its complexity.

Since typewriters do not have the keys to type case fractions except for the most basic forms such as ½ and ¼, most fractions in running text are typed in solidus form (as 2 5/12 or 2-5/12). The editor deletes any hyphen and closes up any space between the whole number and the fraction, circles the whole figure, and writes a note to the compositor to "set case fraction" (or simply "case"). The result will be printed on the line as $2\frac{5}{12}$ or 2⁵⁄₁₂.

Editors need to exercise some care here, because the term *case* has two different meanings among typesetters and editors. Originally, the term *case* was used to refer to any fraction that existed as a single piece of type. It could refer, therefore, to $\frac{1}{2}$ or ½. The term *piece fraction*, on the other hand, has been used to refer to a fraction that is assembled from two pieces of type, a raised and reduced figure for the numerator and a lowered and reduced figure for the denominator. However, the term *case* is now often used to refer to fractions that take the form $\frac{1}{2}$, and the term *piece* often refers to fractions that take the form ½. To reduce this confusion, the term *special fraction* is sometimes used to refer to fractions that take the form ½. However, confusion is still possible, and editors should make sure that they are using these terms in the same way as they are understood by their typesetter.

Where the typist has closed up elements of a mathematical expression that should be open, the editor inserts a vertical line drawn in such a way as not to be misconstrued as part of the copy. The space symbol # is usually not added here because conventionally it stands for word space—the space between words in a line of text. Instead, in the margin the editor may write and circle "Insert thin #" or "Insert hair #." These are the spaces more commonly used in mathematical copy.

If general spacing instructions are written at the beginning of the copy, the editor can indicate spacing by drawing vertical lines through only the first equation or so, just to show how the instructions apply. On the other hand, if the copy is closed up where it should be spaced, these lines are drawn throughout the copy. General instructions would cover such matters as the amount of spacing around signs of operation and relationship. Less common specifications should be typemarked throughout the manuscript by the use of vertical lines, em quads, and margin notations.

Reference notes to mathematical copy use the system of asterisks and daggers described on page 191 in Chapter 8, "Notes and Documentation of Sources," because superior numbers or letters could easily be mistaken for part of the copy. If possible, a footnote reference symbol should be placed next to a word instead of a numeral or other symbol to prevent misinterpretation. The expression may have to be rewritten to accomplish this.

Typeset multiplication signs are different from the capital or lower-case letter x. Where the typist has typed the letter x, the editor crosses over it, making it larger. For reinforcement, the term "multi" or "times sign" is circled in the margin, but usually only at the first appearance of the multiplication sign on each page.

Finally, the copy should be searched for other instances where symbols could be misinterpreted. In equations, for example, the letter l is distinguished from the numeral 1 by being italicized; but in some cases it may help to add a circled "ell" nearby. Likewise, there are cases where the capital letter O might be mistaken for a zero. In these and similar cases, a circled note of clarification may serve to prevent a typesetting error.

Galley Proofs

A manuscript that is sent to the typesetter usually returns to the publisher in the form of *galley proofs* or *galleys*—long strips of paper on which are printed text and headings set the full width of the type page. This stage of production is sometimes omitted. For example, a neatly typewritten manuscript with a very simple format may be returned to the publisher as page proofs without the intermediary galleys. In most cases, however, galley proofs provide a useful transitional tool.

Not all copy is included on the galleys. Page numbers, of course, cannot be set until later. Illustrations are handled separately; for a full discussion of their handling during production see pages 339–342. Other

PM 438$$$$$95

5
6

7 Chapter 11

7 # Production Techniques

9 CONTENTS

16
16
19 The term *production* is an editorial term that refers to the processes by
20 which a publication is produced: from the completion of the manuscript
21 to the making of the plates from which the pages will be printed. During
22 production, the author's copy is edited to increase its accuracy and read-
23 ability and is marked up in such a way that it can be readily typeset. The
24 typeset copy is proofread, fitted on pages along with any illustrations or
25 other material that could not be set in type, and reproduced as film neg-
26 atives. The negatives are used to make the printing plates, which lay
27 down ink on paper on a printing press.
28 Depending upon the size of the publishing house, editorial produc-
29 tion may be handled by a large staff of specialists or by a single person.
30 Large book publishers employ staffs of acquisitions editors, general edi-
31 tors, copy editors, production editors, fact-checkers, designers, proof-
32 readers, and artists. On the other hand, a small company publication may
33 require only one editor to handle all production tasks. In this chapter, the
34 tasks are somewhat arbitrarily allocated to an *editor* (who has overall
35 charge of getting the author's manuscript into copy that the typesetter
36 can interpret), a *designer* (who makes decisions about typography, layout,
37 and the physical appearance of the publication), and a *proofreader* (who
38 checks any newly typeset proofs against the copy from which type was
39 set). In actual situations, any one of these jobs may be handled by two or
40 more specialists, or all of them may be managed by only one person.

41

41
43 ## Overview of the Process

44 The production process usually encompasses all or most of the steps
45 listed below. Each of these steps is discussed either in this chapter or in
46 Chapter 12, "Design and Typography," or in Chapter 13, "Composition,
47 Printing, and Binding."
48
50 1. The author submits a manuscript.
51 2. The manuscript—also called *typescript* or *copy*—is read by at least one
53 editor, who makes corrections and other revisions.
54 3. The revised manuscript may be sent to the author at this point for
56 approval or the answering of queries.
58 4. The designer chooses typography and page format.
59 5. The editor may ask the typesetter for *sample pages* of the copy to see
60 how the designer's choices actually look in print. Sample pages should
61 include examples of all kinds of copy that will appear in the book,
62 including headings, figure captions, tables, and running heads, to en-
64 sure that the various kinds of type look good together on the page.
65 6. The manuscript is typemarked according to the designer's spec-
66 ifications.
68 7. The edited and marked-up manuscript is sent to a typesetter, or *com-*
69 *positor*, who sets it according to the editor's instructions.
71 8. The typesetter returns at least two sets of proofs, usually in the form
73 of galleys.
74 9. The editor may send a set of galley proofs to the author, who makes
76 corrections and returns the galleys to the editor.
77 10. A proofreader corrects the galley proofs and carries any other cor-
78 rections from the author to a *master galley proof*, which is returned to
80 the typesetter.
81 11. Material for illustrations, having been made camera-ready, is sent to
83 the typesetter.
84 12. The typesetter makes the corrections indicated on the master galley
86 by resetting parts of the copy.
87 13. Page layouts, or *dummies*, are made by the designer or by the type-
88 setter.
90 14. The compositor makes up page proofs by combining the typeset ma-
91 terial from the galleys with any illustrations; these proofs are sent to
93 the publisher.
94 15. The editor either approves the pages or asks for revised pages; no
page receives final approval until the editor has seen an acceptable

Figure 11.3. A galley proof

types of copy such as footnotes, tables, and sometimes running heads are set on the galleys, but not necessarily in proper position; their final position will be known only when the material is fitted onto pages. Footnotes may be set together on a separate galley, or they may be set directly below the line which contains the footnote reference symbol and separated from the text by lines of space. Indexes are not ordinarily set in galleys at all. To save time, an index is typeset directly in page format.

Galleys are usually returned in groupings so that the publisher can proofread the galleys while the compositor continues to typeset another grouping. The compositor sends two copies or more of each galley proof. One of these is designated the master proof or master galley; that is the one that will be returned to the compositor with all corrections neatly marked on it. Another may be sent to the author for final corrections, or it may be handled by the production department at the publisher's office. A division of labor there might include a proofreader who compares the galley with the manuscript and an editor who marks the galley to show where tables, footnotes, and art should be positioned. Whenever more than one person works on a galley proof, it is essential that each use an identifiable color of pencil or pen. And the editor or proofreader must take special care, before the master proof is returned to the compositor, that all revisions and instructions from all people who handled the proofs are properly transferred, or *carried,* to the master galley.

Like any proofs, galleys will have physical flaws, such as light or blurry type, which should not concern the proofreader. Most galley proofs that are received in publisher's offices today are not real proofs but photocopies of the compositor's proofs, and the photocopy process may further distort the printed image.

At the top of each galley will be a series of identification codes which should not concern the proofreader. The galley number, however, will be included in the codes, and the proofreader may need to refer to this number when communicating with the compositor or the editor.

Revisions at this stage of production should be kept to a minimum because it is expensive to make changes in galleys. The resetting of lines in most composition systems means that the new line must be recomposed and spliced in with the original typesetting from which the galley proof was made. For this reason, a proofreader is usually told to "read proof" only—that is, to compare the galley proof with the manuscript copy and mark the necessary corrections on the galley, and not to make other revisions. Any other revisions that are considered necessary by the editor or proofreader at this stage are usually made in such a way as to minimize the number of lines that have to be reset and thus to minimize the cost of revision.

Revisions by the Author

A set of galley proofs is often sent to the author along with a request to read it through and verify such things as the spellings of proper names, the accuracy of mathematical material and tabular data, content of bibliography and footnote items—things easily missed by a copy editor. The edited manuscript should be included with the galleys to make comparison and checking easier. Authors should always be asked to keep corrections to a minimum; they should be advised how expensive revisions are, especially if the cost of revision will be charged to them.

Galleys are usually sent to the author after the proofreader has read proof. The proofreader's corrections are carried to the author's copy so that the author can concentrate on substantive matters. It is not advisable to have authors write directly on the master galley; their comments may run long and take up margin space that is needed for instructions to the typesetter. It is better for the editor to carry the author's corrections to the master galley in a form that the typesetter can quickly comprehend.

The proofreader's queries to the author are usually written in the margin, preceded by *Au:* or *Qu:* or a question mark, and circled. The common procedure is for the proofreader to make the correction, then ask for confirmation in the margin, as *Au: ?* The author is then instructed in a cover letter to cross out the question mark (or the word *query*) and let the correction stand if it is acceptable. If the proofreader's suggested change is not acceptable, the author is instructed to cross out the whole query, including the suggested change, in the margin and then to add either "OK as set" or an alternate revision. The abbreviation *OK* by itself should be avoided in the query because the typesetter may not be able to figure whether it is the original or the revision that is "OK."

The author should be instructed not to erase any marks that are written on the galleys. A large X drawn over a notation will indicate that it is unacceptable without obliterating it.

Proofreading the Galley

The main job of a proofreader is to *read proof*, or to compare copy with proof, by reading small sections of copy first, then the corresponding sections of proof, character by character, and to mark the galley proofs so that they follow the copy and its typesetting instructions. A small ruler or an index card can be used to help the eyes focus on one line at a time. In a second reading, the proofreader concentrates on the sense of the material and prepares queries for the author or editor. Proofreaders do not show concern for literary style. Their job is to correct typographical errors, to correct obvious errors that were missed by the copy editor, and to point out to the editor or author any other problems in the galley proofs.

It used to be that proofreaders spent time examining lines for evidence of broken letters or letters set slightly out of alignment. With today's typesetting equipment, however, these printing errors are rare.

The correction marks used by proofreaders are listed on page 327. Copy editors use these symbols as well, but there is a major difference in how the symbols are used. Unlike the copy editor's revisions, all proofreader's marks occur in the margin opposite the affected line, with only a corresponding caret or deletion line in the text to show where the correction should be made. When two or more corrections occur in a line, diagonal marks are used to separate the symbols in the margin. The symbols are written in the same sequence as the errors in the line, reading from left to right. Proofreading symbols are usually written in the right margin, but the left margin may also be used. Sometimes there is not enough room in the margin to indicate a large number of revisions; in these cases the symbols or instructions may be written elsewhere in the margin, but a guideline must be drawn that clearly connects the symbol or instruction with the point in the line that it refers to.

One reason for placing all proofreading marks in the margin is that typeset lines are single-spaced, and there is simply no room for the interlinear marks used by copy editors. But the main reason is that compositors look for proofreading marks only in the margins. When they set text from manuscript copy, they read everything in sequence and can easily follow revisions written above the line. But when they revise a galley that has already been typeset, there is no need for them to reread the whole text, and if a proofreader inserts a mark in the text without a corresponding symbol in the margin to alert the typesetter, that mark may not even be seen.

Proofreaders' Marks

The following paragraphs describe the use of the marks listed on page 327.

Delete Cross out the line or part of the line (use a diagonal to delete a single letter), then place a delete sign in the margin. Place the delete sign within a close-up sign only when letters are deleted from the middle of a word. The delete sign is not used when a substitution is written in the margin to replace a part of the line that has been crossed out. A large section of type such as a paragraph may be deleted neatly by outlining the whole section, placing large X's over the text, and writing a single delete sign in the margin.

Close-up sign Place this sign at the appropriate point in the text and repeat it in the margin.

Caret Use this to point out the exact place in the text where something needs to be inserted. Write the insert in the margin.

Space sign Place a vertical mark on the line to show where space should be added. Write the space symbol in the margin. This symbol may also be used to instruct the typesetter to add space between lines, or as shorthand for the word *space* in any instructions to the typesetter.

Equal space Place carets or vertical lines in the text and the notation *eq.* # in the margin to ask for even spacing between words in a particular line.

Transpose Use the curving line within the lines of text, and add the circled notation *tr* in the margin.

Move left or move right Place the appropriate mark in the text and in the margin in order to instruct the typesetter to move a section of type left or right.

Center Enclose the word or phrase to be centered within a move-right mark on the left and a move-left mark on the right. Repeat the symbol in the margin or write and circle "center." Sometimes the instruction needs to be more specific, as "Center below heading of column 1."

Stet Place dots below the inadvertently deleted material in the text and write *stet* in the margin. Or, if deleting a proofreading notation in the margin, simply cross out the notation.

Align Use in the text to show where type should be aligned. In the margin, repeat the symbol, write the word, "align," or give specific instructions about what is to be aligned, such as "Align column heads." This symbol is used chiefly in the proofreading of tabular matter.

Imperfect character Use in the margin to denote a broken or otherwise imperfectly printed character; circle the character in the line.

Indent or insert one em space Draw the symbol in the margin. In the text, repeat the symbol or use a caret to show its location on the line. To indicate more than one em of indention, insert the number 2, 3, and so on within the symbol, or repeat the symbol for each em of indention that is being requested.

Paragraph Use in the margin to indicate a new paragraph. In the text, use either this symbol or a line-break symbol illustrated on page 312 to mark where the line should be broken to form a new paragraph. To join paragraphs that are separated in the galley, write *no* ¶ in the margin and connect the separated paragraphs with a line.

Spell out Circle the typeset number or abbreviation and write this symbol in the margin. If there is any ambiguity, however, write the spelled-out form in the margin instead.

Capital letter Draw three lines under lowercase type in the text; write *cap* or *uc* in the margin.

Small capitals Draw two lines under lowercase or capitalized type in the text; write and circle *sm cap* or *sc* in the margin.

Lowercase Draw a diagonal line through the capital letter in the text; write and circle *lc* in the margin.

Proofreaders' Marks

ℰ or ⸀ or ⁊ delete; take it out

⌒ close up; print as one word

ℰ⌒ delete and close up

∧ or ⟩ or λ caret; insert here ⌐(something

insert a space

ℰℓ# space evenly where indicated

stet let marked text stand as set

tr transpose; change order the

[⌊ set farther to the left

⌉ set⌊ farther to the right

= straighten alignment

∥ ∥ straighten or align

✗ imperfect or broken character

▢ indent or insert em quad space

¶ begin a new paragraph

(SP) spell out ⟨set 5 lbs. as five pounds⟩

cap set in capitals ⟨CAPITALS⟩

sm cap or *s.c.* set in small capitals ⟨SMALL CAPITALS⟩

lc set in lowercase ⟨lowercase⟩

ital set in italic ⟨*italic*⟩

rom set in roman ⟨roman⟩

bf set in boldface ⟨**boldface**⟩

= or -/ or ⌢ or /H/ hyphen

$\frac{1}{N}$ or *en* or /N/ en dash ⟨1965–72⟩

$\frac{1}{M}$ or *em* or /M/ em — or long — dash

∨ superscript or superior ⟨2 as in πr^2⟩

∧ subscript or inferior ⟨2 as in H_2O⟩

⌃ or ✕ centered ⟨· for a centered dot in $p \cdot q$⟩

↴ comma   ⦂ or ⨀ colon

ↄ apostrophe   ⸌⸍ or ⸜⸝ quotation marks

⨀ period   (/) parentheses

⁏ or ;/ semicolon   [/] brackets

Italic Draw one line below that part of the text to be italicized; write and circle *ital* in the margin.

Roman Circle the affected part of the text; write and circle *rom* in the margin.

Boldface Draw a wavy line below the affected text; write and circle *bf* in the margin.

Hyphen Use any of these symbols in the margin; place a caret in the text to show where the hyphen should be inserted.

En dash Use this symbol in the margin; place a caret in the text to show where the dash should be inserted.

Em dash Use this symbol in the margin; place a caret in the text to show where the dash should be inserted.

Superscript Use this symbol below a number in the margin to ask for the addition of or a change to a superior or superscript number; circle the affected number in the text. Also, use below quotation marks and apostrophes that are written in the margin.

Subscript Use this symbol above a number in the margin to ask for a change to an inferior or subscript number; circle the affected number in the text. Also, use above commas that are written in the margin.

Centered dot Draw the symbol with dot in the margin and draw the symbol above and below the dot in the text.

Change or add punctuation To change punctuation, draw a vertical line through incorrect punctuation and write the correct punctuation in the margin. To add punctuation, draw a caret at the point in the line where the punctuation should be inserted and write the punctuation in the margin. Use the symbols for punctuation marks listed in the table.

Further Preparation of Galley Proofs

In addition to reading proof from manuscript copy, the proofreader attends to other matters while handling galley proofs. One of these jobs is seeing that the galley conforms to the design specifications that accompanied the manuscript. Another is preparing the galley type for positioning on pages.

The proofreader measures the width of the type page; the amount of spacing around headings, equations, enumerations, and other types of displayed copy; and the amount of indention for extracts, to ensure that design specifications were followed. After taking initial measurements on the first galleys, the proofreader merely checks to see that the spacing around similar items matches. (The units of measurement used in design specifications are described in Chapter 12, "Design and Typography.")

Each new typographic change is also checked for conformity to specifications. After the initial measurements, similar items such as headings are simply compared to ensure that the same size and face of type was used.

Word division For the sake of consistency, a single dictionary should be chosen and consulted for the division of words at the end of a line. Specialized dictionaries should be consulted for the division of proper names. The proofreader corrects any faultily divided words, usually by inserting a line-break symbol within the word and repeating the symbol or writing "break as shown" in the margin.

Paragraph endings Printing conventions require that the last word of a paragraph not be divided at the end of the line. Also, a very short word should not occur by itself on the last line of a paragraph. To correct these visual problems an editor may be called upon to insert a word or two in the next-to-last line (preferably no earlier in the paragraph, because the fewer the number of lines revised, the less expensive the revision) so that it runs over to the last line. Or the proofreader may insert a line-break symbol that forces a word or part of a word to run over.

The last line of a paragraph should have at least an em of space following the last word to avoid the appearance of having been left unjustified in error. If the space is less than an em quad, the proofreader uses the "set farther right" symbol and instructs the typesetter to justify the line.

Headings The proofreader sees that runover lines in a heading break at a logical point. Words within headings should not be divided at all. Headings should also be checked for visual appeal. Those that are set all in capitals or in very large type, for example, may require the insertion of extra space between words.

Footnotes, tables, and illustrations If the specifications indicate that notes are to be set as footnotes and not as endnotes, the galleys should be checked to see where the footnotes are located. The proofreader should make a note in the margin of the galley next to the line where a footnote reference occurs, such as "Ftn 2 here." Similarly, notations in the margins of the manuscript that concern tables and illustrations are carried to the galley margins. The typesetter will see these instructions on the galleys—"Insert Fig. 3 about here" or "Ftn 2 here"—and will plan the page formats accordingly.

Lists Lists consisting of brief items that have been set in a single column but that should appear as two or more columns on pages are identified in the margin with a notation to "set two columns in pages."

Lengthy insertions Occasionally the proofreader will have to insert lengthy material that the compositor has inadvertently omitted or will have to carry to the master proof some addition from the author.

Lengthy material that does not fit at the bottom of the galley should be typed on a separate page and identified as "Insert A," "Insert B," and so on. The precise point of insertion should be marked with a caret on the galley and a note circled in the margin, such as "Insert A attached; run in." The page should be stapled or taped to the *front* of the galley so that the compositor will readily find it.

Printer's errors Frequently, but not always, the proofreader is asked to distinguish between typographic errors (typos or *printer's errors*) which result from misreading of copy or incorrect keyboarding, and *author's* (or editor's) *alterations*. This extra job requires that an additional symbol—*PE* or *AA*—be written and circled next to each correction in the galley margins. The distinction between the two types of corrections is made only for cost-allocation purposes. Examples of printer's errors include misspelled words, omission or repetition of words or of whole lines, setting the wrong type, and errors in spacing and alignment. The proofreader should never label an error with a *PE*, however, unless the copy and the instructions were absolutely clear. The typesetter may certainly be excused for misspelling a sloppily written insert that is hard to read. Author's alterations are labeled *AA* only if they are made after the copy is set in type, and the cost of making these revisions is charged to the author.

Running heads If running heads were not included with the manuscript copy and thus are not set on the galleys, the editor prepares them at this point. These heads are written on the galleys or in a cover letter to the typesetter with the instruction to "set running heads." Running heads are a design feature that is discussed in Chapter 12, "Design and Typography."

Carrying instructions All instructions from the editor to the typesetter, such as those concerning the position of tables and footnotes, must be carried from the manuscript to the galley proofs as long as those instructions are still pertinent. One example would be an instruction regarding the continuation of long tables, such as "Comp: repeat title and column heads on new page." Other instructions that should be carried to galley proofs include the number of the manuscript page on which a cross-reference can be found when the galley refers the reader to "page 999."

The editor or the proofreader at this stage also gives the typesetter instructions regarding the placement of type on the page. For example, the typesetter could be told to begin each chapter on a right-hand page; in this case, the phrase "recto page" would be written in the margin next to the chapter title. Or the typesetter could be instructed to begin a certain section on a "new page."

Estimation of length While galley proofs are in hand, the editor may wish to confirm the estimated length of the book by counting the number of pages that can be obtained from the type on the galley proofs. If the length greatly exceeds the limit, the editor may approve the deletion of whole paragraphs, while it is still relatively inexpensive.

Revised galleys Sometimes the galleys are so heavily corrected that it is necessary to request revised galleys, sometimes called *revises*, from the compositor. To reduce costs, only those galleys that are marked up heavily are sent back for revision. The purpose of this extra step is to provide a legible galley from which the compositor can make up pages, and thereby reduce the number of errors likely to be made on the page proofs.

The master set of corrected galleys is returned to the compositor in the next step of production, along with the camera-ready artwork and instructions as to where and how to insert the illustrations into the text.

Layout

When sending the galleys to the compositor, the publisher may include a set of *dummies*. Dummies are made by dividing up the galleys into portions that correspond to pages in the finished publication, and mounting those portions onto *boards*. Boards are pieces of heavy paper at least the size of two facing pages of the final book. On them are printed lines that outline the type area as well as each line of text, and that show the position of folios and running heads. Pieces of the galley are cut out and pasted or taped on these forms, and blank lines are left as specifications require. Photocopies of the artwork and proofs of the captions are pasted down, although sometimes a blank space, or *hole*, is simply measured and left for each illustration with the illustration's identification number written in the hole. Galleys are pasted on the dummy page line for line.

The purpose of the dummy is to provide a layout of each set of facing pages and to provide a place where the designer may mark specific instructions concerning the position of artwork and captions. Dummies are often made up by the compositor instead of the publisher. Dummies are very useful when the copy contains many headings, tables, or pieces of artwork; they are not necessary for material composed entirely of text lines.

Page Proofs

In the next stage of production, the compositor makes the revisions requested by the publisher. Then, the revised text is organized into page proofs, or *pages*, which show for the first time just what each page of the book will look like. If the book contains artwork, it is at this stage that film or proofs of the illustrations, which have been photographed from the camera-ready artwork, are finally combined with film or proof of the text to produce the pages. Page proofs are usually printed on large pieces of paper that show a set of two facing pages just as the reader will see them, only with larger margins. The proofreader at this point is not concerned with such imperfections as fuzzy type or lines printed on a slant. The proofs are made cheaply, and what is sent back to the publisher is often only a photocopy of a proof.

The typesetter sends back the marked-up galleys along with two copies of the new page proofs—a master proof for the editor and a copy for the indexer.

Proofing the Pages

Again the proofreader reads proof—this time comparing the marked-up galleys and the layout instructions with the new page proofs—and ensures that all instructions to the compositor have been carried out. If so instructed, the proofreader again adds *PE* and *AA* symbols where appropriate.

Proofreading pages is essentially the same process as proofreading galleys, but it goes faster. First, there are likely to be many fewer errors on the pages, since the original errors were presumably corrected. Second, the proofreader does not need to reread sections of material for which no corrections were requested; one can assume that this part of the typesetting was left intact. But wherever corrections were asked for on the galley, the proofreader must reread the whole paragraph in which the error occurred, paying special attention not only to the line where the correction was made but to all subsequent lines of that paragraph if they have been altered by the correction. This is essential because often, in the process of correcting one error, the typesetter introduces a different one. Even though the compositor's proofreader will already have read proof on these pages, the publisher's proofreader should carefully double-check any material that might have been reset.

Editorial Checklist

In addition to reading proof, the proofreader or the editor ensures that the typeset material fits the page properly. There is also a variety of other final checks to be made, and it is a very good idea for the editor to keep a checklist so that every job can be checked off as each page of proof is read. Most editors find that the most efficient way to handle these numerous final checks is to do each job separately. For example, after reading proof, the editor goes back and checks all the pages just for folios and running heads, then all the pages just for alignment, and so forth. This process includes the following jobs.

1. Examine every correction marked on the galley to be sure that the copy has been corrected as requested without additional, unwanted alterations. Examine the copy that surrounds the correction, especially the lines below it.
2. Be sure that all other instructions to the compositor that were written on the galleys, on the layouts, or in a cover letter have been carried out.

3. Look for cross-references within the text and follow up on each one to see that it refers the reader to the correct place. If the cross-reference is to the title of a chapter, be sure the wording of the title matches that of the cross-reference. If the cross-reference is to a page number which until now has probably been recorded as "page 000," insert the correct page number. If you do not know how to find the pertinent page, look at the original manuscript, where the author or editor will have written the original page number in the margin. If the cross-reference is to a passage that has not yet been set in pages, you will have to make a note in the margin to insert the reference later. In these situations, however, it is better to avoid referring to a specific page number and instead refer to a chapter or section title. If the book has a table of contents, the page numbers are inserted at this stage.

4. If tables and illustrations are referred to in the text without specific identification numbers, read the text carefully, watching for references to phrases like "the figure above." Make sure that the figures or tables are so positioned. If there is a discrepancy, revise the phrase rather than repositioning the illustration or table.

5. Check the sequence of footnote and endnote numbers, letters, or other symbols and compare each text reference carefully with its corresponding note to be sure that they match. Footnotes must begin on the same page with their corresponding text reference symbols; however, a long footnote may run over to the following page if necessary, as long as two lines or more of the note are carried over. It is also a good idea to break such a note in mid-sentence so the reader will know that it continues on the next page.

6. Check the footnotes for conformity to design specifications and for consistency of form, including size and face of type, indention, measure of space above and below each note, etc. If necessary to save space, more than one short footnote may be set on one line. Footnotes are separated from the text either by extra space or by a short rule extending from the left margin. A footnote on the last page of a chapter is usually separated from the text in the same way. It is usually set just below the last line of text, not at the bottom of the page.

7. Watch for columns and lists of brief items that were typeset on the galleys as a single column but that are now displayed in more than one column. Be sure that the list is complete, that it is arranged according to instructions, and that it looks properly balanced.

8. Following the guidelines presented on pages 336–342 of this chapter and pages 362–365 in Chapter 12, "Design and Typography," check illustrations and tables very carefully for accuracy, completeness, and position on the page.

9. Read the *folios* and *runnings heads* on each page. Folios are page numbers; running heads (abbreviated *rh* in editorial notation) are those brief headings at the top of each page that identify the book or a particular section of the book. Sometimes running heads are chosen by

the editor in time to be set on the galley proofs; sometimes they are written in on the dummies or the layout. Be sure that folio numbers are in sequence. Also, if the specifications so instruct, be sure that folios and runnings heads do not appear on pages that contain chapter beginnings, full-page illustrations or tables, or illustrations set at the top of the page. Running heads should not be so long as to run into the folio, and they never run over to a second line.

10. Look at each set of facing pages as a whole to make sure that they balance. The last line of type must align across the bottom of the two pages. If the lines are not quite in alignment, draw the double horizontal lines to indicate horizontal alignment and write in the margin, "Align bottom of page."

11. Examine the bottom of each page. For reasons of appearance, a heading should never be placed at the bottom of a page without at least two lines of text below it. To fix a mispositioned head, use the techniques described below either to add lines below the head and cut some above, or to add lines above the head in order to move it to the next page. (Remember, however, that to save costs corrections should be limited to as few pages as possible.)

12. Examine the top of each page and make revisions as necessary to avoid *widows,* which are partial lines of text (as at the end of a paragraph) that are set all alone. Either carry over one or two lines from the preceding page (which will require additional fitting on that page) or add words to the widow to fill it out. Also to be avoided at the top of a page are any short indented items, as an item on a list, by itself; a single line of text, even a full line, above a heading; and any mark that indicates repetition, such as a ditto mark in a column or a dash at the beginning of a bibliography entry.

13. If passages of poetry are broken at the bottom of a page, try to break the lines between stanzas, or at least between sets of rhymed lines.

14. Be especially careful in handling tables that continue to a second page or more. See that the copy editor's instructions concerning the use of the word *continued* at the bottom of the page and at the top of the new page have been followed. For more on the handling of continued tables, see pages 337–338 in this chapter.

15. Examine the last page of all chapters. Unless new chapters are supposed to begin on the same page as the previous one, the last page should contain at least five lines of text in order to avoid an excessive amount of white space on the page.

Fitting Pages

It is expensive to make corrections on page proofs, so when changes must be made—either to correct a typographical error or for esthetic reasons or when a previous correction results in a line gained or lost—these revisions are made in places and in ways that will cause the least number of lines to be reset. One avoids adding a line or two to a page that will cause the lines at the bottom of that page to run over to the next page, and lines on that page to run over to the next, and so forth to the end of the chapter. As much as possible, every line added to a page must be compensated for in some way on that page—either by deleting another line or by reducing the amount of space somewhere, as above or below a table. Likewise, every line deleted from a page must be compensated for—by adding either a line of text or a line of space elsewhere on the page.

It is acceptable to print an extra line on a page, or to delete a line, thus reducing or enlarging the size of the bottom margin on that page, but each change of this sort alters the alignment of the two facing pages. Therefore, a change must be made on the opposite page. A line added to one page must be balanced by a line added to its facing page; a line cut from one must be matched by a line cut from the other. If an illustration is set at the bottom of the opposite page, however, absolute alignment of its bottom edge with the text lines opposite is not necessary.

Whenever the editor chooses to alter the bottom margin the compositor should be notified that the change is intentional. A notation at the bottom such as "1 li short OK" will suffice.

Compositors also make adjustments in an effort to make the material fit the page. Often they automatically add or delete space if they can do so without making it too obvious. Sometimes they add leading between lines of text. But usually, to avoid widows or badly positioned headings, the compositor will deliberately set a page long (with too many lines) or short (with too few lines) and stamp *long* or *short* at the bottom of the page proof. This tells the editor to fix the situation.

There are several things an editor can do. He or she can choose to adjust the space around illustrations, tables, footnotes, or displayed passages if the result is not too noticeable. Or the editor can alter the text.

The least costly way to gain lines is to extend the last line of a paragraph over to a new line by adding words (or sometimes extra word space). These additions should be made as near as possible to the end of the paragraph, because adding words in this position results in the need to reset only the last two or three lines of a paragraph rather than the whole paragraph. Similarly, when lines must be lost, the cuts should be made near the end of a paragraph.

Determining just how many words to add to a paragraph to make it run over and form a new line can be tricky for an inexperienced editor. There is no set number of characters per printed line because of (1) the varying widths of different characters such as *l* and *m*, (2) the varying word spaces caused by the need to justify lines, and (3) the limited number of places within a word where end-of-line division is possible. To ensure that one's intention will be met, one can always use the margin to add an instruction to the compositor such as, "Add word space as needed to ensure that paragraph gains one line."

Another problem that can face an editor is trying to correct an error in a page proof without disturbing any other lines. In this case, the correction must fit in the space of the error. This can often be done by counting all the characters, marks of punctuation, and word spaces to be deleted and trying to phrase the correction so that it has exactly the same number of characters, punctuation marks, and word spaces. A total of 15 characters deleted, however, does not always equal 15 characters added, because of such variables as the width of the characters and the necessity of dividing words only at certain syllables. On the other hand, the compositor can help out by adjusting word spaces to help accomplish the editor's purpose.

Final Proofs

One last set of proofs comes to the publisher. In most cases, these final proofs are film proofs, also known as *blues, Ozalids, Dyluxes,* etc. They are made from the film, usually a negative, that the compositor will send to the printing plant to make printing plates from. In some cases, however, the people doing the printing make the negatives. In this case, the final proofs that the compositor provides are reproduction proofs, called *repros.* These are high-quality, camera-ready positive prints of the page, and it is from these that the negatives are made. Either kind of proof coming to the publisher should be examined carefully for scratches, stray marks, or partial opaquing of letters in the text. Repros should be handled with great care; any stray mark or scratch that gets on a repro has to be repaired, or there is a good chance that it will show up on the printed page.

At this point, editors work very fast, usually accepting or rejecting the final proofs within a day. Only those pages requiring corrections are returned to the compositor; for the rest, a note is sent (or a telephone call made) saying that they are acceptable.

Tables and Illustrations

Chapter 9, "Tables and Illustrations," presents guidelines to authors on how to prepare tables and illustrations for inclusion with their manuscript. This section discusses most aspects of how an editor handles these materials from their receipt from the author to their placement in page proofs. However, the typographical aspects of tables and illustrations, including their markup for the compositor, are described in Chapter 12, "Design and Typography." That chapter also presents a few guidelines relating to the layout of pages with illustrations.

Copyediting Tables

All the tables within the copy should be edited together so that any inconsistencies in phrasing or departures from standard style, as it was described in Chapter 9, will likely be noticed. The editor may decide first that some tables are irrelevant and ask the author if they can be deleted. Some might duplicate the text, for instance; others may have to be combined or made more compact. If the author has included tabular matter within the manuscript, the editor makes a photocopy of each table on a separate page and crosses out the table that is in the manuscript. These table pages are then numbered separately from the text pages.

Correspondence of tables and text When the editor is certain that each table's general form is suitable, all the tables are edited, first in terms of their correspondence to the text, according to the following procedures:

1. Make sure that each table that is on its own separate sheet is properly identified with a production number (which may not be the same as the identification number used in the caption), the author's last name or a short title of the work or both, and the page of the manuscript that first refers to the table.
2. Check the identification number in the captions of the tables to ensure that they are consecutive in terms of the first reference to them in the text. In a text with just a few short tables, the tables may be unnumbered, because they can more easily be inserted where they logically fit in the text. Most long tables should be numbered.
3. Make sure that the margins of the manuscript are marked at the points where the tables will be inserted.
4. Closely check all text references to the tables against the actual tables. The text references should be logical and consistent.

Structure and content of tables Having ensured a proper correspondence between tables and text, the editor then reviews the structure and content of each table by asking the following questions:

1. Do column heads and stub items make sense?
2. Does the title or caption accurately summarize the table's contents? Is it brief and clearly phrased?
3. Is there any inconsistency within the table or within a set of similarly constructed tables? Look at patterns of alignment, rules, indention, capitalization, italicization, abbreviation, and the like.
4. Are both vertical and horizontal alignments consistent? Are figures aligned and commas used with numbers of four digits or more?
5. Is the use of rules necessary?
6. Is the use of abbreviations necessary and are the abbreviations themselves understandable?
7. Is there a logical pattern to the use of the symbols that indicate blank cells?
8. Do the footnotes make sense? Do they correspond with the reference marks in the table? Does each reference mark lead to a footnote? Are they in proper sequence and consistently styled?
9. Are similar tables styled alike? Are similar subjects similarly phrased?
10. Do all number totals add up correctly?

Oversized Tables

The editor watches for tables that may be too long or too wide to fit the printed page. These tables are often formatted as parallel tables or continued tables. (For a description of these and other oversized tables, see pages 238–240 in Chapter 9, "Tables and Illustrations.") If a parallel or continued table is going to be used, the compositor is instructed to "Position table on facing pages." If a count of the columns or lines shows that it is necessary to continue a table to yet another page, the editor writes, "Position on facing pages plus next left page." A table that is only sightly too long can sometimes be extended up into the top margin or down into the bottom margin.

Continued tables require special care because the point at which the table breaks on the manuscript will probably not be the same as the point at which it breaks on the printed page. Thus, the editor usually circles (to indicate deletion of) any repeated title or table number, column heads, or the word *continued* on the manuscript. Then a note is written telling the typesetter to use these repeated heads and *continued* lines over any column where the table happens to break on the printed page. The word *continued* should be typemarked so that the compositor will know if it should be italicized, abbreviated, or enclosed in parentheses.

At the same time, the editor adds "continued on next page" in italics or parentheses at the bottom of any table continued on the manuscript, circles it, and instructs the compositor again: "Position at bottom of page wherever table breaks." This line is usually set flush right.

Tables in Galley and Page Proofs

Proofing tables in galley proofs requires special attention to alignment, spacing, and typography. Also, any editorial notations written on the copy that concerns the layout of the table may have to be carried to the galleys, so that the compositor sees them while making up the pages.

Following the instructions on the manuscript, the editor marks the galley proofs to show the place where each table should be inserted, usually with a phrase in the margin such as "Insert Table 3 about here." The table number must be included. Whoever lays out the pages—whether editor, designer, or typesetter—will then be responsible for fitting the table as closely as possible to the text reference. If references like " the table below" appear in the text, they are checked for accuracy and the references are rephrased if necessary. On those pages that contain a full-page table, the running head and folio are usually omitted.

Parallel tables need to be looked at in page proofs to ensure that column heads, rules, and rows of data align across the two pages.

Copyediting Illustrations

Copyediting illustrations includes the following steps:

1. The editor makes a list of all items received from the author and notes any items indicated in the manuscript that are missing.
2. The art is checked for usefulness. If any piece is of doubtful value, it is deleted or replaced.
3. Each piece is examined to see if it is properly identified. If any information is missing—figure number, author and short title, manuscript

page number—the editor supplies it. The identification number is circled if it is only temporary.

4. If the original identification numbers change considerably as a result of copyediting, the illustrations have to be renumbered. A simple change such as the dropping of one illustration can be noted instead by adding to the manuscript a page representing the missing art. On the page is written something like "Figure 6 deleted. Figure 7 follows Figure 5."

5. The separate page of captions, legends, and credit lines received from the author is examined next. If the captions are in the wrong position (such as on the back of the illustrations or in the manuscript), the editor types them properly on a caption and legend page, numbered and double-spaced to facilitate copyediting and in sequence according to their first mention in the text.

6. Captions, legends, and credit lines are copyedited and typemarked according to the publication's style sheet.

7. After editing the list of captions and legends, the editor makes a copy for reference because the original will go to the typesetter.

8. The manuscript is searched for references to the illustrations. If the author has failed to write a circled figure number in the margin opposite a text reference, the editor supplies it. Each reference is read carefully with attention to consistency between reference, figure, caption, legend, and labels. The references must also be in the same order as the numbered illustrations.

9. The editor prepares a *type list* on a separate page from the list of captions and legends. On this page are listed all the words, numbers, and mathematical symbols that form the labels on the figures and that are going to be typeset rather than hand-lettered by the artist or applied from stick-on or transfer lettering sheets. The editor types the characters and words and next to each one or each group notes the size and face of type desired. Later, this type will come back to the editor as camera-ready copy which can be cut out and pasted on the figure before it is photographed.

10. The editor estimates as closely as possible the amount of space that each illustration will take, and then the total space to be taken by all illustrations.

11. Each illustration is checked to ensure that permission has been obtained for copyrighted material being reproduced or adapted, and that the information needed for a credit line has been obtained. Photographs of identifiable people usually require a written release to be signed by those people.

Preparing the Artwork

Illustrations must be put into camera-ready form before being filmed for reproduction. Photocopies, computer-generated graphics, and blueprints do not reproduce well enough. Photographs should be in the form of glossy prints. Whether drawn by a professional or put together by an amateur with the help of press-on letters, the artwork must have the clarity and contrast needed to reproduce well.

Art that is being prepared for publication is handled separately from text. If it is camera-ready, it is handled very carefully, for the slightest tear, smudge, or speck can show up on the plate and on the printed page. For this reason it is suggested that artwork be kept in manila envelopes when not being worked with. All the art for a particular chapter or section should be kept in one envelope, and the outside of the envelope should list the contents.

Illustrations retain their identification numbers throughout the production process. This number, together with the notations placed on the illustration at various stages, should be readily visible without being written directly on the art. A tissue overlay meets this need. It not only protects the art from scratches and dirt, it provides a writing surface as well. However, the tissue should not be written on when it is in position over the artwork except when cropping. If it is necessary to write on the tissue over the art, a light pencil is used, never a ballpoint pen. The tissue is taped to the back of the illustration and folded over so that it covers the front. An alternative to writing on tissue is to write identification and instructions on a label and affix that label to the back of the illustration. Nothing should ever be glued, stapled, or clipped to the art.

Artwork is often mounted on heavy paper for easier handling and prevention of creases. If an expert is not available to do the mounting, the art may be kept between pieces of cardboard.

When the illustrations are ready to be sent to a photographer, a photocopy is made. The copy is kept for reference in the publisher's office and it can also be used to plan layouts.

Cropping Most photographs benefit from cropping—the cutting away of unwanted background detail in order to give a new focus to the picture. To crop a photograph, one first determines the "picture within a picture." This is done with the use of two L-shaped pieces of cardboard called *cropper's L*'s. Moving the cropper's L's over the picture, one can frame any desired shape of rectangle within the photograph.

Crop marks are then made in the margin—never on the photograph itself—with a grease pencil that can be wiped off the glossy surface. A soft erasable pencil is used in the margins of other types of artwork. Only two margins, one vertical and one horizontal, need to be marked. If no margin is available, the crop marks may be drawn on a tissue placed over the photograph.

The marked photograph is sent to a photographer to obtain a new print that shows only the desired area. Sizing instructions usually accompany the picture; the new size can be written between the crop marks in the margin if there is room.

Sizing Artwork is usually reduced, or *shot down,* to fit the pages of the book. A typical reduction is 50 percent. On the occasions that the art is not to be reduced or enlarged, the editor writes *S/s* (for *same size*) in the margin of the illustration.

Reduction accomplishes two purposes: it minimizes any flaws in the art, and it also allows the artist to work on a more comfortable scale. On the other hand, too extreme a reduction can cause loss of detail and legibility. The dimensions of the page will necessarily set certain limits on the size of the illustrations, but another consideration is that illustrations that are parallel in significance should be printed on approximately the same scale.

Artwork for typewritten publications   Artwork for publications that are not typeset but instead published in typewritten form is handled differently. Camera-ready line drawings, graphs, and charts can be photographically reduced and pasted directly on the page, with or without accompanying text lines. These illustrations are photographically reproduced along with the text on the rest of the page.

Captions and Legends

Captions, legends, and credit lines are always set separately from the rest of the text, since their position on the page cannot be known until pages are made up. They are ultimately combined with the illustrations in one of two ways.

In one method, the typed list of captions, legends, labels, and credit lines, properly typemarked or keyed, is sent to a photographer (who may be the compositor or another photographic printing service) with instructions to set camera-ready (or repro) type. When the list of captions is returned, set clear and black on glossy paper, the artist cuts out each caption, legend, and credit line and affixes it to the camera-ready illustration. Since this requires a steady hand and a good visual sense, it is a job best left to a professional artist. Then the illustration, which is now complete, is ready to be photographed to make the final printing plate.

A second method is for the typesetter to set the captions, legends, and credit lines separately along with text and tables so that they can be proofread on galleys. Then, following the layout instructions as to the position of the art and all its parts, the compositor strips in the parts of the three different negatives or repro—text, artwork, and caption-legend-credit line-label combination—to produce a single negative or repro.

In the first method, the captions are considered part of the figure; in the second, they are outside the figure area. In both cases, they are separated from the illustration during editorial stages and must therefore be typed all together on a sheet separate from the illustrations and from the manuscript.

Art Proofs

The photographer returns to the publisher a set of proofs of the illustrations, or perhaps photocopies of proofs. Each art proof is checked to see that it has been cropped and sized according to instructions, to see that it has not been *flopped* (printed backward, as if the negative had flopped over), and to see that no new flaws have appeared on the artwork as a result of mishandling. If corrections are needed, the artwork is returned.

If any changes have been made within an illustration up to this point, the editor must reread caption, legend, and corresponding text references to make sure that they are all still logically related.

Galley and Page Proofs

Little work is done with illustrations at the galley proof stage except to carry any notations about the position of illustrations from the margins in the manuscript to the margins of the galleys. It is also a good idea to recheck the text references because the text may have been revised so that it is inconsistent with one of the figures or its caption, legend, or labels.

Page proofs usually offer the editor a last chance to check the accuracy of the artwork. Even small changes that might have been made in the text, artwork, caption, or legend will affect one another, so again the editor has to compare each illustration with its caption, legend, and text reference, as well as with similar illustrations, to ensure that nothing inconsistent or illogical or bewildering has occurred. Specifically, the editor is expected to do the following:

1. When illustrations are not numbered, read the text carefully for such phrases as "the next figure," and correct the phrase if it is inaccurate.
2. If the artwork was not combined with the text in the page proofs and "holes" have been left for the illustrations, measure these holes carefully to see that the art will fit, along with captions and the white space necessary to properly frame the illustration. Then, write on the page within the hole the identification number of the illustration and add, where appropriate, caption, legend, and credit line. The platemaker will combine these negatives of text matter with the negatives of illustrations, guided by the editor's instructions. It is thus extremely important for the editor to describe exactly which piece of art goes in each hole, in what position, and with what amount of space above and below. Measurements are based on the layout instructions.
3. If the art was ready when pages were made, art proofs may appear in position on each page. Again check the position of the art and its parts. Examine the illustration to ensure that it has been reproduced properly—not flopped or upside down. Any apparent flaw on the proof may not really be in the illustration, but it is acceptable to point it out and query the compositor in the margin: "Negative OK?"

Chapter 12

Design and Typography

CONTENTS

The word *design,* when used in connection with books, magazines, and other printed materials, refers to the arrangement of elements on the printed page. In addition to the typographical elements, such as the size and style of type, the length of lines, and the space between lines, the design of the page often includes tables, illustrations, and the use of color. Although some aspects of designing pages with illustrations are discussed in the section on Tables and Illustrations in this chapter, the chapter focuses mainly on typographical elements of page design. More information about designing pages can be found under the heading Production, Design, and Printing in the Bibliography at the back of this book.

As was pointed out in the preceding chapter, books, magazines, and other printed materials are often designed by professional graphic designers; however, writers and editors are often called upon to work in consultation with designers. And in some cases, writers and editors are required to design materials on their own. It is to meet these two basic needs—to help writers and editors communicate with designers and to help writers and editors design materials for themselves when it is necessary to do so—that this chapter has been written.

The Aspects of Letters

This section of the chapter introduces the vocabulary that is used to describe typeset letters of the alphabet. Terms having to do with the measurement or spacing of type are introduced in the following section. For terms relating to the composition process itself, see the section on Composition, beginning on page 376, in Chapter 13, "Composition, Printing, and Binding," or the Glossary at the end of this book.

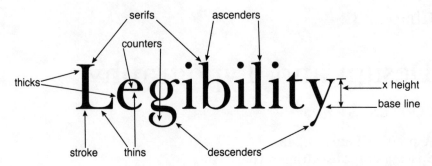

Figure 12.1.   The parts of letters

Parts of Letters

The illustration on this page labels the parts of letters that are most frequently referred to in discussions of typography. Each of the elements labeled in the illustration is defined below.

Ascender An ascender is the part of a lowercase letter that rises above the x height of the letter. The term *ascender* is also used to refer to a lowercase character that has an ascender.

Base line The base line is an imaginary line on which the body of the letter rests.

Counter A counter is an area within a letter that is wholly or partly enclosed by strokes.

Descender A descender is the part of a lowercase letter that descends below the base line. The term *descender* is also used to refer to a lowercase character that has a descender.

Serif A serif is a short line that stems from the upper or lower end of the stroke of a letter.

Stroke A stroke is one of the lines of a letter of the alphabet.

Thick A thick is a thick stroke.

Thin A thin is a thin stroke.

X height The x height is the height of a lowercase x. It represents the height of the main body of a lowercase letter.

Forms of Letters

Later in this chapter we will describe and illustrate different typefaces, such as Helvetica, Bondoni, and Optima. However, within each of these styles of type, letters may take different forms. Most obviously letters may be either uppercase or lowercase, as illustrated below. In addition they may be set in boldface or lightface type, in italic or roman, or in small capitals. Each of these forms is described below.

upper case
A B C D E F G H I J K L M N O P Q R S T U V W X Y Z

lower case
a b c d e f g h i j k l m n o p q r s t u v w x y z

Lightface roman Lightface roman is the form that letters most commonly take. The sample alphabet set above is in lightface roman, as is most of the text of this book. The term *lightface* refers to the width of the strokes, and it means that each stroke is thinner than it would be in boldface. When speaking about the width of strokes for most styles of type, one usually speaks of either lightface or boldface type. However, some typefaces that have relatively thick strokes as part of their design (as the Clarendon type shown below), are available in lightface, medium, and boldface.

Clarendon Light
Typography can be defined as the style, arrangement, and appearance of typeset matter.

Clarendon (medium)
Typography can be defined as the style, arrangement, and appearance of typeset matter.

Clarendon Bold
Typography can be defined as the style, arrangement, and appearance of typeset matter.

Lightface italic Italic type is type in which the strokes of the letters are slanted so that the tops of letters are farther to the right than their bases. In addition, italic type is often more ornamented than roman type. Compare, for example, the line of Baskerville Italic typeset below with the regular Baskerville used to illustrate uppercase and lowercase letters on this page.

Baskerville Italic
A B C D E F G H I J K L M N O P Q R S T U V W X Y Z
a b c d e f g h i j k l m n o p q r s t u v w x y z

Clarendon Italic
Typography can be defined as the style, arrangement, and appearance of typeset matter.

Boldface roman Boldface type uses thick strokes, especially for parts of the letter that are normally thick. Boldface type is seldom used for extended pieces of text, but it is useful for setting individual words or sentences that are meant to stand out, such as headings in a text or important words in a notice.

Application forms are available in the registrar's office. In order to be accepted applications must be completed and returned to the office by April 15. **The application fee must accompany the completed form.**

Boldface italic Boldface italic type features strokes that are both slanted and thicker. Boldface italic type is used infrequently, but it is sometimes useful for providing a greater contrast than can be provided by lightface italic or boldface roman type.

Baskerville Bold Italic
A B C D E F G H I J K L M N O P Q R S T U V W X Y Z
a b c d e f g h i j k l m n o p q r s t u v w x y z

Clarendon Bold Italic
Typography can be defined as the style, arrangement, and appearance of typeset matter.

Small capitals Regular capital letters are uppercase letters. Small capital letters have the same shape as regular capital letters, but they are smaller. Small capital letters are often no higher than the x height of lowercase letters, although they are sometimes designed to be taller than the x height but shorter than the height of a capital letter. Small caps (as they are usually called) are often combined with regular capitals, but they are sometimes used on their own. (For some examples of small capital letters used in context, see the section on Other Uses of Capitals, beginning on page 69, in Chapter 2, "Capitals, Italics, and Quotation Marks.")

caps and small caps
WEBSTER'S STANDARD AMERICAN STYLE MANUAL

Spacing and Measuring Type

The three most important considerations to keep in mind when designing with type are the size of the type, the spacing between lines of type, and the length of the lines of type. In discussing each of these aspects of typography, designers and typesetters use units of measure that are unfamiliar to most people. Therefore, before beginning our discussion of the size and spacing of type, we will first introduce and describe the units of measure most commonly used in reference to type.

Units of Measurement

Of all the units of measure used in typography only two, the *pica* and the *point*, are fixed; that is, they always represent the same amount of space no matter what kind of type is being used. All of the other units vary in the amount of space they represent, depending on the size of the type that is being used. The *thin space* and the *hair space* described below are discussed further on pages 306–307 in Chapter 11, "Production Techniques." Those pages also include a description of letterspacing and the use and marking of word spaces. Editorial uses of em and en spaces are discussed on page 312 in Chapter 11.

Pica A pica is approximately equal to one-sixth of an inch. Picas are commonly used to measure the length of a line of type or the depth of a page. The lines of type in this book, for instance, are 28 picas long. Another way of saying this is that the text block is 28 picas wide. The depth of this page, from the top of the top line to the base line of the last line, is 43 picas.

Point A point is one-twelfth of a pica. Points are most commonly used when referring to the vertical size of type or the amount of space between lines of type. For instance, most of the type used in this book is 10-point type.

Em space An em space is as wide as the point size of the type. When you are setting in 10-point type, an em space is 10 points wide. An em space is sometimes referred to as an *em quad.*

En space An en space is one half of an em space. An en space is sometimes referred to as an *en quad.*

Thick space A thick space is one-third of an em. It is sometimes referred to as a *three-to-the-em space* or, confusingly, a *three-em space.*

Thin space A thin space is usually one-fourth of an em space, although some people use the term to mean one-fifth of an em. (Hence thin space is referred to as a *four-to-the-em space, four-em space, five-to-the-em space,* or *five-em space.*)

Hair space The term *hair space* is variously used to refer to one-fifth of an em, one-sixth of an em, or, as a fixed unit, a space that is one-half point in width.

Unit A unit is a variable measure used by composition equipment for measuring the width of letters and spaces. The size of a unit varies from machine to machine but usually ranges from one-tenth to one-eighteenth of an em.

Size of Type

As we said above, the size of type is measured in points. The size of type used for most of the text in this book is 10-point type. What this means in the typeface we are using, which is Baskerville, is that the distance from the top of the tallest letter to the bottom of the lowest descender is ten points. In some type styles the distance from the top to the bottom

Figure 12.2.   Samples (from left to right) of 72-point Garamond, Times Roman, Bodoni, and Helvetica

will be slightly less than its stated point size, but in no case will it be greater. The illustration on this page demonstrates the variety of actual sizes that correspond to a same point size for a selection of typefaces. Note how much the x height varies in each of these styles. This is an important factor to keep in mind when deciding how much space to leave between lines of type, as will be explained below.

In addition to its vertical dimension, type also has a horizontal dimension, which varies from letter to letter. The capital *M* or capital *W* is usually the widest letter; the lowercase *i* is usually the narrowest. The only good way, then, to think about the width of characters is in terms of an average, usually given as the average number of characters that can be set per pica. For example, the 10-point Baskerville on this page averages 2.55 characters per pica.

Spaces between Lines

All typefaces are designed with a certain amount of space above and below so that the descenders on one line do not crash into or even touch the ascenders on the following line. However, the amount of space left over varies widely, as the illustration on this page points out. A face like Helvetica leaves almost no space between the descenders of one line and the ascenders of the next; Times Roman leaves a good deal of space.

No matter what style of type is being used, page designers usually add some additional spaces between lines in order to improve the legibility of the page and to keep it from looking too crowded. The amount of additional space that is used between the lines is referred to as *leading*. Like so many terms in typography, *leading* is a term that dates back to the time when typesetters set type by positioning pieces of metal type inside trays called galleys. In order to add spacing between lines of type they would add thin strips of lead between the rows. (For more on how type was and now is set, see Chapter 13, "Composition, Printing, and Binding.") The amount of space that is actually necessary between lines will vary with the size of the type, the length of the line, and to some extent, individual taste. In general, the smaller the type and the longer the line, the greater the spacing ought to be in relation to the size of the type.

Also, the taller the x height of a lowercase letter in relation to point size, the denser the type will appear. Adding additional space between the lines can alleviate that denseness. Helvetica, with its high x height, is almost always set with extra space around it. Times Roman, on the other hand, can be set without extra spacing, although most designers add at least some.

Another way to describe the spacing of lines of type is to use the term *body*. Ten-point type set with no additional leading is said to be set on a 10-point body. If two points of leading are added, the type is said to be set on a 12-point body. Ten-point type set on a 12-point body is referred to as *10 on 12* or *10/12*. Most of the type in this book is 10/11 Baskerville.

When type is set with no extra space between the lines, it is said to be *set solid*.

Space between Words

The amount of space that is inserted between words varies according to the point size of the type and whether or not the lines are *justified*. Justified lines are lines into which extra space is added between words in order to make each line of type exactly the same length. Lines that are not justified are referred to as *ragged right*, and they generally have uniform spacing between words. That spacing can be adjusted, but in the most common type sizes (10-, 11-, and 12-point), the space is usually around one fourth of an em. In smaller type sizes relatively more space, as measured in ems, is placed between words. In larger type, fewer ems are required.

Line Length

The length of the line used in a page of type is related to the size of the type and the width of the page. Lines of type that have more than around 75 characters per line become difficult to read. This book, as we said earlier, is set in 10-point Baskerville, which is a style of type that averages 2.55 characters per pica, and it is set on a 28-pica line. That means it averages 71.4 characters per line. If we had been setting in Times Roman, which gets 2.85 characters per pica, our 28-pica line would have averaged nearly 80 characters per line, and it probably would have been best to shorten the line by a pica or a pica and a half.

Typefaces

The purpose of this section is to acquaint readers with the range of choices that are available to anyone choosing a typeface and to introduce some of the vocabulary and ways of thinking about type that can be useful when designing with type. The typefaces mentioned and illustrated in this section represent only a fraction of the total number that are available in many commercial typesetting houses, and anyone seriously involved with designing a publication should begin only after carefully examining the type catalog of the typesetter who will be doing the work. One reason for doing this is that the typesetter may have a typeface available that the designer had not previously thought of using, and looking at the type catalog may suggest new possibilities to the designer. Another and even more important reason for looking at the typesetter's catalog is that typefaces going by the same name will vary somewhat from typesetter to typesetter, depending on who the typesetter bought the type from.

Variations in Typefaces

Most books on typography offer their readers a classification system which attempts to categorize typefaces on the basis of their historical development and their most obvious visual aspects. However, such attempts usually end up being more confusing and frustrating than they are helpful to the newcomer to this field. Therefore, rather than attempt any such classification scheme here, this chapter simply describes some of the aspects of letters that are particularly prone to variation and that are a part of most classification systems. The chapter also includes samples of 18 different typefaces that illustrate how these aspects vary from typeface to typeface.

Serif One of the most obvious aspects of any typeface is whether or not the letters have serifs. Typefaces that lack serifs are called *sans serif* typefaces. In the samples that follow, Helvetica, Optima, Trade Gothic, and Univers are sans serif typefaces. Among the typefaces that have serifs, there is considerable variation in the shape of the serif. Most commonly, serifed typefaces have what is called a *bracketed serif,* meaning that the serif is joined to the stroke with a curved line. In the samples that follow, Baskerville, Caledonia, Century Schoolbook, Garamond, Goudy Old Style, Palatino, and Times Roman have bracketed serifs. Other kinds of serif include the hairline serif used in the Bodoni typeface and the square serif used in Clarendon and Memphis.

Thicks and thins Another very noticeable feature in a typeface is the contrast in the relative width of thick and thin strokes. In the samples that follow, Garamond and Goudy Old Style show relatively less contrast between thicks and thins; Baskerville and Bodoni show more. Most sans serif faces have no contrast between any of the strokes; however, Optima, which is a sans serif typeface, does show a contrast between thicks and thins.

Cap height and ascender height The *cap height* is the height of a capital letter in a typeface. The *ascender height* is the height of the highest ascender. In some typefaces, such as Times Roman or Helvetica, the cap height and ascender height are the same; in others, such as Caledonia or Electra, the ascender height is taller than the cap height.

Sample Typefaces

As we said earlier in this section, the typefaces illustrated here represent only a fraction of the hundreds that are available to graphic designers. It is also worth repeating that typefaces of the same name will vary from typesetter to typesetter: what follows is simply the form these faces take at the typesetting house that set this book. It is also worth pointing out that some typesetters will have very similar versions of these typefaces available under a different name. This is another reason why carefully examining a typesetter's catalog is always the best way to begin a designing project.

What these samples are intended to do is to help the newcomer to this field get used to looking at type and recognizing the variations between typefaces. The most important aspect of any face is the overall feeling it gives as you look at it; however, there are some aspects of individual letters that one can look at to get an idea of what the typeface is like and to aid in quick recognition of the typeface.

Lowercase g In some sans serif and square-serif typefaces the lowercase g simply has a curved tail for a descender; in most serifed faces the lowercase g has two loops, one above the base line, the other mostly below. Among typefaces that have the two-loop g, there is a noticeable variety in the shape of the loops, the angle and thickness of the stroke that connects them, and the angle and shape of the *ear* that extends from the upper-right corner of the upper loop.

Lowercase t In serifed faces, most lowercase t's have a pointed top which does not extend very far above the x height. However, in some serifed faces, such as Bodoni, Caledonia, Electra, and Melior, the t has a square top and may extend up nearly to the cap height. Century Schoolbook has a t with a pointed top that extends up considerably above the x height.

Lowercase y Lowercase y's display variety in whether their descenders have a rounded thickening at the bottom and in how far they curve to left.

Uppercase A In some typefaces, such as Caslon, the broad stroke of the uppercase A has a slight concavity.

Uppercase E and F The crosspieces in uppercase E's and F's vary in their relative length. In some typefaces, such as Palatino, the crosspieces are of nearly equal length; in others like Century Schoolbook and Clarendon, the top and bottom pieces of the E are the same length, while the middle piece is much shorter. And in some typefaces, such as Baskerville, the bottom piece is longest, the top piece somewhat shorter, and the middle piece shortest of all.

Uppercase *J* In some typefaces the uppercase *J* extends below the base line; in others it rests on the base line.

Uppercase *Q* The uppercase *Q* is often the most distinctive letter in the typeface. The tail may cross the loop at an angle, as it does in most sans serif typefaces. It may cross the loop after first doing a little loop itself, as in Century Schoolbook or Clarendon. Or the crosspiece may exist in any number of forms from the simplest to the fanciest but all outside of the loop.

Uppercase *R* Uppercase *R*'s vary in whether their right leg appears to support the upper loop by joining it at the lower-right corner of the loop or whether the leg angles more to the left and joins the left leg at the lower-left corner of the upper loop.

Uppercase *T* In some serifed faces, such as Garamond, the uppercase *T* has pointed serifs on the crossbar that extend up above the cap height.

Punctuation Quotation marks, question marks, and commas all vary from typeface to typeface. Most often the opening and closing quotation marks have different forms. But in some typefaces, such as Palatino, both marks are the same. The question marks can vary in the shaping of the upper cup, in the curvature below the upper cup, and in the relative weighting of thicks and thins. The comma may appear like a period with a tail, or it may simply look like a short, angled stroke.

A note on the samples Each of the samples that follow includes a line of lightface roman, a line of lightface italic, and a line of boldface roman. The lightface roman line is set in 18-point type; the italic and boldface lines are set in 16-point type. The text passage is set in 12-point type on a 13-point body. In cases where a typeface includes light, medium, and bold face versions, the lightface version has been used in order to help the reader see the range of degrees of boldness the typeface provides.

In the samples that follow, typefaces designated ® or ™ are trademarks of the Linotype Company. Typefaces designated ITC are licensed by the International Typeface Corporation.

Baskerville

abcdefghijklmnopqrstuvwxyz1234567890
ABCDEFGHIJKLMNOPQRSTUVWXYZ

abcdefghijklmnopqrstuvwxyz1234567890
ABCDEFGHIJKLMNOPQRSTUVWXYZ

abcdefghijklmnopqrstuvwxyz1234567890
ABCDEFGHIJKLMNOPQRSTUVWXYZ

The word *design*, when used in connection with books, magazines, and other printed materials, refers to the arrangement of elements on the printed page. In addition to the
typographical elements, such as the size and style of type, the
length of lines, and the space between lines, the design of the

Bodoni

abcdefghijklmnopqrstuvwxyz1234567890
ABCDEFGHIJKLMNOPQRSTUVWXYZ

abcdefghijklmnopqrstuvwxyz1234567890
ABCDEFGHIJKLMNOPQRSTUVWXYZ

abcdefghijklmnopqrstuvwxyz1234567890
ABCDEFGHIJKLMNOPQRSTUVWXYZ

The word *design*, when used in connection with books, magazines, and other printed materials, refers to the arrangement of
elements on the printed page. In addition to the typographical
elements, such as the size and style of type, the length of lines,
and the space between lines, the design of the page often includes

Caledonia®

abcdefghijklmnopqrstuvwxyz1234567890
ABCDEFGHIJKLMNOPQRSTUVWXYZ

abcdefghijklmnopqrstuvwxyz1234567890
ABCDEFGHIJKLMNOPQRSTUVWXYZ

abcdefghijklmnopqrstuvwxyz1234567890
ABCDEFGHIJKLMNOPQRSTUVWXYZ

The word *design*, when used in connection with books, magazines, and other printed materials, refers to the arrangement of
elements on the printed page. In addition to the typographical
elements, such as the size and style of type, the length of lines,
and the space between lines, the design of the page often in-

Caslon

abcdefghijklmnopqrstuvwxyz1234567890
ABCDEFGHIJKLMNOPQRSTUVWXYZ

abcdefghijklmnopqrstuvwxyz1234567890
ABCDEFGHIJKLMNOPQRSTUVWXYZ

abcdefghijklmnopqrstuvwxyz1234567890
ABCDEFGHIJKLMNOPQRSTUVWXYZ

The word *design*, when used in connection with books, magazines, and
other printed materials, refers to the arrangement of elements on the
printed page. In addition to the typographical elements, such as the size
and style of type, the length of lines, and the space between lines, the
design of the page often includes tables, illustrations, and the use of

Century Schoolbook

abcdefghijklmnopqrstuvwxyz1234567890
ABCDEFGHIJKLMNOPQRSTUVWXYZ

abcdefghijklmnopqrstuvwxyz1234567890
ABCDEFGHIJKLMNOPQRSTUVWXYZ

abcdefghijklmnopqrstuvwxyz1234567890
ABCDEFGHIJKLMNOPQRSTUVWXYZ

The word *design,* when used in connection with books, magazines, and other printed materials, refers to the arrangement of elements on the printed page. In addition to the
typographical elements, such as the size and style of type,
the length of lines, and the space between lines, the design

Clarendon™

abcdefghijklmnopqrstuvwxyz123456
ABCDEFGHIJKLMNOPQRSTUVWXY

abcdefghijklmnopqrstuvwxyz1234567890
ABCDEFGHIJKLMNOPQRSTUVWXYZ

abcdefghijklmnopqrstuvwxyz123456789
ABCDEFGHIJKLMNOPQRSTUVWXYZ

The word *design,* when used in connection with books,
magazines, and other printed materials, refers to the arrangement of elements on the printed page. In addition
to the typographical elements, such as the size and style
of type, the length of lines, and the space between lines,

Electra®

abcdefghijklmnopqrstuvwxyz1234567890
ABCDEFGHIJKLMNOPQRSTUVWXYZ

abcdefghijklmnopqrstuvwxyz1234567890
ABCDEFGHIJKLMNOPQRSTUVWXYZ

abcdefghijklmnopqrstuvwxyz1234567890
ABCDEFGHIJKLMNOPQRSTUVWXYZ

The word *design*, when used in connection with books, magazines, and other printed materials, refers to the arrangement of elements on the printed page. In addition to the typographical elements, such as the size and style of type, the length of lines, and the space between lines, the design of the page often includes tables, illustra-

ITC Friz Quadrata

abcdefghijklmnopqrstuvwxyz1234567890
ABCDEFGHIJKLMNOPQRSTUVWXYZ

abcdefghijklmnopqrstuvwxyz1234567890
ABCDEFGHIJKLMNOPQRSTUVWXYZ

abcdefghijklmnopqrstuvwxyz1234567890
ABCDEFGHIJKLMNOPQRSTUVWXYZ

The word *design,* when used in connection with books, magazines, and other printed materials, refers to the arrangement of elements on the printed page. In addition to the typographical elements, such as the size and style of type, the length of lines, and the space between lines, the design of the

Garamond

abcdefghijklmnopqrstuvwxyz1234567890
ABCDEFGHIJKLMNOPQRSTUVWXYZ

abcdefghijklmnopqrstuvwxyz1234567890
ABCDEFGHIJKLMNOPQRSTUVWXYZ

abcdefghijklmnopqrstuvwxyz1234567890
ABCDEFGHIJKLMNOPQRSTUVWXYZ

The word *design,* when used in connection with books, magazines, and other printed materials, refers to the arrangement of elements on the printed page. In addition to the typographical elements, such as the size and style of type, the length of lines, and the space between lines, the design of the page often includes tables, illustrations, and the use

Goudy Old Style

abcdefghijklmnopqrstuvwxyz1234567890
ABCDEFGHIJKLMNOPQRSTUVWXYZ

abcdefghijklmnopqrstuvwxyz1234567890
ABCDEFGHIJKLMNOPQRSTUVWXYZ

abcdefghijklmnopqrstuvwxyz1234567890
ABCDEFGHIJKLMNOPQRSTUVWXYZ

The word *design,* when used in connection with books, magazines, and other printed materials, refers to the arrangement of elements on the printed page. In addition to the typographical elements, such as the size and style of type, the length of lines, and the space between lines, the design of the page often includes ta-

Helvetica®

abcdefghijklmnopqrstuvwxyz1234567890
ABCDEFGHIJKLMNOPQRSTUVWXYZ

abcdefghijklmnopqrstuvwxyz1234567890
ABCDEFGHIJKLMNOPQRSTUVWXYZ

abcdefghijklmnopqrstuvwxyz1234567890
ABCDEFGHIJKLMNOPQRSTUVWXYZ

The word *design,* when used in connection with books, magazines, and other printed materials, refers to the arrangement of elements on the printed page. In addition to the typographical elements, such as the size and style of type, the length of lines, and the space between lines, the design of the page

Melior®

abcdefghijklmnopqrstuvwxyz1234567890
ABCDEFGHIJKLMNOPQRSTUVWXYZ

abcdefghijklmnopqrstuvwxyz1234567890
ABCDEFGHIJKLMNOPQRSTUVWXYZ

abcdefghijklmnopqrstuvwxyz1234567890
ABCDEFGHIJKLMNOPQRSTUVWXYZ

The word *design,* when used in connection with books, magazines, and other printed materials, refers to the arrangement of elements on the printed page. In addition to the typographical elements, such as the size and style of type, the length of lines, and the space between lines, the design

Memphis®

abcdefghijklmnopqrstuvwxyz1234567890
ABCDEFGHIJKLMNOPQRSTUVWXYZ

abcdefghijklmnopqrstuvwxyz1234567890
ABCDEFGHIJKLMNOPQRSTUVWXYZ

abcdefghijklmnopqrstuvwxyz1234567890
ABCDEFGHIJKLMNOPQRSTUVWXYZ

The word *design*, when used in connection with books, magazines, and other printed materials, refers to the arrangement of elements on the printed page. In addition to the typographical elements, such as the size and style of type, the length of lines, and the space between lines, the

Optima®

abcdefghijklmnopqrstuvwxyz1234567890
ABCDEFGHIJKLMNOPQRSTUVWXYZ

abcdefghijklmnopqrstuvwxyz1234567890
ABCDEFGHIJKLMNOPQRSTUVWXYZ

abcdefghijklmnopqrstuvwxyz1234567890
ABCDEFGHIJKLMNOPQRSTUVWXYZ

The word *design*, when used in connection with books, magazines, and other printed materials, refers to the arrangement of elements on the printed page. In addition to the typographical elements, such as the size and style of type, the length of lines, and the space between lines, the design of the page

Palatino®

abcdefghijklmnopqrstuvwxyz1234567890
ABCDEFGHIJKLMNOPQRSTUVWXYZ

abcdefghijklmnopqrstuvwxyz1234567890
ABCDEFGHIJKLMNOPQRSTUVWXYZ

abcdefghijklmnopqrstuvwxyz1234567890
ABCDEFGHIJKLMNOPQRSTUVWXYZ

The word *design*, when used in connection with books, magazines, and other printed materials, refers to the arrangement of elements on the printed page. In addition to the typographical elements, such as the size and style of type, the length of lines, and the space between lines, the design of the

Times Roman®

abcdefghijklmnopqrstuvwxyz1234567890
ABCDEFGHIJKLMNOPQRSTUVWXYZ

abcdefghijklmnopqrstuvwxyz1234567890
ABCDEFGHIJKLMNOPQRSTUVWXYZ

abcdefghijklmnopqrstuvwxyz1234567890
ABCDEFGHIJKLMNOPQRSTUVWXYZ

The word *design*, when used in connection with books, magazines, and other printed materials, refers to the arrangement of elements on the printed page. In addition to the typographical elements, such as the size and style of type, the length of lines, and the space between lines, the design of the page often includes tables, illustrations, and

Trade Gothic®

abcdefghijklmnopqrstuvwxyz1234567890
ABCDEFGHIJKLMNOPQRSTUVWXYZ

abcdefghijklmnopqrstuvwxyz1234567890
ABCDEFGHIJKLMNOPQRSTUVWXYZ

abcdefghijklmnopqrstuvwxyz1234567890
ABCDEFGHIJKLMNOPQRSTUVWXYZ

The word *design,* when used in connection with books, magazines, and other printed materials, refers to the arrangement of
elements on the printed page. In addition to the typographical elements, such as the size and style of type, the length
of lines, and the space between lines, the design of the page often

Univers®

abcdefghijklmnopqrstuvwxyz12345678
ABCDEFGHIJKLMNOPQRSTUVWXYZ

abcdefghijklmnopqrstuvwxyz1234567890
ABCDEFGHIJKLMNOPQRSTUVWXYZ

abcdefghijklmnopqrstuvwxyz1234567890
ABCDEFGHIJKLMNOPQRSTUVWXYZ

The word *design,* when used in connection with books, magazines, and other printed materials, refers to the arrangement
of elements on the printed page. In addition to the typographical elements, such as the size and style of type, the length of
lines, and the space between lines, the design of the page

Tables and Illustrations

Tables

Tables are normally set in roman type that is smaller than that of the text, with extra space above and below the table to set if off. Column heads are usually of the same size as the other parts of the table, although sometimes they are set one point smaller if there is a need for them to fit a narrow page.

Titles of tables are usually marked for setting in the same size as the titles of illustrations, if there are any; these titles are sometimes set in type larger than that used for the body of the table. Captions, however, are likely to be set in the same size as that for the table body. Titles and captions should be styled consistently throughout the work.

Differences in typeface are commonly used to differentiate the parts of a table, and each of these differences must be individually marked or keyed. Title and caption, for instance, are often set in boldface or italic type to set them apart from the text. However, any caption set this way should not be lengthy, because large amounts of italic or bold type tend to clutter the page and make reading difficult. A subtitle is sometimes set in smaller or italic type, and sometimes within parentheses. A change of typography may be used in other ways to emphasize the various parts of a table. Column heads are often set boldface, subheads sometimes italic. Total numbers and also the word *total* in the stub may be bold. Subheads within a stub are often distinguished by italic or bold type as well as by their position.

The editor typemarks or keys all of these elements with notations in the margin. If the design of the table includes many such variations in typography, it is a good idea to develop key symbols for the various kinds of type needed, to avoid cluttering the copy with editorial notations. A set of general instructions could describe in detail the specific type needed for a table body (TB), table title (TT), column head (CH), column subhead (CH2), table number (TN), source note (TSN), head for a source note (TSNH), or footnote (TFN). For more on typemarking a manuscript, see the section on Manuscript Markup later in this chapter.

Runover lines The compositor has to know how to handle runover lines. A general instruction is usually written for this. If the copy differs from the specifications, it is marked to confirm the instructions by showing the proper indention or alignment.

Table footnotes Source notes and general notes are usually introduced by the word *Source* or *Note* (or *Sources* or *Notes*), specific notes by the reference symbol used in the table. The introductory word is often marked to be set in a style different from the note itself, as italic or capitals and small capitals. A source note may be further distinguished by being set all in italic and separated from the other notes like the credit line of an illustration.

Footnotes to tables are often set one point smaller than text footnotes, and one to two point sizes smaller than the type used in the body of the table. A typical 8-point table, for example, may have footnotes set in 6- or 7-point type.

Rules The editor either typemarks or keys each rule used in a table to tell the typesetter its desired size. Conventional rules are a half point in size, but heavier ones of a point and larger may be used to set off larger divisions of a table or to fit in with the total design of the book. A very complex table may have both double (parallel) and single horizontal rules to separate large and smaller categories of data. A double rule could be drawn below the caption and at the end of the table, for example, with single rules set below column heads, decked heads, and cut-in heads.

Typography of Captions, Legends, and Credit Lines

Captions are sometimes set in boldface type, but in books roman and italic are more common. A bold typeface should be avoided if the caption is more than two lines long. Capitals and small capitals were once used frequently for figure captions, but they are considered a bit old-fashioned now.

A legend that follows a caption is often distinguished from it by its typography. It is very common, for example, for a boldface caption to be followed by a legend set in roman type of the same size. Other indications such as differences in capitalization, indention, or position can also be used to distinguish caption from legend.

With illustrations that are preceded by identification numbers, the word *Figure* is often set in italic or in capitals and small capitals. And when an identification number is followed immediately by a legend without a caption, the legend is run in and both are usually set roman. Captions are often set in type about two points smaller than text type. The copy editor marks the credit line so that the compositor will know exactly how to set it. The conventional position of a brief credit line is below, and very close to the edge of, the illustration, either flush left or flush right. It is often printed in very small type when it is set in this position (4-point is a common size). But it may also run vertically up an edge. In these positions it is often set in italic, without a period. In a few publications, the credit line is set as the last part of a legend.

Layout of Illustrations and Captions

The first rule of layout is that an illustration and the text reference to it are set as close together as possible. It is the editor's decision whether an illustration must be printed on the same page as its reference, on a facing page, or on another page. Any illustration that is explained in the text should be visible without any need to turn pages back and forth. If that is not possible, the illustration should be referred to by number.

Layouts of illustrations are usually determined by an artist or designer. The artist always looks at facing pages, not just single pages, to plan a layout. The position of figure captions and legends in relation to the figures varies widely. In some modern publications, designers seem to have explored and exercised nearly every possibility. But no matter how free-wheeling the design of the publication, specifications are written and adhered to. Some specialized elements of layout are described in the following paragraphs.

Runarounds Runarounds are very small illustrations with text on three sides and a margin (usually a side margin) on the other. Runarounds are rarely used because they are expensive to set correctly.

Margin cuts Margin cuts are small illustrations set within a side margin next to the text.

Broadside cuts Broadside cuts are requested when the picture has to be laid on its side to fit the page. The left side of the illustration goes on the bottom of the page; any caption or legend is usually set below the illustration, at the right side of the page. Running heads and folios are omitted. These illustrations are best printed on a left-hand page, because the holder of a book reads that page most easily when the book is turned and held sideways.

Other special effects may be ordered by the designer, such as bleeding a photograph—that is, running the picture into the margin and apparently off the page. To accomplish this, the illustration is positioned so that the edge extends a small fraction of an inch beyond the outside trim edge. Borders may also be drawn around text pictures, or other special effects may be created by the artist.

Some of the standards for positioning art on the page include the following guidelines:

1. A full-width illustration with lines of text above or below it should be positioned so that no parts of it are confused with the text. This means that there should be enough lines of text above or below so that they will not look like a caption or a legend; the caption must be clearly set off from the text both by its typography and its position. The line of text immediately below an illustration should always be set full measure. If necessary, these problems can be solved by moving the illustration to the top or bottom of the page.
2. Full-page art is much easier to handle than several pieces of small art. Folios and running heads are usually omitted with full-page art unless a lengthy series of such illustrations requires folios to aid the reader.
3. Artists prefer to set illustrations at the top of a page rather than at the bottom and, if they are less than full measure, next to outside margins rather than inside margins. But a common position for illustrations that are less than full measure is in the center with extra-large side margins.
4. A series of small, related illustrations may be grouped across a full

page and separated by thin lines of space. This is especially efficient if all the figures can be explained in one caption. The single caption may be set the width of the group as a whole, or under one of the figures only, whichever looks best.

5. Captions and legends do not normally extend past the width of the figure unless the figure is nearly as wide as the page.

6. Captions are frequently not set across the full width of the page because of the difficulty of reading small type across a wide column. Another reason for not justifying these captions is to avoid having a very small runover line that contrasts with an extremely long line above it.

7. The traditional position for a caption is centered above the illustration, especially if it is no more than two lines long. However, the trend in today's publications is to set the caption below the artwork, along with the legend and any source note. Flush left styling is common now; flush right is used occasionally if the illustration is flush against the right margin of the page. Captions are frequently set alongside illustrations when there is room. These captions should either be set deliberately about mid-picture, or else the last line of the caption should exactly align with the bottom of the cut. These decisions are all called for in the design specifications, although sometimes the artist takes liberties as needed to fit the art on the page in the most legible and artistic way possible.

8. Design specifications also determine whether captions are to be justified or ragged when lines run over, and whether the runovers are indented. The conventional style is for a caption to be flush left, ragged right, with runovers aligned left. Many publications set captions flush right and ragged left when the cuts are set on the right-hand page, and flush left and ragged right on the left-hand page.

Other Design Elements

In addition to choosing a size and style of type for the main body of text, designers are also responsible for such page-design elements as running heads, folios, headings, and margins. Each of these elements is described in the paragraphs that follow. This section of the chapter also includes instructions on how to mark up a manuscript in such a way that the typesetter will know what size and style of type to use for each of these elements and where to place each of these elements on the page.

Running Heads

Running heads are the short phrases that appear at the top of the page in most books. In some books the running head on the left hand page (often referred to as the *verso* page) is simply the title of the book or a shortened form of the title. In such books, the running head on the right-hand page (often called the *recto* page) is usually the chapter title or a shortened form of it. In books in which the chapters have numerous subdivisions, the running head on the verso page is the chapter title; the running head on the recto page is the subheading within the chapter that covers the contents of the recto page. The latter is the style followed in this book. Running heads may be centered or set flush left or flush right. If a flush-left and flush-right styling is chosen, one of two designs is usually used. Either both sets of running heads are set at the inside margin (i.e., verso running heads at flush right and recto running heads at flush left) or both running heads are set at the outside margin (verso running heads at flush left and recto running heads at flush right). Most books that have running heads have them on both recto and verso pages, but sometimes a successful page design can be made with running heads on only one page of a two-page spread.

Running heads are usually set in the same typeface as the main text; however, the form the typeface takes may vary. Boldface, italic, all-capital, small-capital, and mixed capital and small-capital stylings are all used in setting running heads. Likewise, the size of the type may vary in comparison with the type in the main text. In some books, the running heads are set in a size of type that is much smaller than the text type. In books in which the running heads are not simply decorative but are meant to be used by readers to help them find a particular portion of the text (as in this book), the running head is usually set larger than the text type. The running heads in this book are set in 11-point type, in contrast with the 10-point type used in the text.

Folios

Folio is a book designer's term for a page number. Folios can be set at the top of the page or at the bottom of the page, flush left, flush right, or centered. As with running heads, the point size and typeface of the folio in relation to the main body of the text will vary from book to book. In books in which readers will often be seeking out a specific page, it is a courtesy to set the folio at the top of the page, at the outside margin, and in a point size that is easy to read.

Headings

Headings are words or phrases that are used to introduce and identify text passages within a publication. The most obvious kind of heading is a chapter title, which is often set in a type size that is significantly larger than the body of the text. In this book, chapter titles are set in 24-point type.

Many books also use headings to separate chapters into their major divisions. These headings are usually referred to as *A heads* or *1-heads*, and they are usually bigger or bolder than the type in the main text. In this chapter, the phrase "Other Design Elements" on page 365 is an A head. A heads in this book are set in 16-point type with a 1-point rule running the width of the text block and set 6 points below the base line of the heading.

Major divisions of a chapter may be further subdivided, and these further subdivisions may be indicated with a *B head* or *2-head*. B heads are usually bigger or bolder than the type in the main text, but they should not be as noticeable as an A head. The phrase "Headings" on page 366 is a B head, and it is set in 11-point boldface.

In some texts, A and B heads are horizontally centered on the page; in this book all headings are set flush left. Specifications for heads and subheads usually require them to have extra leading above and below. Less space is usually required below the head, since a head is considered to belong to the text below it, not above.

Still smaller portions of text within a chapter are indicated by headings that are less noticeable than A and B heads. This book makes use of C heads, which are set in 10-point boldface and run in with the text, and D heads, which are set in 10-point italic and also run in with the text. Heads that are run in in this way are referred to as *side heads* or *shoulder heads*.

Other types of side heads include *margin heads,* which are set in the outside margin in a typeface other than that of the text and usually with a sentence-style capitalization. The designer must decide whether the type is to be justified or aligned on the right or left side. (Justifying both sides, when the lines are so short, would result in awkward spaces between words.) Margin heads are not used too often because they are expensive to set. Even more expensive to set are *cut-in side heads*. These are set inside the paragraph in a hole framed by the lines of text, which must be set in varying widths.

Margins

Margins are a design element that can have a great impact on the overall appearance of a page. Margins that are too narrow give a cramped appearance and can mar the look of a page that is otherwise well designed. In general, the width of margins should be made proportional to the size of the page. For instance, a book whose pages measure six inches by nine inches (a typical book size) will usually look best with top, outside, and bottom margins of about an inch or a little less. The inside margin is usually a little narrower than the outside margin, and the top margin a little narrower than the bottom. However, designers have some flexibility in regard to margins. If space is at a premium, the margins can be made slightly narrower. If, for one reason or another, the lines of the text need to be shortened or lengthened slightly, the margins can be widened or narrowed to compensate. If a book is being designed for maximum visual appeal, the margins are often made extra-wide.

Rules

Vertical rules are uncommon in the page designs of most contemporary books; however, horizontal rules are quite common. Rules are commonly set at the top of a page underneath the running head, underneath chapter titles, between major sections of a chapter, and at the foot of a page, separating the text from any footnotes. Rules should be used sparingly however, as too many rules in a text can make the text cluttered and confusing.

Rules vary in their thickness, and they are usually referred to in terms of their point size. Some representative samples of rules are included below.

½-point rule _____
1-point rule _____
1½-point rule _____
2-point rule _____

Indention and Paragraphs

Most publications contain paragraphs whose first lines are indented and whose remaining lines are flush left. The amount of paragraph indention is often specified by the designer; if not, the compositor will choose a commonly used space, usually one or two ems.

Some kinds of copy require reverse, or hanging, indention, in which the first line of a paragraph is flush left and the others indented. These flush-and-hang paragraphs are used in bibliographies and other alphabetical listings where it is important for the first word of the paragraph to catch the reader's eye. The editor writes above the copy an instruction such as "Set items flush and hang; indent runovers 1½ ems."

A few publications use block-style paragraphs, which are not indented at all but instead are separated by extra leading. Block styling should be specified in the designer's instructions if desired.

Manuscript Markup

Marking up the manuscript is one of the final steps in the preparation of copy for the typesetter. The purpose of the markup is to communicate to the typesetter the size, style, and position of each typographical element on the page. There are two methods that are commonly used for marking up the manuscript. One method is to write out in full the size, style, and position of each element on a page each time it appears. This method is illustrated in the sample on page 369. It is really practical only when there are just a few pages to mark up or when one is handling special situations. The other method is simply to label or code the elements on the page. The labels or codes refer the typesetter to a specifications sheet, which gives the details of size, style, and position for each labeled or coded part. A marked-up manuscript using the label method is illustrated on page 371. A coded manuscript would look the same as the labeled manuscript except that the labels, such as "Chapter Number" and "Chap-

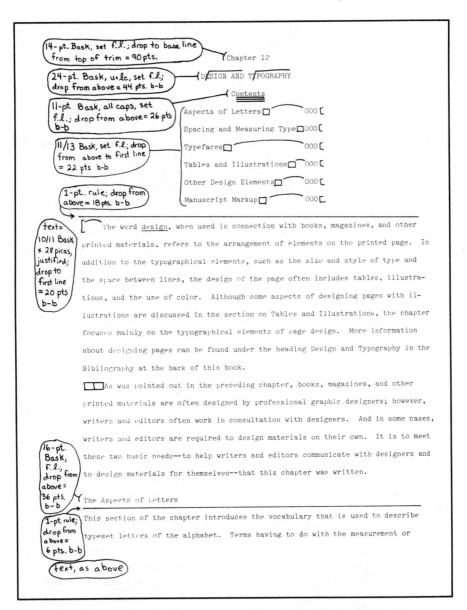

The word _design_, when used in connection with books, magazines, and other printed materials, refers to the arrangement of elements on the printed page. In addition to the typographical elements, such as the size and style of type and the space between lines, the design of the page often includes tables, illustrations, and the use of color. Although some aspects of designing pages with illustrations are discussed in the section on Tables and Illustrations, the chapter focuses mainly on the typographical elements of page design. More information about designing pages can be found under the heading Design and Typography in the Bibliography at the back of this book.

As was pointed out in the preceding chapter, books, magazines, and other printed materials are often designed by professional graphic designers; however, writers and editors often work in consultation with designers. And in some cases, writers and editors are required to design materials on their own. It is to meet these two basic needs--to help writers and editors communicate with designers and to design materials for themselves--that this chapter was written.

The Aspects of Letters

This section of the chapter introduces the vocabulary that is used to describe typeset letters of the alphabet. Terms having to do with the measurement or

Figure 12.3.　A marked-up manuscript with full specifications

ter Title," would be replaced with simple codes, such as *S-1* or *S-2*. The specifications sheet that the labeled manuscript refers to is shown on page 372. To see how the samples on pages 369 and 371 appear in typeset form, see page 343.

These methods of marking up (sometimes called *speccing*) the manuscript are not mutually exclusive. Editors and designers often use more than one method within a single manuscript. For the convenience of the person doing the markup and to reduce the clutter on the page, the labeling or coding method is used wherever it can be. However, each element that is labeled or coded must be on the specifications sheet, and there may sometimes be elements that are left off of the specifications sheet, either because they come up quite infrequently (as the vertical drop between two extracts with no text intervening) or because they always require special handling (as poetry quotations set as extracts). In such cases as these, writing full instructions at each occurrence may be the best course, even though more common typographical elements are labeled or coded.

Sometimes, especially when the design is complex, it makes sense to send the typesetter a layout of the page in addition to the marked page and the specifications sheet. The layout is a drawing of the page that shows the approximate size and position of each element on the page and that includes additional instructions, dimensions, and specifications that help the typesetter understand the designer's wishes. A sample layout is illustrated on page 374.

No matter what kind of instructions are being sent to the typesetter, the purpose is the same: to describe clearly and fully the style, size, and location of each element on the page. Ways of describing these elements are explained in the following paragraphs.

Style

The most important style element that a typesetter needs to know is the typeface or typefaces in which a page is to be set. When the typeface is indicated on the manuscript, the notation is often abbreviated, as *Times* or *TR* for Times Roman, *Pal* for Palatino, or *Helv* for Helvetica.

In addition, the typesetter needs to know whether to use lightface, boldface, roman, or italic type. Italic type is usually indicated by an underline under the element to be italicized, and boldface is usually indicated by a wavy underline under the element that is to be emboldened. However, sometimes this method of marking is reinforced by a marginal notation, such as *ital* for italics and *bold* or *bf* for boldface. Lightface and roman elements usually do not have to be marked as such, but when they are, *light* or *lf* stands for lightface, and *rom* stands for roman.

Beyond that, sometimes the capitalization or lowercasing of letters is not clear from the manuscript without additional marking. In this case *caps, all caps,* or *uc* can be used to indicate that the words are to be set in all capitals. The designation for lowercase is *lc*. A combination of upper-case and lowercase letters is marked as *ulc* or *clc* (for "capitals and lower-

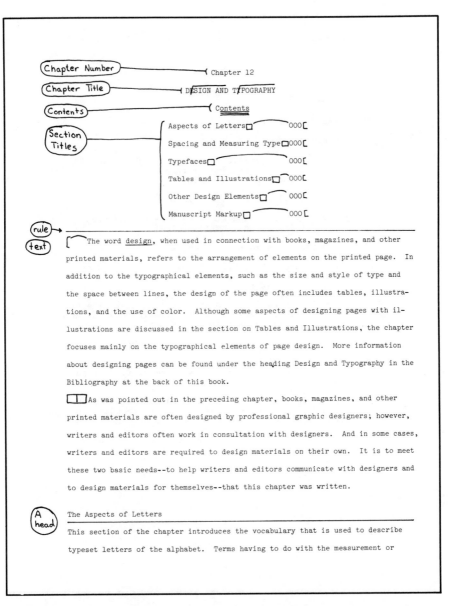

The word <u>design</u>, when used in connection with books, magazines, and other printed materials, refers to the arrangement of elements on the printed page. In addition to the typographical elements, such as the size and style of type and the space between lines, the design of the page often includes tables, illustrations, and the use of color. Although some aspects of designing pages with illustrations are discussed in the section on Tables and Illustrations, the chapter focuses mainly on the typographical elements of page design. More information about designing pages can be found under the heading Design and Typography in the Bibliography at the back of this book.

As was pointed out in the preceding chapter, books, magazines, and other printed materials are often designed by professional graphic designers; however, writers and editors often work in consultation with designers. And in some cases, writers and editors are required to design materials on their own. It is to meet these two basic needs--to help writers and editors communicate with designers and to design materials for themselves--that this chapter was written.

The Aspects of Letters

This section of the chapter introduces the vocabulary that is used to describe typeset letters of the alphabet. Terms having to do with the measurement or

Figure 12.4.   A marked-up manuscript using labels

```
                      Specification Sheet


   Trim Size:  6 1/2 inches x 9 1/2 inches

   Text Page:  28 picas x 43 picas

   Margins:    top:  1 1/8 inches (7/8 inch from top of
               trim to base line of running head); front:
               1 inch; bottom:  1 inch

   Text:       10/11 Baskerville x 28 picas

   Examples:   type size and style as marked, indented
               1 1/2 picas from flush left

   Chapter Opener:  as marked on layout

   A Head:     16-point Baskerville u&lc with a 1-point
               rule 6 points below b-b and running the
               width of the text page; 50-point drop from
               preceding text to base line of first line
               of A head; 20-point drop from base line of
               rule to first line of following text or to
               base line of following B head

   B Head:     11-point Times Roman boldface u&lc; 20-
               point drop from preceding text to base
               line of B head; 14-point drop from base
               line of B head to base line of first line
               of following text

   C Head:     10-point Times Roman boldface, run in; 10-
               point drop from base line of preceding
               text or B head to base line of C head

   Folios and Running Heads:  11-point Times Roman bold-
               face
```

Figure 12.5.   A specifications sheet

case"). Small capitals are indicated by the designation *sm caps* or *sc*. A combination of capitals and small capitals is indicated by the notation *c/sc*.

Size

The size of most typographical elements on a page is given in points. The specifications for the size of type for elements that require more than one line includes not only the size of the type but also the spacing between lines. As explained earlier in this chapter, the size and spacing of type is indicated by expressions such as 10/12, which means 10-point type set on a 12-point body or, put differently, 10-point type set with a 12-point drop from the base line of one line of type to the base line of the next line.

Location

Every element on the page has a location that can be described either by reference to the edge of the paper; the edge of the *type block,* which is the area that the main text fills; or some other element on the page. Because the location of some elements is given in terms of the edge of the paper or the edge of the type block, it is important that the typesetter be given these dimensions on the specifications sheet, on a layout, or in a cover letter accompanying the text.

The size of the sheet of paper on which a page is to be printed is referred to as the *trim size.* The top of the text block is usually described in terms of its drop from the top of the paper, commonly referred to as the *top of the trim.* The drop is measured either to the top of the first line or to the base line of the first line. The width of the text block is equal to the length of the longest line that is to be set. The location of the edge of the text block is described in terms of its distance from the outer edge of the paper.

Type that is intended to begin at precisely the left edge of the text block is said to be set at *flush left,* which is abbreviated as *fl.* Type that is intended to end at precisely the right edge of the text block is said to be set at *flush right,* abbreviated *fl rt.* Indention or horizontal spacing between elements is often given in em spaces. Em spaces are indicated by a small square drawn at the spot where the indention or spacing should fall.

When describing the position of one element in terms of another, the relationship is usually described in terms of its drop in points, and the drop is usually measured from the base line of one element to the base line of the other. (Even rules can be thought of as resting on a base line.) Measurements of this sort are usually indicated by adding the notation *b to b, b-b,* or *b/b.*

Sometimes the best way to specify the horizontal position of an element is to ask that it be centered in the type block. This position is indicated by putting center marks around the element. (Center marks are described and illustrated on pages 326 and 327 in Chapter 11, "Production Techniques."

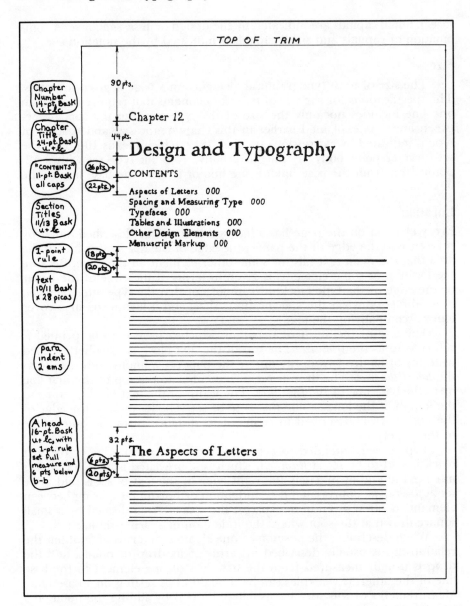

Figure 12.6.   A sample layout

Examples The following examples are taken from the sample on page 369.

24-pt Bask, ulc, set fl; drop from above = 44 pts b-b Set this in 24-point upper and lowercase Baskerville type. Position so that the left edge of the first letter is at flush left and the base line of the letters is 44 points below the base line of the line above.

11-pt Bask, all caps, set fl Set in 11-point Baskerville capital letters.

10/11 Bask × 28 pica, justified Set in 10-point Baskerville type on an 11-point body. Make the line 28 picas long. Justify all lines except the last line of a paragraph.

Chapter 13

Composition, Printing, and Binding

CONTENTS

Most written material that is going to be distributed to a large audience goes through the processes of composition, printing, and binding. As the preceding two chapters have shown, authors and editors often become involved with composition. The printing and binding processes, however, are usually more remote. The purpose of this chapter is to give writers, editors, and other production people an overview of these processes and to introduce some of the concepts and vocabulary relating to them.

Throughout this chapter, composition, printing, and binding are described in terms of book manufacturing. It should be understood, however, at least with composition and printing, that the processes described are the same for books, magazines, pamphlets, or single sheets of paper.

The descriptions that follow are extremely simplified. They are intended to give those writers, editors, and production people who know virtually nothing about book manufacturing a very brief introduction to the processes that go on after manuscript editing and markup is complete. Readers who anticipate having major responsibilities regarding the supervision of a book or other publication through any of the processes described in this section are urged to consult one or more of the books listed under the heading Production, Design, and Printing in the Bibliography at the end of this book.

Overview of the Processes

Traditionally, discussions of the composition, printing, and binding processes begin with an explanation of handset type and letterpress printing, despite the fact that most of today's writers and editors will probably never encounter either of them. Handset type is type that is set by a worker who assembles individual pieces of metal type, one piece for each letter on the page, into frames that hold a page's worth of type. Letterpress printing is done by inking the raised surfaces of those pieces of type and pressing the pieces of paper that are to become the pages of the book against them. Handsetting and letterpress printing were once common in the printing industry, and many of the concepts and much of the vocabulary involved with modern composition and printing are derived from these earlier processes. However, the technology of composition and printing has proceeded so far that the connection between today's processes and earlier processes is becoming more and more remote. This chapter will focus on some typical composition, printing, and binding systems that are in use today. Readers who are interested in some of the earlier processes should consult the sources listed under the heading Production and Printing in the Bibliography at the end of this book.

Book manufacturing, in the typical arrangement that we are describing in this chapter, involves first a typesetting company, often referred to as the *compositor,* that takes the author's edited manuscript and the designer's specifications and from these two sources creates a high-quality, black-and-white image of each page of the book exactly as it will appear in its final form. Through a series of steps, some of which may be carried out in the typesetter's shop but most of which are done in the printing plant, this high-quality picture is transferred to a printing plate that will be used for laying down ink on paper. This plate is mounted on a printing press and inked. The ink is transferred to paper by pressing the inked plate against the paper, which is fed into the printing press either as single sheets or on a continuous roll. After the paper has been printed on both sides, it is folded, trimmed, and bound together.

All of the processes mentioned in the preceding paragraph can take place within one shop, but more typically a publication will be typeset by one company and printed and bound by another. Within a publishing company, these processes may be supervised by a manufacturing manager or a production manager. A common arrangement involves the production department's being responsible for typesetting and the manufacturing department's overseeing all printing and binding.

No matter how the actual work is handled, the processes can be conceptually divided into three distinct stages: composition, platemaking and printing, and binding. These three stages are discussed separately in the following pages.

Composition

The high-quality black-and-white picture of the page in its final form that was mentioned in the preceding section is referred to as a *reproduction proof*, or more commonly, a *repro*. It is called a reproduction proof because it presents an image of the page in which all of the elements are dark enough and sharp enough that, once the image has been transferred to a printing plate, pages of the printed book can be reproduced from it. Some typesetters can also provide their customers with a negative print of the repro, which can then be used in making the printing plate. However, the typesetting process as we are describing it here ends with the making of the repro. This section of the chapter tells how that repro is made.

Hot-metal Composition

At least some mention should be made of the so-called *hot-metal* composition systems, although few readers of this book will ever encounter this older method of composition.

The kinds of machines that were best known among hot-metal composition systems were the Linotype and Monotype machines. In both of these systems, the typesetting process began with an operator sitting at a typewriter-like keyboard and retyping, or keyboarding, the manuscript. The systems are referred to as hot-metal typesetting because, in both cases, each keystroke made by the operator is actually an instruction to the machine to inject molten lead into a mold that will shape the lead into a piece of type.

The principal difference between Linotype and Monotype is the amount of type that is cast in one piece. In Linotype composition all of the molds necessary for a line of type are assembled, and then lead is injected into all of them so that a single piece of lead that constitutes the entire line is molded. In Monotype composition, each piece of type is separately cast as it is arranged into a line.

In both systems, the completed lines are assembled into trays that are called *galleys*. The proofs that are sent to the publisher for proofreading are made by inking the raised surfaces of these pieces of type in the tray and pressing a piece of paper against the inked surfaces. After the contents of the galleys have been corrected and approved, the lines of type are rearranged into the format that they will take on the printed page. Once again, a proof is made and sent to the publisher for approval. This proof not only shows all of the lines of text in place on the page but it also includes the rules, running heads, and page numbers that are to be part of the page. Once the publisher has approved this page proof, the compositor makes the repro-quality page proof. The repro proof is made in the same way that the page proof was made, but extra care is taken in making it, and a better grade of paper is used.

Photocomposition

In a photocomposition system at its simplest, type is set by shining a light through a cutout that is the size and shape of a letter onto a piece of light-sensitive paper. The photocomposition machine includes drums or discs on which cutouts for all of the characters in a font are included. It also includes prisms and mirrors so that the letters can be aimed at precisely the right spot and in precisely the right size on the light-sensitive paper to produce properly aligned lines of type. After the light-sensitive paper has been exposed to the letters, it is developed like any other photograph. The output of the phototypesetter is of repro quality, but often it is not in page format.

The essential elements of any photocomposition system are the keyboard where the manuscript is retyped, as it also is in Linotype or Monotype composition; a computer in which the keyboarded, machine-readable version of the manuscript is stored; and the phototypesetting machine which we have just described.

Input The task of the keyboard operator is to turn the author's edited and marked-up manuscript into a machine-readable form. In doing so, the operator may be creating a punched paper tape that will later be fed into a computer, or the operator may be entering data directly onto a computer disc. One way or the other, the operator is creating a file that includes not only the text of the manuscript but also all of the codes necessary to instruct the phototypesetting machine how to set the type in accordance with the designer's specifications.

At the input stage, most of the instructions are made through generic coding, i.e., with codes that indicate the beginning of running text, the end of a paragraph, words and phrases that should be set apart from the text as headings, text that should be set as an extract, and so forth. In addition, the file would include codes to indicate special characters that are not on the keyboard, such as an accented *é* or a pound sign £. The file would also include codes to indicate that portions of the running text are to be set in italic, boldface, or small capital letters.

Once this file, often called the master file, has been completed, all of the design specifications can be entered into the computer, such as what size and style of type to use for each of the text elements identified through a generic code, how long to set each line, how much space to leave between each line, and how many lines to set on each galley proof or page proof. With these specifications entered, the master file can then be read into the computer, and the output will be a typesetting file complete with all of the instructions necessary for running the phototypesetting machine, including where to break words at the end of lines and, if requested, how much space to insert between words in order to justify the lines.

In recent years, publishers have turned more and more to creating their own master files and submitting to the compositor not a manuscript but a computer file on tape or disc along with a written description of the design specifications that correlates to each of the text elements identified on the tape. The typesetting file itself is still created by the compositor, because only the people in the compositor's shop know the kinds of instructions that the phototypesetter will need.

In theory this practice should work out perfectly; however, before deciding to send a computer file to a compositor, the publisher should be sure that the compositor can use the tape or disc. This means first that the file must be in a format that the compositor's computer can read or that the compositor can make usable without great difficulty. Many compositors now have conversion machines that enable them to accept computer files in a wide range of formats, but it is still best to check before embarking very far on such a project. The publisher should also be sure that the master file includes all of the coding that is necessary for making the typesetting tape. This means that each text element should have a unique code that cannot be confused with any other element in the file. Inadequate planning and failure to consult with the compositor ahead of time can result in the compositor's having to make a printout of the publisher's file, re-mark it with adequate coding, and reenter the file manually.

Proofing and page makeup The output of the phototypesetter is typically a long sheet of paper like the galley proofs that come from the Linotype and Monotype process, and the output is usually referred to as *galley proofs* or simply *galleys*. The typesetting on these galleys is usually of repro quality, so the proofs themselves usually do not leave the compositor's shop. Photocopies are sent to the publisher for proofreading. When these photocopies, proofread and marked for correction, are returned to the compositor, the corrections are entered into the master file and those portions of the master file affected by the correction—sometimes as little as a single line—are run through the phototypesetter again. The output is the line or lines in their corrected form. These lines are in repro form, so they can be stripped down into the galley. In the stripping process, the new line or lines can simply be pasted down over the old lines. Better yet, the old lines can be cut out of the galley proof altogether and new lines pasted down in their place.

After the galley proof has been corrected, the type can be arranged into page format. This is done by creating what is called a *mechanical*. A mechanical is assembled on a board big enough to hold all of the type required on a page or frequently on a two-page spread. Onto this board are pasted all of the elements, in repro form, that go on the page: the basic text, the folios, the running heads, and in some cases illustrations. The mechanical is assembled with extreme care. Each element is placed in the exact position in which it should appear on the printed page, because it is from the mechanical that the negative, and ultimately the printing plate, will be made.

In some phototypesetting systems, the output of the phototypesetter can be in page format. In that case, no mechanical need be made.

Proofs of the mechanical or the phototypeset pages are sent to the publisher for approval. Once these proofs are approved, the compositor sends the mechanicals or the repro pages to the printing plant. Or they may be sent to the publisher, who gives them one more inspection and then sends them on to the printing plant. Alternatively, as was mentioned earlier, the compositor can make a negative of the pages and send only the negative to the printer. In this case, the mechanicals or repro pages are set aside in storage either at the compositor's shop or in the publisher's offices.

CRT Composition

CRT composition systems are so called because they make use of a cathode-ray tube, which is like a television picture tube but with much sharper resolution. CRT systems differ from phototypesetting systems in that there are no cutouts for individual letters. All the characters used in a CRT system exist simply as digital information stored within the system. Like a phototypesetter, the CRT system reads characters from a typesetting tape. But unlike the phototypesetter that then proceeds to find the characters on a disk or drum and then shines light through it, the CRT system translates the characters and electronically assembles them into a picture of the typeset lines and then projects that picture in the form of a stream of electrons at the cathode-ray tube's screen. The image of the typeset lines is displayed on the screen, from which it is transferred to photosensitive paper which becomes the repro.

The important advantage of CRT systems over photocomposition systems is the elimination of the turning disc or drum. Discs and drums can stick, jump, or get out of alignment. Thus, when material is being recomposed, errors can be introduced into typeset lines that previously had no errors. This means that any time new repro is made by a phototypesetter, all of the text in the new repro should be re-proofread. In a CRT system, generally only that portion of the new repro that represents new keyboarding needs to be proofread again. However, even in a CRT system, if there were any computer-generated errors in the original galleys or pages (caused, for instance, by a defect in the page-makeup program) that were fixed by hand or through some other kind of special intervention, these errors will reappear in the new repro. Also, if any aspect of the program has been altered between production phases (as between galleys and pages or between first pages and revised pages), another proofreading may be required to ensure that the program modifications are not creating new problems (such as breaking words differently at the end of lines).

Platemaking and Printing

There are three ways in which a printing plate can be made to transfer ink to paper. The plate can have raised surfaces which can be inked and pressed against paper. This is the method used in letterpress printing and in making proofs from hot-metal composition machines. Alternatively, the plate can be etched so that ink settles into recesses in the plate. Once again the ink is transferred as paper is pressed against the plate. This kind of printing is known as *gravure* printing. Finally, the plate may have neither raised nor lowered surfaces but simply specially treated areas to which ink will adhere. In this system, the ink on the plate is transferred first to a rubber roller and then from the roller onto paper. This process is known as *offset lithography*. It is the most common method for printing books and magazines, and it is described in more detail in this section.

Figure 13.1.   Side views of printing plates: (from left to right) letterpress, gravure, offset. Shaded areas represent ink.

Platemaking

The printing plates used in offset lithography are usually big enough to print several pages at one time. Depending on the size of the page and the kind of the printing that is being done, the printing plate will be large enough to hold all of the pages necessary to print a signature or half a signature. A *signature* is the term for the grouping of pages that are printed on a single sheet which is folded, trimmed, and bound together with other signatures. The number of pages on the printing plate is commonly 32, but 8, 16, 24, and other numbers are sometimes also possible.

There are a number of ways to make the printing plate. Most commonly, the process begins with the making of a full-size negative of the mechanical or repro page. The negative is opaque for all those portions of the page that are not to print and transparent for parts of the page that correspond to the image of the letters or other text elements that are meant to print. As we pointed out in the preceding section, this negative is sometimes made in the compositor's shop. If it is, whoever orders the negatives should be sure that they are ordered in the form in which the printer needs them.

A common way of ordering negatives is to specify that they be opaqued, right-reading, emulsion side down. *Opaqued* means that the negatives should be free of any area through which light could shine except for those elements which are supposed to print. The *emulsion side* is the side of the negative that has the photographically sensitive coating on it. *Right-reading, emulsion side down* means that the text of the negative can be read normally when the negative is positioned with its emulsion side down.

Once the individual page negatives have been made, they are taped down onto a sheet that is big enough to hold all of the negatives for the 16, 24, or 32 pages that will be printed from one plate. The sheet, called

These lines of type are right-reading.	These lines of type are wrong-reading.

a *flat,* is opaque, but it has cutouts that are big enough to allow light to shine through all of the transparent areas on the page negatives. The taping down of the negatives is referred to as the *imposition,* or as *imposing* or *stripping.* The imposition is done with extreme care, because it is from these finished flats that the printing plate will be made.

The negatives are imposed to the flat in a special sequence that is referred to as the *printing layout.* The purpose of the printing layout is to make it possible to take the sheet of paper that is printed from the plate, to fold it and trim off its edges, and to have all of the pages appear in the correct reading order.

A proof of this flat may be sent to the publisher. The proof is folded and trimmed so the publisher can see that the pages are in order and properly positioned in the flat.

In the final stage of the platemaking process, the negative images on the flat are photographically transferred to a grained sheet of metal that will act as the printing plate. In this final stage, for reasons that will become clear in the following paragraphs, the images of the letters and other text elements that have been transferred to the plate are treated in such a way that they repel water.

Bear in mind that there are other methods of making the printing plate. Some rely on making miniature negatives of each page; some avoid individual page negatives altogether. In each of these methods, however, the end product is a printing plate big enough to print multiple pages at the same time and treated to repel water from the letters and other text elements.

Printing

Offset printing is based on the fact that ink will not stick to a wet metal surface. During the printing process, the printing plate is constantly wetted. The water rolls off the images that were treated to repel water and to print; the water adheres to all of the background areas. After it is wetted, the plate is inked, and the ink sticks only to the dry spots. The plate, which is wrapped around a cylinder, is then rolled against another cylinder with a rubber coating. The ink is transferred to this second cylinder, called a *blanket cylinder,* so that the image is now wrong-reading. The *blanket cylinder* in turn is rolled against the paper and lays down a right-reading image.

The paper is fed through the press either as individual sheets that are the size of the printing plate or in a continuous roll, referred to as a *web.* In order for the paper to be printed on both sides, it either goes through the printing press once, being printed on both sides as it goes; or it goes through twice, being printed on one side at a time.

Printing on both sides at once is called *sheetwise* printing, and in this process, the sheet is pressed against two different blanket cylinders on its way through the press. Half of the pages in the signature (the ones that will appear on one side of the printed sheet) are on one of the plates, the other half of the pages (those that will appear on the other side of the printed sheet) are on the other plate. The sheets that come off this press are then ready for folding and trimming into a signature after just one pass through the press.

Printing one side at a time is called *work-and-turn* printing. In work-and-turn printing, the paper is pressed against just one plate as it goes through, but the plate holds all of the pages necessary for printing both the front and the back of the sheet. This is done by dividing the plate into two halves, one section for the front of a sheet, the other section for the back of a sheet. After these sheets come off the press, they are turned over and sent back through the press and past the same plate, but this time in such a way that the part of the paper that was printed from the section of the plate corresponding to the front of the sheet is now printed from the section of the plate corresponding to the back of the sheet, and vice versa. As these sheets come off the press, they are cut in half, each half having been printed with a front and a back.

One advantage of *work-and-turn* printing is that a smaller portion of the book is printed on each pass through the press. This often allows publishers to add or subtract half a signature from a printing without wasting paper.

Printing in Color

Pages printed in color are printed on presses with four different printing plates that are inked from four different ink supplies. Each plate lays down tiny dots of a single color: one lays down dots of yellow, another dots of greenish blue (called *cyan*), another dots of purplish red (called *magenta*), and another dots of black. All color printing is done by laying down combinations of these colors.

The four printing plates are made from four different negatives. In order for these negatives to be made, the colors in the original artwork need to be broken up electronically or through a series of filters into the four printing colors. This process is referred to as *color separation*, and it is usually done by the compositor or in a special color-separating shop. After the color separation, publishers usually receive four proofs, one for each of the negatives produced.

Binding

After the sheets have been printed they are sent through another set of machines that fold the sheets into signatures and trim the sheets down to the size in which they will be bound. Stacks of folded and trimmed signatures are then loaded onto a gathering machine which can take one copy of a signature from each stack and assemble the picked-up signatures into new stacks, each new stack corresponding to an individual book. These gathered signatures are now ready for binding. There are many different methods of binding books. The process described first is *case binding,* which is the method used for most trade books.

Case Binding

The pages within each signature in a casebound book are first sewn together through the folds, and then each signature is sewn to the next signature. This kind of sewing is done by machine and is referred to as *Smythe sewing.* After the signatures have been sewn together, the end sheets, which are sheets of heavier paper, are glued on, and a coat of glue is applied to the spine. A piece of heavy gauze that is wider than the spine is then glued to the spine, and a piece of heavy paper that is the width of the spine is glued over the gauze. At this point, the bound pages have been sewn and glued together, encased in end sheets, and a piece of heavy gauze extends from each edge of the spine.

In case binding, the book's cover, or case, is completely assembled before it is attached to the book. The case itself is made of a back board, a front board, and a backstrip running up the spine, all usually in the form of laminated cardboard. The boards are positioned on and glued to the cover cloth, which is folded over the boards to cover their edges.

The completed case is then attached to the pages by first giving the endpapers a coat of glue and then folding the case around the pages and squeezing the book tight. The ends of the piece of heavy gauze that were extending from the edge of the spine are thus effectively glued between the endpapers and the front and back boards and function as hinges for the covers.

Alternative Binding Methods

Some of the other ways of binding books or other publications include perfect binding, saddle wiring or saddle stitching, side wiring or side stitching, and loose-leaf binding.

Perfect binding *Perfect binding* is a binding method in which the signatures are trimmed in such a way that the area of the page that includes the fold is cut off after the signatures have been collated. The book at this point is, then, simply a stack of separate pages. The pages are held together tightly and the trimmed spine is roughed up and coated with flexible glue. A paper cover is then wrapped around the book. This type of binding is most common for paperback books, but it is also used for catalogs, directories, and some magazines.

Saddle wiring and side wiring *Saddle wiring* and *side wiring* are binding methods that make use of metal staples. In saddle wiring, the staples (usually two or three) are run through the pages from the outside to the inside directly at the fold. In side wiring, the signatures are trimmed in the same way as they are for perfect binding, and the staples go through the pages from side to side. In *saddle stitching* and *side stitching,* thread replaces the staples. These methods are used for small publications, such as pamphlets and magazines.

One important difference between publications with saddle wiring and those with side wiring is that the publication with saddle wiring will always be left with a rounded spine and with staples exposed along the fold of the cover and between the two middle pages. The publication with side wiring has a squared-off spine and hence a separate cover can be put over it and glued on to cover the staples.

Loose-leaf binding *Loose-leaf binding* refers to a style of binding in which pages are trimmed on all four sides, as in perfect binding, and then have holes punched or drilled through them in the inside margin. The pages are then held together by a metal or plastic spiral or by plastic fasteners.

Glossary

This glossary is intended primarily to provide brief definitions of words used in this book that may be unfamiliar or whose meaning may be unclear to readers. In addition, the glossary contains entries for a few words relating to style, editing, or production that are not used elsewhere in this book but that are sufficiently common that readers of this book may encounter them. Most potentially confusing words relating to style, editing, and production that are used in definitions in this glossary are also entered and defined; however, no glossary of this size can be self-contained, and readers may well need to consult a regular dictionary in order to understand fully some definitions in this glossary. For readers who desire a more extensive glossary of terms relating to book production, the section on Production, Design, and Printing in the Bibliography that follows includes entries for a number of book-length glossaries.

AA—see AUTHOR'S ALTERATION

absolute phrase   A phrase that stands apart from and has no syntactical relation to other elements of the sentence. An absolute phrase usually consists of a noun or pronoun and a participle, as in "*Our business being concluded,* we adjourned for refreshments." It may also be a prepositional phrase, as in "*In fact,* we had more than enough room," or a verbal phrase, as in "*Generally speaking,* the summers are quite hot."

accent   A mark (as ´, `, or ^) used in writing or printing to indicate a specific sound value, stress, or pitch, to distinguish words otherwise identically spelled, or to indicate that an ordinarily mute vowel should be pronounced.

acronym   A word (as *radar* or *scuba*) formed from the initial letter or letters of each of the major parts of a compound term.

adjective   A word typically used to modify a noun.

adverb   A word typically used to modify a verb, an adjective, or another adverb.

adverbial clause   A subordinate clause that modifies a verb, an adjective, or an adverb, as in "*If the weather is good,* we'll go on a picnic."

adverbial phrase   A phrase that modifies a verb, an adjective, or an adverb, as in "*In 1919,* his family left Russia and moved to this country," and "We were eager *to start the game.*"

affix   One or more letters occurring as a bound form attached to the be-ginning or end of a word, base, or phrase and serving to produce a derivative word (as in develop*ment*) or inflectional form (as in jump*ed*).

alphabet length   The total width of the 26 lowercase unspaced letters in a particular font. The alphabet length is usually given in points and is used as an indicator of the relative width of the typeface.

appendix   Supplementary material (as tables, charts, documents, etc.) usually placed at the end of a piece of writing.

appositive   A noun or its equivalent that is adjacent to another noun which it identifies, explains, or renames. An appositive can be restric-tive, as in "My cousin *Bill* visited us," or nonrestrictive, as in "Bill, my *cousin,* came to visit us."

Arabic numeral *or* **Arabic number**   One of the number symbols 0, 1, 2, 3, 4, 5, 6, 7, 8, 9.—compare ROMAN NUMERAL

array   A number of mathematical elements arranged in rows and columns.

article   Any of a small set of words (as *a, an,* and *the*) used with nouns to limit or give definiteness to the application.

artwork   Material (as a drawing or photograph) prepared for reproduc-tion in printed matter.

ascender   **1**   The part of a lowercase letter (as *d, f,* and *k*) that rises above the x height of the letter.   **2**   A lowercase character that has an as-cender.—compare DESCENDER

ascender height   The height of the highest ascender in a typeface.

atomic number   A number that indicates the number of protons in the nucleus which in a neutral atom equals the number of electrons out-side the nucleus.

attributive   An adjective or adjective equivalent that immediately pre-cedes the noun it modifies.

author's alteration   An alteration made to typeset copy (as at the galley or page-proof stage) that is not caused by a printer's error.—called also *AA;* compare PRINTER'S ERROR

backbone—see SPINE

back margin   The inside margin of a page.

back matter   Matter (as a bibliography or index) that follows the main text of a book.

back strip   A paper strip that is glued to a piece of binding cloth to form the spine in a case-bound book.

bad break   **1**   The dividing of a word at the end of a line at an incorrect place within the word.   **2**   The dividing of text between pages in a way that leaves a widow at the top of one page or not enough copy at the bottom of another.

base line   An imaginary line on which the body of a typeset letter rests.

bibliography   A list of works referred to in a text or consulted by the author in its production.

binary number   A number in a system of numbers having 2 as its base and consisting of the digits 0 and 1.

binomial nomenclature   A system of naming plants and animals in which each species receives a name of two terms of which the first identifies the genus to which it belongs and the second the species itself. Both terms are New Latin words and are italicized. The genus name is capitalized, while the species name is lowercased. In this system, for example, the binominal for the leopard is *Felis pardus*.

blanket   A rubber sheet in an offset press that receives the inked impression from the printing plate and transfers it to the surface being printed.

blanket cylinder   The cylinder of an offset press that carries the rubber blanket.

blind carbon copy   A carbon copy of a letter that is sent to someone other than the addressee and without the knowledge of the addressee. On such a copy the abbreviation "bcc" is added, followed by a colon and the initials of the recipient.

block quotation—see EXTRACT

board   The stiff foundation piece for the side of a book cover.

body   The vertical space that is occupied by a line of type in a given font. The body of a given font is measured from the top of the tallest ascender to the bottom of the deepest descender; however, a line of type can be set on a body that is larger than that actually occupied by the font in order to give the effect of leading between successive lines of type. The 10-point type in this book has a 10-point body, but it is set on an 11-point body.

body copy   The text of a page as opposed to the headings.

boldface   1 A heavy-faced type. **2** Printing in boldface.—compare LIGHTFACE

bound form   A combination of letters always occurring in combination with a word or with another bound form (as -*metry* in *telemetry*, *un*- in *unknown*, and -*er* in *speaker*).

bracketed serif   A serif that is joined to the stroke with a curved line.

brand name   A name that is given by a manufacturer or merchant to an article or service to distinguish it as produced or sold by him and that may be used and protected as a trademark.—called also TRADE NAME

broadside cut   An illustration or table laid on its side to fit the page, the left side being at the bottom of the page.

built-up fraction   A fraction whose numbers are set in the same point size as the surrounding text and occupy more than one line of vertical space. The fraction $\frac{1}{2}$ is a built-up fraction; the fractions $\frac{1}{2}$, ½, and 1/2 are not.—compare CASE FRACTION

camera-ready   Ready to be photographed for platemaking.

cap   A capital letter.

cap height   The height of a capital letter in a typeface.

capitals and small capitals   Two sizes of capital letters used together. The larger capital letters are the capital letters ordinarily used with the font; the smaller capital letters replace ordinarily lowercase letters and are usually the height of or slightly taller than the x height of the font.

caption   1 The heading especially of an article or document. **2** The identification or explanatory comment accompanying a pictorial illustration.

cardinal number   A number (as 1, 5, 15) that is used in counting and that indicates how many elements there are in an assemblage.—compare ORDINAL NUMBER

caret   A wedge-shaped mark made on written or printed matter to indicate the place where something is to be inserted.

case   1   A shallow tray divided into boxes for holding printing type.   **2**   A book cover that is made complete before it is affixed to a book.

case binding   Binding in which sewn signatures with end sheets glued on are fastened to a cover with gauze and glue.

case fraction   A simple fraction whose numbers are set one above the other in smaller type so as to be contained in one line of type. The term *case fraction* can refer to a fraction that takes the form $\frac{1}{2}$ or ½; however, some people use *case fraction* to refer only to a fraction that takes the form $\frac{1}{2}$. The term *piece fraction* is also used to describe both forms of fractions; however, some people use *piece fraction* to refer only to a fraction that takes the form ½.—compare BUILT-UP FRACTION

castoff   1   The process of calculating the number of characters in a given manuscript in order to determine the number of pages it will require when printed.   **2**   The result of making a castoff.

catalyst   A substance (as an enzyme) that initiates a chemical reaction and enables it to proceed under different conditions than otherwise possible.

character   A letter, symbol, numeral, or mark of punctuation. For some purposes, the spaces between words are also considered characters.

circle graph—see PIE CHART

citation, legal   1   The citing of a previously settled case at law.   **2**   The formal caption by which such a case is designated.

classical name   A proper name associated with ancient Greece or Rome (as *Hercules, Zeus, Virgil, Jupiter*).

clause   A group of words containing a subject and predicate and functioning as part of a sentence.

close punctuation   A pattern of punctuation that makes liberal use of punctuation marks, often including one wherever the grammatical structure of the sentence will allow it.—compare OPEN PUNCTUATION

code   A combination of letters, numbers, and symbols used as instructions for a typesetting system.

collective noun   A noun denoting a number of beings or things considered as one group or whole (as *family* or *flock*).

color separation   The isolation on separate photographic negatives by the use of filters and scanners of the parts of full-color artwork that are to be printed in given colors.

combining form   A word element that is used only to form compounds or derivatives and is not a prefix or suffix (as *mini-* in *minibike* and *-graphy* in *biography*).

comma fault   The misuse of a comma between coordinate main clauses not connected by a conjunction.—called also COMMA SPLICE

comma splice—see COMMA FAULT

common noun   A noun that may occur with limiting modifiers (as *a* or *an*, *some*, *every*, and *my*) and that denotes any one of a class of beings or things (as *child*, *cat*, or *toaster*).

complement   A word or word group that completes the meaning of a subject, an object, or a verb.

complex sentence   A sentence consisting of a main clause and one or more subordinate clauses.

complimentary close   The words (as *sincerely yours*) that conventionally come immediately before the signature of a letter and express the sender's regard for the receiver.

compose   To produce by composition.

composition   The production of type or typographic characters arranged for printing.

compositor   A person who sets type.

compound-complex sentence   A sentence having two or more main clauses and one or more subordinate clauses.

compound predicate   A predicate consisting of two or more verbs and often their associated objects and modifiers.

compound sentence   A sentence having two or more main clauses.

computer language   A system of signs and symbols for programming and interacting with a computer.

condensed *of a typeface* Having letters that are narrower than those of a typeface not so characterized.—compare EXPANDED

conjunction A word that joins together sentences, clauses, phrases, or words.

conjunctive adverb An adverb that relates and connects main clauses and modifies the whole sentence or the clause in which it occurs (as *accordingly, however, therefore,* and *thus*).

continuous-tone *of a piece of artwork* Having gradations of tone from dark to light.

contraction A word form produced by joining two or more words and replacing omitted letters in one or more of them with an apostrophe.

coordinating conjunction A conjunction that connects words, phrases, or clauses of equal grammatical rank (as *and, but, or, for, nor, so*).

copy Matter that is to be set or photographed for printing.

copyediting The usually last editing of a manuscript before it is set in type.

copyright page A page of a book bearing the copyright notice, including the proprietor's name and the date of copyright.

correlative conjunction A conjunction consisting of paired elements (as *both . . . and, either . . . neither,* and *not only . . . but also*) used to connect words, phrases, or clauses.

counter An area within a letter that is wholly or partly enclosed by strokes.

credit line A line, note, or name that acknowledges the source of an item (as an illustration).

cropping The cutting away of unwanted background detail in a photograph to give a new focus to the picture.

cross-reference A notation or direction at one place (as in a book, glossary, or filing system) to pertinent information at another place.

CRT composition Typesetting in which type images are electronically produced and displayed on a cathode-ray tube's screen from which they are transferred to film or photosensitive paper.

cut-in heading *or* **cut-in head**   A heading set on a horizontal space that cuts across the full width of a table and is often set off by rules.—called also *table spanner*

cyan   A greenish blue color.—used in photography and color printing of one of the primary colors

decked heads   A spanner head and its subordinate column heads.

declination   Angular distance north or south from the celestial equator given in degrees, minutes, and seconds of arc.

dependent clause—see SUBORDINATE CLAUSE

descender   **1** The part of a lowercase letter that descends below the base line.   **2** A lowercase character that has a descender.—compare ASCENDER

designer   A person who makes decisions about typography, layout, and the physical appearance of a publication.

determinant   A square array of numbers bordered on either side by a straight line whose value is the algebraic sum of all the products that can be formed by taking as factors one element from each row and column such that no two elements in a given product are in the same row or column and giving the products a sign by rule.

diacritic   A mark used with a letter or group of letters to indicate a sound value different from that given the unmarked or otherwise marked letter or group of letters.

diagonal—see VIRGULE

dingbat   A typographical symbol or ornament.

direct address   A word or phrase that indicates the person, group, or thing addressed, as in "When are you taking your vacation, *Bob?*"

direct discourse   Discourse consisting of or quoting the exact words of a speaker or writer. —compare INDIRECT DISCOURSE

direct question   A question consisting of or quoting the exact words of a speaker or writer, as in "The mover asked, 'Where do you want the sofa put?'"—compare INDIRECT QUESTION

display   Copy (as a heading) that is set apart from the text in larger type.

dot matrix   A pattern of dots in a grid from which characters can be formed (as in printing).

double hyphen   An editorial mark that is made by adding a second hyphen below a typewritten or handwritten hyphen and is used to make it clear to the typesetter that a hyphen is being asked for.

drop   The vertical distance (as on a page) from one typographic or design element to another.

drop folio   A page number that is located at the bottom of a page.

dummy   1   A set of heavy paper boards made up to show the size, shape, and general style of a planned publication, including the positions of text, artwork and captions.   **2**   A bound, unprinted, or only partially printed sample of a planned publication to show its size, shape, and general appearance.

elite   A typewriter type providing 12 characters to the linear inch and 6 lines to the vertical inch. —compare PICA

elliptical construction   A construction in which words are omitted but understood because they appear in a nearby construction.

em dash   A dash that is as wide as the point size of the type.

em quad—see EM SPACE

em space   A space as wide as the point size of the type.—called also *em quad*

en dash   A dash that is shorter than the em dash but slightly longer than the hyphen and is used for the hyphen in some situations.

endnote   A note placed at the end of a text (as of an article or chapter).

en quad—see EN SPACE

en space   A space that is one-half of an em space.—called also *en quad*

epigraph   A quotation set at the beginning of a literary work or a division of it to suggest its theme.

expanded   *of a typeface* Having letters that are wider than those of a typeface not so characterized.—called also *extended;* compare CONDENSED

exponent   A symbol written above and to the right of a mathematical expression to indicate the operation of raising to a power.

extended—see EXPANDED

extract   A long quotation that is set off from the text and set in type that is slightly smaller than that of the text.—called also *block quotation*

final proof   A proof made by the compositor from the film, usually a negative, that he will send to the printer to make printing plates from.

five-em space—see THIN SPACE

five-to-the-em space—see THIN SPACE

flat   An opaque sheet to which negatives are stripped in correct order and orientation and from which a printing plate is made.

flowchart   A diagram that shows step-by-step progression through a procedure or system.

flush-and-hang indention—see HANGING INDENTION

flush left   *of a column or page of type*   Aligned vertically along the left margin.

flush right   *of a column or page of type*   Aligned vertically along the right margin.

folded and gathered sheets   Sheets that have been folded into signatures and collected into the correct order for binding.

folio   A page number.

font   An assortment or set of type all of one size and style.

foot margin   The bottom margin of a page.

footnote   A note of reference, explanation, or comment usually placed below the text on a printed page.

four-em space—see THIN SPACE

four-to-the-em space—see THIN SPACE

front margin   The outside margin of a page.

front matter Matter (as an introduction or preface) that precedes the main text of a book.

full measure The full width of the type page or column.

galley A proof of typeset material especially in a single column before being made into pages.

generic term A name common to a whole group or class (as *lake, river, avenue, bridge*).

genus name The name of a biological classification ranking between the family and the species and designated by a Latin capitalized singular noun which is italicized.

grammar 1 The study of the classes of words, their inflections, and their functions and relations in the sentence. **2** The facts of language with which grammar deals.

gravure printing Printing done from a plate in which the image is sunk below the surface in ink-filled depressions.

gutter A white space formed by the adjoining inside margins of two facing pages.

hair space A space that is one-fifth of an em, one-sixth of an em, or one-half point in width.—compare THIN SPACE

halftone An image that represents continuous-tone artwork (as a photograph) through the use of a pattern of dots of varying size.

H & J Hyphenation and justification.

hanging indention Indention of all the lines of a passage or index except the first line, which is set flush with the left-hand margin. —called also *flush-and-hang indention*

head A word or series of words often in larger letters placed at the beginning of a passage or at the top of a page or column in order to introduce or categorize.—called also *heading*

heading—see HEAD

headline 1 A head of a newspaper story or article usually printed in large type and giving the gist of the story or article. **2** Words set at the head of a passage or page to introduce or categorize.

head margin   The top margin of a page.

headnote   A note of comment or explanation that prefaces a text.

hot-metal composition   The setting of cast metal type set either by hand or by machine.

hyphenate   **1**   To connect (as two words) with a hyphen.   **2**   To divide (as a word at the end of a line of print) with a hyphen.

identification line   The line at the end of a business letter on which the initials of the writer and typist appear.

impose   To arrange (as pages) in the proper order and orientation for printing.

imposition   The order or arrangement of imposed pages.

indefinite pronoun   A pronoun designating an unidentified person or thing (as *anyone, something, everybody*).

independent clause—see MAIN CLAUSE

index   A list of items (as topics or names) treated in a printed work that gives for each item the page number where it may be found.

indirect discourse   Discourse that states what someone said or wrote but not in the exact words. —compare DIRECT DISCOURSE

indirect question   A statement reporting what someone has asked but not in the exact words, as in "The mover asked where we wanted the sofa put." —compare DIRECT QUESTION

inferior   Relating to or being a subscript.—compare SUPERIOR

infinitive   A verb form often used with *to* that serves as a noun or as a modifier and at the same time may take objects and have adverbial modifiers. In the sentence "We have nothing to do," *to do* is an infinitive.

inflected form   A variant of a word that indicates a distinction in its meaning or use. Inflection in English indicates such things as number (*goose* or *geese*), case (as *we* or *us*), tense (as *drive* or *drove* and *driving* or *driven*), and comparison (as *happier* or *happiest*).

interjection   A short utterance usually lacking grammatical connection and expressing an emotion.

interpolation   A word or words inserted into a text or a quotation and enclosed in square brackets.

interrogative pronoun   A pronoun (as *who, which,* and *what*) used to introduce a question.

ion   An atom or group of atoms that carries a positive or negative charge as a result of having lost or gained one or more electrons.

isotope   Any of two or more species of atoms of a chemical element with the same atomic number but with differing atomic mass or mass number and different physical properties.

italic   Of, relating to, or being a type style with characters that slant upward to the right, as in *"these words are italic."*—compare ROMAN

justify   To space a line of type so that it comes out flush right and left.

keyboard   **1**   To operate a machine (as for typesetting) by means of a keyboard.   **2**   To capture or set (as data or text) by means of a keyboard.

key word   A significant word from a text that is used as an index to its content.

layout   The final arrangement of matter to be reproduced especially by printing.

leaders   Dots or sometimes hyphens (as in a table or index) used to lead the eye horizontally across a space to the right word or number.

leading   Extra space inserted between lines of type.

legend   **1** An explanatory list of the symbols used on a map or chart or in an illustration.   **2** Explanatory remarks that accompany an illustration.

letterpress   The process of printing from an inked, raised surface, especially when the paper is impressed directly upon the surface.

letterspacing   Insertion of space between the letters of a word.

ligature   A printed character (as *fi*) consisting of two or more letters or characters joined together.

lightface   **1**   A typeface having comparatively light thin lines.   **2**   Printing in lightface.—compare BOLDFACE

line drawing   A drawing made with a pen or other pointed instrument in solid lines or solid masses.

line graph   A graph in which points representing values of a variable for values of an independent variable are connected by a line.

Linotype   A trademark used for a keyboard-operated typesetting machine that uses circulating matrices and produces each line of type in the form of a solid metal slug.

locator   Information provided with a reference or index entry that gives the location (as the page, column, paragraph, verse, or line) of the cited material or indexed term.

loose-leaf binding   A style of binding in which pages are trimmed and then have holes punched or drilled through them. The pages are held together by a metal or plastic spiral or by plastic fasteners.

lowercase   Small-letter type used in printing.—compare UPPERCASE

machine-readable   Directly usable by a computer.

magenta   A deep purplish red.—used in photography and color printing of one of the primary colors.

main clause   A clause that can stand independently as a complete statement, as in "While we were eating, *the doorbell rang*."—called also *independent clause* and *principal clause*.

makeup   The arranging of typeset matter, including running heads and illustrations, into pages.

margin   The unprinted area of a page.

margin cut   A small illustration set within a side margin next to the text.

markup   The process of marking on a manuscript all the directions for typesetting.

master proof   A set of proofs bearing all corrections and alterations of both the printer and author.

masthead   **1** The printed matter in a newspaper or periodical that gives the title and pertinent details of ownership, advertising rates, and subscription rates. **2** The name of a publication displayed at the top of the first page.

matrix   1 The mold in which hot-metal letters are cast in Linotype machines. **2** A rectangular array of mathematical elements that can be combined to form sums and products with similar arrays having an appropriate number of rows and columns.

mechanical A board on which a page is formatted with all the type and artwork from proofs carefully pasted in place. It is from a mechanical that the negative is made.

microfiche A sheet of microfilm containing rows of microimages of pages of printed matter.

microfilm A film bearing a photographic record on a reduced scale.

microform   1 A process for reproducing printed matter in a much reduced size. **2** Matter reproduced by microform. **3** a photographic copy in which graphic matter is reduced in size (as on microfilm).

Monotype   —A trademark used for a keyboard-operated typesetting machine that casts and sets type in separate characters.

New Latin Latin as used since the end of the medieval period, especially in scientific description and classification.

nonrestrictive Of, relating to, or being a descriptive clause or phrase that adds information to a sentence but is so loosely attached to the main clause as not to be essential. Such a clause or phrase is marked off by commas, as in "The opera, which was sung in Italian, was about bohemians in Paris," and "They decided, much to my chagrin, to sell the house to someone else."—compare RESTRICTIVE

noun A word that is the name of a person, place, or thing.

nut An en space.

object   1 A noun or noun equivalent denoting someone or something that the action of a verb is directed toward. **2** A noun or noun equivalent in a prepositional phrase.

oblique—see VIRGULE

offset printing A printing process in which an inked impression from a plate is first made on a rubber-blanketed cylinder and then transferred to paper.

opaque To paint over any translucent areas on a negative that are not wanted on the printing plate.

open compound   A compound word whose elements are separated by a space (as *general delivery*).—compare SOLID COMPOUND

open punctuation   A pattern of punctuation that makes sparing use of punctuation marks, usually only to separate main clauses and to prevent misreading.—compare CLOSE PUNCTUATION

ordinal number   A number designating the place (as first, second, or third) occupied by an item in an ordered sequence.—compare CARDINAL NUMBER

overbar   A horizontal line that forms the extension of a radical sign over a mathematical expression from which a root is to be extracted.

oxidation number   The degree of or potential for oxidation of an element or atom that is usually expressed as a positive or negative number representing the ionic or effective charge.

page proof   A proof of typeset material that has been made up into a page.

parallelism   A similarity of grammatical form of coordinated word groups especially for rhetorical effect or rhythm.

participle   An inflected form of a verb (as *woven* or *steaming*) having the characteristics of both verb and adjective.

particle   **1**   A unit of speech expressing some general aspect of meaning or some connective or limiting relation and including the articles, most prepositions and conjunctions, and some interjections and adverbs.   **2**   An element (as a prefix or suffix) that resembles a word but that is used only in composition (as *un-* in *unfair* and *-ward* in *backward*).

PE—see PRINTER'S ERROR

perfect binding   A binding process in which collated signatures are trimmed at the back and a glue applied to the cut and roughened edges. A usually paper cover is then wrapped around the book.

personification   Representation of a thing or an abstract idea as a person or by the human form.

phoneme   One of the set of the smallest units of speech that serve to distinguish one utterance from another. They are often set off by virgules. For example, the /p/ of *pat* and the /f/ of *fat* are two different phonemes in English.

photocomposition   The setting of type directly on film or photosensitive paper for reproduction.

photocopy   A photographic reproduction of graphic matter.

phrase   A group of two or more grammatically related words that form a sense unit.

pica   1   12-point type.   **2**   A unit of about ⅙ of an inch used in measuring typographical material.   **3**   A typewriter type providing 10 characters to the linear inch and 6 lines to the vertical inch. —compare ELITE

piece fraction—see CASE FRACTION

pie chart   A circular chart cut by radii into segments illustrating relative magnitudes or frequencies. —called also *circle graph*

platemaking   The making of printing plates for offset printing.

point   A unit of typographical measurement that is 1/12 of a pica (about 1/72 of an inch) and that is used especially in measuring the vertical size of type or the amount of space between lines of type.

possessive case   The grammatical case that denotes possession or an analogous relationship, as in "The *soldier's* weapon," and "an *hour's* time."

possessive pronoun   A pronoun that derives from a personal pronoun and denotes possession or an analogous relationship, as in "That pen is *mine*."

predicate   The part of a sentence or clause that expresses what is said of the subject.

predicate adjective   An adjective that follows a linking verb and modifies or refers to the subject, as in "The author is *unknown*."

predicate nominative   A noun or pronoun that follows a linking verb and refers to the subject, as in "He is the *leader*."

predicate noun   A noun that follows a linking verb and refers to the subject, as in "The fire fighter was a *hero*."

prefix   An affix occurring at the beginning of a word.

preposition   A word that combines with a noun or pronoun to form a phrase.

prepress   The process by which individual page negatives are transferred into a printing plate.

principal clause—see MAIN CLAUSE

printer's error   An error in typeset copy (as errors caused by incorrect keyboarding or a program malfunction) that is the responsibility of the typesetter. —called also *PE;* compare AUTHOR'S ALTERATION

production   The processes by which a publication is produced. These extend from the completion of the manuscript to the making of the plates from which the pages will be printed.

pronoun   A word that is used as a substitute for a noun.

proof   A copy (as of typeset text) made for examination or correction.

proofreader   A person who reads and marks corrections in typeset material and checks corrected proofs to ensure that all corrections have been made.

proper adjective   An adjective formed from a proper noun. Such adjectives are capitalized, as in "*Mexican* food."

proper noun *or* **proper name**   A noun that names a particular person, place, or thing and is capitalized (as *Joshua, Venice,* and *United Nations*).

public domain   The realm embracing property rights that belong to the community at large, are unprotected by copyright or patent, and are subject to appropriation by anyone.

quad   A space in typesetting that is one en or more in width.

ragged left   A column or page of type set with the left side unjustified.

ragged right   A column or page of type set with the right side unjustified.

recto   A right-hand page. —compare VERSO

reduplication   Repetition of a word part occurring usually at the beginning of a word and often accompanied by change of the vowel (as *razzle-dazzle* and *wishy-washy*).

reference mark   A conventional symbol (as an asterisk or a dagger) or a superior number or letter placed in a text for directing attention to a footnote.

relative pronoun   A pronoun (as *who, which,* and *that*) that introduces a subordinate clause, as in "The parade, *which* was due to begin at noon, was delayed."

repro *or* **reproduction proof**   A high-quality, camera-ready, positive print from which a negative is made for making printing plates.

restrictive   Of, relating to, or being a clause or phrase that is essential to the meaning of a sentence because it limits the word it modifies, as in, "The book *that you ordered* is out of print," and "That house *on the corner* is the one we want to buy."—compare NONRESTRICTIVE

revised galley   A galley having the corrections and alterations marked on a previous galley. A revised galley is requested usually when the revisions have been extensive.

right ascension   The arc of the celestial equator between the vernal equinox and the point where the hour circle through the given body intersects the equator that is commonly reckoned in hours, minutes, and seconds.

right-reading   Having the correct right-to-left orientation.—compare WRONG-READING

river   An irregular streak running through several lines of close-set printed matter and caused by a series of wide spaces that appear to form a continuous line.

roman   Of or relating to a type style with upright characters.—compare ITALIC

Roman numeral   A numeral (as I, V, X, C, M) in a system of notation that is based on the ancient Roman system and used in certain formal contexts (as in numbering acts and scenes in a play). —compare ARABIC NUMERAL

rule   **1** A metal strip with a type-high face that prints a linear design. **2** A line or linear design produced by or as if by such a strip.

runaround   Type set in lines shorter than full measure in order to fit around an illustration.

run back   To transfer text from the beginning of one line to the end of the preceding line.

run down   To transfer text from the end of one line to the beginning of the following line.

run in   To make (typeset matter) continuous without a paragraph or other break.

running head   A headline repeated on consecutive pages.

run-on sentence   A sentence containing two or more main clauses joined with no punctuation or conjunction or with only a comma between them.

runover   Typeset material that exceeds the space estimated or allotted.

saddle-stitched—see SADDLE-WIRED

saddle-wired   Secured by a stitch made by driving wire staples through the center fold and clinching them on the inside. This kind of binding is also referred to as being *saddle-stitched,* especially when thread is substituted for the staples. —compare SIDE-STITCHED

salutation   The word or phrase of greeting (as *Gentlemen* or *Dear Madam*) that conventionally comes immediately before the body of a letter.

sans serif   A letter or typeface with no serifs. —see SERIF

self-evident compound   A compound word or word group whose meaning can be readily understood from the meanings of its elements and thus does not need definition (as *nonathlete* and *prearrange*).

sentence   A grammatically self-contained speech unit that expresses an assertion, a question, a command, a wish, or an exclamation.

sentence fragment   A word, phrase, or clause that usually has in speech the intonation of a sentence but lacks the grammatically self-contained structure usually found in the sentences of formal composition.

serial comma   The final comma before the conjunction in a series. Its use is optional, but omitting it can sometimes result in ambiguity.

serif   Any of the short lines stemming from and at an angle to the upper and lower ends of the strokes of a letter.

service mark   A mark or device used to identify a service (as transportation or insurance) offered to customers. —compare TRADEMARK

sheet-fed press   A press that prints individual sheets of paper—compare WEB PRESS

sheetwise   Relating to a method of printing in which the front of a sheet is printed from one plate and the back from another.

shilling mark—see VIRGULE

side-stitched   Secured by passing a wire or thread from side to side through a complete book or magazine before covering.—called also *side-wired;* compare SADDLE-WIRED

side-wired—see SIDE-STITCHED

signature   A printed sheet with usually 8, 16, 24, or 32 pages, which is folded, trimmed, and bound with other signatures.

sinkage   The distance from the top of the top line on a text page to the first line of text.

slant—see VIRGULE

slash—see VIRGULE

slash mark—see VIRGULE

small capital   A letter having the form of but smaller than a capital letter.

Smyth sewing   A method of attaching the signatures of books by means of threads passed through the folds.

software   The entire set of programs, procedures, and related documentation associated with a computer system.

solid compound   A compound word whose elements are joined without a hyphen (as *waterproof*).—compare OPEN COMPOUND

solidus—see VIRGULE

solidus fraction   A fraction whose numbers are separated by a solidus.

source note   A note set below or sometimes above a table that gives the source of the information in the table.

spanner head   A head which is set on top and spans the width of two or more subordinate column heads.

species name   The name of the biological classification ranking immediately below the genus or subgenus and designated by a Latin lowercased italicized noun or adjective agreeing grammatically with the genus name.

spine   The back of a bound book that connects the front and back covers.—called also *backbone*

spiral binding   Binding in which a continuous spiral wire or plastic strip is passed through holes at the gutter margin.

step-and-repeat   Of, relating to, or employing a method in which successive exposures of a single image are made on a printing surface.

stet   An editorial mark, meaning "let it stand," that is used to indicate that words crossed out in copy or proof are to be restored. This is written in the margin and heavy dots are placed under the affected words.

strip   To arrange (as negatives) in proper position on a flat.

stroke   One of the lines of a letter of the alphabet.

stub   A vertical column at the left edge of a table usually containing items of subject matter that are treated in vertical columns to its right.

stubhead   A heading over the stub of a table.

style sheet   A compilation of detailed style rules (as in regard to punctuation, hyphenation, and abbreviations) to be followed consistently throughout a manuscript.

subheading   A heading of a subdivision (as in an outline or index).

subject   A noun or noun equivalent about which something is stated by the predicate.

subordinate clause   A clause that is used as a noun, adjective, or adverb and cannot stand independently as a complete statement.—called also *dependent clause*

subscript   A distinguishing symbol (as a letter or number) written immediately below or below and to the right or left of another character. —compare SUPERSCRIPT

suffix   An affix occurring at the end of a word.

superior   Relating to or being a superscript.—compare INFERIOR

superscript A distinguishing symbol (as a letter or number) written immediately above or above and to the right or left of another character.—compare SUBSCRIPT

syntax The way in which words are put together to form phrases, clauses, or sentences.

table spanner—see CUT-IN HEADING

taxonomic name The name of an organism as established by the system of binomial nomenclature.

tear sheet A page cut or torn from a publication.

tensor A generalized vector with more than three components.

text page—see TYPE PAGE

thick A thick stroke.

thick space A space that is one-third of an em. —called also *three-to-the-em space* or *three-em space*

thin A thin stroke.

thin space A space that is one-fourth of an em space but sometimes used to mean one-fifth of an em. —called also *four-to-the-em space, four-em space, five-to-the-em space,* or *five-em space;*—compare HAIR SPACE

three-em space—see THICK SPACE

three-to-the-em space—see THICK SPACE

title page A page of a book bearing the title and usually the names of the author and publisher and the place and sometimes the date of publication.

trademark A device (as a word) that points distinctly to the origin or ownership of merchandise to which it is applied and that is legally reserved to the exclusive use of the owner as maker or seller.—compare SERVICE MARK

trade name—see BRAND NAME

transposition sign A proofreader's mark that is a line curving over one element and under another to indicate transposition of characters, words, phrases, or sentences.

trigonometric function   A function (as the sine, cosine, tanget, cotangent, secant, or cosecant) of an arc or angle expressed in terms of the ratios of pairs of sides of a right-angled triangle.

trim marks   Marks placed on a page proof or page negative to show where the edge of the page will be after the printed signatures have been trimmed to their final size.

trim size   The actual size (as of a book page) after excess material required in production has been cut off.

type list   A list of all the words, numbers, and mathematical symbols that form the labels on the figures and that are going to be typeset rather than hand-lettered or applied.

typemark   To specify on the manuscript how type is to be set.

type page *or* **text page**   The area of a page that includes all of the copy measured from the ascender of the top line to the descender of the bottom line. The term *type page* is usually taken to include the running head and folio (but not a drop folio), but it is used by some to refer to just the text, excluding the running heads and folio. The term *text page* is usually synonymous with *type page;* however, some who use the term *type page* to refer to the area that includes the running heads and folios use the term *text page* to refer to the area that includes just the text.

typescript   A typewritten manuscript and especially one that is intended for use as printer's copy.

typesetter   **1** A person who sets type. **2** A device that produces the type from keyboarded instructions.

typography   The style, arrangement, and appearance of typeset matter.

underscore   A line drawn under a word or line especially for emphasis or to indicate intent to italicize.

unit   A variable measure usually ranging from $\frac{1}{10}$ to $\frac{1}{18}$ of an em that is used by composition equipment for measuring the width of letters and spaces.

uppercase   Capital-letter type used in printing.—compare LOWERCASE

valence   The degree of combining power of an element or radical as shown by the number of atomic weights of a univalent element (as hydrogen) with which the atomic weight of the element will combine or for which it can be substituted.

vector A quantity that has magnitude and direction and is commonly represented by a directed line segment whose length represents the magnitude.

verb A word that characteristically is the grammatical center of a predicate and expresses an act, occurrence, or mode of being.

verso A left-hand page.—compare RECTO.

vinculum A straight horizontal mark placed over two or more members of a compound mathematical expression and equivalent to parentheses or brackets about them.

virgule A slanted line / used chiefly to represent a word (as *or* or *per*) that is not written out, to separate or set off certain adjacent elements of text, and to set off phonemic transcriptions.—called also *diagonal, oblique, shilling mark, slant, slash, slash mark, solidus*

vocative Of, relating to, or being a word or word group that denotes the person or entity being addressed, as in "*Waiter,* we're ready to order."

web press A press that prints a continuous roll of paper.—compare SHEET-FED PRESS

widow A single short last line (as of a paragraph) separated from its related text and appearing at the top of a printed page or column.

word processing The production of typewritten documents (as business letters) with automated and usually computerized typing and text-editing equipment.

word processor A keyboard-operated terminal usually with a video display and a magnetic storage device for use in word processing.

work-and-turn printing Printing one side of a sheet, turning it over, and printing the other side. Two copies of the pages are produced when the sheet is cut in half.

wrong-reading Having a reversed right-to-left orientation.—compare RIGHT-READING

x height The height of a lowercase x used to represent the height of the main body of a lowercase letter.

Bibliography

This bibliography includes references to books on a variety of topics that are of interest to writers and editors. In order to help readers find references to books on a particular topic, the bibliography has been divided into nine sections under the following headings:

Copyright and Libel
Illustrations
Language and Editing
Production, Design, and Printing
Publishing
Reference Books
Secretarial Practice
Style Manuals
Word Processing

No list of this length can be comprehensive of all the valuable books in any of these categories, and some very good books have probably been omitted. It is also worth noting that some of the categories represent fields in which opinions can vary widely about quite basic issues, and the references in this bibliography are meant to reflect that diversity. For this reason, a reader who is coming to any of these topics for the first time is urged to consult more than one of the sources listed.

Copyright and Libel

Crawford, Tad. *Legal Guide for the Visual Artist*. New York: Hawthorn, 1980.

_____. *The Writer's Legal Guide*. New York: Hawthorn, 1979.

Johnston, Donald F. *Copyright Handbook*. 2d ed. New York: Bowker, 1982.

Latman, Alan. *The Copyright Law: Howell's Copyright Law Revised and the 1976 Act*. Washington, D.C.: Bureau of National Affairs, 1979.

Phelps, Robert H., and E. Douglas Hamilton. *Libel: Rights, Risks, Responsibilities*. Rev. ed. Mineola, New York: Dover, 1978.

Sack, Robert D. *Libel, Slander, and Related Problems*. New York: Practising Law Institute, 1980.

Seltzer, Leon E. *Exemptions and Fair Use in Copyright: The Exclusive Rights Tensions in the 1976 Copyright Act.* Cambridge, Mass.: Harvard Univ. Press, 1978.

Strong, William S. *The Copyright Book: A Practical Guide.* Cambridge, Mass.: MIT Press, 1981.

Illustrations

Evans, Hilary, et al. *The Picture Researcher's Handbook.* New York: Scribner, 1975.

Hill, Mary, and Wendell Cochran. *Into Print: A Practical Guide to Writing, Illustrating and Publishing.* Los Altos, Calif.: William Kaufmann, 1977.

Houp, Kenneth W., and T. E. Pearsall. *Reporting Technical Information.* 4th ed. New York: Macmillan, 1980.

Klemin, Diana. *The Illustrated Book: Its Art and Craft.* Greenwich, Conn.: Murton, 1983.

McDarrah, Fred W., ed. *Photography Market Place.* 2d ed. New York: Bowker, 1977.

———. *Stock Photo and Assignment Source Book: Where to Find Photographs Instantly.* New York: Bowker, 1977.

Quick, John. *Artists' and Illustrators' Encyclopedia.* 2d ed. New York: McGraw-Hill, 1977.

Ridgway, John Livesy. *Scientific Illustration.* Stanford, Calif.: Stanford Univ. Press, 1938.

Thomas, T. A. *Technical Illustration.* 3d ed. New York: McGraw-Hill, 1978.

White, Jan V. *The Graphic Idea Notebook.* New York: Watson-Guptill, 1980.

———. *Using Charts and Graphs.* New York: Bowker, 1984.

Zweifel, Frances W. *A Handbook of Biological Illustration.* Chicago: Univ. of Chicago Press, 1961.

Language and Editing

Business Communications

Barry, Robert E. *Business English for the Eighties.* 2d ed. Englewood Cliffs, N.J.: Prentice-Hall, 1985.

Brock, Luther A. *How to Communicate by Letter and Memo.* New York: McGraw-Hill, 1974.

Brown, Leland. *Effective Business Report Writing.* 4th ed. Englewood Cliffs, N.J.: Prentice-Hill, 1985.

Brusaw, Charles T., Gerald J. Alred, and Walter E. Oliu. *Handbook of Technical Writing.* 2d ed. New York: St. Martin's, 1982.

Ewing, David W. *Writing For Results in Business, Government, the Sciences, the Professions.* 2d ed. New York: Wiley, 1979.

Fallon, William K., ed. *Effective Communication on the Job.* 3d ed. New York: American Management Associations, 1981.

Gallagher, William J. *Writing the Business and Technical Report.* New York: Van Nostrand Reinhold, 1980.

Janis, J. Harold. *Writing and Communicating in Business.* 3d ed. New York: Macmillan, 1978.

_____. *Modern Business Language and Usage in Dictionary Form.* New York: Doubleday, 1984.

Keithley, Erwin, and Margaret H. Thompson. *English for Modern Business.* 4th ed. Homewood, Ill.: Richard D. Irwin, 1982.

Lewis, David V. *Secrets of Successful Writing, Speaking, and Listening.* New York: American Management Associations, 1982.

Poe, Roy W. *The McGraw-Hill Guide to Effective Business Reports.* New York: McGraw-Hill, 1982.

_____. *The McGraw-Hill Handbook of Business Letters.* New York: McGraw-Hill, 1983.

Poe, Roy W., and R. T. Fruehling. *Business Communication: A Problem-Solving Approach.* 2d ed. New York: McGraw-Hill, 1978.

Sigband, Norman B. *Communication for Management and Business.* 3d ed. Glenview, Ill.: Scott, Foresman, 1982.

Wolf, Morris P., and Shirley Kuiper. *Effective Communication in Business.* 8th ed. Cincinnati, Ohio: South-Western, 1984.

Editing and Proofreading

Beach, Mark, *Editing Your Newsletter.* 2d ed. New York: Van Nostrand Reinhold, 1982.

Bentley, Garth. *Editing the Company Publication.* Westport, Conn.: Greenwood, 1972.

Butcher, Judith. *Copy-Editing: The Cambridge Handbook.* 2d ed. New York: Cambridge Univ. Press, 1981.

DeBakey, Lois. *The Scientific Journal: Editorial Policies and Practices—Guidelines for Editors, Reviewers, and Authors.* St. Louis: C. V. Mosby, 1976.

Ferguson, Rowena. *Editing the Small Magazine.* 2d ed. New York: Columbia Univ. Press, 1976.

Garst, Robert E., and Theodore M. Bernstein. *Headlines and Deadlines: A Manual for Copy Editors.* 4th ed. New York: Columbia Univ. Press, 1982.

Gibson, Martin L. *Editing in the Electronic Era.* Ames, Iowa: Iowa State Univ. Press, 1979.

International Association of Business Communicators. *Without Bias: A Guidebook For Nondiscriminatory Communication.* 2d ed. New York: Wiley, 1982.

Judd, Karen. *Copyediting: A Practical Guide.* Los Altos, Calif.: William Kaufmann, 1982.

Kent, Ruth. *The Language of Journalism: A Glossary of Print-Communications Terms.* Kent, Ohio: Kent State Univ. Press. 1970.

McNaughton, Harry H. *Proofreading and Copyediting: A Practical Guide to Style for the 1970's.* Communications Arts Books. New York: Hastings House, 1973.

Miller, Casey, and Kate Swift. *The Handbook of Nonsexist Writing.* New York: Barnes & Noble, 1981.

Moore, Charles B., and William F. Blue, Jr. *Editing and Layout for the Company Editor.* Indianapolis, Ind.: Ink Art, 1979.

Nelson, Jerome L. *Libel: A Basic Program for Beginning Journalists.* Ames, Iowa: Iowa State Univ. Press, 1974.

O'Neil, Carol L., and Avima Ruder. *The Complete Guide to Editorial Freelancing.* 2d ed. New York: Barnes & Noble, 1984.

Plotnik, Arthur. *The Elements of Editing.* New York: Macmillan, 1982.

Grammar, Usage, and Composition

Bailey, Edward P., Jr., *Writing Clearly.* Columbus, Ohio: Charles E. Merrill, 1984.

Baker, Sheridan. *The Complete Stylist and Handbook.* 3d ed. New York: Harper & Row, 1984.

_____. *The Practical Stylist.* 5th ed. New York: Harper & Row, 1981.

Bernstein, Theodore M. *The Careful Writer: A Modern Guide to English Usage.* New York: Atheneum, 1977.

_____. *Dos, Don'ts & Maybes of English Usage.* New York: Times Books, 1977.

_____. *Miss Thistlebottom's Hobgoblins: The Careful Writer's Guide to the Taboos, Bugbears, and Outmoded Rules of English Usage.* New York: Simon & Schuster, 1984.

_____. *Watch Your Language.* New York: Atheneum, 1965.

Bremmer, John B. *Words on Words.* New York: Columbia Univ. Press, 1980.

Copperud, Roy H. *American Usage and Style: The Consensus.* New York: Van Nostrand Reinhold, 1980.

Curme, George Oliver. *A Grammar of the English Language.* Essex, Conn.: Verbatim, 1983.

Day, Robert A. *How to Write and Publish a Scientific Paper.* 2d ed. Philadelphia: ISI Press, 1983.

Ebbitt, Wilma R., and David R. Ebbitt. *Writer's Guide and Index to English.* 7th ed. Glenview, Ill.: Scott, Foresman, 1982.

Elsbree, Langdon, et al. *The Health Handbook of Composition*, 10th ed. Lexington, Mass.: Heath, 1981.

Evans, Bergen, and Cornelia Evans. *A Dictionary of Contemporary American Usage*. New York: Random House, 1957.

Flesch, Rudolf. *The ABC of Style: A Guide to Plain English*. New York: Harper & Row, 1980.

————. *The Art of Readable Writing*. Rev. and enlarged ed. New York: Harper & Row, 1974.

————. *Lite English: Popular Words That Are OK to Use*. New York: Crown, 1983.

————. *Look It Up: A Deskbook of American Spelling & Style*, New York: Harper & Row, 1977.

Follett, Wilson. *Modern American Usage: A Guide*. Edited and completed by Jacques Barzun and others. New York: Hill and Wang, 1966.

Fowler, H. W. *A Dictionary of Modern English Usage*. 2d ed. Revised by Sir Ernest Gowers. New York: Oxford Univ. Press, 1965.

Gorrell, Robert M., and Charlton Laird. *Modern English Handbook*. 6th ed. Englewood Cliffs, N.J.: Prentice-Hall, 1976.

Graves, Robert, and Alan Hodge. *The Reader Over Your Shoulder: A Handbook for Writers of English Prose*. 2d ed. New York:Random House, 1979.

Hodges, John C., and Mary E. Whitten. *Harbrace College Handbook*. 9th ed. New York: Harcourt Brace Jovanovich, 1984.

Irmscher, William F. *The Holt Guide to English: A Comprehensive Handbook of Rhetoric, Language, and Literature*. 3d ed. New York: Holt, Rinehart & Winston, 1981.

Lamberts, J. J. *A Short Introduction to English Usage*. Melbourne, Fla.: Krieger, 1981.

Menzel, Donald H., Howard Mumford Jones, and Lyle G. Boyd. *Writing a Technical Paper*. New York: McGraw-Hill, 1961.

Mitchell, John H. *Writing for Professional and Technical Journals*. New York: Wiley, 1968.

Morris, William, and Mary Morris. *Harper Dictionary of Contemporary Usage*. New York: Harper & Row, 1975.

Partridge, Eric. *Usage and Abusage: A Guide to Good English*. Baltimore: Penguin Books, 1963.

Perrin, Porter G. *Reference Handbook of Grammar and Usage*. New York: Morrow, 1972.

Quirk, Randolph, and Sidney Greenbaum. *A Concise Grammar of Contemporary English*. New York: Harcourt Brace Jovanovich, 1973.

Strunk, William, Jr., and E. B. White. *The Elements of Style*. 3d ed. New York: Macmillan, 1979.

Success with Words. Pleasantville, N.Y.: Reader's Digest, 1983.

Trelease, Sam F. *How To Write Scientific and Technical Papers*. Cambridge, Mass.: M.I.T. Press, 1969.

Warriner, John E., and Francis Griffith. *English Grammar and Composition: Complete Course*. New York: Harcourt Brace Jovanovich, 1977.

Zinsser, William. *On Writing Well: An Informal Guide to Writing Nonfiction*. 2d ed. New York: Harper and Row, 1980.

Language and the English Language

Allen, Harold B., and Michael D. Linn. *Readings in Applied English Linguistics*. 2d ed. New York: Knopf, 1981.

Baron, Dennis E. *Grammar and Good Taste: Reforming the American Language*. New Haven, Conn.: Yale Univ. Press, 1982.

Baugh, Albert C., and Thomas A. Cable. *A History of the English Language*, 3d ed. Englewood Cliffs, N.J.: Prentice-Hall, 1978.

Bloomfield, Leonard. *Language*. Chicago: Univ. of Chicago Press, 1984.

Bolinger, Dwight. *Language: The Loaded Weapon*. New York: Longman, 1980.

Bolinger, Dwight, and Donald A. Sears. *Aspects of Language*. 3d ed. Harcourt Brace Jovanovich, 1981.

Bryant, Margaret M. *Current American Usage: How Americans Say It and Write It*. New York: T.Y. Crowell, 1965.

Daniels, Harvey A. *Famous Last Words: The American Language Crisis Reconsidered*. Carbondale, Ill.: Southern Illinois Univ. Press, 1983.

Farb, Peter. *Word Play: What Happens When People Talk*. New York: Knopf, 1973.

Finnegan, Edward. *Attitudes toward English Usage: A History of the War of Words*. New York: Teachers College Press, 1980.

Gleason, Henry A. *Introduction to Descriptive Linguistics*. Rev. ed. New York: Holt, Rinehart & Winston, 1961.

Jespersen, Otto. *Growth and Structure of the English Language*, 10th ed. Chicago: Univ. of Chicago Press, 1982.

Joos, Martin. *The Five Clocks*. New York: Harcourt Brace Jovanovich, 1967.

Laird, Charlton. *Language in America*. Englewood Cliffs, N.J.: Prentice-Hall, 1972.

Language in the USA. Ed. Charles A. Ferguson and Shirley Brice Heath. New York: Cambridge Univ. Press, 1981.

Marckwardt, Albert H. *American English*. 2d ed. Ed. J.L. Dillard. New York: Oxford Univ. Press, 1980.

Mencken, Henry L. *The American Language: An Inquiry into the Development of English in the United States*. 4th ed., and two supplements. Abridged with annotations and new material by Raven I. McDavid, Jr. New York: Knopf, 1963.

Pyles, Thomas. *Origin and Development of the English Language*, 3d ed. New York: Harcourt Brace Jovanovich, 1982.

———. *Words and Ways of American English*. Norwood, Pa.: Telegraph Books, 1983.

Pyles, Thomas, and John Algeo. *English: An Introduction to Language*. New York: Harcourt Brace Jovanovich, 1970.

Sapir, Edward. *Language*. New York: Harcourt Brace Jovanovich, 1955.

Strang, Barbara. *A History of English*. New York: Methuen, 1970.

Sturtevant, Edgar. *Introduction to Linguistic Science*. New York: AMS Press, 1976.

Production, Design, and Printing

Arnold, Edmund C. *Ink on Paper Two: A Handbook of the Graphic Arts*. New York: Harper & Row, 1972.

_____. *Modern Newspaper Design*. New York: Harper & Row, 1969.

Bevlin, Marjorie Elliott. *Design through Discovery*. 4th ed. New York: Holt, Rinehart & Winston, 1984.

Association of American University Presses, ed. *One Book—Five Ways: The Publishing Procedures of Five University Presses*. Los Altos, Calif.: William Kaufmann, 1978.

Biegeleisen, J. I. *The ABC of Lettering*. 5th ed., rev. and enlarged. New York: Harper & Row, 1976.

Blumenthal, Joseph. *Art of the Printed Book, 1455–1955*. Boston: David R. Godine, 1973.

Bookman's Glossary. 6th ed. Ed. Jean Peters. New York: Bowker, 1983.

Chappell, Warren. *A Short History of the Printed Word*. Boston: David R. Godine, 1980.

Cockerell, Douglas. *Bookbinding and the Care of Books*. New York: Taplinger, 1978.

Cogoli, John E. *Photo-Offset Fundamentals*. 4th ed. Bloomington, Ill.: McKnight, 1980.

Comparato, Frank E. *Books for the Millions: A History of the Men Whose Methods and Machines Packaged the Printed Word*. Harrisburg, Pa.: Stackpole, 1971.

Craig, James. *Designing with Type: A Basic Course in Typography*. Rev. ed. Ed. Susan E. Meyer. New York: Watson-Guptill, 1971.

_____. *Phototypesetting: A Design Manual*. Ed. Margit Malmstrom. New York: Watson-Guptill, 1978.

_____. *Production for the Graphic Designer*. New York: Watson-Guptill, 1974.

Dair, Carl. *Design with Type*. Toronto: University of Toronto Press, 1982.

Dennis, Ervin A., and John D. Jenkins. *Comprehensive Graphic Arts.* 2d ed. New York: Bobbs-Merrill, 1983.

Diehl, Edith. *Bookbinding: Its Background and Technique.* 2 vols. New York: Hacker, 1979.

Glaister, Geoffrey. *Glaister's Glossary of the Book: Terms Used in Paper-Making, Printing, Bookbinding, and Publishing.* Berkeley, Calif.: Univ. of California Press, 1979.

Goudy, Frederic W. *The Alphabet and Elements of Lettering.* Rev. ed. Gloucester, Mass.: Peter Smith, Inc., n.d.

––––––. *Typologia: Studies in Type Design and Type Making.* Berkeley, Calif.: Univ. of California Press, 1977.

King, Jean Callan, and Tony Esposito. *The Designer's Guide to Text Type.* New York: Van Nostrand Reinhold, 1980.

Jaspert, W. Pincus, et al. *The Encyclopaedia of Type Faces.* 5th rev. ed. New York: Sterling, 1984.

Latimer, Henry C. *Preparing Art and Camera Copy for Printing.* New York: McGraw-Hill, 1977.

Lawson, Alexander S. *Printing Types: An Introduction.* Boston: Beacon, 1974.

Lee, Marshall. *Bookmaking: The Illustrated Guide to Design, Production, Editing.* 2d ed. New York: R. R. Bowker, 1979.

Lehmann-Haupt, Hellmut, et al. *Bookbinding in America.* New York: Bowker, 1967.

Lewis, John. *Typography: Design and Practice.* New York: Taplinger, 1978.

Lieberman, J. Ben. *Type and Typefaces.* 2d ed. New Rochelle, N.Y.: Myriade Press, 1978.

Longyear, William. *Type and Lettering.* 4th ed. New York: Watson-Guptill, 1966.

McMurtrie, Douglas C. *The Book: The Story of Printing and Bookmaking.* 3d ed. New York: Oxford Univ. Press, 1943.

Mintz, Patricia Barnes. *Dictionary of Graphic Arts Terms: A Communication Tool for People Who Buy Type and Printing.* New York: Van Nostrand Reinhold, 1981.

Moran, James. *Printing Presses: History and Development from the 15th Century to Modern Times.* Berkeley, Calif.: Univ. of California Press, 1973.

National Association of State Textbook Administrators, et. al. *Manufacturing Standards and Specifications for Textbooks.* Stamford, Conn.: Advisory Commission on Textbook Specifications, 1978.

Ogg, Oscar. *Twenty-Six Letters.* Rev. ed. New York: T. Y. Crowell, 1971.

Orne, Jerrold. *The Language of the Foreign Book Trade: Abbreviations, Terms, Phrases.* 3d ed. Chicago: American Library Association, 1976.

Pocket Pal: A Graphic Arts Production Handbook. 12th ed. New York: International Paper Co., 1979.

Rice, Stanley. *Book Design.* 2 vols. New York: Bowker, 1978.

Rosen, Ben. *Type and Typography: The Designer's Type Book.* Rev. ed. New York: Van Nostrand Reinhold, 1976.

Sanders, Norman. *Graphic Designer's Production Handbook.* Illus. William Bevington. New York: Hastings House, 1982.

Silver, Gerald A. *Modern Graphic Arts Paste-up.* 2d ed. New York: Van Nostrand Reinhold, 1983.

Stone, Bernard, and Arthur Eckstein. *Preparing Art for Printing.* Rev. ed. New York: Van Nostrand Reinhold, 1983.

Stevenson, George A. *Graphic Arts Encyclopedia.* 2d ed. New York: McGraw-Hill, 1979.

Strauss, Victor. *Graphic Arts Management.* New York: Bowker, 1973.

Thomson, Susan Otis. *American Book Design and William Morris.* New York: Bowker, 1977.

Tinker, Miles A. *Legibility of Print.* Ames, Iowa: Iowa State Univ. Press, 1963.

Updike, Daniel B. *Printing Types: Their History, Forms and Use.* 2d ed. 2 vols. Mineola, N.Y.: Dover, 1980.

White, Jan V. *Editing by Design: A Guide to Effective Word-and-Picture Communication for Editors and Designers.* 2d ed. New York: Bowker, 1982.

_____. *Mastering Graphics: Designs and Production Made Easy.* New York: Bowker, 1983.

Wilson, Adrian. *The Design of Books*. Layton, Utah. Gibbs M. Smith, 1974.

Zapf, Hermann. *Manuale Typographicum: 100 Typographical Arrangements with Considerations about Types, Typography, and the Art of Printing*. Cambridge, Mass.: MIT Press, 1970.

————. *Typographic Variations*. New Rochelle, N.Y.: Myriade Press, 1978.

Publishing

Appelbaum, Judith, and Nancy Evans. *How to Get Happily Published*. New York: Harper & Row, 1978.

Bailey, Herbert S. *The Art and Science of Book Publishing*. Austin, Texas. Univ. of Texas Press, 1980.

Dessauer, John P. *Book Publishing: What It Is, What It Does*. 2d ed. New York: Bowker, 1981.

The Business of Publishing. Ed. Arnold W. Ehrlich. New York: Bowker, 1976.

Grannis, Chandler B., ed. *What Happens in Book Publishing*. 2nd ed. New York: Columbia Univ. Press, 1967.

Greenfield, Howard. *Books: From Writer to Reader*. New York: Crown, 1976.

Smith, Datus C., Jr. *A Guide to Book Publishing*. New York: Bowker, 1966.

Tebbel, John W. *A History of Book Publishing in the United States*. 4 vols. New York: Bowker, 1972–1981.

Reference Books

Abbreviations

Crowley, Ellen T., ed. *Acronyms, Initialisms, and Abbreviations Dictionary*. 8th ed. 3 vols. Detroit: Gale, 1982.

De Sola, Ralph. *Abbreviations Dictionary*. 6th ed. New York: Elsevier, 1981.

Paxton, John, ed. *Dictionary of Abbreviations*. Totowa, N.J.: Rowman & Littlefield, 1973.

Pugh, Eric. *Pugh's Dictionary of Acronyms and Abbreviations: Abbreviations in Management, Technology and Information Science*. Phoenix, Ariz.: Oryx Press, 1982.

Rybicki, Stephen A. *Abbreviations: A Reverse Guide to Standard and Generally Accepted Abbreviated Forms*. Ann Arbor, Mich.: Pierian Press, 1971.

Webster's Guide to Abbreviations. Springfield, Mass: Merriam-Webster, 1985.

Biography

American Men and Women of Science: Physical and Biological Sciences. 14th ed. 8 vols. Ed. Jacques Cattell Press. New York: Bowker, 1979.

American Men and Women of Science: Social and Behavioral Sciences. 13th ed. Ed. Jacques Cattell Press. New York: Bowker, 1978.

Dictionary of American Biography, 20 vols. and 6 suppls. Published under the auspices of the American Council of Learned Societies. New York: Scribners, 1956–1980.

Gillispie, Charles C., ed. *Dictionary of Scientific Biography*. 16 vols. Published under the auspices of the American Council of Learned Societies. New York: Scribners, 1970.

International Who's Who. London: Europa Publications, published annually.

Webster's American Biographies. Ed. Charles Van Doren. Springfield, Mass.: Merriam-Webster, 1984.

Webster's New Biographical Dictionary. Springfield, Mass: Merriam-Webster, 1983.

Who's Who: An Annual Biographical Dictionary. New York: St. Martin's, published annually.

Who's Who in America. Chicago: A.N. Marquis, published biennially

Computers

Chandor, Anthony. *The Facts on File Dictionary of Microcomputers*. New York: Facts on File, 1981.

Dictionary of Computing. New York: Oxford Univ. Press, 1983

Graham, John. *The Facts on File Dictionary of Telecommunications.* New York: Facts on File, 1983.

Office Automation: A Glossary and Guide. Ed. Nancy MacLellan Edwards. Comp. Carmine Shaw and Patricia King. White Plains, N.Y.: Knowledge Industry, 1982.

Rosenberg, Jerry M. *Dictionary of Computers, Data Processing, and Telecommunications.* New York: Wiley, 1984.

Sippl, Charles J. *Microcomputer Dictionary.* 2d ed. Indianapolis, Ind.: Howard W. Sams, 1981.

Sippl, Charles J., and Roger J. Sippl. *Computer Dictionary and Handbook.* 3d ed. Indianapolis, Ind.: Howard W. Sams, 1980.

English-language Dictionaries and Spellers

9,000 Words: A Supplement to Webster's Third New International Dictionary. Springfield, Mass.: Merriam-Webster, 1983.

Webster's Collegiate Thesaurus. Springfield, Mass.: Merriam-Webster, 1976.

Webster's New Dictionary of Synonyms. Springfield, Mass.: Merriam-Webster, 1984.

Webster's Ninth New Collegiate Dictionary. Springfield, Mass.: Merriam-Webster, 1985.

Webster's Third New International Dictionary. Springfield, Mass.: Merriam-Webster, 1981.

Webster's Instant Word Guide. Springfield, Mass.: Merriam-Webster, 1980.

Webster's Legal Speller. Springfield, Mass.: Merriam-Webster, 1978.

Webster's Medical Speller. Springfield, Mass.: Merriam-Webster, 1975.

General and Miscellaneous

Bell, Marion V., and Swidan, Eleanor A. *Reference Books: A Brief Guide.* 8th ed. Baltimore: Enoch Pratt Free Library, 1978.

British Books in Print: The Reference Catalogue of Current Literature. New York: Bowker, published annually.

Encyclopedia of Associations. 20th ed. 3 vols. Ed. Katherine Gruber. Detroit: Gale, 1985.

Gates, Jean Key. *Guide to the Use of Libraries and Information Sources.* 5th ed. New York: McGraw-Hill, 1974.

Literary Market Place. New York: Bowker, published annually.

The New Encylopaedia Britannica. 15th ed. 32 vols. Chicago: Encyclopaedia Britannica, Inc., 1985.

Publisher's Trade List Annual. New York: Bowker, published annually.

Sheehy, Eugene P. *Guide to Reference Books.* 9th ed. Chicago: American Library Association, 1976.

The Statesman's Year-Book: Statistical and Historical Annual of the States of the World. Ed. S. H. Steinberg. New York: St. Martin's, published annually.

Ulrich's International Periodicals Directory 1984: A Classified Guide to Current Periodicals, Foreign and Domestic. 23d ed. New York: Bowker, 1984.

United States. Department of Labor. Employment and Training Administration. *Dictionary of Occupational Titles.* 4th ed. Washington, D.C.: GPO, 1977.

United States. Office of the Federal Register. *The United States Government Manual.* Washington, D.C.: GPO, 1983.

The World Almanac and Book of Facts. New York: Newspaper Enterprise Association, published annually.

Geography

Columbia Lippincott Gazetteer of the World. Ed. Leon E. Seltzer. New York: Columbia Univ. Press, 1952. Supplement, 1961.

Hammond Ambassador Atlas. Maplewood, N.J.: Hammond, 1982.

National Geographic Atlas of the World. 5th ed. Washington, D.C.: National Geographic Society, 1981.

New International Atlas. Chicago: Rand McNally, 1981.

Rand McNally Road Atlas: United States, Canada, Mexico. Chicago: Rand McNally, published annually.

Webster's New Geographical Dictionary. Springfield, Mass.: Merriam-Webster, 1984.

Law

Black, Henry Campbell. *Black's Law Dictionary.* 5th ed. St. Paul, Minn.: West, 1979.

Literature

Benet, William Rose. *The Reader's Encyclopedia,* 2d ed. New York: T. Y. Crowell, 1965.

Brewer, Ebenezer C. *Brewer's Dictionary of Phrase and Fable,* Rev. Ivor Evans. New York: Crown, 1978.

————. *The Reader's Handbook of Famous Names in Fiction.* New ed., rev. and enlarged. New York: Gordon, 1966.

Harvey, Sir Paul. *The Oxford Companion to English Literature.* 4th ed. Rev. Dorothy Eagle. New York: Oxford Univ. Press, 1967.

Holman, Clarence Hugh. *A Handbook of Literaure.* 4th ed. New York: Bobbs-Merrill, 1980.

The Reader's Adviser: A Layman's Guide to Literature. 12 ed., rev. and enlarged. Ed. Sally Prakken. New York: Bowker, 1974–79.

Scott, Arthur F., ed. *Current Literary Terms.* New York: St. Martin's 1965.

Zimmerman, John E. *Dictionary of Classical Mythology.* New York: Harper & Row, 1964.

Medicine

Blakiston's Gould Medical Dictionary. 4th ed. New York: McGraw-Hill, 1979.

Campbell, Robert J. *Psychiatric Dictionary.* 5th ed. New York: Oxford Univ. Press, 1981.

Dorland's Illustrated Medical Dictionary. 26th ed. Philadelphia: W. B. Saunders, 1980.

Marler, E. E. J. *Pharmacological and Chemical Synonyms: A Collection of Names of Drugs, Pesticides, and Other Compounds Drawn from the Medical Literature of the World.* 7th ed. New York: Elsevier, 1983.

The Merck Index: An Encyclopedia of Chemicals and Drugs. 10th ed. Ed. Martha Windholz. Rahway, N.J.: Merck & Co, 1983.

Nomenclature Committee of the International Union of Biochemistry. *Enzyme Nomenclature 1978.* New York: Academic, 1979.

Physician's Desk Reference. 39th ed. Oradell, N.J.: Medical Economics, 1985.

Stedman's Medical Dictionary. 24th ed. Baltimore: Williams and Wilkins, 1982.

Quotations

Bartlett, John. *Familiar Quotations: A Collection of Passages, Phrases, and Proverbs Traced to Their Sources in Ancient and Modern Literature.* 15th ed., rev. and enlarged. Ed. Emily Morison Beck. Boston: Little, Brown, 1980.

Mencken, Henry L., ed. *A New Dictionary of Quotations on Historical Principles from Ancient and Modern Sources.* New York: Knopf, 1942.

The Oxford Dictionary of Quotations. 3d ed. New York: Oxford Univ. Press, 1979.

Stevenson, Burton. *Home Book of Quotations, Classical and Modern.* 10th ed. New York: Dodd, Mead, 1967.

Science and Technology

McGraw-Hill Encyclopedia of Science and Technology. 5th ed. New York: McGraw-Hill, 1982.

Hopkins, Jeanne. *Glossary of Astronomy and Astrophysics.* 2d ed. Chicago: Univ. of Chicago Press, 1981.

McGraw-Hill Dictionary of Scientific and Technical Terms. 3d ed. Ed. Sybil P. Parker. New York: McGraw-Hill, 1983.

Stearn, W. T. *Botanical Latin: History, Grammar, Syntax, Terminology, and Vocabulary.* New York, Hafner, 1966.

Secretarial Practice

Adams, Dorothy, and Margaret A. Kurtz. *Legal Terminology and Transcription.* New York: McGraw-Hill, 1981.

Adams, Dorothy, and Margaret A. Kurtz. *Technical Secretary: Terminology and Transcription.* New York: McGraw-Hill, 1967.

Byers, Edward E. *Gregg Medical Shorthand Dictionary.* New York: McGraw-Hill, 1975.

Curchack, Norma, Herbert F. Yengel, and Katherine H. Hannigan. *Legal Typist's Manual.* 2d ed. New York: McGraw-Hill, 1981.

Davis, Phyllis, E., and N. L. Hershelman. *Medical Shorthand.* 2d ed. New York: Wiley, 1981.

Sardell, William. *Encyclopedia of Corporate Meetings, Minutes, and Resolutions.* Rev. ed. 2 vol. Englewood Cliffs, N.J.: Prentice-Hall, 1978.

Shorthand Guide to Legal Terminology. Binghamton, N.Y.: Gould Publications, 1983.

Webster's Legal Secretaries Handbook. Springfield, Mass.: Merriam-Webster, 1981.

Webster's Medical Secretaries Handbook. Springfield, Mass.: Merriam-Webster, 1979.

Webster's Secretarial Handbook. 2d ed. Springfield, Mass.: Merriam-Webster, 1983.

Style Manuals

Biology

Council of Biology Editors. Style Manual Committee. *CBE Style Manual: A Guide for Authors, Editors, and Publishers in the Biological Sciences.* 5th ed. Bethesda, Md.: Council of Biology Editors, 1983.

Chemistry

American Chemical Society. *Handbook for Authors.* Washington, D.C.: American Chemical Society, 1978.

General

Hart's Rules for Compositors and Readers at the University Press, Oxford. 39th ed. New York: Oxford Univ. Press, 1983.

Hutchinson, Lois Irene. *Standard Handbook for Secretaries.* 8th ed. New York: McGraw-Hill, 1969.

Keithley, Erwin M., and Philip J. Schreiner. *A Manual of Style for the Preparation of Papers and Reports.* 3d ed. Cincinnati, Ohio. South-Western, 1980.

The McGraw-Hill Style Manual. Ed. Marie Longyear. New York: McGraw-Hill, 1983.

Manheimer, Martha L. *Style Manual: A Guide for the Preparation of Reports and Dissertations.* Books in Library and Information Science, vol. 5. New York: Marcel Dekker, 1973.

Turabian, Kate L. *A Manual for Writers of Term Papers, Theses, and Dissertations.* 4th ed. Chicago: Univ. of Chicago Press, 1973.

Skillin, Marjorie E., and Robert M. Gay. *Words into Type.* 3d ed. Englewood Cliffs, N.J.: Prentice-Hall, 1974.

U.S. Government Printing Office Style Manual. Rev. ed. Washington, D.C.: GPO, 1973.

University of Chicago Press. *The Chicago Manual of Style.* 13th ed. Chicago: Univ. of Chicago Press, 1982.

Van Leunen, Mary-Claire. *A Handbook for Scholars.* New York: Knopf, 1978.

Geology

U.S. Geological Survey. *Suggestions to Authors of the Reports of the United States Geological Survey.* 6th ed. Washington, D.C.: GPO, 1978.

Journalism

The Associated Press Stylebook. Ed. G. P. Winkler. New York: Associated Press, 1977.

Jordan, Lewis, ed. *The New York Times Manual of Style and Usage: A Desk Book of Guidelines for Writers and Editors.* New York: Times Books, 1976.

Literature

Gibaldi, Joseph, and Walter S. Achtert. *MLA Handbook for Writers of Research Papers, Theses, and Dissertations.* 2d ed. New York: Modern Language Association of America, 1984.

Mathematics

American Mathematical Society. *A Manual for Authors of Mathematical Papers.* 7th ed. Providence, R.I.: American Mathematical Society, 1980.

Swanson, Ellen. *Mathematics into Type: Copyediting and Proofreading of Mathematics for Editorial Assistants.* Rev. ed. Providence, R.I.: American Mathematical Society, 1979.

Medicine

American Medical Association. *Manual for Authors & Editors.* Chicago: American Medical Association, 1981.

Physics

American Institute of Physics. *Style Manual for Guidance in the Preparation of Papers.* 3d rev. ed. New York: American Institute of Physics, 1978.

Psychology

American Psychological Association. *Publication Manual of the American Psychological Association.* 3d ed. Washington, D.C.: American Psychological Association, 1983.

Science, General

American National Metric Council. *Metric Editorial Guide.* 3d ed. Bethesda, Md.: American National Metric Council, 1980.

American National Standard for the Preparation of Scientific Papers for Written or Oral Presentation. New York: American National Standards Institute, 1979.

Dunford, Nelson J. *A Handbook for Technical Typists.* New York: Gordon & Breach, 1964.

Word Processing

Cecil, Paula B. *Word Processing in the Modern Office.* 2d ed. Menlo Park, Calif.: Benjamin/Cummings, 1980.

Kleinschrod, Walter, et al. *Word Processing: Operations, Applications, and Administration.* Indianapolis, Ind.: Bobbs-Merrill, 1980.

Layman, N. Kathryn, and Adrienne G. Renner. *Word Processors: A Programmed Training Guide with Practical Applications.* Englewood Cliffs, N.J.: Prentice-Hall, 1981.

Lobuz, Ronald A. *How to Typeset from a Word Processor.* New York: Bowker, 1984.

Mason, Jennie. *Introduction to Word Processing.* Indianapolis, Ind.: Bobbs-Merrill, 1979.

Rosen, Arnold, and Rosemary Fielden. *Word Processing.* 2d ed. Englewood Cliffs, N.J.: Prentice-Hall, 1982.

Stultz, Russell A. *The Word Processing Handbook.* Englewood Cliffs, N.J.: Prentice-Hall, 1981.

Waterhouse, Shirley. *Word Processing Fundamental.* New York: Harper & Row, 1979.

Wheeler, Carol A., and Marie Dalton. *Word Processing Simulations for Electronic Typewriters and Text Editors.* New York: Wiley, 1982.

Zarrella, John. *Word Processing and Text Editing.* Fairfield, Calif.: Microcomputer Applications, 1980.

Index

A (in type), 351
a, an, 100
A head, 366–367
AA (author's alteration), 330, 332
Abbreviations, 4, 96–108, 299
  alphabetizing of, 281
  with apostrophe, 5
  of Bible books, 212
  in binomial nomenclature, 152–153
  capitalization of, 98
  in chemistry copy, 141–143, 145, 146
  in compound words, 99
  in computer terminology, 156–157
  copyediting changes, 310–311, 326
  in documentation of sources, 209–210, 212
    bibliographies, 199, 200, 201, 203, 204
    journal titles, 203
    Latin terms, 189–190
    parenthetical references, 195, 196, 197
    source notes, 183, 185–186, 187
  hyphen in, 32
  in index entries, 259, 270, 281–282
  inflected forms, 5
  Latin, 71, 189–190
  in legal citations, 210–211
  within parentheses, 33–34
  plural forms, 74, 98–99
  possessive forms, 82, 99
  of proper nouns and adjectives, 53
  punctuation of, 37, 96, 97–98
  purpose of, 96
  in small capitals, 306
  standard and nonstandard, 238
  as subscripts and superscripts, 136
  in tables, 221, 228, 229, 238
  of units of measurement, 130, 148, 149
  variations in styling of, 96
  with virgule, 47
Absolute clause, 15
Abstractions, capitalization of, 53
Accent marks. See Diacritics

Accounting losses in parentheses, 35
Acknowledgment of sources, 232, 250–252, 302–303. See also Documentation of sources
Acknowledgments page, 303
Acronyms. See Abbreviations
Act, of play, 115, 211–212
Acute accent, 311
A.D., 100, 122–123
Additions, editorial. See Insertions, editorial
Addresses, 128
  abbreviations in, 101, 103, 104
  numbers in, 119–120
  punctuation of, 21
  virgule as divider in, 48
Adjectives
  within compound words, 85, 86
  as index headings, 256
Adjectives, compound, 87–90
Adjectives, proper. See Proper adjectives
Adjustment of lines on page, 334–336
Administration, capitalization of, 57
Adverbs
  within compound words, 88, 91
  as modifiers of compounds, 90
Adverbs, compound, 90–91
Adverbs, conjunctive, 45
Adverbial clauses and phrases, 13–15
Agency names. See Organizations, names of
Aggregation, signs of, 136–137, 138
  and line breaks, 133
A.H., 123
Alicyclic compounds, 148
Alignment
  of facing pages, 334, 335
  of inclusive numbers, 226, 227
  of lists, 314
  of poetry quotations, 173–174
  within tables, 224–230, 235
  dates, 228
  decimal fractions, 226
  dollar signs, 225
  footnote symbols, 231, 234

Webster's Standard American Style Manual

Designed by the editors of Merriam-Webster Inc.

Composed in Linotron Baskerville with Times Roman boldface by P&M Typesetting, Inc., Waterbury, Connecticut

Printed on 50-pound P. H. Glatfelter Supple Offset Antique and bound by Arcata Graphics / Fairfield, Fairfield, Pennsylvania